Access 2000
Programming

Blue Book

Wayne Brooks

Lars Klander

Publisher
Keith Weiskamp

Acquisitions Editor
Stephanie Wall

Marketing Specialist
Diane Enger

Project Editor
Toni Zuccarini

Technical Reviewers
Derrel Blain
Amy Sticksel

Production Coordinators
Wendy Littley
Jon Gabriel

Cover Design
Jody Winkler

Layout Design
April Nielsen

CD-ROM Developer
Robert Clarfield

The Coriolis Group, LLC
14455 North Hayden Road, Suite 220
Scottsdale, Arizona 85260

480/483-0192
FAX 480/483-0193
http://www.coriolis.com

Library of Congress Cataloging-in-Publication Data
Brooks, Wayne F., 1957–
    Access 2000 programming blue book / by Wayne Brooks and Lars Klander.
        p.   cm.
    ISBN 1-57610-328-5
    1. Database management.   2. Microsoft Access.   I. Klander, Lars.   II. Title.
QA76.76.S64B76   1999
005.75'65 — dc21   98-32428
                                                                                        CIP

Printed in the United States of America
10 9 8 7 6 5 4 3 2 1

CORIOLIS

14455 North Hayden Road, Suite 220 • Scottsdale, Arizona 85260

Dear Reader:

Coriolis Technology Press was founded to create a very elite group of books: the ones you keep closest to your machine. Sure, everyone would like to have the Library of Congress at arm's reach, but in the real world, you have to choose the books you rely on every day *very* carefully.

To win a place for our books on that coveted shelf beside your PC, we guarantee several important qualities in every book we publish. These qualities are:

- *Technical accuracy*—It's no good if it doesn't work. Every Coriolis Technology Press book is reviewed by technical experts in the topic field, and is sent through several editing and proofreading passes in order to create the piece of work you now hold in your hands.

- *Innovative editorial design*—We've put years of research and refinement into the ways we present information in our books. Our books' editorial approach is uniquely designed to reflect the way people learn new technologies and search for solutions to technology problems.

- *Practical focus*—We put only pertinent information into our books and avoid any fluff. Every fact included between these two covers must serve the mission of the book as a whole.

- *Accessibility*—The information in a book is worthless unless you can find it quickly when you need it. We put a lot of effort into our indexes, and heavily cross-reference our chapters, to make it easy for you to move right to the information you need.

Here at The Coriolis Group we have been publishing and packaging books, technical journals, and training materials since 1989. We're programmers and authors ourselves, and we take an ongoing active role in defining what we publish and how we publish it. We have put a lot of thought into our books; please write to us at **ctp@coriolis.com** and let us know what you think. We hope that you're happy with the book in your hands, and that in the future, when you reach for software development and networking information, you'll turn to one of our books first.

Keith Weiskamp
President and Publisher

Jeff Duntemann
VP and Editorial Director

Look For These Other Books From The Coriolis Group:

Access 2000 Developer's Black Book

Access 2000 Client/Server Gold Book

Visual Basic 6 Programming Blue Book

Visual Basic 6 Black Book

Visual Basic 6 Core Language Little Black Book

Visual Basic 6 Object-Oriented Programming Gold Book

Visual Basic 6 Client/Server Programming Gold Book

Visual C++ 6 Programming Blue Book

This book is dedicated to the memory of Otto Sims, Sr. and Stanley E. Holmes, Jr.
—Wayne Brooks

To Brett: Through all the problems, and the trials, and the tribulations,
you have always been there at my side—I can't thank you enough
for everything you have meant and been to me.
I will love you always.
—Lars Klander

ò.

About The Authors

Wayne F. Brooks (waynebrooks@nolla.org) is an IT professional, Web technology consultant, and author. He has over 15 years experience in information technology, and is founder/president of Interactive Learning Technologiez, a Maryland-based technology consulting company. Wayne is the author of *FrontPage 97 Sourcebook* and *Active Server: A Developer's Guide*, and is co-author and technical editor of *Special Edition Using Asymetrix Multimedia ToolBook*. Mr. Brooks is also author/instructor of *Client/Server Fundamentals* and *FrontPage Fundamentals*, two Web-based technology training courses published and distributed online by DigitalThink.

Lars Klander, MCSE, MCSD, MCT **(lklander@lvcablemodem.com)** is the author or co-author of over half-a-dozen books, including *1001 Visual Basic Programmer's Tips*, the winner of the 1997 *Visual Basic Programmer's Journal* Reader's Choice award. A professional network security consultant and Microsoft Certified Trainer, Klander has written on a wide variety of programming and network security topics, ranging from books about C/C++ programming to books about creating speech applications. Klander has been a professional author and trainer for several years and a computer professional for over 15 years.

Acknowledgments

Finishing a book is like running a marathon and crossing the finish line. Even though you're physically exhausted, your spirit is soaring from the accomplishment. Moreover, knowing that this book is part of the new Coriolis Blue Book series only adds to the thrill of victory. Projects like this one aren't completed in a vacuum. There are numerous people whose hard work, dedication, support, and encouragement have made the difference in an always challenging process.

I would like to extend thanks and appreciation to Margot Maley and the folks at Waterside Productions for their continued support. Many thanks also to Stephanie Wall, Toni Zuccarini, Wendy Littley, Jon Gabriel, Jody Winkler, April Nielsen, and the rest of the Coriolis team for their dedication and cooperation. Thanks also to the tech reviewers, Derrel Blain and Amy Sticksel, for their attention to detail. Special thanks to Lars Klander for the fantastic job on Chapters 12, 13, 18, 19, 20, 21, 24, and 25. Lars, your efforts in making this project a success are greatly appreciated.

I'd also like to take this opportunity to say thank you to Rochelle Clemons, Antoine Brooks, Russell Stokes, Doug and Claudette Berry, and John Kapke for their support and encouragement during the course of this project.

On a personal note, thanks to Mike Campbell, Marc Webster, and James Williams—your benevolence and support is greatly appreciated.

Special thanks to my wife Tanya for love and support on a daily basis, and to Brittney, Colette, Nicolas, Ashley, and Wesley for their motivation.

Frances B. Brooks, you're the best!

—*Wayne Brooks*

Acknowlegments

In publishing, like any other business, you learn quickly that the people around you can make you look good or they can make you look bad. While Wayne's and my names are the only ones that appear on the front of the book, it takes a lot of people to put together all the text that makes up something of this size. While the number of contributors is too great to mention, I would like to thank several people who played key roles in the finishing of this book. First and foremost, Toni Zuccarini, the Project Editor for the book, has been wonderful to work with and very patient in dealing with my need to question every little thing in the finalization of the text. Wendy Littley and Jon Gabriel, the Production Coordinators, and their team of layout professionals managed to take often-dry text and present it in a manner appealing to the eye and easy to read. Robert Clarfield, the CD-ROM Developer; Jody Winkler, the Cover Designer; and April Nielsen, the Layout Designer, helped put together crucial add-ons for the book, including all the CD-ROM contents and the back and inside covers.

But the real kudos go to our editors. Our Copy Editor, Bart Reed, who spent many hours reading each chapter and making changes that improved the presentation while making sure that my original text wasn't lost. Just as marvelous was our Technical Editor, Amy Sticksel, who not only made sure the code was perfect, but provided valuable suggestions for additional technical notes that the reader might find helpful. This is my second opportunity to work with Amy, and I can't say enough about the quality of the work she does—so I will leave it at "you're the best."

Hal Ross and the team at R&R Michada here in Las Vegas provided me with a new laptop on about a day's notice that was crucial to my finishing the book—Hal and his team know that I value their contribution greatly, and now everyone else does, too.

Last but not least, Stephanie Wall, the Acquisitions Editor for the project, and David Fugate, my agent, put me together with Wayne, providing me with the opportunity to contribute some valuable content to his book. Thanks to you both—working with the two of you almost makes publishing contracts easy.

—Lars Klander

Table Of Contents

Introduction

Welcome to the *Access 2000 Programming Blue Book*. The pages that follow will introduce you to the latest incarnation of Microsoft's popular relational database management system and show you how to extend its capabilities using the power of Visual Basic for Applications. If you've always been curious about what it would it take to write an Access program, but weren't sure of how to go about it, then this book is for you. If you're an Access user who wants to move from simple data storage and retrieval to sophisticated data interaction, then this book will help you do just that. If you're an experienced Access developer, then you're going to discover how Access 2000 can increase your productivity with enhancements that support integration with Microsoft Office, as well as the Web.

Access 2000 has undergone significant changes since its last release, as you'll notice when you see its new Office 2000-style user interface. You'll also notice the changes in the standard Access datasheet, as you're introduced to the product's new subdatasheet feature that allows related data to be edited in the same window.

Another exciting feature of Access 2000 is the debut of data access pages. This feature facilitates data sharing by allowing you to create data-bound HTML pages that extend the power of your desktop applications to the Internet or the corporate intranet. You'll encounter these and other features as you learn techniques such as:

- How to use a structured methodology to guide your programming efforts
- How to program using Access SQL

- How to interact with your data using Visual Basic for Applications
- How to create your own class modules
- How to build and program data access pages

This book is written from a "Do It, Then Review It" point of view. Consequently, you'll gain hands-on programming experience as you walk through the process of building a variety of practical applications. Once you've finished the building process, you'll review the work you've done and explore the concepts and techniques that support the completed application.

The intent of this book is to be a multipurpose text. As such, it contains 27 chapters and 4 appendixes full of procedures, discussions, figures, tips, questions and answers, and online resources to help you get the most out of your Access 2000 programming experience. In addition, this book contains a companion CD-ROM with the databases, source code, and support files used to create the book's applications, as well as demo versions of various development tools and utilities.

As the IT community moves toward Internet-enabled business applications that extend the desktop to the Web, the ability to understand and use technologies like Access 2000 can place the power to support the future at your fingertips. This book will move you closer to that end.

Seize the day.

Chapter 1

Access 2000: A New Beginning

With the Millenium just around the corner, Microsoft is breathing new life into its Office business productivity suite, and Access 2000 is a major beneficiary of the results.

Access 2000 is the latest incarnation of Microsoft's venerable relational database management system. It represents somewhat of a new beginning for the application. This Access upgrade contributes a number of new enhancements designed to improve its usefulness to the developer. In this chapter, I'll provide an overview of these new enhancements. I'll also introduce you to a development methodology for building both simple and complex programs in a structured, orderly fashion. So, let's get this show on the road!

What's Different About Access 2000?

Access 2000 differs from its predecessors due to enhancements in the following areas:

- Productivity
- Programmability
- Objects
- Client/Server
- Jet 4.0 Database Engine

NOTE

The presumption in this book is that you're familiar with the Access world. However, if you aren't, don't worry. By the time you're done with this book, you'll have a pretty good handle on the important stuff and the enhancements may or may not be that significant to you.

Productivity Enhancements

Productivity enhancements are typically designed to make our jobs easier than we could imagine. With Access 2000, Microsoft pushes the productivity envelope once again with a few significant improvements, beginning with its interface.

The Access Database Window

One of the most obvious changes in the new version of Access is the Access database window (see Figure 1.1). This primary interface now sports a framed design similar to the Microsoft Outlook mail client (see Figure 1.2). The new design follows the updated look and feel of the Microsoft Office 2000 application suite.

Other changes to the database window include:

- A new section for data access pages (more about these later)

- New sections for views, stored procedures, and database diagrams

- An Internet Explorer 4.0 Listview control that lists available objects

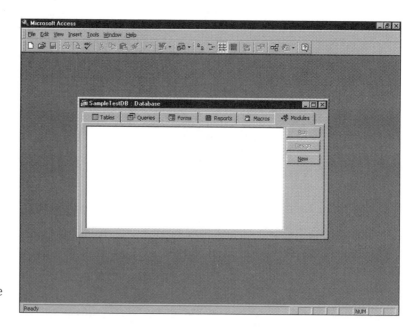

Figure 1.1
The Access 97 database window uses tabs.

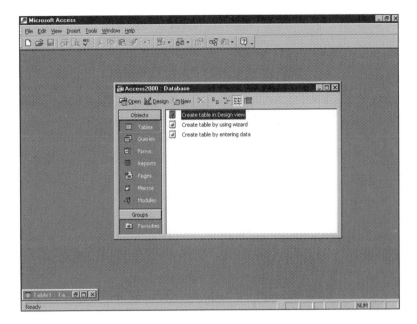

Figure 1.2
Access 2000 features a redesigned database window.

- New object items in the list of objects
- The ability to create user-defined groups containing any object type

The Name AutoCorrect Feature

Access 2000 automatically fixes common errors that may occur when you change user-defined names through the Access user interface. This is possible because Access 2000 stores name mapping information along with a unique identifier for each new object. Consequently, when Access detects that an object has changed since the last execution of Name AutoCorrect, it performs this operation again on all items for the object.

Subdatasheets

The addition of subdatasheets is one of the more interesting enhancements to Access 2000. Subdatasheets allow users to browse table, query, form, or subform data hierarchically in the datasheet view. As a result, users can now see data related to a single table or a higher-level record. Figure 1.3 illustrates the hierarchical structure of the categories table using subdatasheet views of the product table and the orders table.

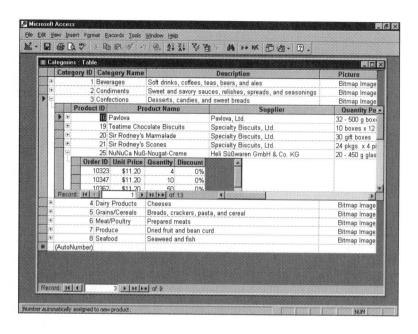

Figure 1.3
Subdatasheets let you browse table data hierarchically.

Multilingual Input

For tighter integration with Microsoft Office 2000, Access now lets you designate a secondary font that supports character sets not available in the primary font. For example, under the English version of Windows NT 4.0, when using the default datasheet of Arial, characters of Korean text would normally appear as boxes when mixed with English text in a table. However, when the Dual Font Support feature is used, Korean text will be displayed alongside the English text.

Programmability Enhancements

Access 2000 makes database programming easier than ever through the seamless integration of Microsoft development tools such as the Visual Basic Editor and the Microsoft Script Editor.

The Visual Basic Editor

Unlike its predecessors, Access 2000 uses the same Visual Basic Editor as Microsoft Word, Microsoft Excel, and Microsoft PowerPoint. As a result, code modules now appear in the Visual Basic Editor instead of the Access Module window.

The Microsoft Script Editor

The Microsoft Script Editor is also new in Access 2000. This component lets you use scripting language in data access pages. This feature is accessible from the Tools menu in all Microsoft Office applications.

Object Enhancements

Access 2000 enhances the object-oriented design model with the introduction of the Data Access Page object.

The Data Access Page Object

As you might expect, Access 2000 is much more Web-aware than its predecessors. This is accomplished through a new object type called the *data access page*. You'll learn a lot more about this object in Chapter 14. For now, all you need to know is that data access pages are HTML documents that bind directly to database data. Data Access Page objects are used like Access forms, but they are designed to run in the Internet Explorer Web browser.

Client/Server Enhancements

The most significant enhancement in the client/server features of Access 2000 is the new concept of the Access Project.

The Access Project

With the Access Project feature, you can build applications that rely on Access panels as the front end, while adding a number of options for the underlying database object. Using the Project feature, you create an Access Project file with the extension .ADP. This file contains all the forms, data access pages, reports, macros, and modules that comprise an application. However, the Project contains no tables or queries. This data, and the processing components of the application (tables, stored procedures, views, and database diagrams), are connected to a back-end store, such as:

- The integrated store that ships with Access 2000

- SQL Server 6.5

- SQL Server 7

Jet 4.0 Database Engine Enhancements

This version of Access includes significant enhancements to the Jet Database Engine that gives it new data types, new extensions, Unicode support, additional commands, and more, in the name of improved compatibility.

Unicode Support

In Access 2000, character data stored under the **Text** and **Memo** data types, as well as the equivalent Microsoft Jet SQL data types **CHAR** and **VARCHAR**, is now saved in the Unicode two-byte character representation format. This enhancement replaces the Database Character Set (DBCS) format previously used for storing non-English-language character data.

NT-Compatible Sorting

Because it now supports Unicode, the Microsoft Jet Database Engine is also able to use a Windows NT-based sorting mechanism. This mechanism uses LCIDs and supports all Windows NT sort orders.

Data Types

Because database scalability (and improved compatibility between Microsoft Jet and Microsoft SQL Server) is a consideration for Access users and developers, Access 2000/Microsoft Jet data types have been enhanced to more closely resemble Microsoft SQL Server data types.

SQL Extensions

In an effort to conform more closely to the ANSI SQL 92 specification, as well as to support improved capabilities, the Microsoft Jet 4.0 SQL implementation now offers enhanced SQL statement compatibility between Microsoft Jet and Microsoft SQL Server.

Tip

In order to keep Microsoft Jet backward compatible, the enhancements to SQL are available only when the database engine is set to operate in ANSI SQL 92 mode.

Views

With the release of Access 2000, Microsoft Jet has been enhanced to support the ANSI standard definition of views. This enhanced capability sits on top of Jet's stored query functionality and establishes portability between Jet and other SQL databases.

NOTE

Although ANSI SQL specifies that a new transaction starts automatically following a COMMIT or ROLLBACK, Microsoft Jet does not follow this model.

Procedures

As with views, Access 2000 enjoys Microsoft Jet's enhancement to support the ANSI standard definition of procedures. Again, this capability rests atop Jet's stored functionality for action queries (for instance, queries based on **UPDATE**, **DELETE**, **SELECT INTO**, and **DROP**) and parameterized **SELECT** queries.

Transactions

Microsoft Jet SQL now supports invocation and termination (committing or rolling back) of transactions.

Tables

The latest version of the Microsoft Jet Database Engine also contains a number of enhancements to improve overall table management. For instance, more flexible syntax for the **CREATE TABLE** and **ALTER TABLE** commands allows business rules to span multiple tables and simplifies changes to column definitions.

Passive Shutdown

A passive shutdown feature has been introduced with Access 2000. Also called a *Connection control*, this feature prevents users from connecting to a database during an administrative event like compacting or updating. Invoking passive shutdown allows connected database users to continue working until they log out. Users are unable to reconnect to the database until passive shutdown is disabled.

User List

Another interesting enhancement to the Microsoft Jet 4.0 Database Engine is the user list feature. This addition lets you determine who is connected to a Microsoft Jet database and the state of their connection. Using the Active Data Objects (ADO) programming interface, the following information is available:

- The name of the user's computer
- The user ID
- Whether the user is currently connected to a database
- Whether the user's database was terminated normally

Lock Promotion

With the release of Access 2000, Microsoft Jet 4.0 has now been enhanced to allow users to open a table for exclusive use and to modify table rows without locks being placed on either the corresponding index or data page. Although this only allows one user to update a table, it increases performance when many rows are being modified.

Row-Level Locking

Microsoft Jet 4.0 now supports row-level locking. This feature increases concurrency and performance by allowing users to lock one row at a time, rather than being forced to lock an entire page containing multiple rows of data.

Replication

To improve compatibility with Microsoft SQL Server, version 4.0 of the Microsoft Jet Database Engine now supports bi-directional replication. With this enhancement, changes made to data in a Microsoft SQL Server database can be replicated to a Microsoft Jet database and vice versa.

Replication Conflict Resolution

With Microsoft Jet 4.0 Replication, synchronization conflicts and synchronization errors are viewed as synchronization conflicts, and a single mechanism is used to record and resolve them. In previous versions, Microsoft Jet Replication differentiated between synchronization conflicts and synchronization errors.

Column-Level Conflict Resolution

In Microsoft Jet 3.5, conflicts were determined at the row level. For instance, if users in two different replicas changed the record for the same customer, but each changed a different field in the record, the two records would conflict when the replicas were synchronized. Microsoft Jet 4.0 implements column-level conflict resolution, in which changes to the same record in two different replicas will cause a synchronization conflict only if the same column or field is changed.

Well, that's about it for enhancements. If you're familiar with the previous versions of Access, I'm sure you'll agree that this version comes packed with some significant improvements. If you're new to Access and application development, then not to worry. You'll be working like a pro in no time at all. All it takes is a little PRACTICE. How's that for a segue?

PRACTICE—A Structured Approach To Developing Access 2000 Programs

Programming, whether in Access or any other language, is about developing solutions. Because best practice in the software industry suggests that the quality of a software product is, by and large, a function of the process used to create it, it seems prudent at the outset to provide you with a viable process for developing good Access solutions. The process I offer is called PRACTICE.

PRACTICE is an acronym for eight activities supporting good solution development, whether you use Access 2000 or any other software development tool. Specifically, PRACTICE means:

- **P**ose a purpose for your program
- **R**esolve what the program needs to do
- **A**llocate how the program can be broken into logical functions
- **C**onsider the process steps
- **T**est each functional code block
- **I**ntegrate and debug
- **C**orrelate to the original purpose
- **E**nd with good documentation

Let's briefly examine each of the PRACTICE activities.

Pose A Purpose For Your Program

Before you write your first line of code, determine why your program is needed and write down that purpose. What is the problem that your program solves? Perhaps there is a business function that requires automated support. For example, you may be recording seminar registrations on paper and need a program to automate the registration process. Posing a purpose for your program establishes the basis for its creation.

Resolve What The Program Needs To Do

After you've determined why your program is necessary, the next step is to determine what your program needs to do. In other words, ask yourself, "What functions must be accomplished to solve the problem at hand in a logical fashion?" Typically, you call this step *requirements definition*, and spend a fair amount of time determining the level of detail needed to describe exactly what you want to accomplish. Whether the program is for your personal use or for a paying customer, good requirements let you focus on designing a solution that supports everyone's expectations. By the way, it's not a bad idea to write down exactly what these expectations are, so you can perform sanity checks against your work as you progress.

Allocate How The Program Can Be Broken Into Logical Functions

So, you know why you need a program and what the program has to do. Now you're ready to allocate your program requirements to functional modules. For example, if you need to collect and store personal information like name, address, and phone number, you might allocate these requirements to a functional module called Collect Personal Data. This practice lets you focus on writing programs in blocks of code that perform one specific task, thereby making your solution easier to debug and maintain.

Consider The Process Steps

After you define logical functions for your program, you'll need to go down a level. At this stage, you'll need to determine the specific steps required to accomplish each of the functions you've identified. This is extremely important because it forms the basis for writing program code. One technique used to support this step is to write pseudocode. *Pseudocode* combines English statements with programming language statements. For example, you might write the following pseudocode to write data to an Access table:

```
IF the name field contains XYZ THEN
   Store the contents of the name field in the ABC table.
END IF
```

As a rule of thumb for this exercise, if any of your program modules seem to contain a large amount of pseudocode, you may want to consider decomposing a large functional module into multiple smaller modules.

Test Each Functional Code Block

As you might expect, you'll need to test each complete block of code. I recommend testing each logical code block by itself. This activity is known as *unit testing* and ensures that each logical function can stand on its own.

Integrate And Debug

Once unit testing is complete, you're ready to bring all the modules together and run them as a single application. This is the program integration step, and it officially begins the debug stage of the process. During this stage, you'll look for and correct any program errors.

Correlate To The Original Purpose

If all goes well during the integration and debug step, then it's time to do a sanity check. In other words, see whether the program you've developed fulfills your initial goal.

End With Good Documentation

Finally, do yourself a favor and document what you've accomplished. Quite often, great programs are lost because they exist in two places—the head of the creator and the code itself. Make it a habit to write down how your program is put together, so that someone else has a shot at maintaining and enhancing it.

Where To Go From Here

In this chapter, we looked at the upgrades that distinguish Access 2000 from its predecessors. With its redesigned database window interface and editing capabilities, enhanced features for Internet support, and greater compatibility with Microsoft SQL Server, Access 2000 evolves from a relational database management system to a database application development environment. You were also introduced to the PRACTICE methodology of solution development. By using this eight-step process, you can have some degree of assurance that your program solutions are as good as you intend them to be.

In the next chapter, you'll try your hand at building your first Access 2000 program.

Chapter 2

Let's Write An Access Program!

Whether you're an experienced programmer or a novice that's new to the game, writing your first program with a new development tool should be fun.

I've heard it said that the best way to start a swimming lesson is to get your feet wet. Well, that's just what you're about to do. In this chapter, you'll develop a simple Access program that you can use to provide password-protected access to your application screens. This is a quick and painless exercise; so don't worry if things move a bit fast. I'll slow down and cover some basics about application design and development a bit later. For now, let's get those feet in the water.

In Case You Didn't Know

A program is simply a set of instructions that tell the computer to perform some task. This instruction set is written using a programming language.

In the case of database management systems like Access 2000, that programming language is usually SQL (pronounced ESS-QUE-ELL or SEE-QWUL). SQL is an acronym that stands for Structured Query Language. However, Access 2000 also supports another programming language called Visual Basic for Applications (VBA). Visual Basic for Applications is the standard programming language for all applications comprising the Microsoft Office suite and is a much more robust development language than SQL. Using a combination of SQL and VBA, you'll be able to create some pretty useful applications.

But, I digress. I'll discuss both SQL and VBA in detail a little later in the book; for now let's get back to the discussion at hand. Before you can begin programming with Access 2000, you'll need to create a database and a table to store some data. So, let's tackle this first.

Creating A Database

If you don't have Access 2000 open, launch it by clicking Start|Programs|Access 2000. When the application launches, you'll be presented with the Microsoft Access dialog box. Create a database using this dialog box by performing the following steps:

1. Select the Blank Access Database radio button, and then click OK to launch the File New Database dialog box, shown in Figure 2.1.

2. Enter "FirstDatabase" in the File Name field. Then click the Create button to launch the Access Database window, which provides a view of the blank datasheet.

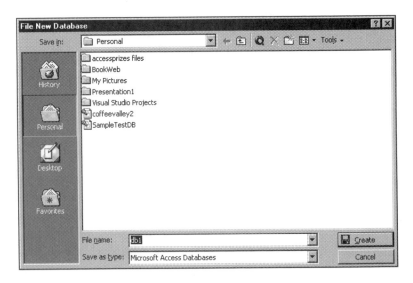

Figure 2.1
The File New Database dialog box has a new look in Access 2000.

Creating And Populating A Table

Next, you'll need to create and populate a table using the blank datasheet view by performing the following steps:

1. Enter "Rosebud" in the column labeled Field1, and then press the Tab key to place the cursor in the Field2 column.

2. Enter "Kane" in the Field2 column, and then select File|Save from the Microsoft Access menu bar to launch the Save As dialog box.

3. Enter "FirstTable" in the Table Name field, and then click OK.

4. When presented with the primary key warning dialog box, click No.

5. Now that there's data in your table, prepare to define your column headers by selecting View|Design View from the Access menu bar.

6. In the Design View dialog box, replace the name "Field1" with "Username", and then Tab to the row with the file name Field2.

7. Replace "Field2" with the name "Password", and then select File|Save from the Access menu bar.

8. Select View|Datasheet View to see your results. Your screen should now look like the one shown in Figure 2.2.

Opening A Module Window

Now that you have a database and some data to work with, it's time to create a program module. As with previous versions of Access, you use modules to hold the VBA instructions that run the applications you produce. Begin the module creation process by opening a module window as follows:

1. Close the FirstTable Datasheet view by selecting File|Close from the Access 2000 menu bar.

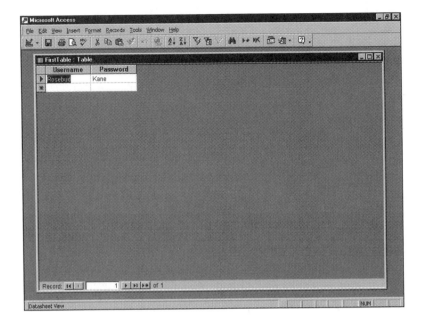

Figure 2.2
Your new database should contain one table with a single record.

2. Click Modules under the Objects button in the leftmost frame of the database window.

3. Click New on the database window's menu bar to launch a Module window inside the Microsoft Visual Basic Editor (see Figure 2.3).

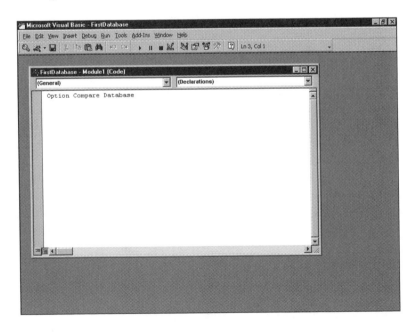

Figure 2.3
The Visual Basic Editor now replaces the traditional Access code editor.

.Project **Let The Coding Begin**

Because the objective of this exercise is to let you code and run your first Access 2000 program quick, fast, and in a hurry, I'll save the explanatory discussion for later. So, if you're ready, let the coding begin by performing the following steps:

1. At the blinking cursor, type:

```
Sub Logon()
'Variable Declaration Section
Dim Username
Dim Password
Dim q1
Dim q2
'Variable Definition Section
Username = InputBox( _
            "You're programming with Access 2000." & _
            Chr(13) & Chr(13) & _
            "Please enter your username.")
Password = InputBox( _
            "You're doing a great job!" & _
            Chr(13) & Chr(13) & _
            "Now, please enter your password")
'Query Execution Section
q1 = DLookup("[Username]", "FirstTable", "[Username] = _
   username")
q2 = DLookup("[Password]", "FirstTable", "[Password] = _
   password")
'Processing Logic Section
   If Username = qresult1 And Password = qresult2 Then
       MsgBox "Congratulations, Give this man a cigar!"
   Else
       MsgBox "Hey! That's not right!" & Chr(13) & _
           "No cigar for you!"
   End If
End Sub
```

2. When you've finished entering the code, select Debug|Compile FirstDatabase on the Visual Basic menu bar.

3. Next, select File|Save FirstDatabase to launch the Save As dialog box.

4. Enter "Logon" in the Module Name field, and then click OK.

5. Select Run|Run Sub/Userform from the Visual Basic menu bar. This action begins program execution, launching the dialog box shown in Figure 2.4.

6. Enter the word "Test" in the Username field, and then click OK to open the Password dialog box shown in Figure 2.5.

7. Enter the word "Test" in the Password field, and then click OK. Because Test is neither a username nor a password in the table you created, clicking OK results in the message box shown in Figure 2.6.

8. Repeat Steps 5 through 7. This time enter "Rosebud" in the Username field, and enter "Kane" in the Password field. This time your actions should result in the message box shown in Figure 2.7.

Let's Review Some Of The Code

You've done well! You've just written and tested your first Access 2000 program. Now let's take a look at what's going on.

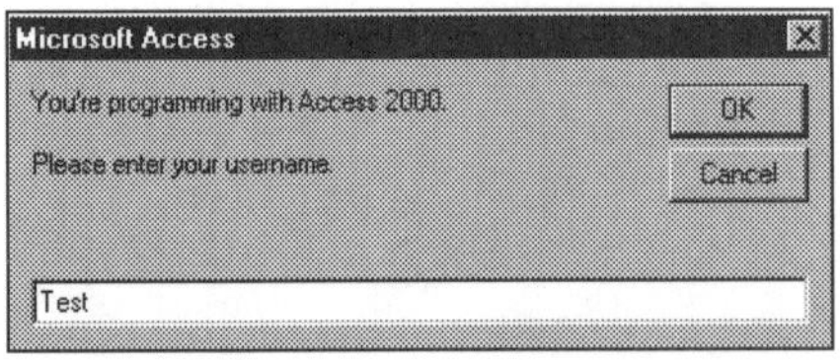

Figure 2.4
Successful program execution launches a prompt for your username.

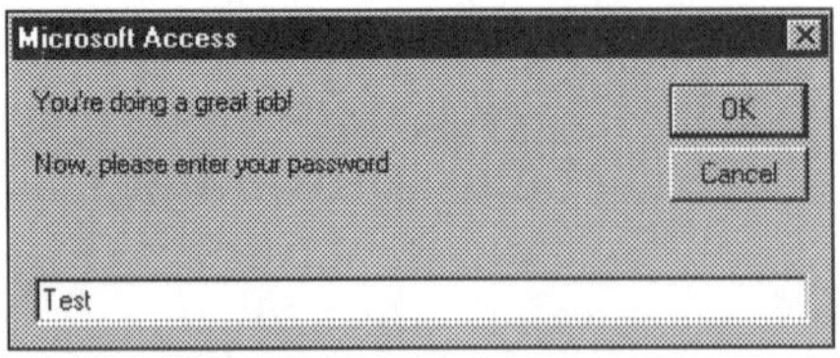

Figure 2.5
The Username prompt is followed by a Password prompt.

Figure 2.6
An unsuccessful logon results in a "No cigar" message.

Figure 2.7
A successful logon presents a congratulatory message.

Option Compare Database

Option Compare Database is the first instruction you see whenever you open a new module window. Functionally, this statement sets the ground rules for how string comparisons are done within a module. With this statement in effect, Access uses the string comparison parameters established by the database's sort order.

Sub Logon()

This statement identifies **Logon()** as a subroutine. A *subroutine* is a group of program statements that collectively perform a specific task. Typically, a subroutine is a functional component of a larger application that can be called from anywhere within the application's program code. The **Logon()** subroutine is a standalone procedure with generic applicability. By the way, **End Sub()** completes a subroutine.

Comment Sections

The inclusion of sections for variable declaration, variable definition, query execution, and processing logic are merely to exercise good programming practice with regard to code comments. Comments in Visual Basic for Applications are annotated with an apostrophe (') followed by the comment string.

Dim

Dim is a Visual Basic keyword used to explicitly declare the creation of a variable. Variables are logical allocations of computer memory used to temporarily reserve space in which to store data for use by a program at a later time. The **Logon()** subroutine allocated memory for four data elements subsequently used by the program: **Username**, **Password**, **q1**, and **q2**.

The InputBox() Function

This is a VBA function designed to prompt and collect data from an end user. Input boxes are modal windows, which means they stay on the screen until a user completes them.

Table 2.1 **Special operators and functions for the Logon() subroutine.**

Symbol	Description
&	Performs concatenation of two or more string expressions.
_	The line continuation character allows an extended text string to be broken and continued on the next line.
Chr(13)	This function lets you add a line break/carriage return to a code block.

Special Operators And Functions

The **Logon()** subroutine makes use of the special operators and functions listed in Table 2.1.

The DLookup() Function

The **DLookup()** function allows you to retrieve and evaluate specific table values using arguments that correspond to the SQL keywords **SELECT**, **FROM**, and **WHERE**. You'll learn more about SQL in Chapter 5.

Message Box (MsgBox)

This is a VBA function designed to display a prompt in a message dialog box. Message boxes also contain buttons used to return an end user's response to the program.

Where To Go From Here

In this chapter, you created and tested your first Access 2000 program. You were also introduced to some of the basic commands, statements, and functions that you'll come to rely on and use as your programming skills begin to mature. In the next chapter, you'll go under the hood a bit for some details on how Access programs are structured and what makes them work.

Chapter 3

What Makes Access Programs Tick?

Does form follow function or does function follow form? In either case, there is a method that dictates the end result.

In the last chapter, you hit the ground running by writing and testing your first Access 2000 program. You learned some new terms, and even gained a little insight into how the pieces of your program fit together to accomplish the task at hand. Now it's time to slow down a bit and discover what really makes Access programs tick.

Pay No Attention To The Man Behind The Curtain

Just as the sound and fury of the Great and Powerful Oz comes from a man behind a curtain, so, too, does the power of Access programs. However, in the case of Access, the man happens to be an Access database and, to a greater extent, Visual Basic for Applications (VBA). As briefly mentioned in Chapter 2, VBA is a programming language integrated with Access; it allows the native capabilities of Access to be extended beyond the boundaries of traditional database management tasks. In the paragraphs that follow, as you examine the characteristics of the Access Development Model, you'll begin to understand the synergistic relationship between Access and VBA.

The Access Development Model is a solution-building paradigm that's driven by three characteristics:

- Database development

- Object-oriented design

- Event-driven programming

Database Development

From the simple to the complex, all Access solutions begin with some form of database development. For this reason, it's important to understand some basics about sound database design. After all, the foundation of your solution depends on the database and its associated structures, indexes, and relationships. From a programmer's point of view, database development most often involves creation of a relational database. A relational database is, at its core, a container. It consists of numerous tables linked by common data elements to allow cross-table data lookup and retrieval. Because the management of multiple tables and their relationships can become quite complex, it's advisable to create a data model during the Resolve step of the PRACTICE methodology (see Chapter 1 for this methodology).

A data model is a graphical depiction of all the tables, fields, indexes, and rules necessary to support the solution you intend to build. So, this is a case where a picture is indeed worth a thousand words. The data model building process involves the following activities:

- Data element identification

- Field definition

- Entity definition

- Table normalization

- Index definition

- Relationship definition

Data modeling is a standard information engineering practice with many facets and is far beyond the scope of this book. However, understanding a few of the basics will allow you to build applications on a more solid foundation. With that said, let's examine the basic data model building activities in a little more detail.

Data Element Identification

The first step in building a data model involves making a list of the data that you want to maintain. For example, if you are planning a database to store the elements for a job posting application, you may want to include items on your list like job number, job title, date posted, post expiration date, point-of-contact name, point of contact phone, point of contact email, and point of contact fax.

Field Definition

After you've built your list of data elements, you'll want to define how each element will reside in the database. This means that name, length, and data type must be defined for each data element. For example, you might define fields for the data elements used for the planned job posting application, as shown in Table 3.1.

Entity Definition

The next step in the process is to define entities that describe the type of information that you'll store. In other words, create specific categories for each type of data you want to maintain. The data elements that you previously defined will become attributes of the entities. This activity results in logical table and field definitions. For example, you might consider having two entities for the job posting application. Entity 1 could be Job Information, and Entity 2 could be Contact Information. Entity 1—Job Information would have the attributes Job Number, Job Title, Date

Table 3.1   Field definitions.

Field Name	Length	Data Type
JobNumber	7 chars	Text
JobTitle	20 chars	Text
Date_Posted	8 chars	Date
PostExp	8 chars	Date
ContactName	12 chars	Text
ContactPhone	13 chars	Text
ContactEmail	25 chars	Text
ContactFax	13 chars	Text

NOTE

A good rule of thumb says that when you have multiple instances of a category of data in an entity, you should create a new entity to accommodate that reoccuring dataset.

Posted, and Post Expiration Date. Entity 2—Contact Information would have the attributes Job Number, Contact Phone, Contact Email, and Contact Fax. The physical equivalent of your logical entities and attributes are database tables and fields. Table 3.2 shows the relationship between entities, attributes, tables, and fields.

Table Normalization

At this point in the process, it's time to look for redundancies and duplication in your tables and entities. This process is called *normalization*. When working with relational databases, you use normalization to apply rules that result in a more efficient database design. Normalization rules are generally expressed to describe three ever-increasing levels of database design efficiency. These levels represent database design efficiency in *normal forms*. The most frequently applied normal forms are First Normal Form, Second Normal Form, and Third Normal Form. Table 3.3 briefly describes each of these.

Index Definition

With your tables and fields defined, it's time to establish indexes to facilitate rapid record location and sorting. Much like a book index, database indexes are lists of references that point to where rows appear in a table. Because indexes generally list values in sorted order, Access uses a table's primary key to determine this

Table 3.2   Entities are logical equivalents of physical database tables.

Entity Name	Entity Attributes	Table Name	Field Name
Job Information	Job Number	JobInfo	JobNumber
	Job Title		JobTitle
	Date Posted		DatePosted
	Post Expiration Date		PostExp
Contact Information	Job Number	ContactInfo	JobNumber
	Contact Name		ContactName
	Contact Phone		ContactPhone
	Contact Email		ContactEmail
	Contact Fax		ContactFax

Table 3.3 Normal forms.

Normal Form	Description
First Normal Form	Every row by column position must contain one and only one value, with no columns duplicating other columns.
Second Normal Form	The First Normal Form criteria are met, and column values should be fully identifiable by the entire primary key. In other words, after First Normal Form conditions are met you should be able to locate any table value by searching the table using a primary key, for example Record Number, SSN, and so on.
Third Normal Form	The Second Normal Form criteria are met, and all non-key columns do not depend on other columns to exist.

Tip

A primary key is a field that contains a unique value for each record in a table.

order. Hence, this is one of many reasons for establishing a primary key for each table you create.

Relationship Definition

Now that your tables are defined and indexed, your last task is to define and establish relationships between the tables that will reside in your database. Relationships allow one table to access and retrieve information stored in another table. Table relationships are established through the identification of a primary key field.

Object-Oriented Design

In the Access Development Model, object-oriented design means that Access solutions are composed of objects. In other words, when you design an application in Access, some portion of your effort is spent creating and manipulating objects on the screen. Now, exactly what does the term "object" refer to? Well, in the physical sense, object refers to the material things that fill our everyday existence, like a book, a lamp, a television, a VCR, or a car. However, in the context of an Access application, object refers to things that comprise the end solution, like tables, queries, forms, reports, pages, macros, and modules. Object can also refer to a container for other objects. For example, a database object contains tables, records, and fields, and a form object contains controls, for instance, buttons, text boxes, and combo boxes.

NOTE

You'll become more familiar with Design View in the next chapter.

Object Properties

An object is defined by its properties. For example, take the book you're reading. What are properties of this Book object? One property would be Title, another Weight, another Number of Pages, yet another would be Paper Color, or Ink Color. So you see, properties are attributes that characterize the nature of an object. Unlike real-world objects, objects in the Access world exist for user modification. Figure 3.1 shows a property sheet. The property sheet is the mechanism by which you modify Access object properties in Design View. The property sheet for an Access object is available by right-clicking on the object, and then selecting the Properties option from the right-click menu.

Object Methods

Although objects are physically characterized by their properties, they are characterized functionally by their methods. One way to understand the concept of object methods is to ask, "What can I do with this object?" For example, take another look at the Book object that we just discussed. What can you do with this object? Well, among other things, you can open it. You can close it. You can read it. You can highlight it. You can dog-ear its pages. The point is that *object methods* define the behavior that an object is capable of demonstrating. This is important because you'll reference object methods, as well as object properties, when you're ready to control Access objects programmatically.

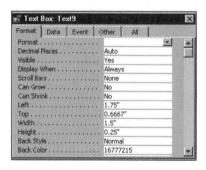

Figure 3.1
Properties in Access are modified in Design View via the property sheet.

Object Classes

Let's say you're looking at a 3.5-inch floppy disk, a recordable CD-ROM, and an external hard drive. Based on what you now understand about object properties and methods, what properties and methods would you say these things have in common? On the property side, all three objects have weight, and they are all portable. On the method side, they all record and store data. Now, if you were to assemble a collection of objects, each with the same properties and methods as the three items in our example, you'd have an *object class*.

In the world of object-oriented design, classes let you establish and describe the qualities of an object. Consequently, you can use classes as a foundation for creating your own custom objects. When you create a custom object, you first create a base copy of an object with the properties and methods that you require. This object base copy is called an *instance*. Instances are created through a process called *instantiation*. When you instantiate an object, you create a new instance of an object belonging to a given class. You then use the new instance to create your own object type. Understanding the concept of object classes is key to understanding the capabilities available to you with Access objects and VBA.

The Access Object Model

Now that you know something about objects, let's take a look at how this applies to Access 2000. Access objects fall into two distinct categories:

- Application objects
- Data Access objects (DAO)

Application Objects

Application objects represent user interface elements maintained by Access itself (see Figure 3.2). In addition, these objects represent open forms, reports, modules, and their associated controls

Figure 3.2
Access-maintained application objects are shown in the Database window.

and sections, as well as objects supporting **DoCmd**, **Application**, **Screen**, **Err**, and **Debug**.

Data Access Objects

NOTE

The "Jet" in the phrase Jet Database Engine is actually an acronym for Joint Engine Technology.

Data Access objects represent the database structure and the data stored in it. These objects are native to the Jet Database Engine, which is the underlying data processing component of Access. Data Access objects are the primary object references you'll use with VBA to programmatically interact with the database. Figure 3.3 illustrates a breakdown of the Access Object Model.

Event-Driven Programming

Although it's debatable as to who should get full credit between Apple and Microsoft, it's a safe bet that both the Mac and Windows operating systems had a significant role in the era of graphical user interfaces (GUIs) with point-and-click functionality.

It's that notion of point-and-click functionality that makes event-driven programming the second tier of the Access Development Model. Access solutions are event-driven. This means that their design basis is cause and effect. As an Access programmer, you'll typically create a form-based front end that contains field and button objects. You'll then modify the properties of the form objects as your requirements dictate. Finally, you'll create macros or write VBA procedures to act as object event handlers for user-triggered events.

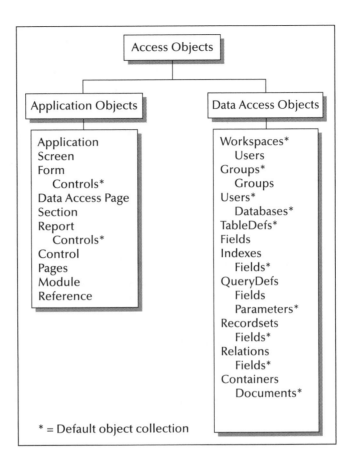

Figure 3.3
The Access Object Model supports Application and Data Access objects.

When a user interacts with your Access solution by pointing to a button object on the form and clicking it, a cause/event is triggered. The triggered event invokes the event handler, which then executes a macro or procedure in response to the **click** event. As a practical example, recall the Logon program in Chapter 2. Although you didn't use forms, you did use objects with built-in methods as a substitute. You then entered data and clicked the OK button on the input box, which triggered execution of a procedure as a response to the **click** event. The effect was confirmation or denial about the validity of the entered username and password.

Event Handlers

In Access, event handlers come in two varieties—macros and procedures. Your choice of which to use often depends on the complexity of the operation you need to perform. A macro is a set of one or more actions, each performing a specific operation, like opening a form or printing a report. Typically, a macro is the event handler of choice when all you need is a generic response to a common event. Procedures are the event handler of choice when you need to have control over the results of an event. Procedures exist as either subroutines or functions.

Subroutines

Subroutines perform a task without returning a value. They begin with the keyword **Sub** and end with the statement **End Sub**. As you may recall from the Logon program, subroutines are represented with the following syntax:

```
Sub SUBROUTINENAME (argument1, argument2, etc.)
    VBA statement n
End Sub
```

Functions

Functions perform a task and return a value when their execution is complete. Similar to subroutines, functions begin with the keyword **Function** and end with the statement **End Function**. Functions are represented with the following syntax:

```
Function FUNCTIONNAME (argument1, argument2, etc.)
    VBA statement n
End Function
```

Modules

The VBA code that powers Access applications resides in modules stored in an Access database. These coded modules can exist in two flavors:

- Standard

- Class

Standard Modules

Standard modules are your garden-variety procedures that may be called and/or run from any point in an application. In other words, they are standalone code blocks that have no dependence on a specific object to work their magic. In its current form, the

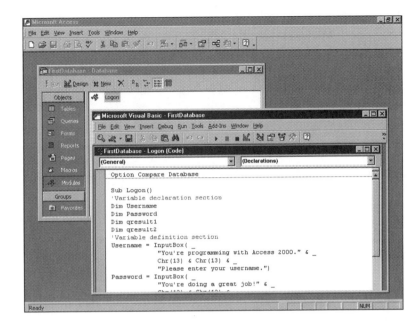

Figure 3.4
Standard modules are listed in the Database window and edited in VBA.

Logon procedure could be classified as a standard module. As shown in Figure 3.4, standard modules are listed in the Access Database window and may be edited within the VBA editor by double-clicking on the module name.

Class Modules

In contrast to standard modules, class modules are associated with specific objects, however they can still exist as standalone code blocks. For this reason, you can use class modules to create your own custom objects.

Where To Go From Here

In this chapter, you took a behind-the-scenes look at what gives Access programs their horsepower. You accomplished this by examining the primary characteristics of the Access Development Model—database development, object-oriented design, and event-driven programming. In the next chapter, you'll build another Access program as you begin to explore form-based applications.

Chapter 4

Let's Create A Form-Based Program

Take a design screen and add some control objects. Mix in some VBA code and a pinch of SQL, and voilà— another Access 2000 program.

In Chapter 2, you wrote a simple Access program to provide password protection for your application screens. This type of standalone program is called a *standard module*. As mentioned previously, standard modules are one of the two module types used to store VBA code in an Access program. However, because most of your Access 2000 programming will be form-based, this chapter walks you through the process of creating forms that use the other type of VBA code module: the class module. In fact, to keep things simple, you'll develop a form-based version of the Logon application we developed in Chapter 2. As you proceed, you'll get a better feel for the practical application of some of the concepts discussed in the previous chapter.

Project Designing A Form

When you're ready to build a form in Access 2000, you have two options: Create Form In Design View or Create Form By Using Wizard (see Figure 4.1). Because I'm sure you want to get your hands dirty, let's use the Design View option.

With the Access database window open and using FirstDatabase as your data source, perform the following steps:

1. Click the Forms option under the Objects button, and then double-click Create Form In Design View to launch the Form window and the Toolbox (see Figure 4.2).

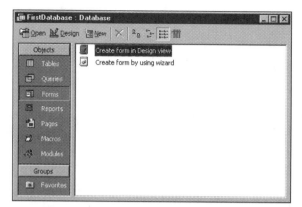

Figure 4.1
Selecting the Forms object presents two form creation options.

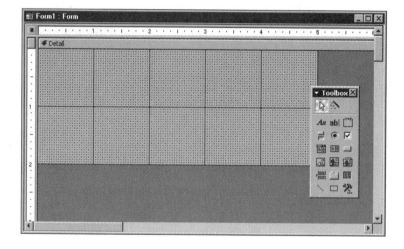

Figure 4.2
The Forms window opens with a floating Toolbox palette.

Figure 4.3
Use the Toolbox palette to select Access control objects.

2. On the Toolbox, click the Text Box control tool (see Figure 4.3).

3. Place the cursor in the Detail section of the form, click, and then hold down the left mouse button, dragging the mouse from left to right to draw a Text Box control (see Figure 4.4). Release the mouse button when the control is the size that you want.

4. Double-click the Text0 label to open its property sheet (see Figure 4.5).

5. Change the Caption in the Label property sheet from Text0 to Username, and also change the name of the field from

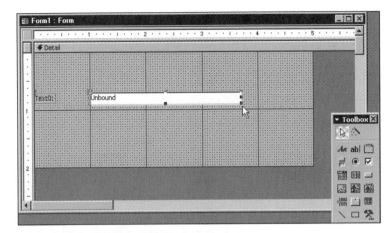

Figure 4.4
Draw control objects in the Form window's Detail section.

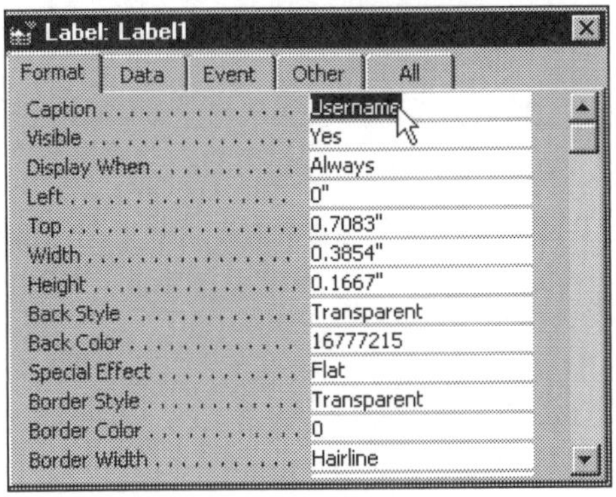

Figure 4.5
Use property sheets to modify object attributes.

Text0 to Username. Then close the property sheet by clicking the close box in the upper-right corner.

6. Adjust the size of the label to see its full contents by clicking the label and dragging its right sizing handle (see Figure 4.6).

7. Draw and place a second Text Box control under the first one by repeating Steps 2 and 3.

8. Double-click the Text1 label to open the Label property sheet for the second control.

9. Change the label caption from Text1 to Password and the field name from Text1 to Password, and then close the dialog

NOTE

You'll notice that each Text Box control contains the word "Unbound." An Unbound control is a control object that is not yet associated with a database field.

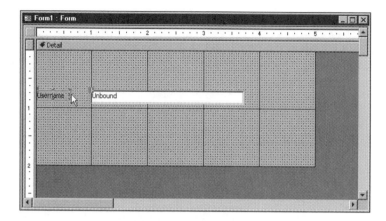

Figure 4.6
Resize control objects by using their sizing handles.

Figure 4.7
Use the Command Button tool as an all-purpose control to trigger program events.

box by clicking the close box in the upper-right corner. Again, adjust the size of the label to see its entire contents.

10. On the Toolbox, click the Command Button control tool (see Figure 4.7).

11. Place the cursor beneath the second Text Box control, and click once to place a Command Button control on the form.

12. Double-click the Command Button control to open its property sheet.

13. Change the caption for the control to Verify, and then close the property sheet.

Your form window should now appear as shown in Figure 4.8.

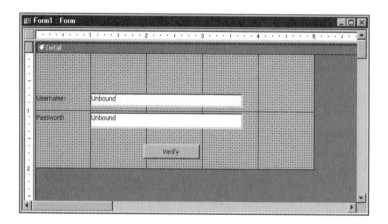

Figure 4.8
The results of our first form project.

 **Creating An Event Handler**

Now that your form design is complete, it's time to create the form's event handler. As you may recall from the previous chapter, event handlers are lines of program code that respond to events like a button click. Because you'll require an event handler that does more than page navigation or simple command execution, in this case we'll use a procedure instead of a macro. As you might expect, the event handler is the starting point for class module creation.

Create an event handler for the Logon form by performing the following steps:

1. Right-click on the Verify button in the Detail window, and then select the Build Event menu option to open the Choose Builder dialog box (see Figure 4.9).

2. Select Code Builder from the Choose Builder dialog box, and then click OK to open the Visual Basic Editor (see Figure 4.10).

3. Place the cursor between the **Private Sub Command4_Click()** and the **End Sub** statements, and enter the following lines of code:

```
'Variable Declaration Section
 Dim db As Database
 Dim result
 Dim SQLline
'Variable Definition Section
 SQLline = "SELECT * FROM FirstTable _
   WHERE Username = [Username] _
   AND Password = [Password];"
 Set db = CurrentDb()
 Set result = db.OpenRecordset(SQLline)
'Processing Logic Section
 If result![Username] = [Username] _
   And result![Password] = [Password] Then
     MsgBox "Congratulations, Your identity _
       has been verified!"
 Else
     MsgBox "Sorry! There's a problem with your ID!" _
       & Chr(13) & "Please try again!"
 End If
 result.Close
```

NOTE

The Visual Basic Editor displays two combo boxes above the coding window. The combo box on the left presents the list of control objects on the active form. Because you're working with the Command Button control object, **Command4** *is the default value. Selecting one of the listed objects displays either the syntax of a new event handler for that object, or the event handler code for the object control. The combo box on the right presents a list of events associated with the current object control.*

Figure 4.9
Create event handlers using the Choose Builder dialog box.

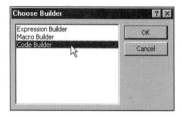

Figure 4.10
Access 2000 integrates the VBA Editor to support code generation.

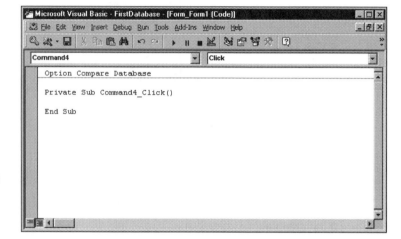

4. On the Visual Basic Editor menu bar, click File|Save FirstDatabase.

5. At the Save As prompt, enter "LogonForm", and then click OK.

Project Fine-Tuning The Form's Appearance

Your Logon form is almost complete but it's not quite ready for prime time. Since you probably want your form to have a more refined appearance, perform the following steps to clean up the form face and to add a few additional features:

1. In Design View, right-click on the Username Text Box object, and then select Properties from the right-click menu.

2. On the Text Box: Username property sheet, click the All tab and set the following property values:

Tip

You'll need to select the Username field in the Expression Builder window.

- *Validation Rule*—"=[Username]"
- *Validation Text*—"Please enter your username."
- *Font Name*—Century Schoolbook or similar font

3. Close the Text Box: Username property sheet.

4. Next, right-click on the Password Text Box object, and then select Properties from the right-click menu.

5. On the Text Box: Password property sheet, click the All tab and set the following property values:

   - *Input Mask*—Password
   - *Validation Rule*—"=[Username]"
   - *Validation Text*—"Please enter your password."
   - *Font Name*—Century Schoolbook or similar font

6. Close the Text Box: Password property sheet.

7. Click anywhere in the form's Detail window to de-select the Password Text Box object.

8. Right-click on the square in the upper-left corner of the Form window, and select Properties from the right-click menu (see Figure 4.11).

9. On the Form property sheet, click the All tab and set the following property values:

   - *Caption*—Access 2000—Logon Program
   - *Scroll Bars*—Neither
   - *Record Selectors*—No
   - *Navigation Buttons*—No
   - *Dividing Lines*—No
   - *Auto Resize*—No
   - *Border Style*—Dialog

10. Close the Form property sheet.

11. Select File|Save, and then select View|Form View from the Access menu bar.

The completed form should appear as shown in Figure 4.12.

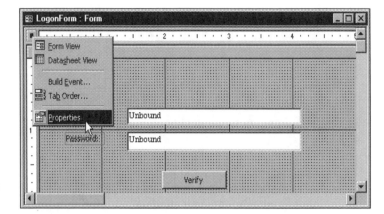

Figure 4.11
Access the form's
Properties from the
upper-left corner of the
Form window.

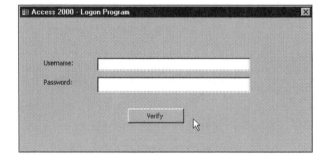

Figure 4.12
The completed
Logon form.

Project Testing The Program

Now that the form and its programming are complete, it's time to
test your handiwork. If all is well, you should be able to perform
the following tests and achieve the noted results:

1. Tab to the Password field without entering a Username.

   You should be prompted to enter your Username.

2. Click the Verify button without entering any values.

   You should be alerted that there is a problem with your ID.

3. Enter a fake Username and Password.

   The Password field should display asterisks, and you should be
   alerted that there is a problem with your ID.

4. Enter "Rosebud" as your Username and enter "Kane" as
   your Password.

   You should be notified that your identify has been verified.

Let's Review Some Of The Code

You're doing great! You've just written and tested your second Access 2000 program. Now, let's look at some of the more significant pieces of the code.

Private Sub Command4_Click()

This line of code introduces you to the **Private** keyword. Using the **Private** keyword dictates that the procedure in use cannot be called from outside the module where it's declared and can only be used by other procedures residing in the same module. This is in contrast to procedures using the **Public** keyword. **Public** procedures are available to any component of an application and may be called regardless of their point of origin. In Access 2000, all form event procedures are made **Private** by default.

db As Database

The significance of this statement lies in the explicit declaration of the **Database** Data Access Object (DAO). In the context of this program, the declaration of **db As Database** establishes a specific reference to the object type that identifies the currently open database.

SQLline = "SELECT * FROM FirstTable WHERE Username = [Username] AND Password = [Password];"

This statement introduces you to Structured Query Language (SQL). I'll cover SQL in detail in the next chapter. However, notice the use of brackets—[ ]—in the code. In this program, the contents of the brackets are field names—they refer to the Text Box control objects residing on the form.

Set db = CurrentDb()

This statement identifies the contents of the declared **db** variable with the current database. This method of reference is preferable to using the entire data object hierarchy path reference **DBEngine.Workspaces(0).Databases(0)**. In addition, the use of

NOTE

*The Database **Data** object type is not available in the Access 2000 DAO object library. In fact, Access 2000 includes DAO objects, methods, and properties that replace those in versions 1.x, 2.0, and 7.0. In order to continue using DAO objects, methods, and properties supported in earlier versions of Access, you need to establish a reference to the Microsoft DAO 2.5/3.5 compatibility library, which offers full backward compatibility. This is done by clicking References on the Tools menu while in Design View. Additional details can be found in the Access 2000 Help files under "DAO Object Library Compatibility."*

CurrentDb() as a shorthand reference creates a new instance of the active database. It also facilitates multiple uses of the **Database** data type, which can be beneficial when developing programs for multiple users.

Set result = db.OpenRecordset(SQLline)

The heart of Access programming lies in the ability not only to add, delete, and update data, but in the ability to retrieve data in a meaningful way. This data retrieval is made possible by the use of **Recordset** objects. Recordsets store data for the purpose of dynamic manipulation using VBA. In other words, you can think of a **Recordset** object as the logical version of the physical database with VBA as its data access language. The **Set result** statement creates a **Recordset** object and fills it with the data resulting from the SQL query named **SQLline**. Table 4.1 presents the three most commonly used recordset types.

If result![Username] = [Username] And result![Password] = [Password] Then…

If the terms "property," "method," or "collection" are unfamiliar to you, refer to Chapter 7.

The significant feature in this statement is the use of the bang (!) identifier. Just as the dot (.) identifier separates an object from a property, method, or object collection, the bang (!) identifier separates an object from the collection in which it resides. For

Table 4.1   Common recordset types.

Recordset Type	Description	Use
Table	Contains recordsets stored in a database table.	Primarily used to perform quick searches using indexes. However, it is limited to local Access tables.
Dynaset	Contains pointers that refer to data in tables or to database queries.	Used to store data from multiple tables from more than one source, as well as data based on a SQL string. Dynaset recordset objects can be updated.
Snapshot	Contains a copy of a recordset as it exists at a fixed point in time.	Used for quick looks at data when updates are not required.

example, **result![Username]** indicates that the **Username** field is contained in the **result** data collection.

result.Close

This statement reinforces good housekeeping when using a recordset. Because the data contained in a recordset is available as long as the recordset remains open, it's good programming practice to close the recordset after use to free resources.

Where To Go From Here

In this chapter, you wrote and tested your second Access 2000 program. This exercise exposed you to the distinction between standard modules and class modules, while familiarizing you with the mechanics of the second and third tiers of the Access Development Model—object-oriented design and event-driven programming, respectively. You also learned a little bit about creating and using SQL-driven recordsets.

Next, you'll get to know VBA's supporting player, Structured Query Language (SQL), and how it's used to manipulate data. By the way, refer back to Chapter 3 if you're unclear on using the Access Development Model.

Chapter 5

Programming With Access SQL

For you to get the most out of programming with Access 2000, you'll need to integrate your VBA code with Structured Query Language (SQL).

So far, you've seen firsthand how VBA and SQL work together to extend the database management capabilities of Access 2000. In this chapter, we're going to split up the dynamic duo and take a closer look at some of the finer points of SQL. First, you'll learn a little about the origin of SQL, and then you'll examine a few syntax conventions for building Access SQL statements. Next, you'll discover the four most frequently used commands for accessing and manipulating data with SQL programming. You'll then take a look at how to build and customize queries, and finally, you'll learn to programmatically manipulate SQL data.

Where Did SQL Come From?

Structured Query Language originated in the early 1970s with the vision of Dr. E.F. Codd, a pioneer in relational databases. In his writings, Dr. Codd described a universal data access and manipulation language for use with relational databases. In 1974, a team of IBM engineers developed what they called *Structured English Query Language* or SEQUEL, based on Dr. Codd's research. This early version of SQL was integrated with IBM's initial relational database management systems. By the late 1980s, SEQUEL had evolved to the point where organizations like the American National Standards Institute (ANSI) and the International Standards Organization (ISO) developed and published usage standards for SEQUEL-like languages. These standards ultimately led to industry acceptance and use of SQL as we know it today.

Understanding SQL Statement Construction

Most programming languages, including SQL, have syntax conventions and rules of thumb that dictate the most correct way to write code. It is good programming practice to use these conventions, and it can also save you debugging time. Here are a few rules of thumb to consider when creating SQL statements:

• Terminate SQL statements with a semicolon.

• Write SQL keywords in uppercase and parameters in lowercase or mixed case.

• Use multiline statements to distinguish keywords from table names.

• Use an asterisk (*) as a wildcard to retrieve all table fields for a SQL dataset.

Let's look at these conventions a little more closely.

Terminate SQL Statements With A Semicolon

Access SQL requires that your SQL statements end with a semicolon. This is an Access peculiarity, as more generic implementations of SQL don't require statements to end with a semicolon. For example:

```
SELECT fieldname FROM tablename;
```

Write SQL Keywords In Uppercase And Parameters In Lowercase Or Mixed Case

SQL statements are not case-sensitive. This means that you could write the statement

```
SELECT fieldname FROM as select fieldname FROM
```

or even

```
select fieldname from
```

It doesn't matter. However, using the uppercase convention for SQL keywords and lowercase or mixed case for statement parameters makes code more readable. For instance:

```
SELECT fieldname FROM tablename WHERE fieldname =
[formfieldname];
```

Use Multi-line Statements To Distinguish Keywords From Table Names

SQL ignores white space, so you can split a SQL statement over multiple lines and not affect how the statement is processed:

```
SELECT
fieldname
FROM
tablename
WHERE
fieldname = [formfieldname];
```

Use An Asterisk (*) As A Wildcard To Retrieve All Table Fields For A SQL Dataset

Rather than keying a sequence of comma-delimited field names after the **SELECT** keyword, to retrieve all table fields, use the asterisk to represent a wildcard. In other words, you can save yourself a few keystrokes by using an asterisk instead of a statement. For instance,

```
SELECT a,b,c,d,e,f,g FROM table name
WHERE fieldname = [formfieldname];
```

is a poor choice over

```
SELECT * FROM table name
WHERE fieldname = [formfieldname];
```

Using the aforementioned general statement conventions produces SQL code that is easy to read, understand, and maintain.

Exploring The SQL Foundational Four

There are effectively four key statements that drive the majority of your SQL programs. I call these statements the SQL Foundational Four, and they include **SELECT**, **INSERT INTO**, **UPDATE**, and **DELETE**. Get these down, and you'll have mastered the fundamentals of SQL programming. Let's explore each of these a little further.

Using The SELECT Statement

The **SELECT** statement is the king of SQL statements. This is because its sole function is to initiate data retrieval queries, which, after all, is a significant part of database interaction. You'll use the **SELECT** statement to construct queries that pull specific rows of table data and retrieve them in a recordset. The **SELECT** statement is built using the following syntax:

```
SELECT (name of one or more table columns)
FROM (name of table containing the specified column(s));
```

There are also two optional clauses for the **SELECT** statement: **WHERE** and **ORDER BY**. The **WHERE** clause specifies a condition that must be met when retrieving table data. For example, let's say that you're at a travel agency telling the travel agent that you want to travel to a location **WHERE** "the sun is always shining." Just as "the sun is always shining" is a **WHERE** condition that must be met by the travel agent, so too are the clauses that follow **WHERE** in SQL statements.

The **ORDER BY** clause specifies a sort order for the records retrieved by the executed query. For example, if you have 10 records each containing a city and a state, the **ORDER BY** clause lets you specify whether the resulting recordset is ordered alphabetically by city or alphabetically by state.

The following **SELECT** statement accesses the Employees table of the Northwind Sample Database. The Northwind Sample

▶Tip

If you need to add data to more than one column, separate each additional column name with a comma.

Database ships with Access 2000. Figures 5.1 and 5.2 show the before and after recordset views.

```
SELECT Employees.*, Employees.Title
FROM Employees
WHERE (((Employees.Title)="Sales Representative")));
```

Using The INSERT INTO Statement

The **INSERT INTO** statement lets you add single records to a table, as well as copy records from tables or copy queries to other tables. Use this statement when you're ready to build an application that requires manual data entry (something you'll do in the next chapter). When adding a single record to a table, the **INSERT INTO** statement is composed of three parts, which follow the **INTO** keyword:

• The name of the table you want to add data to

• The name(s) of the column in which you want to insert data values

• The values to be added designated by the keyword **VALUES**

```
INSERT INTO table name [column name]
VALUES (value1, value2};
```

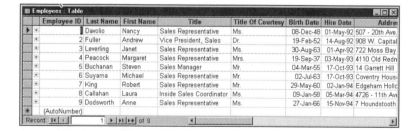

Figure 5.1
The Employees table prior to running the **SELECT** statement.

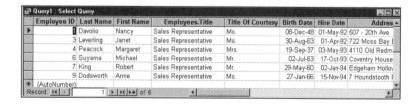

Figure 5.2
The recordset resulting from the execution of the **SELECT** statement.

When you want to copy a record from a table or query to another table, the **INSERT INTO** statement has two parts:

- The name of the table where the data is going

- A **SELECT** statement

```
INSERT INTO table name
SELECT statement
```

Let's look at a project containing code samples that demonstrate the two primary uses of the **INSERT INTO** statement. The first sample adds a record to the FirstTable table of the FirstDatabase database. The second code sample copies a record from a query of the FirstTable table and adds it to the FirstEmployees table. Because Access 2000 doesn't provide a command line interface for testing SQL statements, perform the following steps to run the code samples.

 *Project* Add A Record To A Table

The steps that follow allow you to add a record to a table using SQL. Again, you're constrained here because using SQL View is the only mechanism provided by Access for testing realtime SQL queries.

1. With the Access 2000 database window open, choose the Queries option under Objects in the database window object selection frame. Then select New from the window's button menu to launch the New Query dialog box shown in Figure 5.3.

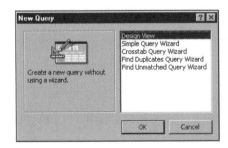

Figure 5.3
The New Query dialog box offers five ways to create a new query.

2. Select Design View, and then click OK to open the Access Query-By-Example grid and the Show Table dialog box (see Figure 5.4).

3. Click the Close button on the Show Table dialog box, and then select View|SQL View from the Access menu bar to open the SQL query window.

4. Select Edit|Delete from the Access menu bar to clear the contents of the query window, and then enter the following code (see Figure 5.5):

```
INSERT INTO FirstTable (Username, Password)
VALUES ("Clark", "Superman");
```

5. Select Query|Run from the Access menu bar. At this point, you'll be alerted that a new record will be appended to the table. When you see this prompt, click Yes (see Figure 5.6).

6. Close the query window by selecting File|Close from the Access menu bar, and click No when prompted to save the current query.

7. Check your result by opening the LogonForm created in Chapter 4, and enter the Username and Password you just

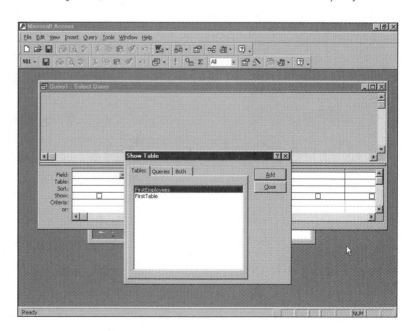

Figure 5.4
Selecting Design View launches the Access Query-By-Example (QBE) panels.

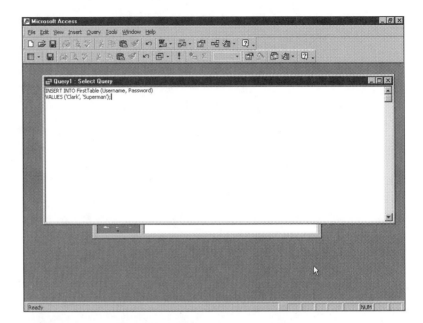

Figure 5.5
SQL View can be used
to evaluate SQL
statements.

Figure 5.6
Access alerts you before
it adds a row to an existing table from a query.

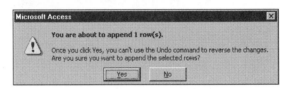

added using **INSERT INTO**. Your ID should be verified with
no problem; however, if you mistyped something, you will get
an error message.

Project Copy Records To Another Table

Before you begin this exercise, you'll need to create a quick table.
So, let's digress for a moment and do this in short order by performing the following steps:

1. Select File|Open from the Access menu bar, and open the
Northwind Sample Database.

2. With the Access 2000 database window open, choose the
Tables option under Objects in the database window object

NOTE

The Northwind Sample Database is located on the Access Program CD, in case you didn't copy it to your hard drive when you installed Access 2000.

selection frame. Then select New from the window's button menu to launch the New Table dialog box shown earlier in Figure 5.3.

3. Select Table Wizard from the New Table dialog box, and then click OK to launch the Table Wizard dialog box (see Figure 5.7).

4. Select Employees from the Sample Tables list box, and select the fields FirstName, LastName, and Title from the Sample Fields list box. Click the right arrow on the dialog box to move these fields to the Fields In My New Table list box, and then click Next.

5. On the new Table Wizard panel, enter "FirstEmployees", accept the remaining defaults, and then click Next twice. Finally, click the Finish button.

6. Close the new table by selecting File|Close from the Access menu bar.

With that done, let's get back to our **INSERT INTO** demonstration.

7. With the Access 2000 database window open, choose the Queries option under Objects in the database window object selection frame. Then select New from the window's button menu to launch the New Query dialog box.

8. Select Design View, and click OK to open the Access Query-By-Example grid and the Show Table dialog box.

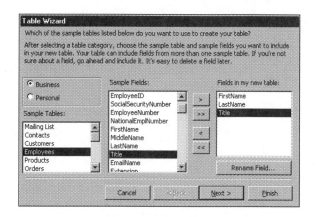

Figure 5.7
The Table Wizard lets you create new tables based on table models.

9. Click the Close button on the Show Table dialog box, and then select View|SQL View from the Access menu bar to open the SQL query window.

10. Select Edit|Delete from the Access menu bar to clear the contents of the query window, and then enter the following code:

```
INSERT INTO FirstEmployees
SELECT LastName, FirstName, Title FROM Employees;
```

11. Select Query|Run from the Access menu bar, and when prompted, click Yes.

12. Close the query window by selecting File|Close from the Access menu bar. Click No when prompted to save the current query.

13. Check your result by opening the FirstEmployees table. It should contain a four-column view of all the records from the Northwind Employees table.

Using The UPDATE Statement

When you need to make sure that the data supporting your applications is as current as possible, you'll frequently call on the **UPDATE** statement. This statement, as the name implies, lets you update data in one or more columns programmatically. In most cases, the **UPDATE** statement requires:

- The name of the table affected by the update

- Use of the **SET** keyword followed by the name of the column or columns to be updated

- An optional **WHERE** clause specifying which table rows to update

The **UPDATE** statement syntax is:

```
UPDATE tablename or queryname
SET column = Some expression
WHERE row-specific criteria
```

The next project contains a code sample that demonstrates how to use the **UPDATE** statement. The exercise allows you to update a record in the FirstEmployees table that you created in the **INSERT INTO** exercise.

Project Update A Record

The first record in the FirstEmployees table is that of Nancy Davolio, who, it just so happens, has been promoted from Sales Representative to Sales Manager. You can update Nancy's title to reflect her promotion by performing the following steps:

1. With the Access 2000 database window open, choose the Queries option under Objects in the database window object selection frame. Then select New from the window's button menu to launch the New Query dialog box.

2. Select Design View, and click OK to open the Access Query-By-Example grid and the Show Table dialog box.

3. Click the Close button on the Show Table dialog box, and then select View|SQL View from the Access menu bar to open the SQL query window.

4. Select Edit|Delete from the Access menu bar to clear the contents of the query window, and then enter the following code:

```
UPDATE FirstEmployees
SET Title = 'Sales Manager'
WHERE LastName = 'Davolio';
```

5. Select Query|Run from the Access menu bar, and when prompted, click Yes.

6. Close the query window by selecting File|Close from the Access menu bar, and click No when prompted to save the current query.

7. Check your result by opening the FirstEmployees table and looking in the Title field of the first record. It should show Sales Manager instead of Sales Representative.

Tip

*Exercise caution with the **DELETE** statement. Its simplicity is also one of its biggest dangers because, once executed, it deletes without warning.*

Using The DELETE Statement

Quite simply, the **DELETE** statement removes table rows. It generally requires:

- The **DELETE FROM** keywords followed by the name of the table from which data will be deleted

- A **WHERE** clause to restrict the deletion process

The syntax for the **DELETE** statement is:

```
DELETE
FROM tablename
WHERE restriction criteria
```

Use the preceding syntax to write your own SQL **DELETE** statement, and then remove a single record from the FirstEmployee table.

*Project* ## Using The Foundational Four

Here's your chance to bring everything together. Take this opportunity to perform a **SELECT** operation, move the results into a new table using the **INSERT INTO** statement, use the **UPDATE** statement to modify one or more rows in the new table, and then remove a few rows from the same table using the **DELETE** statement.

Where To Go From Here

In this chapter, you learned what Structured Query Language, a.k.a. SQL, is. You also saw some guidelines for correct construction of SQL statements, and how to use SQL to programmatically manipulate table data using the SQL Foundational Four: **SELECT**, **INSERT INTO**, **UPDATE**, and **DELETE**.

In the next chapter, you'll undertake the task of building a market research tool that calculates and stores research results. Take note of how Access, SQL, and VBA work together to produce a very useful application.

Chapter 6

Let's Build A Market Research Tool

Access allows you to design and build real-world solutions for many types of programming needs.

You've covered quite a lot of ground so far. Now, it's time to take what you've learned and apply it to the real world. In this chapter, I'll walk you through designing and building a simple market research tool, using the concepts and techniques that you acquired from the previous chapters. The goals are to reinforce what you've learned and to give you a sense of how a programming methodology helps to add structure and form to your development activities. I'll also introduce aggregate functions.

We'll begin by making you a consultant who's been called in to develop a productivity program for a fictional marketing team. As you proceed through this chapter, you'll find yourself wearing a number of different hats.

PRACTICE In Practice

In Chapter 1, you were introduced to a methodology called PRACTICE. As you may recall, PRACTICE is an acronym for the following eight solution development activities:

- **P**ose a purpose for your program.

- **R**esolve what the program needs to do.

- **A**llocate what the program needs to do to logical functions.

- **C**onsider the process steps.

- **T**est each functional code block.

57

- Integrate and debug.
- Correlate to the original purpose.
- End with good documentation.

You are going to use a streamlined version of PRACTICE to assess what work must be done and how you'll go about doing it. First, you'll need to determine the program's purpose. Your preliminary discussions with the marketing team have determined the goals that follow.

The Program's Purpose

You have been asked to build a program to increase the productivity of the marketing team by automating the team's market survey process. Team members have requested the solution because they currently use paper to collect and tally market research data. They find this to be both inefficient and cost-prohibitive.

What The Program Needs To Do

Because marketing team members have chosen to retire their paper data collection method, they want their new survey tool to provide an automated data collection and query capability. The program must allow them to collect market research data at their desktop, and to determine response percentages for each survey question at the click of a button. For this reason, the team has emphasized that the automated solution must provide a graphical user interface (GUI) to supply simple interaction with the survey data. Now that you know what the program needs to do, you've determined you'll use Access 2000 to build a prototype solution for demonstration purposes.

Allocate What The Program Must Do To Logical Functions

You'll begin your development activity by allocating the program into functional modules. You've decided that you need a program module to collect data, another to calculate data, another to retrieve data, and yet another to display the results. Now you have to find out the nature of the data your program needs to work with. After further discussions with the marketing team, you find that the paper survey consists of five statements; each statement is rated from -3 to 3. The survey statements are:

- Child safety seats should be mandatory for all automobiles.

- Auto dealers should provide all families with small children child safety seats at no cost.

- Wearing seat belts should not be mandatory for adults.

- Automobile airbags are more of a safety hazard than a safety help.

- Red automobiles are involved in more accidents than automobiles of any other color.

The rating scale for the questions is:

- -3   Strongly Disagree

- -2   Disagree

- -1   Somewhat Disagree

- 0   Don't Know

- 1   Somewhat Agree

- 2   Agree

- 3   Strongly Agree

Project Developing A Prototype

At this point, you begin developing a prototype for the new survey tool. Because you're familiar with the Access Development Model, your first task is to build the database that will store the survey responses. Create a database for the new market survey tool by performing the following steps:

1. Launch Access 2000.

2. Select the Blank Access Database radio button from the opening dialog box, and then click OK to launch the File New Database dialog box (see Figure 6.1).

3. Select the Desktop button in the Save In frame of the File New Database dialog box, and then type "Survey" in the File

▶Tip

Access 2000 now integrates desktop and Web browser functions.

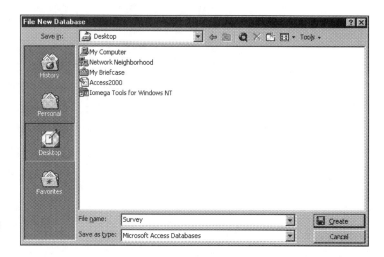

Figure 6.1
The File New Database dialog box.

**Tip**

Design View in Access 2000 has not changed from previous versions of Access.

Refer back to Chapter 3 for more on primary keys.

Name field. Click the Create button to open a new database called Survey with a blank table displayed in Datasheet View.

4. To define the data elements for the new table, select View|Design View from the Access menu bar.

5. Enter the data shown in Table 6.1 in the table's Design View, leaving the Description field blank (see Figure 6.2).

6. Select File|Save on the Access menu bar, and then enter "Responses" in the Save As dialog box. Click OK.

7. When Access prompts you to create a primary key, select Yes. You'll notice that the **RespondentID** field is the default primary key because of the key icon that appears to the left of the field name.

Table 6.1   Structure of the survey table.

Field Name	Data Type
RespondentID	AutoNumber
Q1	Number
Q2	Number
Q3	Number
Q4	Number
Q5	Number

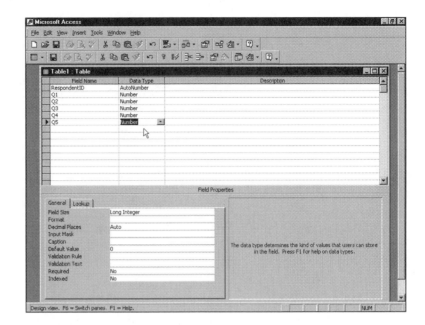

Figure 6.2
Use Design View to modify the structure of Access tables.

Project   Creating A Prototype User Interface

Now that your database and table have been created, it's time to advance to the next tier of the Access Development Model—object-oriented design. Create a prototype user interface for the new survey tool by performing the following steps:

1. Select File|Close on the Access menu bar to close the Responses table and reveal the Access Database Window.

2. Select the Forms button in the Objects frame of the Database Window. Then double-click Create Form By Using Wizard to open the first panel of the Form Wizard.

3. Select all fields for use on the form by clicking the double arrow button (see Figure 6.3), and then click Next to advance to the next Wizard panel.

The Form Wizard lets you choose from 10 standard form styles.

4. Select Justified in the Form Layout panel, and then click Next to advance.

5. Select Blueprint from the Form Wizard Style panel. Then click Next to advance to the final Form Wizard panel.

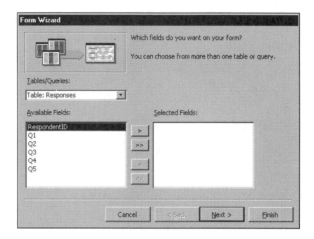

Figure 6.3
Use the >> button to select all fields for use on the form.

6. Enter "Market Research Survey Response Sheet" in the title field of the last Form Wizard panel (see Figure 6.4). Select the Modify The Form's Design radio button, and then click Finish. When you're done, your screen should appear as shown in Figure 6.5.

Customizing The Prototype User Interface

Now that your prototype user interface has a form layout, some minor customization is in order. Perform the following steps to customize the newly created form:

1. Select Edit|Select All to select every label and text field on the form.

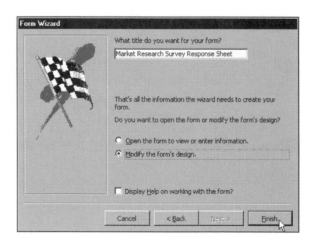

Figure 6.4
The last Form Wizard panel gives you additional customizing options.

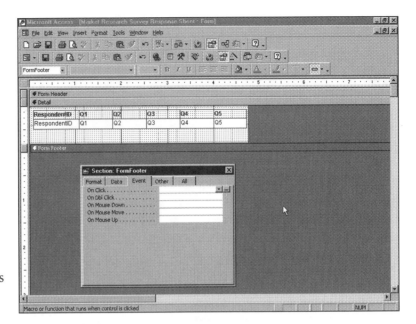

Figure 6.5
The form layout appears in the Detail section of the Design View.

2. Right-click on any selected field to open the right-click menu.

3. Select Special Effect: Sunken from the right-click menu (see Figure 6.6) to add some depth to each form field. A tool tip appears when you mouseover the selection, so you can see the name of each button.

4. Right-click on the form grid to open the form's right-click menu, and then select Toolbox to open the floating Toolbox palette (see Figure 6.7).

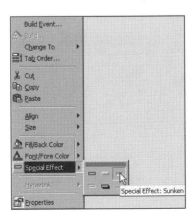

Figure 6.6
Use the Special Effect option to add depth or shading to form fields.

Figure 6.7
The floating Toolbox palette offers access to more than 30 form controls.

5. Select the Command Button control on the floating Toolbox palette, and click on the form grid to create five command buttons that will handle events (see Figure 6.8).

6. Select the first Command Button, select the Format tab on the Command Button property sheet, and then change the Caption property to "AVG Q1" (see Figure 6.9).

7. Select the Other tab on the Command Button property sheet, change the Name property to "AVG Q1", and then select File|Save from the Access menu bar. Save the form with the name "Market Research Survey Response Sheet".

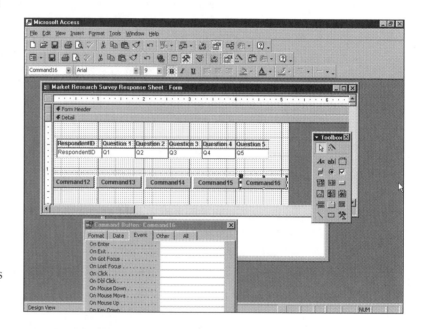

Figure 6.8
Use Command Buttons to trigger form event handlers.

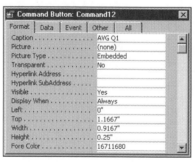

Figure 6.9
Change the Caption label with the Command Button property sheet.

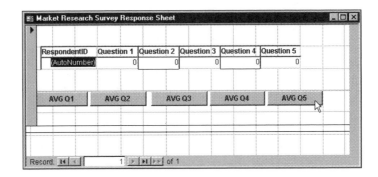

Figure 6.10
The Market Research Survey user interface prototype.

8. Repeat Steps 6 and 7 for each remaining command button. When you're done, select View|Form View from the Access menu bar. Your form should be similar to the one shown in Figure 6.10.

Consider The Process Steps

Now you're ready to consider the process steps needed to accomplish the functions you identified earlier: data collection, data calculation, data retrieval, and results display. The data collection function is a snap—it's accomplished using the form you just created. In addition, Access lets you append a blank record to the active table by clicking the right arrow button on the form status bar (see Figure 6.11).

The data retrieval and display functions should be familiar to you from the programs you created in Chapters 2 and 4. I'll skip the pseudocode for these routines—they're not very complex. The data calculation function, however, is a little more complex. In order to average the data stored in the columns for each survey question, the program we're working on right now will need some basic data summarization. This data summarization is called *aggregation*, and Access provides two function sets for performing it—SQL aggregation functions and domain aggregation functions.

Figure 6.11
Use the status bar to append a blank record to your table.

The two function sets essentially produce the same results; however, you should be aware of some differences.

SQL Aggregation Functions

Basically, there are three types of queries in Access SQL that support aggregation functions. Each produces a read-only recordset. These three query types are:

- Simple aggregation using a **SELECT** statement without a **GROUP BY** clause:

```
SELECT Sum(Q1)
FROM Responses
```

- **GROUP BY** queries involving a **SELECT** statement and a **GROUP BY** clause:

```
SELECT Sum(Q1)
FROM Responses
GROUP BY RespondentID
```

- Crosstab queries using the **TRANSFORM** statement:

```
TRANSFORM
SELECT Sum(Q1)
FROM Responses
GROUP BY RespondentID
```

Each of these query types uses some aggregate function with a **SELECT** clause. Table 6.2 lists the aggregate functions that are valid in Access 2000.

Domain Aggregate Functions

Domain aggregate functions let you perform an SQL summary query outside of a query object, namely in a form, report, or module. In fact, domain aggregate functions are considered to be a form of SQL statement because they perform an SQL operation on a table to return a value. Also, their arguments correspond to those in an SQL query. Take a look at the following examples; they both yield the same result:

NOTE

Domain aggregate functions have a reputation for being slow. Therefore, it's advisable to use them when speed is not your primary consideration.

Table 6.2   SQL aggregate functions.

Function Name	Operation
Avg()	Returns the average of all non-null column values
Count()	Returns the number of records in a table
First()	Returns the value of the first record in a recordset
Last()	Returns the value of the last record in a recordset
Max()	Returns the largest value in a recordset
Min()	Returns the smallest value in a recordset
Sum()	Returns the total of all records in a table
STDev()	Returns the sample standard deviation for a column
STDevP()	Returns the population standard deviation for a column
Var()	Returns the sample variance for a column
VarP()	Returns the variance deviation for a column

Table 6.3   Domain aggregate functions.

Function Name	Operation
DAvg()	Returns the average of all non-null column values
DCount()	Returns the number of records in a table
DFirst()	Returns the value of the first record in a recordset
DLast()	Returns the value of the last record in a recordset
DMax()	Returns the largest value in a recordset
DMin()	Returns the smallest value in a recordset
DSum()	Returns the total of all records in a table
DSTDev()	Returns the sample standard deviation for a column
DSTDevP()	Returns the population standard deviation for a column
DVar()	Returns the sample variance for a column
DVarP()	Returns the variance deviation for a column

```
DAvg("Q5", "Responses")

SELECT Avg(Q5) FROM Responses;
```

Table 6.3 shows you the domain aggregate functions that are valid in Access 2000.

With this said, let's get back to our prototype survey program.

.Project Creating The Program Event Handlers

One of the requirements for this program is that it determine percentages for each survey question at the click of a button. As you might expect, you will need to program a button event handler. Create an event handler for each of the buttons on the user interface prototype by performing the following steps:

1. Select View|Design View from the Access menu bar, and then right-click on the button labeled AVG Q1.

2. Select Build Event from the right-click menu, choose Code Builder from the Choose Builder dialog box, and then click OK to open the Visual Basic Editor (see Figure 6.12).

3. Enter the following code between the **Sub** and **End Sub** statements for **AVGQ1_Click()**:

```
'Variable Declaration Section
    Dim Stats1
'Variable Definition Section
    Stats1 = DAvg("q1", "Responses")
'Processing Logic Section
    MsgBox "The average response for Question 1 is " &
        Stats1
```

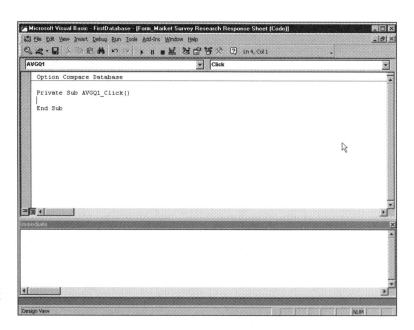

Figure 6.12
Use the Visual Basic Editor to create and test your event handlers.

4. Select File|Save Survey from the Visual Basic Editor menu bar, and then select Debug|Compile Survey. You should find no errors.

5. Select File|Close And Return To Microsoft Access on the Visual Basic Editor menu bar.

Project Testing Each Functional Code Block

Now you're ready to test your code block. If it works, you'll simply duplicate the code and modify it for the other button controls on the form. Test the code block by performing the following steps:

1. With the Market Research Survey Response Sheet in Form View, enter the following numbers into records 1 through 7 in the column labeled Question 1:

   "3", "2", "1", "0", "-1", "-2", "-3"

   Advance from record to record by clicking the right arrow button on the Form Status bar after you've entered the numeric value.

2. After you've entered all the values, click the AVG Q1 button. If all is well, you should see a message box that displays the average of all responses for Question 1 (see Figure 6.13).

3. Copy and modify the clean code block to each of the remaining control buttons. Make sure you modify each new code block to reflect the appropriate table column, and then test each newly created code block in isolation.

Figure 6.13

A successful test gives you the average of all Question 1 responses.

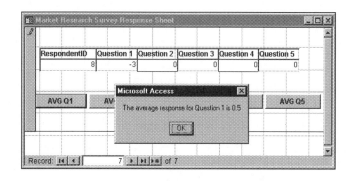

Integrating And Debugging

It should be all easy from here. Because this is not a complex program, and because each code block is a duplicate of the other, program integration for your Market Research prototype is a breeze. As far as debugging, congratulations, you're bug free. If you're a relative novice to programming, then rest assured— bug-free module integration is typically the exception and not the rule.

Correlating To The Original Purpose

You be the judge. Does the program prototype accomplish its purpose? Will it increase the productivity of the marketing team? Does the prototype allow the team to collect market research data at their desktop and to determine response percentages for each survey question at the click of a button? If you've answered yes to these questions, I'd say you were right. Congratulations, the marketing team should be very happy.

Ending With Good Documentation

This one's a no-brainer. You're reading the documentation for your prototype. Now, it's up to you to build a final version of the market research tool, documenting the bells and whistles that have yet to be added. Make generous use of comments in your code—use the section divisions from the examples you've completed as a guide. In addition, document any changes you make to your clean code blocks. This will pay big dividends down the road.

Where To Go From Here

In this chapter, you wrote and tested your third Access 2000 program. As I mentioned earlier, this chapter served to reinforce what you've already learned, to give you practical experience using a programming methodology to add structure and form to your development activity, and, finally, to introduce you to aggregate functions. Next, we'll get up close and personal with the fundamentals of Visual Basic for Applications. See you in the next chapter.

Chapter 7

VBA Programming Fundamentals

Even though you've written a little code and seen some functions work, it never hurts to reacquaint yourself with a few basics.

This chapter is a refresher for the experienced programmer and a primer for the novice. It will also come in handy when you need a quick VBA reference. As mentioned in previous chapters, Visual Basic for Applications is the standard programming language for Access 2000 and the other applications in the Office 2000 productivity suite. Because of VBA's integration with Access, mastering the programming nuances of either application gives you a good foundation in the other.

Getting Acquainted With VBA

VBA is a subset of the Visual Basic programming environment. When used with Access 2000, the VBA user interface replaces the familiar Access module window. As you know by now, the VBA interface is used for your code editing and debugging activities. The VBA user interface also includes additional features like the Properties window, the Project Explorer, and the Object Browser (see Figure 7.1). With the integration of VBA, Access is exposed to a more robust feature set that includes support for OLE automation and ActiveX controls. If you're already familiar with the syntax and capabilities of Visual Basic, you're ahead of the crowd. However, if Access 2000/VBA is your first exposure to Visual Basic programming, then you'll have to endure a slight learning curve. Not to worry though; you'll pick this stuff up in no time.

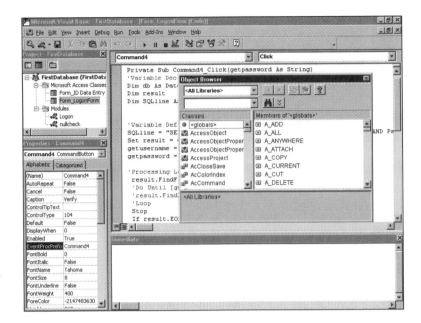

Figure 7.1
The VBA user interface gives Access a more robust feature set.

Understanding Methods, Properties, And Collections

Working with VBA requires an understanding of the way in which objects are referenced. For this reason, let's take a moment to examine the relationship between *methods*, *properties*, and *collections*.

In Chapter 3, you learned that Access development involves the use of object-oriented design and that an object is a term used to describe something tangible. For example, Car, Tire, and Door all represent physical objects in our environment. When thinking of objects in the Access/VBA world, you should view them in terms of:

• What you can do with them

• How they appear and what they're made of

When you think of what you can do with an object, you're thinking about an object's methods. For example, think of what you can do with a car. You can Start, Stop, Turn, Move Forward, or Move Backward. All of these things are methods of a Car object. In the VBA world, you would represent the object and its method with the object type followed by a dot, followed by the method. For instance, here are three objects with three different methods

- **CAR.START**
- **TIRE.ROLL**
- **DOOR.OPEN**

You can also refer to objects by the way they appear. When you refer to an object in this way, you are considering an object's properties. What are some properties of a car? Cars have color, they have engines, they have trunks, and they have brakes. Just as with methods, you would represent the object and its properties with the object type, followed by a dot, followed by the property:

- **CAR.COLOR = "Blue"**
- **CAR.ENGINE = "V-8"**

When you put together a group of objects with various methods and properties, you have a collection. As you may recall from Chapter 3, Access object collections are grouped as databases, tables, and forms. When the objects in a collection have similar properties and methods, they are referred to as a class. Hence, the notion of the Class module, which contains procedures that define the methods and properties of user-defined objects.

I'll discuss Class modules further in Chapter 10.

Now that you understand the concept of objects, methods, properties, and collections, let's take a look at variables.

Understanding VBA Variables

Think of variables as imaginary storage boxes that allow you to reference a location in your computer's memory. These storage boxes let you define and hold information that your program uses during its execution. Therefore, your programs are able to store data in a variable and access that same data by referencing the particular variable's name.

Creating Variables

You can create VBA variables using either the *explicit* method or the *implicit* method. When creating a variable with the explicit method, use the keyword **Dim** (short for dimension) followed by a variable name. For example, to create a variable called **Name**, you'd type the following VBA code

```
Dim Name
```

and you're done. You can also create more than one variable by following the **Dim** keyword with a string of variable names separated by commas. For example:

```
Dim Name, City, State
```

You can also create variables using the implicit method. With this method, you eliminate the use of keywords and simply declare a variable name and give it a value. For example

```
Month = September
```

automatically creates a variable called **Month** and assigns it the value **September**.

Generally, you should avoid mixing variable declaration methods, as it may be confusing to someone trying to maintain your code. For this reason, VBA provides a way to establish a consistent approach to variable declaration using the **Option Explicit** command. By using **Option Explicit** as the first line of code in

Following The Rules

In VBA, variable names must adhere to the following conventions:

- They must begin with a letter
- They can contain only letters, numbers, and the underscore character
- They must be 40 characters or less
- They cannot be a VB reserved word

In addition, VBA variables must be unique in their scope. *Scope* refers to a variable's availability with a given procedure. For example, when a variable is declared within a procedure, it is said to have *local* scope because it's only available to code in the procedure where it was declared. Conversely, when a variable is declared outside of a procedure but not within another procedure, that variable is said to have *public* scope, and it is available to all procedures in a given program. Local scope variables remain until their host procedure executes. Public variables exist until their host program has finished execution.

your programs, you disable the capability to declare variables using the implicit method. In other words, you'll be forced to use the **Dim** keyword each time you want to declare a variable.

Understanding VBA Data Types

VBA uses a number of different data types and subtypes to create variables. Some of the more commonly used data types include Currency, Decimal, Array, and Variant. Typically, variants hold strings and numbers; however they are not limited in this regard because of their ability to embrace data subtypes. Some common VBA data subtypes include:

- *Boolean*—Allows variables to be set as either True, with a value of -1, or False, with a value of 0.

- *Byte*—Allows the storage of integer values between 0 and 255.

- *Double*—A floating-point data type that has a range of $4.9E^{-324}$ to $1.8E^{308}$ for positive numbers, and a range of $-4.9E^{-324}$ to $-1.8E^{308}$ for negative numbers.

- *Date/Time*—Allows storage of date and/or time in a predefined format.

- *Empty*—Used for variables that have been created but not assigned a data value.

- *Error*—Used for error handling and debugging.

- *Integer*—Allows the storage of numbers that fall within the range -32,768 to 32,767 but cannot contain a decimal point.

- *Long*—Allows the storage of integers that fall within the range -2,147,483,648 to 2,147,683,647.

- *Null*—Used for variables specifically set to contain no data.

- *Object*—Allows variables to reference OLE automation objects.

- *Single*—Allows the storage of decimals or floating-point numbers in the range $1.4E^{-45}$ to $3.4E^{38}$ for positive numbers and $-1.4E^{-45}$ to $-3.4E^{38}$ for negative numbers.

- *String*—Used to store alphanumeric data.

For the most part, you can store most any kind of data in a variant variable, and it handles the data type appropriately.

Understanding VBA Operators

Operators are symbols that cause either a specific mathematical operation to be performed on a variable or cause a variable to be compared to one or more other variables. In VBA you'll encounter three classifications of operators: arithmetic operators, comparison operators, and logical operators (see Table 7.1). When you perform multiple operations in an expression, each operation is executed in *operator precedence*. In effect, this means that there is a predetermined order to the way operators are applied for evaluation within a program. Arithmetic operators are evaluated first, comparison operators are evaluated next, and logical operators are evaluated last (see Table 7.2).

Table 7.1   Standard VBA operators.

Operator	Operator Function	Operator Class
+	Addition.	Arithmetic
-	Subtraction.	Arithmetic
*	Multiplication.	Arithmetic
/	Division.	Arithmetic
^	Exponentiation.	Arithmetic
\	Integer Division.	Arithmetic
Mod	Modulo arithmetic.	Arithmetic
=	Tests if a variable is equal to another.	Comparison
<>	Tests if a variable is not equal to another.	Comparison
> and <	Tests if a variable is greater than or less than another.	Comparison
>= and <=	Tests if a variable is greater than or equal to, or less than or equal to, another.	Comparison
Is	Tests if two object references in an expression refer to the same object.	Comparison
And	Compares two or more variables as a test.	Logical
Or	Compares operators to see what condition must occur for an operation to proceed.	Logical
Not	Negates an expression.	Logical
XoR	Checks if only one condition is true.	Logical
Eqv	Checks for equality between two variables.	Logical
Imp	Performs a logical implication on two expressions.	Logical

Table 7.2   VBA operator precedence.

Operator	Operator Function	Precedence
+	Addition	3
-	Subtraction	3
*	Multiplication	2
/	Division	2
^	Exponentiation	1

Understanding VBA Control Constructs

When you're ready to write programs that make decisions or invoke repetitive code execution, then you'll use statements called *control constructs*. Program control constructs supported in VBA include:

If-Then

This control construct evaluates whether a condition is true, then performs some action. The syntax for the **If-Then** control construct is:

```
If your condition = True Then
    Statement to execute when your condition is true
End If
```

If-Then-Else

This control construct determines whether a condition is true, then performs some action based on the true condition or another action based on the false condition. The syntax for the **If-Then-Else** control construct is:

```
If your condition = True Then
    Statement to execute when your condition is true
Else
    Statement to execute when your condition is not true
End If
```

If-Then-ElseIf

This construct determines whether a condition is true. Then it performs some action based on the true condition or checks to see if there is another true condition.

```
If firstcondition Then
    Statement to execute when firstcondition is true
ElseIf secondcondition Then
    Statement to execute when firstcondition is false,
    and secondcondition is true
End If
```

The Select Case Construct

This construct lets you evaluate a value and perform an action based on that value. The syntax for the **Select Case** control construct is:

```
Select Case Your_Expression
    Case Expression-1
        Statement to execute if Expression-1
        matches Your_Expression
    Case Expression-2
        Statement to execute if Expression-2
        matches Your_Expression
    Case Else x
        Statement to execute if Expression-x
        matches Your_Expression
End Select
```

The For-Next Loop

This control construct executes a series of program statements x number of times. The syntax for the **For-Next** loop control construct is:

```
For countervariable = start to end
    Statement to be repeated
Next
```

The Do-While Loop

This control construct executes a series of program statements while a condition is true. In other words, a given condition is established that will change during execution of a program loop. When execution of the program loop causes the **While** condition to be false, the loop ends and the program continues to execute the next coded statement. The syntax for the **Do-While** loop control construct is:

```
Do While condition
    Statement to be executed within the loop
Loop
```

The Do Until Loop

This construct executes a series of program statements until a condition becomes true. With the **Do Until** construct, program execution begins and executes at least once before a condition to end loop execution is encountered. The syntax for the **Do Until** loop control construct is:

```
Do Until condition
    Statement to be executed within the loop
Loop
```

The Do-Loop Until Loop

This causes an action and then executes the action repeatedly until a condition is true. The syntax for the **Do-Loop Until** loop control construct is:

```
Do
    Statement to be executed within the loop
Loop Until condition
```

The Do-Loop While Loop

This construct causes an action and then executes the action repeatedly while a condition becomes true. The syntax for the **Do-Loop While** loop control construct is:

```
Do
    Statement to be executed within the loop
Loop While condition
```

Understanding VBA Procedures

Procedures are groups of code statements called by name to perform a given task within a program. In VBA, there are two types of procedures: subroutines and functions.

Understanding Subroutines

A *subroutine* acts as host for a series of VBA statements. Once you declare the block of code representing your subroutine in a program, that subroutine can be referenced and run at any time during program execution. Once a subroutine completes its function, control returns to the program that called it, and program execution resumes from the point at which that subroutine was called. Subroutines are declared using the beginning keyword **Sub** and the closing **End Sub** statement. The following example shows the structure of a typical subroutine

```
Sub SubroutineName
    Code statement within the subroutine
End Sub
```

wherein **SubroutineName** is, in fact, the subroutine's name. Subroutine names should be as descriptive as possible.

Understanding Functions

The second type of VBA procedure is known as a *function*. Functions are like subroutines, however they return a value to the calling block of code. You can declare a function using the keyword **Function**, and the statement **End Function**. The structure of a typical function is:

```
Function YourFunctionName()
    Code statement within the function
End Function
```

VBA In Action

In the paragraphs that follow, we'll take a closer look at some VBA features in context and see how they might apply to practical programming. As an aid to understanding, each of these features are presented with the following details:

- *Feature Name*

- *Feature Description*

- *Keywords*—The VBA words or symbols associated with the subject feature.

- *Code Sample*—A code block that you can run in the Access Visual Basic Editor to demonstrate the feature described.

Array Handling

This feature provides statements and functions that let you declare and manipulate array variables. An array is a variable construct that allows you to access a group of related data items using the same name. For instance, using an array you could refer to red, white, and blue, as **color(1)**, **color(2)**, **color(3)**. With an array, you can also access a particular data element using a unique index. Array indexes always identify the first element in the array as 0. Keywords for array handling include:

- **Array**
- **Dim**
- **Private**
- **Public**
- **ReDim**
- **IsArray**
- **Erase**
- **LBound**
- **Ubound**

The following code sample illustrates how an array might be used:

```
Option Compare Database

Sub ArrayTest()
Dim Month
Month = Array("January", "February", "March", _
              "April", "May", "June", "July")
a = Month (0)
b = Month (1)
c = Month (2)
d = Month (3)
e = Month (4)
f = Month (5)
g = Month (6)
Debug.Print a, b, c, d, e, f, g
End Sub
```

Assignments

This feature allows you to assign an object type to a VBA variable. The keyword used for assignment is **Set**:

```
Private Sub CodeTest()
'Variable Declaration Section
Dim db As Database
```

NOTE

Remember that an underscore character (_) is used as a line break character in VBA.

```
Dim result
Dim SQLline As String

getpassword = "result!Password"
'Variable Definition Section
SQLline = "SELECT * FROM FirstTable WHERE _
Username = [username] AND Password = [password];"
Set result = _
  CurrentDb.OpenRecordset(SQLline, dbOpenDynaset)
Debug.Print result!Username
result.MoveNext
Debug.Print result!Username
End Sub
```

Comments

This feature provides the capability to add explanatory text to programming code. The important keyword here is **Rem**. (It was originally short for "Remark.")

```
Private Sub Command4_Click()
Rem    Variable Declaration Section
       Dim db As Database
       Dim result
       Dim SQLline As String
Rem    Variable Definition Section
       SQLline = "SELECT * FROM FirstTable;"
       Set result = _
       CurrentDb.OpenRecordset(SQLline, dbOpenDynaset)
Rem    Processing Logic Section
End Sub
```

*The apostrophe can be used instead of **Rem** to denote a comment.*

Constant

This feature allows you to use special values that never change. For example, -1 is always equal to True and 0 is always equal to False. You can create your own constants by initializing variables and never changing their value. The code sample that follows executes a test to determine whether the declared variable is empty or full. The keywords involved include:

• **Empty**

• **Nothing**

• **Null**

*Constants can be evaluated using the **IsNull()** and **IsEmpty()** functions.*

- True

- False

The following code illustrates how a constant might be used:

```
Sub ConstantTest()
Rem This program tests the value of Constants.
Dim ConstantTest
ConstantTest = 10
If IsEmpty(ConstantTest) = True Then
    Debug.Print "This variable is empty."
Else
    Debug.Print "This variable contains data."
End If
End Sub

Sub ConstantTest()
Rem This program tests the value of Constants.
Dim ConstantTest
Rem ConstantTest = 10
If IsEmpty(ConstantTest) = True Then
    Debug.Print "This variable is empty."
Else
    Debug.Print "This variable contains data."
End If
End Sub
```

Control Flow

This feature provides the capability to introduce decision logic into your programs. Control flow constructs let you create blocks of code that can repeat or execute based on decision conditions in the code. Keywords for control flow include:

- Do...Loop

- For...Next

- For Each...Next

- If...Then...Else

- Select Case

For code examples, see the other samples in this section.

Procedures

VBA procedures are characterized by subroutines, which perform actions, and by functions, which perform a calculation and return a single value. Keywords include:

- **Call**

- **Function**

- **Sub**

Note that in the following code sample, you use the **Call** keyword to reference the **ArrayTest** procedure you used earlier.

```
Private Sub Command4_Click()
'Variable Declaration Section
Dim db As Database
Dim result
Dim SQLline As String
Dim getpassword As String

getpassword = "result!Password"
'Variable Definition Section
SQLline = "SELECT * FROM FirstTable WHERE _
  Username = [username] AND Password = [password];"
Set result _
  = CurrentDb.OpenRecordset(SQLline, dbOpenDynaset)
'Processing Logic Section
Do Until result!Password = Me!Password
    result.MoveNext
Loop
If result.EOF Or IsNull("password") Or _
    result!Password <> Me!Password Then
    MsgBox "This ID is not on file!"
Else
    MsgBox "Your ID has been verified"
End If
result.Close
Call ArrayTest
End Sub
```

When you run this code sample, verify that the procedure **ArrayTest** has executed by looking in the Debug window of the Visual Basic Editor.

Where To Go From Here

In this chapter, you explored some basics of Visual Basic for Applications. You learned about methods, properties, collections, variables, data types, operators, program control constructs, and procedures. This chapter also provided you with a number of examples to help you get a practical feel for how VBA can add versatility to your Access 2000 programs. Next, we'll take an in-depth look at recordsets and how they're used to retrieve data.

Chapter 8

Let's Work With Recordsets

*Now, it's time
to take a look
at how to write
Access 2000
programs
to navigate
your data.*

Aside from its rich feature set, Access 2000 is fundamentally a tool for storing, retrieving, and manipulating data. Consequently, Access programming allows you to extend the capabilities of the tool by automating common Access tasks. To demonstrate that, in this chapter, we'll build a Control Panel utility to automate data navigation and recordset retrieval. If you need a refresher about recordsets before you get started, take another look at Chapter 4.

.Project Designing The Control Panel

The Control Panel that you're about to build is a utility that you can use to quickly navigate through a given recordset. It should come in handy when you want to scan the data in a table or just familiarize yourself with the concepts of programmatic navigation. To use the utility, you'll simply need to go into the code and make adjustments for the table you want to work with. Perform the following steps to design the Control Panel form:

1. With the Access Database window open to FirstDatabase, click the Forms option under the Objects button, and then double-click Create Form In Design View to launch the Forms window.

2. Select View|Toolbox to display the Toolbox palette, if it's not already visible.

Figure 8.1
Use the Rectangle control to create form borders.

3. On the Toolbox, click the Rectangle control tool (see Figure 8.1).

4. Place the cursor in the upper-left corner of the form's Detail section, then click and hold down the left mouse button, dragging the cursor to the right corner of the Detail section.

5. Release the mouse button to complete the rectangle creation task (see Figure 8.2).

6. On the Toolbox palette, click the Command Button control tool.

7. Place the cursor inside the rectangle you just created, and then click once to place a Command Button control on the form.

8. Repeat Step 7 until you have created two rows, each with four command buttons.

9. Adjust the spacing of the button controls, and adjust the size of the rectangle so that there is enough space to place a label at the top of the form (see Figure 8.3).

10. On the Toolbox palette, click the Label control (see Figure 8.4).

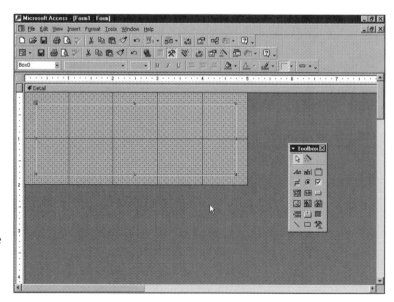

Figure 8.2
The completed rectangle should be centered on the form's Detail section.

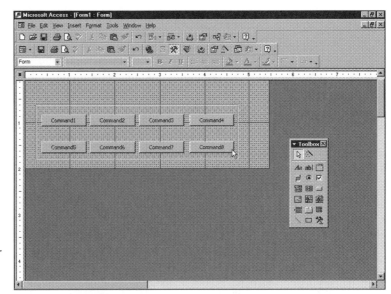

Figure 8.3
Your form should contain two rows of four buttons bound by a rectangle.

Figure 8.4
Use the Label control to add text-based labels to your forms.

11. Place the cursor on the form, just above the rectangle, and then, while holding down the left mouse button, drag the mouse down and to the right to create a label field.

12. At the blinking cursor inside of the Label field, type the words "Recordset Control Panel". When you're done typing, press the Enter key.

13. On the Access Formatting toolbar, select 18 from the Font Size drop-down menu.

14. Save the form as "Navigation Panel", by selecting File|Save As from the Access menu bar. Your form should look like the one shown in Figure 8.5.

.Project Enabling The Control Panel Buttons

Each of the eight buttons inside the rectangle must now be programmed to perform a different recordset navigation function. In the next sections, we'll enable the Control Panel buttons with the following recordset navigation capabilities: MoveLast, MoveFirst, MoveNext, MovePrevious, Move n Records, Seek,

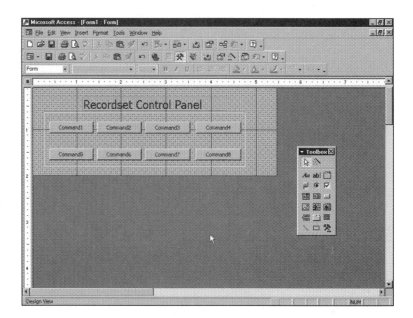

Figure 8.5
Your form should contain Label, Rectangle, and Button controls.

RecordCount, and PercentPosition. The details of each of these will be examined in the next chapter. For now, let's begin by enabling the MoveLast control button.

Creating The MoveLast Button

Your first task is to convert the Command1 button to the MoveLast button. You can accomplish this by performing the following steps:

1. Right-click the button labeled Command1, and then select Properties from the button's right-click menu to open the button's property sheet.

2. Select the All tab on the property sheet, and then move the tab's scrollbar to the top until you see the Name and Caption property fields (see Figure 8.6).

3. Change the button's Name and Caption properties from "Command1" to "MoveLast".

4. Scroll down the property sheet until you find the button's On Click property field.

5. Select the On Click property field, and then choose Event Procedure from the field's drop-down menu.

NOTE

Be advised that the activities you'll perform in this chapter are repetitive by design. The intent is to reinforce the construction process with each new recordset navigation command introduced. Although it may seem a bit redundant, take the time to execute each step of each activity. When you're done, not only will you have a reusable utility for record-set navigation, you'll understand what it takes to move through a record-set programmatically.

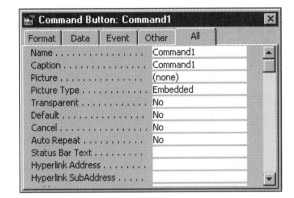

Figure 8.6
The first two button property entries on the All tab are Name and Caption.

NOTE

The code is broken here and in other examples for clarity; however, as a rule, do not break the lines of code associated with the **MsgBox** *or* **Input Box** *commands.*

6. Click the square button with three dots that appears to the right of the property field drop-down menu to launch the Visual Basic Editor.

7. Place the following code between the **Sub** and **End Sub** statements for the **MoveLast** click event:

```
'Variable Declaration Section
    Dim db As Database
    Dim recordsource
'Variable Definition Section
    Set db = CurrentDb
    Set recordsource = db.OpenRecordset("FirstEmployees")
'Processing Logic Section
    recordsource.MoveLast
    MsgBox "The last record in this table contains " &_
        "the Last Name: " & recordsource("LastName")
```

8. Select File|Close And Return To Microsoft Access from the Visual Basic Editor menu bar, and then close the form's property sheet.

9. Select View|Form View from the Access menu bar, and then click the MoveLast button. A message box should appear, as shown in Figure 8.7.

Creating The MoveFirst Button

Your next task is to convert the Command2 button to the MoveFirst button. You can accomplish this by performing the following steps:

Figure 8.7
Clicking the MoveLast
button displays a name
for the last table record.

1. Right-click the button labeled Command2, and then select Properties from the button's right-click menu to open the button's property sheet.

2. Select the All tab on the button's property sheet, and then move the tab's scrollbar to the top until you see the Name and Caption property fields.

3. Change the button's Name and Caption properties from "Command2" to "MoveFirst".

4. Scroll down the property sheet until you find the button's On Click property field.

5. Select the On Click property field, and then choose Event Procedure from the field's drop-down menu.

6. As before, click the square button with three dots that appears to the right of the property field drop-down menu to launch the Visual Basic Editor.

7. Place the following code between the **Sub** and **End Sub** statements for the **MoveFirst** click event:

```
'Variable Declaration Section
    Dim db As Database
    Dim recordsource
'Variable Definition Section
    Set db = CurrentDb
    Set recordsource = db.OpenRecordset("FirstEmployees")
'Processing Logic Section
    recordsource.MoveFirst
    MsgBox "The first record in this table " &_
      "contains the Last Name: " &
    recordsource("LastName")
```

8. Select File|Close And Return To Microsoft Access from the Visual Basic Editor menu bar, and then close the form's property sheet.

9. Select View|Form View from the Access menu bar, and then click the MoveFirst button. A message box should appear, as shown in Figure 8.8.

Creating The MoveNext Button

This time you'll convert the Command3 button to the MoveNext button. As you might expect, the steps you'll perform are as follows:

1. Right-click the button labeled Command3, and then select Properties from the button's right-click menu to open the button's property sheet.

2. Select the All tab on the button's property sheet, and then move the tab's scrollbar to the top until you see the Name and Caption property fields.

3. Change the button's Name and Caption properties from "Command3" to "MoveNext".

4. Scroll down the property sheet until you find the button's On Click property field.

5. Select the On Click property field, and then choose Event Procedure from the field's drop-down menu.

6. Click the square button with three dots that appears to the right of the property field drop-down menu to launch the Visual Basic Editor.

Figure 8.8
Clicking the MoveFirst button displays a name for the first table record.

7. Place the following code between the **Sub** and **End Sub**
   statements for the **MoveNext** click event. You'll notice that
   this time the code is slightly different, as you are incorporat-
   ing a **Do While** loop:

```
'Variable Declaration Section
    Dim db As Database
    Dim recordsource
'Variable Definition Section
    Set db = CurrentDb
    Set recordsource = db.OpenRecordset("FirstEmployees")
'Processing Logic Section
    Do While recordsource.EOF = False
    recordsource.MoveNext
        If recordsource.EOF = True Then
        MsgBox "End of File, " &_
            "Please Click the MovePrevious Button"
        Else
        MsgBox "This record contains the " &_
            "Last Name: " & recordsource("LastName")
        End If
    Loop
```

8. Select File|Close And Return To Microsoft Access from the
   Visual Basic Editor menu bar, and then close the form's
   property sheet.

9. Select View|Form View from the Access menu bar, and then
   click the MoveNext button. You'll notice that this time the
   message box displays the name of each record in the selected
   table, as illustrated by Figures 8.9 and 8.10.

Creating The MovePrevious Button

This time you'll convert the Command4 button to the
MovePrevious button. You can accomplish this by performing the
following steps:

1. Right-click the button labeled Command4, and then select
   Properties from the button's right-click menu to open the
   button's property sheet.

2. Select the All tab on the button's property sheet, and then
   move the tab's scrollbar to the top until you see the Name
   and Caption property fields.

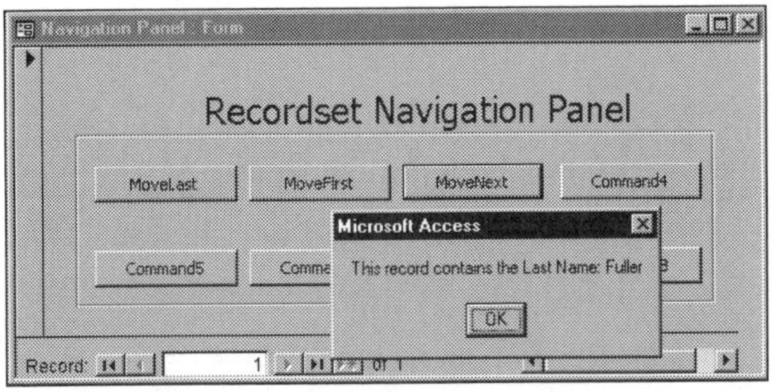

Figure 8.9
Clicking the MoveNext button invokes a loop displaying each table record.

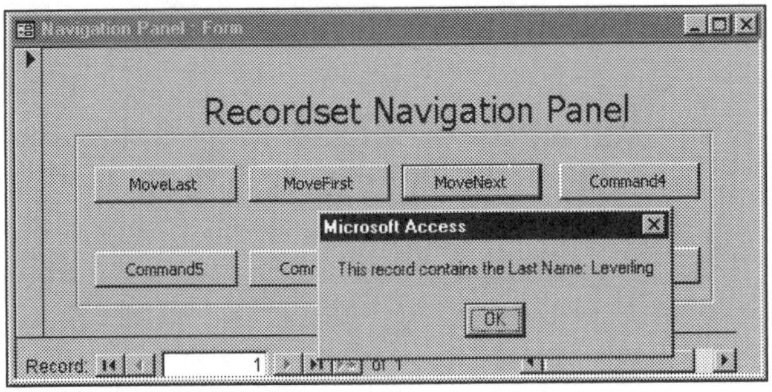

Figure 8.10
You'll notice that the record for Leverling follows the record for Fuller.

3. Change the button's Name and Caption properties from "Command4" to "MovePrevious".

4. Scroll down the property sheet until you find the button's On Click property field.

5. Select the On Click property field, and then choose Event Procedure from the field's drop-down menu.

6. Click the square button with three dots that appears to the right of the property field drop-down menu to launch the Visual Basic Editor.

7. Place the following code between the **Sub** and **End Sub** statements for the **MovePrevious** click event:

```
'Variable Declaration Section
    Dim db As Database
    Dim recordsource
'Variable Definition Section
    Set db = CurrentDb
    Set recordsource = db.OpenRecordset("FirstEmployees")
'Processing Logic Section
  recordsource.MoveLast
```

```
Do While recordsource.BOF = False
  recordsource.MovePrevious
     If recordsource.BOF = True Then
     MsgBox "Beginning of File, Please Click the " &_
        "MoveNext Button"
     Else
     MsgBox "This record contains the " &_
        "Last Name: " & recordsource("LastName")
     End If
  Loop
```

8. Select File|Close And Return To Microsoft Access from the Visual Basic Editor menu bar, and then close the form's property sheet.

9. Select View|Form View from the Access menu bar, and then click the MovePrevious button. This time you'll notice that the message box displays records in the reverse order from the way they appeared using the MoveNext button.

Creating The Move n Records Button

You've completed the first row of buttons for the Control Panel, so let's forge ahead by converting the Command5 button to the Move n Records button. You'll accomplish this by performing the following steps:

1. As before, right-click the button labeled Command5, and then select Properties from the button's right-click menu to open the button's property sheet.

2. Select the All tab on the button's property sheet, and then move the tab's scrollbar to the top until you see the Name and Caption property fields.

3. Change the button's Name property to "MovenRecords", and then change the button's Caption property to "Move n Records".

4. Scroll down the property sheet until you find the button's On Click property field.

5. Select the On Click property field, and then choose Event Procedure from the field's drop-down menu.

6. Click the square button with three dots that appears to the right of the property field drop-down menu to launch the Visual Basic Editor.

7. Place the following code between the **Sub** and **End Sub** statements for the **MovenRecords** click event:

```
'Variable Declaration Section
Dim db As Database
Dim recordsource
Dim Advance As Integer
'Variable Definition Section
Set db = CurrentDb
Set recordsource = db.OpenRecordset("FirstEmployees")
Advance = InputBox("Enter the number of rows you " &_
    "wish to move ahead")
'Processing Logic Section
    If IsEmpty(Advance) Then
    MsgBox "Please enter a value!"
    Else
    recordsource.Move Advance
    MsgBox "This record contains the " &_
        "last name " & recordsource("LastName")
    End If
```

8. Select File|Close And Return To Microsoft Access from the Visual Basic Editor menu bar, and then close the form's property sheet.

9. Select View|Form View from the Access menu bar, and then click the Move n Records button. An input box should appear, as shown in Figure 8.11.

10. Enter "5" in the input box, and then click OK. You should see a message box that displays the name Suyama for the record associated with the value 5 (see Figure 8.12).

Creating The Seek Button

Your next task is to convert the Command6 button to the Seek button. You'll accomplish this by performing the following steps:

1. Right-click the button labeled Command6, and then select Properties from the button's right-click menu to open the button's property sheet.

2. Select the All tab on the button's property sheet, and then move the tab's scrollbar to the top until you see the Name and Caption property fields. Change the button's Name and Caption properties from Command6 to "Seek".

▶Tip

Entering a negative number for Step 10 will generate an error.

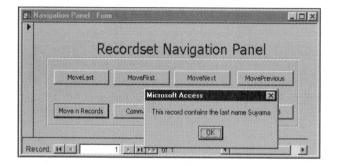

Figure 8.11
Clicking the Move n Records button prompts you to enter a value.

Figure 8.12
Suyama is the name associated with table record 5.

3. Scroll down the property sheet until you find the button's On Click property field.

4. Select the On Click property field, and then choose Event Procedure from the field's drop-down menu.

5. Click the square button with three dots that appears to the right of the property field drop-down menu to launch the Visual Basic Editor.

6. Place the following code between the **Sub** and **End Sub** statements for the **Seek** click event:

```
'Variable Declaration Section
Dim db As Database
Dim recordlist
Dim SeekIt As String
Dim MatchMsg
'Variable Definition Section
Set db = CurrentDb
Set recordlist = db.OpenRecordset("FirstEmployees")
SeekIt = InputBox("Enter the last name for " &_
    "the employee whose status you wish to check.")
MatchMsg = "The last name you entered is " &_
    "an authorized employee. "
```

```
'Processing Logic Section
        recordlist.Index = "LastName"
        recordlist.Seek "=", SeekIt
    If recordlist.NoMatch = True Then
        MsgBox "We have no employee on file " &_
            "with the last name " & SeekIt
    Else
    MsgBox MatchMsg
    End If
End Sub
```

7. Select File|Close And Return To Microsoft Access from the Visual Basic Editor menu bar, and then close the form's property sheet.

8. Select View|Form View from the Access menu bar, and then click the Seek button. An input box should appear, as shown in Figure 8.13.

9. Enter "Peacock" in the input box, and then click OK. You should see a message box that confirms the presence of Peacock in the table (see Figure 8.14).

Figure 8.13
Clicking the Seek button prompts you for the record you want to locate.

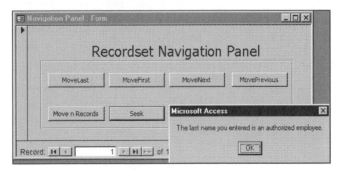

Figure 8.14
A confirmation message indicates that your Seek was successful.

Creating The RecordCount Button

Only two more tasks to go! This time you'll convert the Command7 button to the RecordCount button. You can accomplish this by performing the following steps:

1. Right-click the button labeled Command7, and then select Properties from the button's right-click menu to open the button's property sheet.

2. Select the All tab on the button's property sheet, and then move the tab's scrollbar to the top until you see the Name and Caption property fields.

3. Change the button's Name and Caption properties from "Command7" to "RecordCount".

4. Scroll down the property sheet until you find the button's On Click property field.

5. Select the On Click property field, and then choose Event Procedure from the field's drop-down menu.

6. As before, click the square button with three dots that appears to the right of the property field drop-down menu to launch the Visual Basic Editor.

7. Place the following code between the **Sub** and **End Sub** statements for the **RecordCount** click event:

```
'Variable Declaration Section
Dim db As Database
Dim recordsource
'Variable Definition Section
Set db = CurrentDb
Set recordsource = db.OpenRecordset("FirstEmployees")
    numrecs = recordsource.RecordCount
'Processing Logic Section
    MsgBox "The number of records in " &_
        "this table is " & numrecs
```

8. Select File|Close And Return To Microsoft Access from the Visual Basic Editor menu bar, and then close the form's property sheet.

9. Select View|Form View from the Access menu bar, and then click the RecordCount button. A message box should appear, as shown in Figure 8.15.

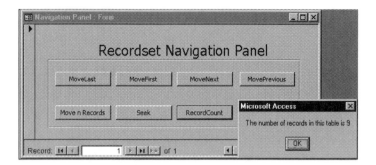

Figure 8.15
Clicking the
RecordCount button
displays the number of
table records.

Creating The PercentPosition Button

For your final task, you'll convert the Command8 button to the
PercentPosition button. Perform the following steps to accomplish this task:

1. Right-click the button labeled Command8, and then select
   Properties from the button's right-click menu to open the
   button's property sheet.

2. Select the All tab on the buttons property sheet, and then
   move the tab's scrollbar to the top until you see the Name and
   Caption property fields.

3. Change the button's Name and Caption properties from
   "Command8" to "PercentPosition".

4. Scroll down the property sheet until you find the button's On
   Click property field.

5. Select the On Click property field, and then choose Event
   Procedure from the field's drop-down menu.

6. Click the square button with three dots that appears to the
   right of the property field drop-down menu to launch the
   Visual Basic Editor.

7. Place the following code between the **Sub** and **End Sub**
   statements for the **PercentPosition** click event:

```
'Variable Declaration Section
Dim db As Database
Dim recordsource
Dim percent
'Variable Definition Section
Set db = CurrentDb
```

```
Set recordsource = db.OpenRecordset("FirstEmployees")
percent = InputBox("Please enter a percentage.")
'Processing Logic Section
    recordsource.PercentPosition = percent
    MsgBox "The record found at this " &_
        position contains the last name " &_
        recordsource("LastName")
```

8. Select File|Close And Return To Microsoft Access from the Visual Basic Editor menu bar, and then close the form's property sheet.

9. Select View|Form View from the Access menu bar, and then click the PercentPosition button. An input box should appear, as shown in Figure 8.16.

10. Enter "20" in the input box, and then click OK. You should see a message box that confirms the presence of Leverling at the 20 percent point in the table (see Figure 8.17).

Now you're all done and your Control Panel utility has been tested! The finished product should appear as shown in Figure 8.18.

Where To Go From Here

In this chapter, you designed, programmed, and tested a recordset navigation utility. Using this utility, you can move through any recordset in a variety of different ways. Coming up next, we'll take a closer look at the navigation commands used in programming the utility click events. We'll also explore how to refine recordset navigation using SQL operators.

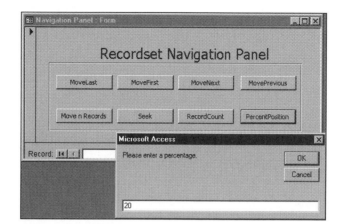

Figure 8.16
Clicking the
PercentPosition button
prompts you for a
percentage value.

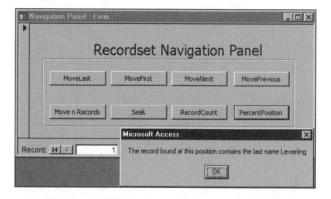

Figure 8.17
A named record is
associated with the
percentage you entered.

Figure 8.18
The Recordset Control
Panel utility.

Chapter 9

Understanding SQL And VBA Operators

Programming in Access 2000 is about interacting more efficiently with data. This means providing you with the capability to easily retrieve the data you want, manipulate the data as you require, and view the data in a variety of ways.

The control panel that you built in the last chapter demonstrated how to use Access 2000 and VBA to programmatically adjust your position in a set of records. Now that you've had a little hands-on experience moving around inside the database programmatically, let's take a look at some alternate methods for getting to the data that you want, and making it do what you need. Before we begin, however, let's take a quick look back at the Recordset Control Panel to gain some insight into coding for automatic record navigation.

Understanding The Recordset Control Panel

The Recordset Control Panel that you created in Chapter 8 is an Access 2000 form containing eight Command Button controls. Each Command Button control triggers an event procedure that allows you to perform some aspect of recordset navigation. Let's begin our look at the Recordset Navigation Control Panel by examining the various methods used to traverse the rows of a recordset. The first four buttons on the Navigation Control Panel demonstrate the four basic navigation methods: **MoveLast**, **MoveFirst**, **MoveNext**, and **MovePrevious**. Because the code for each of the first four buttons is similar, you can get a feel for how these methods are invoked by examining a representative procedure. Listing 9.1 numbers the lines of code to make discussing the code easier.

Listing 9.1   Examining the MoveLast procedure.

```
1    'Variable Declaration Section
2    Dim db As Database
3    Dim recordsource
4    'Variable Definition Section
5    Set db = CurrentDb
6    Set recordsource =
          db.OpenRecordset("FirstEmployees")
7    'Processing Logic Section
8    recordsource.MoveLast
9    MsgBox "The last record in this
          table contains the Last Name: "
          recordsource("LastName")
```

Line 1 of the **MoveLast** procedure is a comment that defines a variable declaration section header. Lines 2 and 3 declare the variables **db** and **recordsource**. **db** is declared as a database object type and **recordsource** is declared as a variant object type. As you may recall from Chapter 3, the Access object model supports application object types and data access object types. The database object type represents the container that holds the data and its associated code. Variants are variables that are capable of storing a variety of different data types; they are not restricted to numbers or letters only. Line 4 presents another section header. This time, the header identifies the area in the code where values are defined for the previously declared variables.

The variable **db** is assigned the value **CurrentDb**. **CurrentDb** not only refers to the current database but also creates a new instance of the current database. Effectively, Line 5 lets Access know that the records to be used by the subroutine are stored in the new instance of the current database. In Line 6, you assigned the variable **recordsource** the values contained in the **FirstEmployees** table. The fact that the **recordsource** variable contains values from an entire table is the result of creating a table-type **Recordset** object and populating the object with the contents of the **FirstEmployees** table. Line 7 denotes the final

NOTE

*For the sake of clarity, be aware that **MoveFirst** immediately jumps you to the first record in a recordset, and **MoveNext** moves you ahead one record at a time. As you might expect, **Move-Previous** moves you backward in a recordset one record at a time.*

section header for the code block and identifies the section as including the procedure's data processing logic.

Line 8 of the code block is what distinguishes each of the buttons on the Recordset Navigation Control Panel—this is where you find the instruction for moving within the recordset known as **recordsource**. In this case, **MoveLast** leapfrogs you to the last record in the generated recordset. Finally, Line 9 launches a message box to let you know the last name of the individual that appears first in the recordset. Although it's not shown here, each of the Recordset Navigation Control Panel procedures begins and ends with the **Sub...End Sub** construct discussed in Chapter 7.

Examining The Move *n* Records Procedure

Although similar to the procedures for the first four panel buttons, the **Move *n* Records** button procedure introduces the **Move** method. When the **Move** method is used to navigate a recordset, an additional parameter is required. This additional parameter calls for the number of rows that you want to move within the specified recordset. Direct your attention to lines 4, 8, and 10 through 13 in Listing 9.2.

Listing 9.2   Code introducing the Move method.

```
1    'Variable Declaration Section
2    Dim db As Database
3    Dim RecordSource
4    Dim Advance As Integer
5    'Variable Definition Section
6    Set db = CurrentDb
7    Set RecordSource =
        db.OpenRecordset("FirstEmployees")
8    Advance = InputBox("Enter the number of rows
                         you wish to move ahead")
9    'Processing Logic Section
10   If IsEmpty(Advance) Then
11   MsgBox "Please enter a value!"
12   Else
13   RecordSource.Move Advance
14   MsgBox "This record contains the last name"
        & RecordSource("LastName")
15   End If
```

Line 4 declares the variable **Advance** as type **Integer**. Line 8 uses an **InputBox** to collect the numeric data value stored in the variable **Advance**. Lines 10 through 12 begin an **If...Then...Else** statement that checks to see if the **Advance** variable contains any data and prompts the user to enter a value if no data is detected. Line 13 provides the **Move** method of the **RecordSource** object with the numeric value required to move forward or backward in the recordset. Entering a positive value, for instance 1 or 2, moves you ahead in the recordset, while entering a negative number has the opposite effect.

Examining The Seek Procedure

One of the most efficient ways to find what you're looking for in a recordset is to use the **Seek** method. Using **Seek** allows Access to take advantage of field indexes, thereby increasing the speed with which a search can be executed. Using the **Seek** method requires that you provide an index field to search on and a record search criteria. Take a look at Lines 4, 9, and 12 through 15 in Listing 9.3.

Listing 9.3   Code introducing the Seek method.

```
1    'Variable Declaration Section
2    Dim db As Database
3    Dim recordlist
4    Dim SeekIt As String
5    Dim MatchMsg
6    'Variable Definition Section
7    Set db = CurrentDb
8    Set recordlist = db.OpenRecordset("FirstEmployees")
9    SeekIt = InputBox("Enter the last name
                        for the employee whose
                        status you wish to check.")
10   MatchMsg = "The last name you
                    entered is an authorized employee."
11   'Processing Logic Section
12   recordlist.Index = "LastName"
13   recordlist.Seek "=", SeekIt
14   If recordlist.NoMatch = True Then
15   MsgBox "We have no employee
                on file with the last name " & SeekIt
16   Else
17   MsgBox MatchMsg
18   End If
```

Line 4 declares the variable **SeekIt** as type **String**. Line 9 uses an **InputBox** to collect the string value stored in the variable **SeekIt** for use as a search criterion. Line 12 specifies the index to use to find the required record. In this case, the first record that has an indexed field equal to **LastName** is specified. Line 13 then uses the **Seek** method to look for the record that has a string value contained in the **SeekIt** variable. Lines 14 and 15 begin an **If...Then...Else** statement that displays (in a message box) the value of the record matching the search criteria.

Examining The RecordCount Procedure

Although the **RecordCount** procedure does not navigate a record-set in the conventional sense of moving forward and back, it does assist you in the navigation process. The **RecordCount** property does not return the actual number of rows in a recordset. Instead, it returns the number of rows that have been accessed. Consequently, in order to find the actual number of rows, first you need to move to the last record in a given recordset, and then invoke the **Record-Count** property. Otherwise, the **RecordCount** property returns 0 for no rows, or 1 if one or more rows exist when the recordset is created. Because the **MoveLast** procedure was previously invoked, Line 7 of Listing 9.4 shows that the variable **numrecs** will store the value returned by the **RecordCount** property.

Listing 9.4   Code introducing the RecordCount property.

```
1    'Variable Declaration Section
2    Dim db As Database
3    Dim recordsource
4    'Variable Definition Section
5    Set db = CurrentDb
6    Set recordsource =
            db.OpenRecordset("FirstEmployees")
7    numrecs = recordsource.RecordCount
8    'Processing Logic Section
9    MsgBox "The number of records in this table is
            & numrecs
```

Examining The PercentPosition Procedure

The **PercentPosition** procedure introduces you to the **PercentPosition** property. This property allows you to find a record by setting a percentage that equates to the total number of records returned by the **RecordCount** property. For the Recordset Navigation Control Panel, the **PercentPosition** property is invoked using lines 4, 8, 10, and 11 of Listing 9.5.

Listing 9.5   Code introducing the PercentPosition property.

```
1    'Variable Declaration Section
2    Dim db As Database
3    Dim recordsource
4    Dim percent
5    'Variable Definition Section
6    Set db = CurrentDb
7    Set recordsource =
         db.OpenRecordset("FirstEmployees")
8    percent = InputBox("Please enter a percentage.")
9    'Processing Logic Section
10   recordsource.PercentPosition = percent
11   MsgBox "The record found at this
             position contains the last name "
         & recordsource("LastName")
```

Line 4 declares the variable **percent** in support of Line 8, which uses **InputBox** to collect the numeric data value stored in the variable. Line 10 invokes the **PercentPosition** property, which then moves through the recordset to supply the value displayed in the message box launched in Line 11.

Recordset Navigation And The Bookmark Property

Although it wasn't demonstrated on the Recordset Navigation Control Panel, the **Bookmark** property provides yet another method for accomplishing recordset navigation. In effect, the **Bookmark** property lets you uniquely identify each individual recordset row and is stored by Access as a four-byte array. Bookmarks should typically be assigned to a **String** or **Variant** data type using the following syntax:

```
Dim myBookmark As String or As Variant
myBookmark = recordsource.Bookmark
```

So that you can see the **Bookmark** property in action, modify the code for the **MoveLast** button on the Recordset Navigation Control Panel as shown in Listing 9.6.

Listing 9.6   Code introducing the Bookmark property.

```
Private Sub MoveLast_Click()
'Variable Declaration Section
    Dim db As Database
    Dim RecordSource
    Dim myBookmark As String
'Variable Definition Section
    Set db = CurrentDb
    Set RecordSource =
    db.OpenRecordset("FirstEmployees")
    myBookmark = RecordSource.Bookmark
'Processing Logic Section
    RecordSource.MoveLast
    MsgBox "The last record in this table contains the
            Last Name: " & RecordSource("LastName")
    RecordSource.MoveFirst
    RecordSource.MoveNext
    RecordSource.Bookmark = myBookmark
    MsgBox "This is a Bookmark test."
            & RecordSource("LastName")
    RecordSource.Bookmark = myBookmark
    MsgBox "A successful Bookmark is
            confirmed by the Last Name:
            & RecordSource("LastName")
```

Understanding SQL Operators

In Chapter 5, we discussed the foundational four SQL statements used to manipulate table data: **SELECT**, **INSERT INTO**, **UPDATE**, and **DELETE**. However, now that we've turned our attention to data navigation and retrieval, SQL has a bit more to offer. SQL supports three special operators used to retrieve records based on multiple match possibilities. These special operators are **BETWEEN**, **IN**, and **LIKE**. I'll briefly discuss each of these in the paragraphs that follow.

The BETWEEN Operator

With the **BETWEEN** operator, you are able to determine whether a value is within the range of two other values. Used as an extension of the SQL **WHERE** clause, the **BETWEEN** operator combines the greater than or equal to (**>=**) and the less than or equal to (**<=**) conditions. The following code snippet uses the **BETWEEN** operator to retrieve only ZIP codes between 90210 and 91210:

```
SELECT * FROM Test WHERE ZipCode BETWEEN 90210 AND 91210
```

The IN Operator

The **IN** operator is used to determine whether a value is a member of a specific dataset. The values belonging to the dataset must be separated by commas and enclosed in parentheses. Using the **IN** operator also allows you to test whether a value is part of the result set of a different **SELECT** statement. The **IN** operator corresponds to using the **OR** operator for each data value. The code snippet that follows retrieves values for handsets made by Nokia, Ericsson, or Motorola:

```
SELECT * FROM Phones
WHERE Manufacturer
IN ('Nokia', 'Ericsson', 'Motorola')
```

The preceding code is equivalent to the following:

```
SELECT * FROM Phones WHERE Manufacturer ='Nokia'
OR Manufacturer= 'Ericsson' OR Manufacturer = 'Motorola'
```

The LIKE Operator

The **LIKE** operator lets you check for string value matches using wild cards. Wild cards are symbols that act as value substitutes in string searches when looking for a specific character pattern. You're probably familiar with the asterisk (*) wild card symbol or the $ wild card symbol. You can also use the percent symbol (%) as a wild card. Using the **LIKE** operator is known to be a performance inhibitor, because searches using **LIKE** usually take longer to complete than other search conditions. The following code snippet uses the **LIKE** operator to retrieve individuals whose last name begins with the letter "P". For a pattern match to occur, a last name must have "P" as the first character:

```
SELECT * FROM AddressBook WHERE LastName LIKE 'P*'
```

The next statement retrieves individuals with a "P" anywhere in their last name:

```
SELECT * FROM AddressBook WHERE LastName LIKE '*P*'
```

The next statement retrieves individuals whose last name ends with a "P":

```
SELECT * FROM AddressBook WHERE LastName LIKE '*P'
```

The next statement retrieves individuals whose last name does not begin with "P". This example shows that the **LIKE** operator is negated when the **NOT** operator is used.

```
SELECT * FROM AddressBook WHERE LastName NOT LIKE 'P*'
```

Understanding VBA Operators

In Chapter 7, you were introduced to the three classes of VBA operators: arithmetic operators, comparison operators, and logical operators. Here, you'll gain a more detailed understanding about these operator classes and how the operators themselves are used.

Understanding Arithmetic Operators

As you might expect, arithmetic operators let you perform simple math calculations on variables. You're probably very familiar with these operators already, as you no doubt encountered them in grade school. At any rate, because you need to know how to handle these operators in your programming life, it never hurts to review them. However, before we begin, let's create a simple application that we'll use and build on throughout the discussion.

First create a new table in the FirstDatabase database called **ShoeOrders**, and give it the structure shown in Table 9.1.

Table 9.1   The structure of the ShoeOrders table.

Field Name	Data Type	Description
OrderID	Autonumber	**OrderID** is the primary key.
DressShoes	Number	
CasualShoes	Number	
RunningShoes	Number	

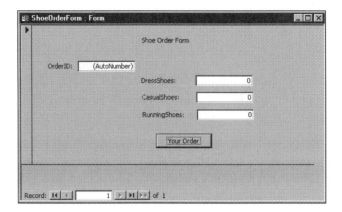

Figure 9.1
The ShoeOrderForm.

Next, create and save a form called ShoeOrderForm using the
ShoeOrders table as your data source. Your screen should appear
as shown in Figure 9.1. You'll notice that values appear in the
fields shown on the ShoeOrderForm. This is because the fields are
bound to the **ShoeOrders** table. If you find that no values appear
in your form's text box fields, then perform the following steps:

1. Right-click on the field to open the right-click menu.

2. Select Properties to open the Text Box Property sheet.

3. Select the All tab on the Text Box Property sheet, and then
   enter the field name from the **ShoeOrders** table in the
   Control Source property field.

4. Select File|Save, and then close the Property sheet.

5. Repeat Steps 1 through 4 as needed.

The Addition Operator

The addition operator (**+**) is used to add values together whether
they are variables, constants, or integers. You'll use this operator
to add two numbers, as in:

```
Total_Orders = 7 + 3
```

Or, you can add a number to a variable and assign it to another variable:

```
Total_Orders = AllShoes + 25
```

Now, let's have some fun. Create an **OnClick** event procedure for the Your Order button on the ShoeOrderForm by adding the following code:

```
Private Sub YourOrder_Click()
'Variable declaration section
Dim Shoes_Ordered
Dim Dress
Dim Casual
Dim Running
'Variable definition section
Dress = CInt(DressShoes.Value)
Casual = CInt(CasualShoes.Value)
Running = CInt(RunningShoes.Value)
Shoes_Ordered = Dress + Casual + Running
'Processing logic section
MsgBox "Your total shoe order is "
   & Shoes_Ordered & " pairs!"
End Sub
```

Enter the value 5 in each of the form fields, and then click the Your Order button. Your result should appear as shown in Figure 9.2.

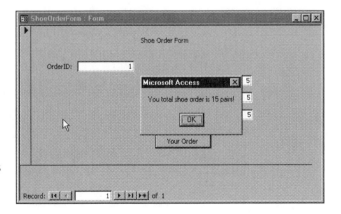

Figure 9.2
A shoe order of 15 pairs illustrates the addition operator in action.

The Subtraction Operator

As you might expect, the subtraction operator (-) is used in the opposite fashion of the addition operator. The subtraction operator subtracts numbers instead of adding them. Modify the code for the Your Order button as follows to see the subtraction operator in action. Your result should appear as shown in Figure 9.3.

```
Private Sub YourOrder_Click()
'Variable declaration section
Dim Shoes_Ordered
Dim Shoes_OutofStock
Dim Dress
Dim Casual
Dim Running
'Variable definition section
Dress = CInt(DressShoes.Value)
Casual = CInt(CasualShoes.Value)
Running = CInt(RunningShoes.Value)
Shoes_Ordered = Dress + Casual + Running
Shoes_OutofStock=Shoes_Ordered - 5
'Processing logic section
MsgBox "Your total shoe order is "
    Shoes_Ordered & " pairs!"
MsgBox "Oops! We're out of Casual Shoes, your order
    is reduced to " & Shoes_OutofStock & " pairs!"
End Sub
```

Notice that the **ShoeOrders** table still has a record of your original order; this is because you modified the code but not the table. Edit the record to reflect 0 Casual Shoes at your convenience. You'll also notice that when you make the change to the table, your order is reduced yet again.

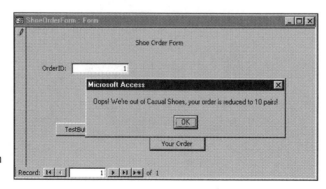

Figure 9.3

A reduced shoe order illustrates the subtraction operator in action.

The Multiplication Operator

The multiplication operator (*) is used to multiply numeric values. Modify the code for the Your Order button as follows to see the multiplication operator in action. Your result should appear as shown in Figure 9.4.

```
Private Sub YourOrder_Click()
'Variable declaration section
Dim Shoes_Ordered
Dim Shoes_OutofStock
Dim Dress
Dim Casual
Dim Running
Dim OrderCost
'Variable definition section
Dress = CInt(DressShoes.Value)
Casual = CInt(CasualShoes.Value)
Running = CInt(RunningShoes.Value)
Shoes_Ordered = Dress + Casual + Running
Shoes_OutofStock=Shoes_Ordered - 5
OrderCost = Shoes_Ordered * 19.95
'Processing logic section
MsgBox "Your total shoe order is "
    Shoes_Ordered & " pairs!"
MsgBox "Oops! We're out of Casual
    Shoes, your order is reduced to
    Shoes_OutofStock & " pairs!"
MsgBox "Your order cost is $" & OrderCost & "."
End Sub
```

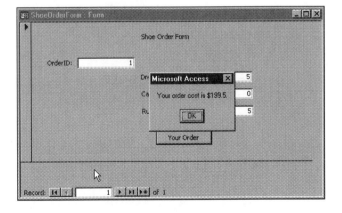

Figure 9.4

An order of $199.50 illustrates the multiplication operator in action.

The Division Operator

The division operator (/) is the last arithmetic operator we'll cover for now. Just as subtraction complements addition, division complements multiplication. As the name implies, the division operator is used to divide numeric values. Modify the code for the Your Order button as follows to see how the division operator is used. Your result should appear as shown in Figure 9.5.

```
Private Sub YourOrder_Click()
'Variable declaration section
Dim Shoes_Ordered
Dim Shoes_OutofStock
Dim Dress
Dim Casual
Dim Running
Dim OrderCost
Dim CostPerPair
'Variable definition section
Dress = CInt(DressShoes.Value)
Casual = CInt(CasualShoes.Value)
Running = CInt(RunningShoes.Value)
Shoes_Ordered = Dress + Casual + Running
Shoes_OutofStock=Shoes_Ordered - 5
OrderCost = Shoes_Ordered * 19.95
CostPerPair = OrderCost / Shoes_Ordered
'processing logic section
MsgBox "Your total shoe order is "
   Shoes_Ordered & " pairs!"
MsgBox "Oops! We're out of Casual
   Shoes, your order is reduced to"
   Shoes_OutofStock & " pairs!"
MsgBox "Your order cost is $" & OrderCost & "."
MsgBox "Your cost per pair is $" & CostPerPair & "."
End Sub
```

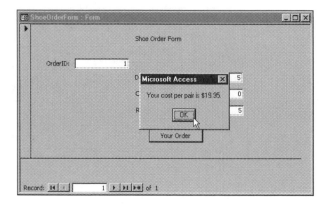

Figure 9.5
$19.95 per pair illustrates the division operator in action.

Understanding Comparison Operators

The next operator class is for comparison operators. These operators are used to compare any combination of variables, numbers, or constants. In this class, you'll find the equality and inequality operators, as well as the operators for less than and greater than. So, let's start from the top.

The Equality Operator

The equality operator (=) is used to test for value equality. Value equality is always used to check a condition, as shown in the following code snippet:

```
If x = y Then
Proceed to Z
Else
End If
```

The Inequality Operator

As the name implies the inequality operator (<>) is used to test for value inequality. As shown in the following code snippet, the construct results in True if inequality exists and False if it does not.

```
If x <> y Then
Proceed to Z
Else
End If
```

Less Than And Greater Than Operators

The less than operator (<) tests that the value on the left is less than the value on the right, while the greater than (>) operator does the exact opposite. The following code snippets illustrate how these opposite operators are used:

```
If x < y Then
Proceed to Z
Else
End If
```

```
If x > y Then
Proceed to Z
Else
End If
```

Less Than Or Equal To And Greater Than Or Equal To Operators

The less than or equal to operator (**<=**) tests that the value on the left is less than or equal to the value on the right, and its companion the greater than or equal to (**>=**) operator tests that the value on the left is greater than or equal to the value on the right. The following code snippets illustrate how these operators are used:

```
If x <= y Then
Proceed to Z
Else
End If

If x >= y Then
Proceed to Z
Else
End If
```

Understanding Logical Operators

The final operator class we'll discuss is the logical operators. This class contains members used to evaluate variables, numbers, or constants as either True or False. You'll find that you use logical operators in both your VBA and SQL statements, so let's wrap up with a look at the members of the operator class.

The Negation Operator

The negation operator (**NOT**) is most often used with the **If...Then** construct as illustrated by the following code:

```
If NOT x Then
MsgBox "Here's Your Answer"
Else
MsgBox "You're Incorrect."
End If
```

The Conjunction Operator

The conjunction operator (**AND**) compares two or more variables as a test. This operator uses this syntax:

```
X = expression1 AND expression2
```

Typically, this operator is used to ensure that two or more conditions are met before proceeding with another operation. Consequently, for the value **X** to be True, **expression1** and **expression2** must be True.

The Disjunction Operator

The disjunction operator (**OR**) compares two or more variables as a test. This operator uses the same syntax as the conjunction operator:

```
X = expression1 OR expression2
```

However, this operator is used when you want to decide where multiple tasks could occur, but only one must occur for an operation to continue. Consequently, for the value **X** to be True, either **expression1** or **expression2** can be True.

The Exclusion Operator

The exclusion operator (**XOR**) is used to test if only one condition alone is True. This operator uses the following syntax:

```
X = expression1 XOR expression2
```

With the exclusion operator, if all expressions are the same, then **X** is False. However, if one expression is different from the other, **X** evaluates to True.

Where To Go From Here

In this chapter, you had the chance to look inside the commands used to support the Recordset Navigation Control Panel. You also examined some alternate methods for retrieving data using SQL operators and manipulating data using VBA operators. Coming up next, you'll gain some experience with programming class modules in Access 2000.

.

Chapter 10

Let's Work With Class Modules

Programming in Access 2000 gives you more control over the solutions you develop. Allowing you to exercise program control is what class modules are all about.

In this chapter, you'll get some hands-on experience with class modules. Specifically, you'll perform tasks that demonstrate how Access 2000 provides all the necessary tools to design, create, instantiate, and use class modules to enhance your programs with custom objects. Don't worry if everything doesn't gel right away. The intent is simply to explore a few possibilities. We'll discuss the intricacies of objects and object-oriented programming in the next chapter. With that said, let's get underway.

What's A Class Module?

Class modules are really just VBA procedures that define a class and the specific properties and methods associated with it. Of course, this statement begs the question, *what is a class?* A class is a generic set of behaviors and attributes used to define and categorize a given object type. For example, consider a class called Telephone. The Telephone class defines objects with the following characteristics:

- A numeric keypad

- A handset for listening and speaking

- A connection to a communications network

The same Telephone class establishes that objects belonging to it exhibit the following behaviors:

- Ringing to indicate that a call is being received

- Continuous tone to indicate that a call may be placed

With this in mind, consider what you now know about VBA procedures. The **Sub** and **End Sub** or **Function** and **End Function** program code that you write defines the *behavior* set for a given class, whereas statements such as **Property Get** and **Property Let** define the *property* set for the class. You haven't encountered the **Property Get** or the **Property Let** statements so far, but you'll get to know them in this chapter.

Creating Class Modules

The tasks that follow walk you through the process of creating two sets of class modules. The first set of class modules is time related and demonstrates the use of the **Property Get** statement. The second set demonstrates the use of the **Property Let** statement.

.Project Creating Time-Based Class Modules

This first set of class modules will show you how to create a DateStamp class, a TimeStamp class, and a DateTimeStamp class. Begin to build the DateStamp class by performing the following steps:

1. Launch Access 2000 and open the FirstDatabase database.

2. Select the Module button under the Objects menu on the Access 2000 database window, and then select Insert|Class Module from the Access 2000 menu bar.

3. When the Visual Basic Editor opens, a new class module is created (see Figure 10.1).

4. Select File|Save FirstDatabase from the Visual Basic Editor menu bar, and then replace the name "Class 1" with "DateStamp" in the Save As dialog box.

5. In the Declarations section of the class module window, type a private string variable with the name "strDateStamp".

6. Select Class from the module window's Object drop-down menu, and then enter the following line of code between the **Sub** and **End Sub** statements for the **Class_Initialize()** procedure:

```
strDateStamp = Date
```

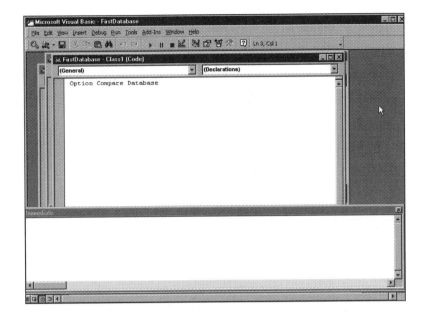

Figure 10.1
Class modules are created in the module window of the VB Editor.

7. Create a **Property** procedure by entering the following code beneath the **Class_Initialize()** procedure (see Figure 10.2):

```
Public Property Get DateStamp() As String
DateStamp = strDateStamp
End Property
```

8. Select File|Save FirstDatabase, and then select File|Close And Return To Microsoft Access. An icon should appear in the Access 2000 database window for the DateStamp class (see Figure 10.3).

9. Select the Module button under the Objects menu on the Access 2000 database window, and then select New from the window's toolbar to launch the VB Editor.

10. In the new module window, enter the following lines of code:

```
Sub ShowDateStamp()
Dim Latest As New DateStamp
MsgBox Latest.DateStamp
Set Latest = Nothing
End Sub
```

11. Select File|Save FirstDatabase, and save the new procedure with the name "ShowDateStamp".

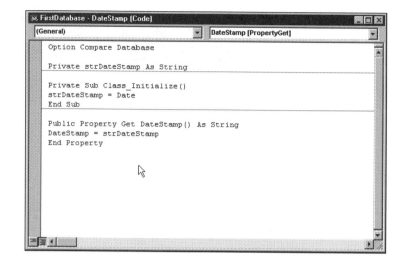

Figure 10.2
Place the **Property** procedure below the **Class_Initialize()** procedure.

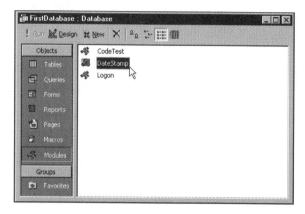

Figure 10.3
The new class module is represented by the DateStamp icon.

12. Select Run|Run Sub/UserForm from the VB Editor menu bar to run the **ShowDateStamp()** procedure. A successful run results in the message box shown in Figure 10.4.

Creating A TimeStamp Class

Now that you've grasped the mechanics of how to build and run a class module, try your hand at building a TimeStamp class module by performing these steps:

Figure 10.4
The result of successfully running the DateStamp class module.

1. Repeat Steps 1 through 4 in the previous procedure, replacing "DateStamp" with "TimeStamp".

2. In the Declarations section of the class module window, create a private string variable with the name "strTimeStamp".

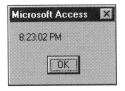

Figure 10.5
The result of successfully running the TimeStamp class module.

3. Select Class from the module window's Object drop-down menu, and then enter the following line of code between the **Sub** and **End Sub** statements for the **Class_Initialize()** procedure:

```
strTimeStamp = Time
```

4. Repeat Steps 7 through 12 of the DateStamp creation process, replacing "DateStamp" with "TimeStamp". Figure 10.5 shows a successful run of the TimeStamp class module.

Creating A DateTimeStamp Class

Give it a go one last time, and try your hand at building a DateTimeStamp class module by performing these steps:

1. Repeat Steps 1 through 4 of the DateStamp creation process, replacing "DateStamp" with "DateTimeStamp".

2. In the Declarations section of the class module window, create a private string variable with the name "strDateTimeStamp".

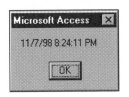

Figure 10.6
The result of successfully running the DateTimeStamp class module.

3. Select Class from the module window's Object drop-down menu, and then enter the following line of code between the **Sub** and **End Sub** statements for the **Class_Initialize()** procedure:

```
strDateTimeStamp = Now
```

4. Repeat Steps 7 through 12 of the DateStamp creation process, replacing "DateStamp" with "DateTimeStamp." Figure 10.6 shows the result of your work with the DateTimeStamp class module.

Project Creating Class Modules Using Property Get

Let's keep the ball rolling by building a second set of class modules. This time you'll use the **Property Get** statement to establish a default value for an object, instead of having the value assigned by system function. Perform the following steps as you forge ahead:

1. With the Access 2000 database window open and the Module button selected, choose Insert|Class Module from the Access 2000 menu bar to launch the VB Editor.

2. Place the cursor in the new module window, and then enter the following code:

```
Private MyClassTest As String
Private Sub Class_Initialize()
MyClassTest = "The name is Bond, James Bond."
End Sub
Property Get MyProperty() As String
MyProperty = MyClassTest
End Property
```

3. Select Debug|Compile FirstDatabase, and then select File|Save FirstDatabase from the VB Editor menu bar.

4. When prompted, save the class module with the name "MyNewObject".

5. Select Insert|Module from the VB Editor menu bar to launch a new module window.

6. Select File|Save FirstDatabase on the VB Editor menu bar, and, when prompted, save the new module with the name "ShowMe". Then enter the following code in the new module window:

```
Sub ShowMe()
Dim MyInstance As New MyNewObject
Dim Line As String
Line = MyInstance.MyProperty
MsgBox Line
Set MyInstance = Nothing
End Sub
```

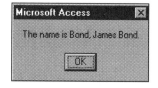

Figure 10.7
The **ShowMe()** routine demonstrates how to assign a value to an object.

7. Select Run|Run Sub/UserForm from the VB Editor menu bar to run the **ShowMe()** procedure. A successful run results in the message box shown in Figure 10.7.

.Project Creating Class Modules Using Property Let

Now that you've seen how to create class modules that use programmatic functions and predefined defaults, let's look at how to customize an object property using the **Property Let** statement. Perform the following steps to undertake this task:

1. With the VB Editor window open, select Window|
   FirstDatabase-MyNewObject (code) from the VB Editor
   menu bar to bring the MyNewObject window to the front.

2. With the cursor beneath the **End Property** statement, enter
   the following code (see Figure 10.8):

```
Property Let MyProperty(Change As String)
MyClassTest = Change
End Property
```

3. Select Debug|Compile FirstDatabase, and then select
   File|Save FirstDatabase from the VB Editor menu bar.

4. Select Window|FirstDatabase-ShowMe (code) from the VB
   Editor menu bar to bring the ShowMe module window to the
   front.

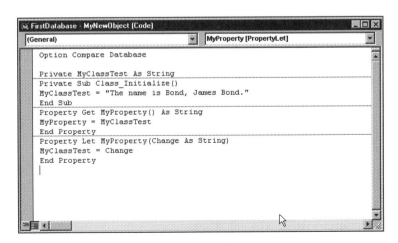

Figure 10.8
Add the **Property Let**
code beneath the
Property Get code.

NOTE

*The **MyInstance.My Property** = statement is broken here for clarity. Do not break it in the actual code.*

5. Revise the ShowMe module by adding the following line of code between:

```
Sub ShowMe()
Dim MyInstance As New MyNewObject
Dim Line As String
MyInstance.MyProperty = _
   "So, we meet again my dear Mr. Rosebud."
Line = MyInstance.MyProperty
MsgBox Line
Set MyInstance = Nothing
End Sub
```

6. Select Run|Run Sub/UserForm from the VB Editor menu bar to execute the procedure. A successful execution presents the message box shown in Figure 10.9.

Using Class Modules

Once you've created a class module and learned to manipulate its properties, you're ready to put the module to use. This involves becoming familiar with object instantiation. *Instantiation* is the process of creating a new instance of an existing class module. You may not have been aware of it, but you instantiated class modules in the preceding exercises. The next section will specifically walk you through the instantiation process.

Figure 10.9
The Macro dialog box prompts you to select a module to run.

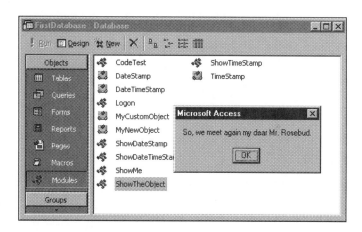

 **Instantiating A Class Module**

Module instantiation is a process of resource allocation and object re-creation. We'll examine this more closely in the next chapter. For now, let's instantiate a copy of MyNewObject by performing the following steps:

1. With the VB Editor open, select Insert|Module to open a new module window.

2. Select File|Save FirstDatabase to save the module with the name "NewObject".

3. At the blinking cursor, enter the following code and press the Enter key to begin a new procedure:

```
Sub NewObject()
```

4. Between the **Sub** and **End Sub** statements, enter the following code:

```
Dim NewOne As New MyNewObject
```

NOTE

*Notice that after you type in **As**, the VB Editor presents you with a list of object types. The same thing occurs after you enter the word **New** or select **New** from the object list.*

The **Dim** statement functions in the same way as if you were declaring a variable. In other words, it allocates space to create the new object. **NewOne** identifies what the object will be called, and **As New MyNewObject** tells you that, when created, the new object will have the characteristics of the existing **MyNewObject** object. Notice however that the object itself has not been created. Actual object creation occurs when a property or method of the identified object is referenced in your procedure. Add the following line of code to the **NewObject** procedure following the **Dim** statement to create the **NewOne** instance of the **MyNewObject** object:

```
NewOne.MyProperty = _
    "Happy Birthday to me, I'm a newborn object"
```

NOTE

Notice that after you type in a dot, the VB Editor presents you with a list of properties for the new object.

5. Enter the following line of code, and then select Debug| Compile FirstDatabase and then Run|Run Sub/UserForm from the VB Editor menu bar to execute the **NewObject** procedure. Your result should appear as shown in Figure 10.10.

```
MsgBox NewOne.MyProperty
```

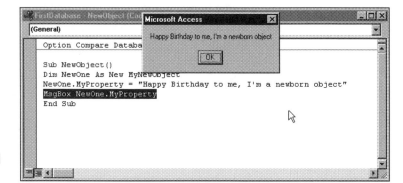

Figure 10.10
Your newly instantiated
class module.

*Project*   Using The Object Browser

By now you've created several class modules and should have a
pretty good handle on what they're all about. However, after
you're done with the modules and put them all away, where do
they go? They're still around, and in case you want to take a look
at where they're hanging out, it's a good idea to get acquainted
with the VB Editor's Object Browser. Let's locate the object
you've created by performing the following steps:

1. With the VB Editor open, press the F2 key to launch the
   Object Browser (see Figure 10.11).

2. Select the first drop-down menu, and choose the First-
   Database library. Completing this action displays a list of all
   classes associated with FirstDatabase (see Figure 10.12).

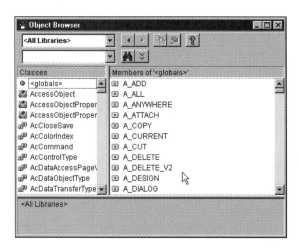

Figure 10.11
The VB Editor Object
Browser.

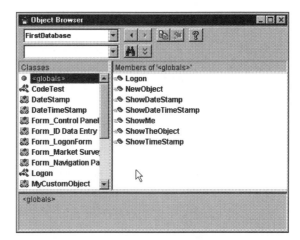

Figure 10.12
The classes available with FirstDatabase.

3. Scroll down the leftmost panel of the Object Browser to find the DateStamp module you created earlier.

4. Double-click DateStamp on the classes list, and you'll launch the DateStamp class module, ready for editing (see Figure 10.13).

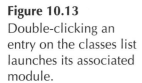*Project* Putting It All Together

Now it's time to have a little fun. In this section, you'll create a control panel that uses the three time-based class modules you built at the beginning of the chapter. When you're done, you'll see how independently created class modules can be linked to an Access form and executed. So let's get started by performing the following steps:

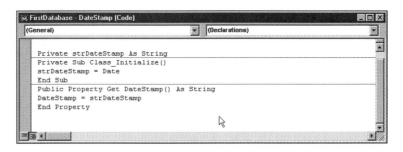

Figure 10.13
Double-clicking an entry on the classes list launches its associated module.

1. With the Access database window open to FirstDatabase, click the Forms option under the Objects button, and then double-click Create Form In Design View to launch the Forms window.

2. Select View|Toolbox to display the Toolbox palette, if it's not visible.

3. On the Toolbox, click the Rectangle control tool.

4. Place the cursor in the upper-left corner of the form's Detail section, click and hold down the left mouse button, and drag the mouse to the right corner of the Detail section.

5. Release the mouse button to complete the rectangle creation task.

6. On the Toolbox palette, click the Command Button control tool.

7. Place the cursor inside the rectangle you just created, and then click once to place a Command Button control on the form.

8. Repeat Step 7 until you have created one row of three command buttons.

9. Adjust the spacing of the button controls, and adjust the size of the rectangle so that there is enough space to place a label at the top of the form.

10. On the Toolbox palette, click the Label control.

11. Place the cursor on the form just above the rectangle, and then, while holding down the left mouse button, drag the mouse down and to the right to create a Label field.

12. At the blinking cursor inside of the Label field, type the words "Class Module Panel", and then press the Enter key.

13. On the Access Formatting toolbar, select 18 from the Font Size drop-down menu.

14. Save the form as "Class Module Panel", by selecting File|Save As from the Access menu bar. Your form should now appear as shown in Figure 10.14.

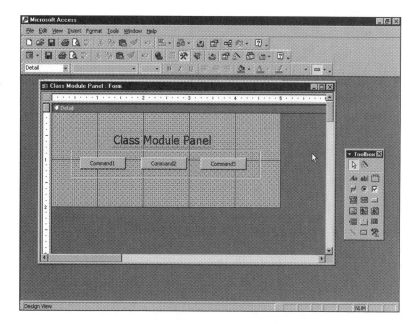

Figure 10.14
Class Module Panel
before button
assignments.

Activating The Class Module Panel Buttons

Now you're ready to assign a class module to each of the three
buttons inside the rectangle. Let's begin by activating the button
labeled Command1 to run the DateStamp class module. You'll
accomplish this by doing the following:

1. Right-click on the button labeled Command1, and then
   select Properties from the button's right-click menu to open
   the button's property sheet.

2. On the button's property sheet, select the All tab, and then
   move the tab's scrollbar to the top until you see the Name
   property field and the Caption property field.

3. Change the button's Name and Caption properties from
   "Command1" to "DateStamp".

4. Scroll down the property sheet until you find the On Click
   property field.

5. Select the On Click property field, and then choose Event
   Procedure from the field's drop-down menu.

6. Click the square button with three dots that appears to the
   right of the property field drop-down menu to launch the
   Visual Basic Editor.

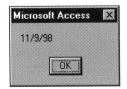

Figure 10.15
The activated
DateStamp button
displays a message
box with the date.

7. Place the following code between the **Sub** and **End Sub** statements for the DateStamp click event:

```
Private Sub DateStamp_Click()
Dim DS As New DateStamp
MsgBox DS.DateStamp
End Sub
```

8. Select File|Close And Return To Microsoft Access from the Visual Basic Editor menu bar, and then close the form's property sheet.

9. Select View|Form View from the Access menu bar, and then click the DateStamp button. A message box should appear, as shown in Figure 10.15.

Now that you've activated the DateStamp button, repeat Steps 1 through 9 for command buttons 2 and 3. Use the following code for the TimeStamp **click** event:

```
Private Sub TimeStamp_Click()
Dim TS As New TimeStamp
MsgBox TS.TimeStamp
End Sub
```

Use this code for the DateTimeStamp **click** event:

```
Private Sub DateTimeStamp_Click()
Dim DTS As New DateTimeStamp
MsgBox DTS.DateTimeStamp
End Sub
```

When you're done, your functional Class Module Panel should appear as shown in Figure 10.16.

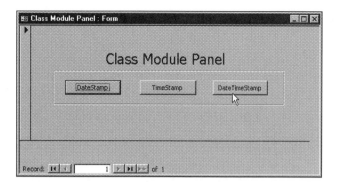

Figure 10.16
The working Class
Module Panel.

Where To Go From Here

In this chapter, you worked with class modules. You discovered
how they are created, how their properties are manipulated, and
how to instantiate them. You also learned how to use the VB
Editor Object Browser to locate class modules as you need them.
Finally, you put it all together by building a control panel that
made use of the time-based class modules. If you need more
practice, try your hand at enhancing the control panel by additional buttons that use the MyCustomObject class.

Coming up next, we'll take a closer look at how everything you've
done in this chapter is standard operating procedure in the world
of object-oriented programming. In addition, we'll cover some
concepts that should help you make a little more sense of how
class modules support their self-contained capability.

Chapter 11

Understanding Object-Oriented Programming With Access 2000

The use of class modules to add object-oriented programming to Access is a lesson in efficiency. No doubt, this is why it's an integral part of the Access Development Model.

Object-oriented programming has been around for quite some time, and, as you've seen, its usefulness as an application design tool is indisputable. However, before you can fully appreciate what this method brings to the table, you'll need to alter your point of view just a bit. Using object-oriented programming techniques means that you'll need to think a bit more about objects and a bit less about processes. You'll need to consider how things are constructed rather than how things work procedurally. Before we delve deeply into this topic, if you feel the need for a brief refresher on object-oriented techniques in a broad sense, take another look at Chapter 3.

Basics Of Object-Oriented Programming

When discussing object-oriented programming (OOP), it's important to understand that OOP, like PRACTICE (see Chapter 1) is a methodology. In other words, OOP is a structured software development approach that focuses on reducing a problem into distinct pieces known as *objects*. Once a problem has been defined in terms of its object makeup, that problem becomes simpler and easier to manage, thereby letting you build a more focused solution. Access 2000 supports the concept of object-oriented development using class modules. As presented in Chapter 10, objects are used to create new instances of a given class. Each class is a template that defines the behavior and attributes of objects created from it. This will become more clear in the following paragraphs as we examine the class modules you built in the previous chapter.

Examining The Time-Based Class Module

Let's take a moment to review the **DateStamp** class module from Chapter 10, paying particular attention to its object composition. Begin by looking at the following code:

```
Private Sub Class_Initialize()
strDateStamp = Date
End Sub
```

With these three lines, you used the **Class_Initialize** procedure to create a class module called **DateStamp**. This procedure is executed each time a new object instance is created using the **DateStamp** class module. Furthermore, you see that the **Class_Initialize** procedure contains **Date** as a default value for the property of the created object. In other words, when you equate the **Date** function with the value **strTimeStamp**, any objects created using the **DateStamp** class module automatically contain the Visual Basic **Date** function as an object property. It's also important to note that the return value for the **Date** function is assigned to a private variable, as indicated by the keyword **Private**. Class module variables are typically declared as private variables to make sure they are unavailable and, therefore, not impacted by procedures that exist outside the class module itself. Next, take a look at following code:

```
Public Property Get DateStamp() As String
DateStamp = strDateStamp
End Property
```

In these three lines of code, you deliberately make your private class module variable available as a property that can be referenced outside the class module. You establish this availability using the **Public Property Get** procedure. The **Public** keyword makes a given property available to procedures both inside and outside a class module. The **Get** keyword tells you that the

Property Get procedure specifies what should occur when a procedure other than **Property Get** wants to use the value stored in the class module variable. The **DateStamp** piece of the procedure tells you the name of the property in use; the **String** keyword identifies the property data type. In effect, the **Public Property Get** procedure creates a publicly available property named **DateStamp** that returns a string value.

So, each time a reference is made to the value of the **DateStamp** object's **DateStamp** property, the **Property Get** procedure is executed. Executing the procedure causes the **DateStamp** class module to assign the value of the private variable **strTimeStamp** to the public property **DateStamp**. You can see how this all fits together by examining the following five lines of code:

```
Sub ShowDateStamp()
Dim Latest As New DateStamp
MsgBox Latest.DateStamp
Set Latest = Nothing
End Sub
```

The first line of this code opens a new standard module called **ShowDateStamp**. The second line creates a new instance of the **DateStamp** object called **Latest**. Of note here is the fact that the **Dim** statement doesn't actually *create* a new **DateStamp** object; rather, it reserves space for the object's creation, just as space is reserved when you declare any variable. The new object instance is actually created when it is referenced in the code as shown in the third line.

The **MsgBox** statement launches the **Class_Initialize** routine, which provides the **Date** function as a default property value for the **DateStamp** class being invoked as a new instance called **Latest**. Notice the last two lines of this procedure:

```
Set Latest = Nothing
End Sub
```

Setting the newly created object variable to **Nothing** releases any resources used by the variable so they cannot be reused. As you might expect, the **End Sub** statement indicates the end of the subroutine.

NOTE

*If you want to refresh yourself about how **Property Get** and **Property Let** are used, check out Chapter 10.*

Using Property Get And Property Let

Before we continue, let's take a quick look at how you used object-oriented programming, specifically **Property Get** and **Property Let**, in Chapter 10 to manipulate object properties. By this time, you're probably a little more familiar with **Property Get** than **Property Let**, so let's start with the former.

Understanding Property Get

You return the value of an object's property by setting the **Property Get** statement name to match the value that you want returned. This will become clearer as you examine the code for the **MyNewObject** class module:

```
Private MyClassTest As String
Private Sub Class_Initialize()
MyClassTest = "The name is Bond, James Bond."
End Sub
```

With the first line of code, you declared a private string variable named **MyClassTest**. Next, you created a class module variable called **MyClassTest** using the **Class_Initialize** procedure. As before, this procedure is executed whenever you use **MyClassTest** to create a new object instance. In the case of this class module, the **Class_Initialize** procedure contains the string **"The name is Bond, James Bond."** as the default value of the object's property. As usual, the **End Sub** statement indicates the end of the **Class_Initialize** subroutine.

After you created the **MyClassTest** class module, you again made your private class module variable available as a property that can be referenced. You established this availability using the **Public Property Get** procedure shown in the following lines of code:

```
Public Property Get MyProperty() As String
MyProperty = MyClassTest
End Property
```

As mentioned, the **Public** keyword allows a given property to be available to procedures both inside and outside a class module. This time, the **Public Property Get** procedure creates a publicly available property named **MyProperty**, which returns a string value. You'll notice that the **Property Get** statement uses the same name as the variable that will hold the value to be returned. Executing the procedure causes the **MyNewObject** class module to assign the value of the private variable **MyClassTest** to the public property **MyProperty**.

With your class module available for reference, you wrote a subroutine called **ShowMe**. This subroutine is shown in the following code:

```
Sub ShowMe()
Dim MyInstance As New MyNewObject
Dim Line As String
Line = MyInstance.MyProperty
MsgBox Line
Set MyInstance = Nothing
End Sub
```

Your first subroutine instruction reserved space for a new instance of the **MyNewObject** object that was called **MyInstance**. Your next instruction reserved space for a string object called **Line**. Then, you assigned the new instance of the **MyNewObject** object class to the string variable **Line**. When **MsgBox** is referenced, the variable line triggers creation of the **MyInstance** object that contains the property **MyProperty**. This property has the value **"The name is Bond, James Bond."**. Finally, you set the **MyInstance** object to **Nothing**, which released any committed resources for reuse, and ended the subroutine with the **End Sub** statement. You can see by this example that you determined the default value of the class module variable using a string that you defined (**"The name is Bond, James Bond."**), rather than having the default value determined by a system function, such as **Date**.

Understanding Property Let

As opposed to **Property Get**, **Property Let** allows users of your object to change the value of the object's property. Take a look at the following code:

```
Property Let MyProperty(Change As String)
MyClassTest = Change
End Property
```

With **Property Let**, you assign an empty string to the class module variable **MyClassTest**, rather than assigning a literal value, like you used with **Property Get**. Consequently, you fill the empty string with a string value that you define from within your program code rather than assigning a value for the empty string ahead of time. This is shown in the following code sample:

```
Sub ShowMe()
Dim MyInstance As New MyNewObject
Dim Line As String
MyInstance.MyProperty = _
    "So, we meet again my dear Mr. Rosebud."
Line = MyInstance.MyProperty
MsgBox Line
Set MyInstance = Nothing
End Sub
```

In the fourth line of the code block, notice that you assign a value to the **MyInstance.MyProperty** object instance before you assign the new instance of the **MyNewObject** object class to the **Line** string variable. The value that you assign fills the empty string variable you established using **Property Let**. Consequently, when you run the revised **ShowMe** subroutine, the value **"The name is Bond, James Bond."** is replaced by the value **"So, we meet again my dear Mr. Rosebud."**

Your work with class modules demonstrates three basic concepts of object-oriented programming: encapsulation, inheritance, and polymorphism. Let's take a closer look at each of these.

Understanding Encapsulation

When you were building your class modules, you created private variables that were unavailable for use by other procedures until you exposed them by using the **Public** keyword. When you did this, you were, in effect, invoking *encapsulation*. Encapsulation, also called *data hiding*, is the notion of being able to use an object while being shielded from its inner workings. For example, you get into a car, insert the key into the ignition, and turn the key. Bingo, the car starts. You don't need to know how the starter, the accelerator, and the engine work together to use the object called car. In this same way, programming objects are self-contained

Tip

Encapsulation is also a data protection mechanism, as it allows the properties of a given object to be established without touching the native object code.

units of capability that allow you to piece together a working solution without knowing the object's innermost details.

Understanding Inheritance

When you used the **Property Let** statement to change the value of an object's property within your code, the only thing that really changed was the value of the string itself. This is because **MyInstance**, which is a new instance of the **MyNewObject** class, inherited the functionality associated with the **MyNewObject** class. Inheritance allows you to reuse objects repeatedly without having to reproduce the object attributes and behaviors each time. Inheritance operates on the notion that once you've created a parent class with a specific set of properties and methods (attributes and behaviors), any offspring of that class possesses the properties and methods of the parent. The offspring will also include its own specific properties and methods.

Understanding Polymorphism

The **Property Let** example also demonstrates another important aspect of object-oriented programming: the concept of *polymorphism*. As you may have noticed in the **Property Let** example, changing the value of **MyInstance.MyProperty** did not require you to change its name. This is because polymorphism allows you to use a variable of a parent class to refer to any classes derived from that parent. So, rather than needing two separate instances—one named **MyInstance.MyProperty1** with the value **"The name is Bond, James Bond."** and another named **MyInstance.MyProperty2** with the value **"So, we meet again my dear Mr. Rosebud."**—polymorphism allows like items to have the same name, as long as the items are distinguished by their specific values.

New Objects In Access 2000

Access 2000 includes a new crop of objects that improve the application's functionality. These objects also allow you, as a programmer, to strengthen your OOP skills. Many of these objects will be familiar to you, as they are actually extensions of existing Access and VB object types. The distinction between the old and new object types lies in the fact that the new object types generally reference a set of like objects to which a specific individual object belongs. This set of like objects is called a *collection* and forms the basis for understanding how data is organized and managed by Access 2000. Let's look at some of the new objects included with Access 2000, their collection designation, and how they're used.

AccessObject

AccessObject objects include information about a single object instance. They also describe forms, reports, macros, modules, data access pages, tables, queries, views, stored procedures, and database diagrams. Respectively, the aforementioned objects belong to the collections: **AllForms, AllReports, AllMacros, AllModules, AllDataAccessPages, AllTables, AllQueries, AllViews, AllStoredProcedures,** and **AllDatabaseDiagram** collections. As a programmer, using **AccessObject** means that you'll have a common way to reference all objects of a given type. In other words, because an **AccessObject** object relates to an existing object, you don't create new **AccessObject** objects or delete existing ones. You typically reference an **AccessObject** object in a specific object collection by its **Name** property. For example in the case of the Logon form you built in Chapter 4, you might reference an instance of the form as an **AccessObject** using the syntax:

```
AllForms("Logon") AllForms![Logon]
```

You can see by this example that the **AccessObject** Logon is part of the **AllForms** collection.

AccessObjectProperty

AccessObjectProperty objects represent a built-in or user-defined characteristic of an **AccessObject** object. The **AccessObjectProperty** object is best understood by saying that each **AccessObject** object contains an **AccessObjectProperties** collection, and that the objects comprising the **AccessObjectProperties** collection are in fact distinct **AccessObjectProperty** objects.

The objects themselves have two built-in properties: the **Name** property, which is a string uniquely identifying the property of the given object, and the **Value** property, which is a variant containing the property setting for the named object.

CodeData

As with the table and form objects that you work with in Access 2000, the code that supports your programs is also stored in your Access 2000 database. When you refer to an **AccessObject** like a table or a form within your code, Access 2000 recognizes these references as **CodeData** objects. **CodeData** objects consist of the **AllTables**, **AllQueries**, **AllViews**, **AllStoredProcedures**, and **AllDatabaseDiagrams** collections.

CurrentData

The **CurrentData** object refers to the objects stored in the current database by the source server application. As with the **CodeData** object, the **CurrentData** object is another way for Access 2000 to recognize references to stored data. However, in the case of the **CurrentData** object, the data being referenced is not limited to data references embedded in your program code.

CurrentProject

In Access 2000, the set of all code modules in a database, including standard and class modules, is called a *project*. Projects typically have the same name as the database that they are associated with. The **CurrentProject** object refers to the Access 2000 entity by which the current Access 2000 project is referenced. You use the **CurrentProject** object just as you have been using the **Currentdb** object in the programs you've written thus far. The difference is that **Currentdb** is a reference to the currently active database, and **CurrentProject** is a reference to the currently active Access 2000 project.

DataAccessPage

A **DataAccessPage** object refers to a particular Access 2000 data access page. You'll get acquainted with data access pages in

Chapter 14. For now, be aware that when you create a data access page, Access 2000 recognizes that page as a **DataAccessPage** object for reference purposes.

DefaultWebOptions

The **DefaultWebOptions** object contains a global set of properties used by Access when you save a data access page as a Web page or open a Web page. When you save a data access page, certain properties like hyperlink color, hyperlink underlines, and settings for HTML encoding are automatically set. The **Default-WebOptions** object contains these properties that affect the characteristics of the overall document. These default properties may be set programmatically to affect all data access pages or specific data access pages.

FormatCondition

The **FormatCondition** object represents a conditional format of a combo box or text box control and is a member of the **FormatConditions** collection.

VBE

The **VBE** object is the root object that contains all other objects and collections represented in Visual Basic for Applications. Use the following collections to access the objects contained in the **VBE** object:

- **VBProjects** accesses the collection of projects.

- **Windows** accesses the collection of windows.

- **CodePanes** accesses the collection of code panes.

- **CommandBars** accesses the collection of command bars.

Tip

Be aware that attribute values differ from one data access page to another, depending on the value at the time the data access page was saved.

WebOptions

A **WebOptions** object refers to the specific Web option properties of an Access 2000 data access page. This object contains attributes used by Access 2000 when you save a data access page as a Web page or when you open a Web page. Using the

WebOptions object, you can return or set attributes at either the application level or the data access page level.

Retained Objects In Access 2000

Although Access 2000 contains several new object types, it also maintains compatibility with previous versions of Access and their object types. The set of Access objects retained in Access 2000 that you're likely to use most often are described in this section.

Application

The **Application** object still contains all Access objects and collections, including the **Forms**, **Reports**, **Modules**, and **References** collections, as well as the new **DataAccessPages** collection. The **Application** object also contains the **Screen**, **DoCmd**, **VBE**, **DefaultWebOptions**, **Assistant**, **CommandBars**, **DBEngine**, **FileSearch**, **ComAddIns**, **AnswerWizard**, and **LanguageSettings** objects. This object is typically used to apply methods or property settings to the entire Access 2000 application.

Control

The **Control** object represents a form, report, or section control that is within or attached to another control. All form or report controls belong to the **Controls** collection for the specific **Form** or **Report** object. Section controls belong to the **Controls** collection for the given section. Controls within a Tab control or Option Group control belong to the **Controls** collection for that control. Similarly, a Label control attached to another control belongs to the **Controls** collection for that control.

DoCmd

The **DoCmd** object has been retained, and its methods are used to run Access actions from Visual Basic. Actions perform tasks like closing windows, opening forms, and setting control values.

Because the **DoCmd** object replaces the now-obsolete **DoCmd** statement, actions formerly used as arguments for the **DoCmd** statement are now methods of the **DoCmd** object.

Form

A **Form** object is a member of the **Forms** collection. The **Forms** collection is the set of all currently open forms. Reference to an individual **Form** object in the **Forms** collection is made by referring to the form by name, or by referring to the form's index within the collection. (Individual forms are indexed beginning with zero.) Each **Form** object has a **Controls** collection, containing all controls used on a given form.

Module

Module objects refer either to a standard module or a class module. The **Modules** collection contains all open **Module** objects, regardless of their type. **Module** objects in the **Modules** collection can be compiled or uncompiled.

Reference

The **Reference** object designates a reference to the type library of another application or project. When you create a **Reference** object, you set a reference dynamically from Visual Basic. The **Reference** object is a member of the **References** collection.

Report

A **Report** object references a specific Access report. These objects are members of the **Reports** collection, which consists of all currently open reports. Inside the **Reports** collection, individual reports are indexed beginning with zero. Consequently, you can refer to an individual **Report** object by referring to the report by name, or by referring to its index within the **Reports** collection.

Screen

Also retained in Access 2000 is the **Screen** object. **Screen** objects reference specific forms, reports, or controls that currently have focus.

Access 2000 Object Collections

As you may have gathered by now, Access 2000 supports DAO objects and their collections. These objects allow you to write programs to create and manipulate database components. Objects and collections contain properties that describe the nature of the components and methods used to manipulate them. Table 11.1 lists the current state of Access object collections by name, object type, and what they contain.

Table 11.1 Access object collections.

Name	Object Type	Description
AllDataAccessPages	AccessObject	Contains **AccessObject** for each data access page in the **CurrentProject** or **CodeProject** object.
AllDatabaseDiagrams	AccessObject	Contains **AccessObject** for each table database diagram in the **CurrentData** or **CodeData** object.
AllForms	AccessObject	Contains **AccessObject** for each form in the **CurrentProject** or **CodeProject** object.
AllReports	AccessObject	Contains **AccessObject** for each report in the **CurrentProject** or **CodeProject** object.
AllMacros	AccessObject	Contains **AccessObject** for each macro in the **CurrentProject** or **CodeProject** object.
AllModules	AccessObject	Contains **AccessObject** for each module in the **CurrentProject** or **CodeProject** object.
AllQueries	AccessObject	Contains **AccessObject** for each query in the **CurrentData** or **CodeData** object.
AllStoredProcedures	AccessObject	Contains **AccessObject** for each stored procedure in the **CurrentData** or **CodeData** object.
AllTables	AccessObject	Contains **AccessObject** for each table in the CurrentData or CodeData object.
AllViews	AccessObject	Contains **AccessObject** for each view in the **CurrentData** or **CodeData** object.
Connections	Connection	Provides data about a connection to an ODBC data source.
Containers	Container	Stores data about predefined object types.
Databases	Database	An open database.
DBEngine	DBEngine	The Microsoft Jet database engine.

(continued)

Table 11.1   Access object collections *(continued)*.

Name	Object Type	Description
Documents	Document	Contains data about saved, predefined objects.
Errors	Error	Contains data about any errors associated with this object.
Fields	Field	A column belonging to a table, query, index, relation, or recordset.
Groups	Group	A group of user accounts.
Indexes	Index	Predefined value ordering and uniqueness in a table.
Parameters	Parameter	A parameter for a parameter query.
Properties	Property	A built-in or user-defined property.
QueryDefs	QueryDef	A saved query definition.
Recordsets	Recordset	The records in a base table or query.
Relations	Relation	A relationship between fields in tables and queries.
TableDefs	TableDef	A saved table definition.
Users	User	A user account (Microsoft Jet workspaces only).
Workspaces	Workspace	A session of the Microsoft Jet database engine.

Where To Go From Here

In this chapter, you took an inside look at object-oriented programming. You also reviewed how the class modules you created in Chapter 10 effectively demonstrated the concepts of encapsulation, inheritance, and polymorphism. Finally, you were introduced to the new Access 2000 objects and collections, as well as objects and collections retained for the sake of backward compatibility. Up next, you'll take on the task of building Access 2000 reports.

Chapter 12

Creating Reports In Access 2000

Creating professional reports in Access 2000 is not a difficult process. With a little practice, you can easily create reports from the extremely simple to the very complex.

As you've already seen in previous chapters, Access 2000 provides a powerful set of tools for you to use when creating databases and applications. However, data is generally only useful when you can do something with it—most data is not useful in-and-of itself, but rather only when you use or present it in conjunction with other data. Although forms, tables, and queries provide you with very powerful methods of interacting with the data while it's in the computer, often you need to generate hardcopy output about the data (for a meeting, for offline records, and so on). In such cases, the most efficient means for presenting the data in a physical form is to generate a report. Reports can take a variety of forms, as you'll see throughout this chapter and the next one. In this chapter, we'll use a database included on the companion CD-ROM as a basis for the creation of a series of reports in different styles and types. In Chapter 13, we'll analyze more closely some of the techniques at your disposal for improving your reports and making them more useful.

.*Project* Opening The Database From The CD-ROM

The CD-ROM contains the Chap12Wine.mdb database. This database is a derivative of, and expansion on, the Wine Collection database created from the template of the same name. To open the database, perform the following steps:

1. Select File|Open to display the Open dialog box.

2. Within the Open dialog box, navigate to the directory where you installed the CD-ROM that came with this book. Double-click on the Chap12Wine.mdb file.

3. Access will open the database and display the Database window, as shown in Figure 12.1.

 **Project** Creating A New Report

You can create a new report in several ways. The most common is to select the Reports tab of the Database window and then click on New. The New Report dialog box will appear, as shown in Figure 12.2. This dialog box allows you to select from the many options available for creating reports. They can be created from scratch in Design View (the first option in the box), but they can also be created with the help of five wizards. The first three wizards help you build standard reports, the next helps you build reports containing charts, and the last wizard automates the process of creating mailing labels. The report wizards are so powerful that most developers use one of them to build the initial foundation for almost every report they create. In the following section, you'll quickly create a report with the Report Wizard, just

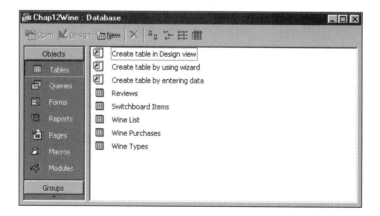

Figure 12.1
The Database window after you open the Chap12Wine.mdb database.

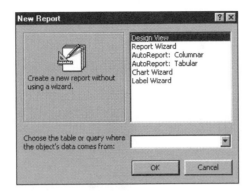

Figure 12.2
The New Report
dialog box.

to see how it works; you'll then delete that report and create a
new report for the database from scratch.

Creating A Report With The Report Wizard

To create a report using the Report Wizard, select Report Wizard
from the New Report dialog box and click on OK. The Report
Wizard is launched. The first step of the Report Wizard prompts
you for the table or query that will supply data to the report. It's
best to base your reports on queries. This improves performance
and enhances your ability to produce reports based on varying
criteria. In this case, however, the report should be based on the
Wine List table.

1. From the drop-down list in the dialog box, select the Table:
   Wine List entry.

2. After you've selected the table, you can select the fields you
   want to include in the report. The fields included in the
   selected table or query are listed in the list box on the left. To
   add fields to the report, double-click on the name of the field
   you want to add, or click on the field name and click the
   right-arrow button (>). In this case, you'll be adding all the
   fields to the report, so click on the double right-arrow button
   (>>). Figure 12.3 shows the dialog box after you add all the
   fields to the report.

3. After you've selected a table or query and the fields you want
   to include on the report, click on Next. The Report Wizard
   will prompt you to specify grouping levels to add to the report.
   Grouping levels add report groupings to the report. Add them

NOTE

*Be advised that, as with
previous chapters, the
activities you'll perform in
this chapter are repetitive
by design. The intent is to
reinforce the construction
process with each new
report you create.
Although it may seem a
bit redundant, take the
time to execute each step
of each activity. When
you're done, not only will
you have developed the
reports, you'll have a
better understanding of
what it takes to create
reports to meet different
needs in your own
environment.*

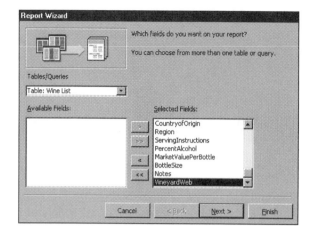

Figure 12.3
The first dialog box of the Report Wizard after you've added fields to the report.

if you need to visually separate groups of data or include summary calculations (subtotals). Click Next to move on to the dialog box that helps you set sorting levels for the report.

4. The third step of the Report Wizard prompts you for sorting levels for your report. Because the order of a table underlying a report is completely ignored by the report builder when the report is run, it's necessary that you designate a sort order. You can add up to four sorting levels using the wizard. In the case of the report you're currently building, the data should be sorted first by Vineyard and then by WineName. Figure 12.4 shows the sorting levels dialog box of the Report Wizard after the sorting fields have been selected. After you select the fields you want to sort on, click on Next.

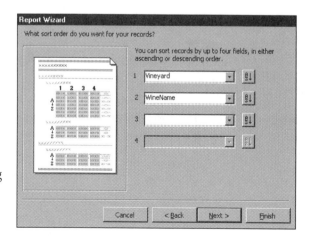

Figure 12.4
The sorting levels dialog box in the Report Wizard after you enter your sort specifications.

5. The fourth step of the Report Wizard prompts you for the layout and orientation of the report. The layout can be set to Vertical or Tabular. The orientation can be set to Portrait or Landscape. This step of the Report Wizard also allows you to specify whether you want Access to attempt to adjust the width of each field so that all the fields fit on each page. In the case of this report, leave the layout defaults and change the alignment to Landscape. Click on Next to move to the next dialog box in the wizard.

6. The fifth step of the Report Wizard enables you to select a style for your report. The available choices are Bold, Casual, Compact, Corporate, Formal, and Soft Gray. Although the style doesn't particularly impact this discussion, select Formal and click on Next.

7. The final step of the Report Wizard prompts you for a title for the report. This title will be used as the name and the caption title for the report. Name the report rptSortedWineList, and click on Finish. Access 2000 will display a preview of the completed report, as shown in Figure 12.5.

You should take note of some important considerations about this report before we modify it in the next section and before you begin to design your own. First, notice how the headers in the report overlap—there are too many fields in the report and not

Figure 12.5
The preview of the completed report.

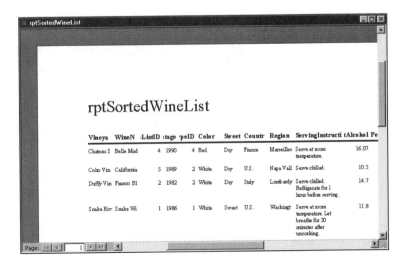

enough space for them all to fit. Notice, as well, how the data in some of the columns is truncated. Finally, note that the WineListID field isn't particularly useful in the output. In the following section, we'll address these issues to fix the Report Wizard-generated report.

Another way to start the Report Wizard is to click on the Tables or Queries tab and then click on the table or query on which you want the report to be based. Use the New Object drop-down list on the toolbar to select Report. The New Report dialog box will appear. Within the New Report dialog box, select Report Wizard. You don't need to use the Tables/Queries drop-down list to select a table or query. The table or query you selected before invoking the wizard is automatically selected for you.

Project Fixing The Report Wizard-Generated Report

Fixing the report is a straightforward process, akin to the form design you've done in previous chapters. Before we can fix the report, however, you must get out of Preview Mode and into Design View. To do so, click on the blue triangle at the top-left corner of the IDE. Access will display the report in Design View, as shown in Figure 12.6.

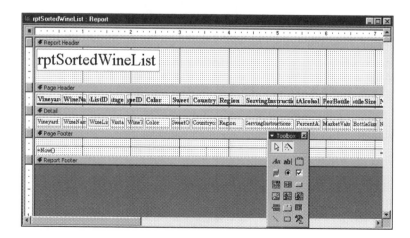

Figure 12.6
The report in Design View.

As mentioned previously, you have several things to fix in the implementation of the report created by the Report Wizard. The first two are simple: correcting the title of the report and removing the WineListID field. The following subsections discuss these tasks, as well as resizing the other fields on the report.

Fixing The Caption

To fix the caption for the report, perform the following steps:

1. Within Design View, click once on the label in the Report Header section. Access will select the label (as indicated by the presence of the sizing blocks) and show a bar cursor. Click again within the label at the end of the text. Access will display a flashing text cursor inside the label.

2. Delete the existing label caption and enter "Wine List Sorted By Vineyard and Wine Name". Press Enter after you type in the new caption. As you can see, Access will automatically resize the label for you.

Removing The WineListID Field

Now that you've fixed the caption, go ahead and delete the WineListID field from the report. To do so, perform the following steps:

1. Within Design View, click once on the WineListID label in the Page Header section. Access will select the label (as indicated by the presence of the sizing blocks) and show a bar cursor. Press the Delete key, or use the Cut button on the toolbar to delete the label.

2. Next, click once on the WineListID label in the Detail section. Access will select the label (as indicated by the presence of the sizing blocks) and show a bar cursor. Press the Delete key, or use the Cut button on the toolbar to delete the label.

When you finish these two sets of actions, your report should look similar to the one shown in Figure 12.7.

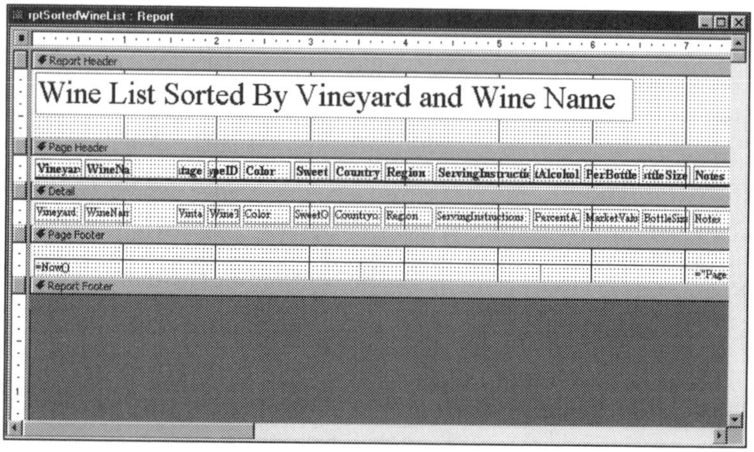

Figure 12.7
The report in Design View after changing two of the problems with the Report Wizard-generated report.

Realigning The Fields On The Report For Clearer Output

Well, as you saw in Figures 12.5 and 12.6, the Report Wizard doesn't exactly lay out the report in the most effective manner. In fact, if your report has sufficient columns, Access may try to cram too many of them into a single row, resulting in truncated captions or data. Such is the case with the rptSortedWineList report created earlier in this chapter. Fixing the report is a slightly longer process, requiring manual action on your part.

Before you start to move labels on the Report Designer, however, let's consider some issues about what's currently on there. For starters, the WineTypeID field is not particularly useful, displaying only a number. In fact, WineTypeID is a foreign key lookup field, and it should pull a text description of the wine type in from that foreign location. Unfortunately, pulling the table directly as we did when designing this report means that you must either change the datasource for the report to a query or join to pull in the lookup value, or you must kill the WineTypeID field because of its meaninglessness. You'll create a query as the basis for a report later in this chapter, so for now, simply delete the WineTypeID field from the report. To do so, perform the following steps:

1. Within Design View, click once on the WineTypeID label in the Page Header section. Access 2000 will select the label (as indicated by the presence of the sizing blocks) and show a bar

cursor. Press the Delete key, or use the Cut button on the toolbar to delete the label.

2. Click once on the WineTypeID label in the Detail section. Access will select the label (as indicated by the presence of the sizing blocks) and show a bar cursor. Press the Delete key, or use the Cut button on the toolbar to delete the label.

Now, with the space created by the deletion of the two fields, you should be able to make the report fit correctly. To do so, perform the following steps:

3. Click on the WineName label in the Page Header section. When the cursor changes to a small hand, drag the label six grid points to the right. Repeat the process for the WineName label in the Detail section.

4. Click on the Vineyard label in the Page Header section. Move the cursor to the right side of the label until Access displays the double sizing arrow, and then drag the right side of the label over until it's a single grid point away from the left side of the WineName label. Repeat the process for the Vineyard label in the Detail section.

5. Make sure the Vineyard label in the Detail section is selected, and then press Alt+Enter to display the Properties dialog box. On the Format tab of the Properties dialog box, select the **Can Grow** property. Change the property's value to Yes.

6. Click on the Vintage label in the Page Header section. When the cursor changes to a small hand, drag the label four grid points to the right. Repeat the process for the Vintage label in the Detail section.

7. Click on the WineName label in the Page Header section. Move the cursor to the right side of the label until Access 2000 displays the double sizing arrow, and then drag the right side of the label over until it's a single grid point away from the left side of the Vintage label. Repeat the process for the WineName label in the Detail section.

8. Make sure the WineName label in the Page Header section is selected, and then press Alt+Enter to display the Properties

dialog box. On the Format tab of the Properties dialog box, select the **Caption** property. Change the property's value to "Wine Name".

9. Click on the Vintage label in the Page Header section. Move the cursor to the right side of the label until Access 2000 displays the double sizing arrow, and then drag the right side of the label over until it's a single grid point away from the left side of the Color label. Repeat the process for the Vintage label in the Detail section.

10. Click the mouse on the gray Detail bar, and hold it down. Drag the bar down toward the bottom of the report page, until the area displayed within the Page Header section is approximately double its previous size.

11. Click once on the solid black line below the header labels, and hold the mouse button down. Drag the bar down until it appears at the bottom of the newly expanded Page Header area.

12. Click on the ServingInstructions label in the Page Header section. Move the cursor to the bottom edge of the label until Access displays the double sizing arrow, and then drag the bottom edge of the label down until it's a single grid point above the solid black line.

13. Make sure the ServingInstructions label in the Page Header section is selected, and then press Alt+Enter to display the Properties dialog box. On the Format tab of the Properties dialog box, select the **Caption** property. Change the property's value to "Serving Instructions".

14. Click on the PercentAlcohol label in the Page Header section. Move the cursor to the bottom edge of the label until Access displays the double sizing arrow, and then drag the bottom edge of the label down until it's a single grid point above the solid black line.

15. Make sure the PercentAlcohol label in the Page Header section is selected, and then press Alt+Enter to display the Properties dialog box. On the Format tab of the Properties

dialog box, select the **Caption** property. Change the property's value to "Percent Alcohol".

16. Click on the MarketValuePerBottle label in the Page Header section. Move the cursor to the bottom edge of the label until Access displays the double sizing arrow, and then drag the bottom edge of the label down until it's a single grid point above the solid black line.

17. Make sure the MarketValuePerBottle label in the Page Header section is selected, and then press Alt+Enter to display the Properties dialog box. On the Format tab of the Properties dialog box, select the **Caption** property. Change the property's value to "Value/ Bottle".

18. Click on the BottleSize label in the Page Header section. Move the cursor to the bottom edge of the label until Access displays the double sizing arrow, and then drag the bottom edge of the label down until it's a single grid point above the solid black line.

19. Make sure the BottleSize label in the Page Header section is selected, and then press Alt+Enter to display the Properties dialog box. On the Format tab of the Properties dialog box, select the **Caption** property. Change the property's value to "Bottle Size".

20. Click on the VineyardWeb label in the Page Header section. Move the cursor to the bottom edge of the label until Access displays the double sizing arrow, and then drag the bottom edge of the label down until it's a single grid point above the solid black line.

21. Make sure the VineyardWeb label in the Page Header section is selected, and then press Alt+Enter to display the Properties dialog box. On the Format tab of the Properties dialog box, select the **Caption** property. Change the property's value to "Vineyard Web Address".

When you finish making all these changes, your report will look similar to the one shown in Figure 12.8 (note that the report is wide enough that your screen will likely not display it in its entirety).

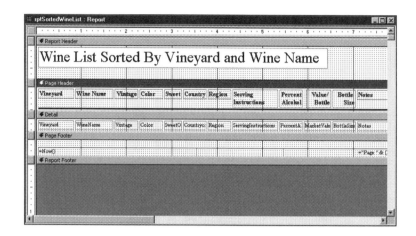

Figure 12.8
The fixed report in
Design View.

You can do many additional things with the report once you've
completed its design—print it, export it to an HTML file for
publication on the Web, and so on. These topics will be discussed
in detail in Chapter 13.

.Project Creating A Report From Design View

Although you'll usually get started with most of your reports using
a report wizard, you should understand how to create a new report
from Design View. To create a report without the use of a wizard:

1. Click on the Reports tab, and then click on New. The New
   Report dialog box appears.

2. Click on Design View, and then click on OK. The Report
   Design window appears.

Designing A Query To Use With The Report

As mentioned previously, you'll often design a custom query to
use with the report. In the case of the report you'll design next,
it's important to create a query, because the fields in the report
will not come from a single table. To create the new query,
perform the following steps:

1. From within the Database window, select the Queries object.
   Within the window, double-click on the Create Query In
   Design View option. Access 2000 will display the Query1

builder, as well as the Show Table dialog box. For simplicity's sake, close the Show Table dialog box and click on the SQL button on the toolbar. Access will display the SQL window.

2. Within the SQL window, enter the following **SELECT** statement:

```
SELECT DISTINCTROW [Wine Types].[WineType],
                   [Wine List].[Vineyard],
                   [Wine List].[WineName],
                   [Wine List].[Vintage],
                   [Wine List].[MarketValuePerBottle],
                   Sum([Wine Purchases].[Quantity])
                        AS [Quantity]
FROM ([Wine Types] RIGHT JOIN [Wine List] ON
        [Wine Types].[WineTypeID] =
            [Wine List].[WineTypeID])
        INNER JOIN [Wine Purchases] ON
            [Wine List].[WineListID] =
                [Wine Purchases].[WineListID]
GROUP BY [Wine Types].[WineType],
         [Wine List].[Vineyard],
         [Wine List].[WineName],
         [Wine List].[Vintage],
         [Wine List].[MarketValuePerBottle];
```

3. Close the SQL window. Access 2000 will prompt you to name and save the query. Name the query qrySelectWineByType and click on OK. Access will save the query.

You'll analyze the qrySelectWineByType query in more detail in Chapter 13; for now, simply understand that it pulls values from the Wine Types, Wine List, and Wine Purchases tables, returning hybrid data for the report.

Now that you've created the necessary query, the next step is to add the fields necessary for the report to the designer.

Adding Fields To The Report

Fields can most easily be added to a report using the Field List window. With it open, click and drag a field from the field list onto the appropriate section of the report. Just as with forms, multiple fields can be added at one time. Use the Ctrl key to select noncontiguous fields or the Shift key to select contiguous

▶**Tip**

One problem with adding fields to a report is that both the data field (a Text Box control) and the attached label for the data field (a Label control) are placed in the same section of the report. This means that if you click and drag fields from the Field List window to the Detail section, both the fields and the attached labels will appear in the report. If you're creating a tabular report, this isn't acceptable. You'll then need to cut the attached labels and paste them within the Page Header section of the report.

fields; then click and drag the fields to the report as a unit. However, you must first associate a datasource with the report before you can open the Field List window. To associate the qrySelectWineByType query with the report you're currently designing, perform the following steps:

1. Click on the gray box just inside the top-left corner of the Report Designer. Access 2000 will put a small black box inside the gray box.

2. Press Alt+Enter to display the Properties window. Access will display the report properties.

3. Within the Properties window, select the Data tab. On the Data tab, click on the drop-down arrow to the right of the **Record Source** property. Access will display a list of available datasources; select the qrySelectWineByType item.

4. Click on the Field List icon on the toolbar to display the Field List window.

To place all the necessary fields on the working report layout, perform the following steps:

5. Within the Field List window, click on the WineType field. Then, hold down the Shift key and click on the Quantity field.

6. Hold down the Ctrl key, and deselect the MarketValuePer-Bottle field. Continue holding down the Ctrl key, click on any of the selected fields, hold down the mouse button, and drag the fields to the Detail area of the report. Access 2000 will display five fields and five labels in two columns.

7. Click off the fields. Then, within the detail area, click on the first of the five labels. Click on the Cut button, or press Ctrl+X to cut the label. Move the mouse cursor up to the Page Header section, and paste the label inside that section. Repeat the process for the remaining four labels. Note that Access will paste all five labels one on top of the other.

8. Before continuing, click on the Print Preview button to display the report in Preview Mode. Next, right-click on the report. Access will display a pop-up menu.

9. Within the pop-up menu, select the Page Setup option. Access will display the Page Setup dialog box.

10. Within the Page Setup dialog box, select the Page tab. On the Page tab, change the orientation selection to Landscape. Click on OK to exit the Page Setup dialog box.

11. Click on the Design button to return the report to Design View. Note that Access 2000 does not automatically widen the size of the page.

12. To widen the size of the page, click on the right margin of the white space on the report and drag its edge until it's at the 9" mark.

Now that the fields are basically in place, let's make some changes to the layout of the report before we finalize the objects on the report. The following section details how to lay out sorting and grouping levels for the report.

Laying Out Sorting And Grouping Levels For The Report

Obviously, we want to make sure the data in the report is organized in a way that's most useful to the people reviewing the report. In this case, there's benefit to both grouping and sorting the data on the report. To set up the sorting and grouping for the report, perform the following steps:

1. Click on the Sorting And Grouping icon on the toolbar. Access 2000 will display the Sorting And Grouping dialog box.

2. In the first row, select the WineType field from the drop-down list. Access automatically defaults to ascending order for the sort. Additionally, when you select the field name, Access makes available five group properties you can set. For the WineType field, set **Group Header** to Yes, **Group Footer** to Yes, and leave the remaining properties unchanged. When you finish, the dialog box will look similar to the one shown in Figure 12.9.

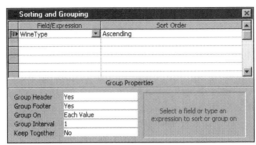

Figure 12.9
The sorting and grouping information for the WineType field.

3. In the second row, select the Vineyard field from the drop-down list. Access 2000 will automatically default to ascending order for the sort. Additionally, when you select the field name, Access makes available five group properties that you can set. Do not set any group properties for the Vineyard field (we are only sorting on this field, not grouping by it).

4. In the third row, select the WineName field from the drop-down list. Access 2000 will automatically default to ascending order for the sort. Additionally, when you select the field name, Access 2000 makes available five group properties that you can set. Do not set any group properties for the WineName field.

5. After you finish setting the sorting and grouping properties, close the dialog box. Note that Access 2000 has added two more sections to the report—the WineType Header and the WineType Footer sections. We'll use both sections to display information about each grouping.

Now that all the sections are on the report, let's work on the layout of each of the report sections, in order.

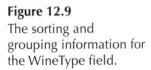

►Tip

If your report does not show the Report Header section, right-click in the designer and select the Report Header/ Footer option from the pop-up menu.

Laying Out The Report Header Section Of The Report

Obviously, placement of the fields and labels on the report in each of the sections is crucial for the report to look appropriate. Laying out each of the sections is somewhat tedious, so let's take them one at a time. To lay out the Report Header section, perform the following steps:

1. If the toolbox is not currently displayed, click on the Toolbox icon on the toolbar. Within the toolbox, click on the Label control icon. When you move the cursor back over the report, Access 2000 displays the label-creation cursor.

2. Click anywhere within the Report Header section, hold down the mouse button, and drag the mouse down and to the right to create a new label. The size of the label is not particularly important; you'll set its properties momentarily from the Properties dialog box.

3. Press the Alt+Enter keyboard combination to display the Properties dialog box.

4. Within the Format tab, change the **Caption** to "Wine By Type". Change the **Left** property to 0.05", the **Top** property to 0.0417", the **Width** property to 1.6563", and the **Height** property to 0.3646".

5. Change the **Fore Color** property to 8388608, the **Font Name** property to Times New Roman, the **Font Size** property to 20, the **Font Weight** property to Bold, and the **Font Italic** property to Yes.

6. When you finish setting the label properties, you must set one additional property for the Report Header section. To do so, click on the gray Report Header bar and then change the **Height** property of the section to 0.6563".

Laying Out The Page Header Section Of The Report

Earlier in this chapter, you placed five labels within the Page Header section of the report. Now, it's time to format those five labels and add a sixth, summary label. You can make the process easier by spreading the five labels out a little bit in the header area in the following order, from left to right: WineType, WineName, Vineyard, Vintage, and Quantity. Let's format each of the five labels before we add the sixth. To format the labels, perform the following steps:

1. Within the Page Header area of the designer, click on the WineType label. Press the Alt+Enter keyboard combination to display the Properties dialog box.

2. Within the Format tab, change the **Caption** to "Wine Type". Change the **Left** property to 0.05", the **Top** property to 0.0417", the **Width** property to 1.9167", and the **Height** property to 0.2188".

3. Change the **Fore Color** property to 8388608, the **Font Name** property to Times New Roman, the **Font Size** property to 11, the **Font Weight** property to Bold, and the **Font Italic** property to Yes.

4. Within the Page Header area of the designer, click on the WineName label. Press the Alt+Enter keyboard combination to display the Properties dialog box.

5. Within the Format tab, change the **Caption** to "Wine Name". Change the **Left** property to 1.95", the **Top** property to 0.0417", the **Width** property to 1.6042", and the **Height** property to 0.2188".

6. Change the **Fore Color** property to 8388608, the **Font Name** property to Times New Roman, the **Font Size** property to 11, the **Font Weight** property to Bold, and the **Font Italic** property to Yes.

7. Within the Page Header area of the designer, click on the Vineyard label. Press the Alt+Enter keyboard combination to display the Properties dialog box.

8. Within the Format tab, change the **Left** property to 3.6042", the **Top** property to 0.0417", the **Width** property to 1.6042", and the **Height** property to 0.2188".

9. Change the **Fore Color** property to 8388608, the **Font Name** property to Times New Roman, the **Font Size** property to 11, the **Font Weight** property to Bold, and the **Font Italic** property to Yes.

10. Within the Page Header area of the designer, click on the Vintage label. Press the Alt+Enter keyboard combination to display the Properties dialog box.

11. Within the Format tab, change the **Left** property to 5.2583",
    the **Top** property to 0.0417", the **Width** property to 0.6354",
    and the **Height** property to 0.2188".

12. Change the **Fore Color** property to 8388608, the **Font Name**
    property to Times New Roman, the **Font Size** property to 11,
    the **Font Weight** property to Bold, and the **Font Italic** prop-
    erty to Yes. Then, change the **Text Align** property to Right.

13. Within the Page Header area of the designer, click on the
    Quantity label. Press the Alt+Enter keyboard combination to
    display the Properties dialog box.

14. Within the Format tab, change the **Left** property to 5.9438",
    the **Top** property to 0.0417", the **Width** property to 1.3194",
    and the **Height** property to 0.2188".

15. Change the **Fore Color** property to 8388608, the **Font Name**
    property to Times New Roman, the **Font Size** property to 11,
    the **Font Weight** property to Bold, and the **Font Italic** prop-
    erty to Yes. Then, change the **Text Align** property to Right.

After you format the five existing labels, you should add the sixth
label to the Page Header section. To do so, perform the following
steps:

16. If the toolbox is not currently displayed, click on the Toolbox
    icon on the toolbar. Within the toolbox, click on the Label
    control icon. When you move the cursor back over the report,
    Access 2000 displays the label-creation cursor.

17. Click anywhere within the Page Header section, hold down
    the mouse button, and drag the mouse down and to the right
    to create a new label. The size of the label is not particularly
    important; you'll set its properties momentarily from the
    Properties dialog box. Enter the caption as "Current Value".

18. Within the Page Header area of the designer, click on the
    Current Value label. Press the Alt+Enter keyboard combina-
    tion to display the Properties dialog box.

19. Within the Format tab, change the **Left** property to 7.3132",
    the **Top** property to 0.0417", the **Width** property to 1.0833",
    and the **Height** property to 0.2188".

20. Change the **Fore Color** property to 8388608, the **Font Name** property to Times New Roman, the **Font Size** property to 11, the **Font Weight** property to Bold, and the **Font Italic** property to Yes. Then, change the **Text Align** property to Right.

Now that the layout of the Page Header section is complete, in the next section of the chapter you'll design the WineType Header section of the report.

Laying Out The WineType Header Section Of The Report

The WineType Header section of the report will contain only a single text box, corresponding to the particular wine type for the grouping. However, this text box should be cut from the text boxes that you put in the Detail section previously. To place the text box in the WineType header, perform the following steps:

1. Within the Detail section, click on the existing WineType text box. Access 2000 indicates your selection by displaying selectors around the box.

2. Cut the text box (using either Ctrl+X or the Cut icon on the toolbar). Paste the text box into the WineType Header section (using either Ctrl+V or the Paste icon).

3. Within the WineType Header area of the designer, click on the WineType text box. Press the Alt+Enter keyboard combination to display the Properties dialog box.

4. Within the Format tab, change the **Left** property to 0.05", the **Top** property to 0.0", the **Width** property to 1.9167", and the **Height** property to 0.2292".

5. Change the **Fore Color** property to 8388608, the **Font Name** property to Times New Roman, the **Font Size** property to 11, and the **Font Italic** property to **Yes**.

6. Select the WineType header (by clicking on the WineType Header gray bar), and change the **Height** property to 0.2708".

Now that the layout of the WineType Header section is complete, you'll design the Detail section of the report.

Laying Out The Detail Section Of The Report

Earlier in this chapter, you placed five text boxes within the Detail section of the report. You subsequently removed one of those text boxes and placed it in the WineType Header section. Now, it's time to format the remaining four text boxes and add a fifth, summary text box. You can make the process easier by spreading the four text boxes out a little bit in the Detail area in the following order, from left to right: WineName, Vineyard, Vintage, and Quantity. Let's format each of these four text boxes before we add the new one. To format the text boxes, perform the following steps:

1. Within the Detail area of the designer, click on the WineName text box. Press the Alt+Enter keyboard combination to display the Properties dialog box.

2. Within the Format tab, change the **Left** property to 1.95", the **Top** property to 0.0", the **Width** property to 1.6042", and the **Height** property to 0.1875".

3. Change the **Font Name** property to Arial and the **Font Size** property to 8.

4. Within the Detail area of the designer, click on the Vineyard text box. Press the Alt+Enter keyboard combination to display the Properties dialog box.

5. Within the Format tab, change the **Left** property to 3.6042", the **Top** property to 0.0", the **Width** property to 1.6042", and the **Height** property to 0.1875".

6. Change the **Font Name** property to Arial and the **Font Size** property to 8.

7. Within the Detail area of the designer, click on the Vintage text box. Press the Alt+Enter keyboard combination to display the Properties dialog box.

8. Within the Format tab, change the **Left** property to 5.2583", the **Top** property to 0.0", the **Width** property to 0.6354", and the **Height** property to 0.1875".

9. Change the **Font Name** property to Arial and the **Font Size** property to 8.

10. Within the Detail area of the designer, click on the Quantity text box. Press the Alt+Enter keyboard combination to display the Properties dialog box.

11. Within the Format tab, change the **Left** property to 5.9438", the **Top** property to 0.0", the **Width** property to 1.3194", and the **Height** property to 0.1875".

12. Change the **Font Name** property to Arial and the **Font Size** property to 8.

After you format the four existing text boxes, you should add the new text box to the Detail section. To do so, perform the following steps:

13. If the toolbox is not currently displayed, click on the Toolbox icon on the toolbar. Within the toolbox, click on the Text Box control icon. When you move the cursor back over the report, Access 2000 displays the text box-creation cursor.

14. Click anywhere within the Detail section, hold down the mouse button, and drag the mouse down and to the right to create a new text box. The size of the text box is not particularly important; you'll set its properties momentarily from the Properties dialog box. Enter the name as "Current Value".

15. Within the Detail area of the designer, click on the Current Value text box. Press the Alt+Enter keyboard combination to display the Properties dialog box.

16. Within the Format tab, change the **Format** property to Currency, the **Left** property to 7.3132", the **Top** property to 0.0", the **Width** property to 1.0833", and the **Height** property to 0.1875".

17. Change the **Font Name** property to Arial and the **Font Size** property to 8.

18. Within the Data tab, change the **Control Source** property to the following:

```
=[MarketValuePerBottle]*[Quantity]
```

19. Select the Detail section (by clicking on the Detail gray bar), and change the **Height** property to 0.2292".

Now that the layout of the Detail section is complete, you'll design the WineType Footer section of the report.

Laying Out The WineType Footer Section Of The Report

The WineType Footer section of the report will contain a single label and three text boxes, which are designed to display summary information corresponding to the particular wine type for the grouping. To design the WineType footer, perform the following steps:

1. Select the WineType Footer section (by clicking on the WineType Footer gray bar), and change the **Height** property to 0.4375".

2. If the toolbox is not currently displayed, click on the Toolbox icon on the toolbar. Within the toolbox, click on the Text Box control icon. When you move the cursor back over the report, Access 2000 displays the text box-creation cursor.

3. Click anywhere within the WineType Footer section, hold down the mouse button, and drag the mouse down and to the right to create a new text box. The size of the text box is not particularly important; you'll set its properties momentarily from the Properties dialog box. Enter the name as "SumField1".

4. Within the WineType Footer area of the designer, click on the SumField1 text box. Press the Alt+Enter keyboard combination to display the Properties dialog box.

5. Within the Format tab, change the **Left** property to 0.05", the **Top** property to 0.0", the **Width** property to 8.9", and the **Height** property to 0.1677".

6. Change the **Font Name** property to Arial, the **Font Size** property to 8, and the **Font Italic** property to Yes.

7. Within the Data tab, change the **Control Source** property to the following:

```
="Summary for " & "'WineType' = " & " " & [WineType] &
    " (" & Count(*) & " " &
    IIf(Count(*)=1, _
        "detail record","detail records") & ")"
```

8. Click anywhere within the WineType Footer section, hold down the mouse button, and drag the mouse down and to the right to create a new text box. The size of the text box is not particularly important; you'll set its properties momentarily from the Properties dialog box. Enter the name as "SumQuantity".

9. Within the WineType Footer area of the designer, click on the SumQuantity text box. Press the Alt+Enter keyboard combination to display the Properties dialog box.

10. Within the Format tab, change the **Left** property to 5.9438", the **Top** property to 0.1979", the **Width** property to 1.3194", and the **Height** property to 0.1979".

11. Change the **Font Name** property to Arial, the **Font Size** property to 8, and the **Font Italic** property to Yes.

12. Within the Data tab, change the **Control Source** property to the following:

```
=Sum([Quantity])
```

13. Click anywhere within the WineType Footer section, hold down the mouse button, and drag the mouse down and to the right to create a new text box. The size of the text box is not particularly important; you'll set its properties momentarily from the Properties dialog box. Enter the name as "SumValue".

14. Within the WineType Footer area of the designer, click on the SumValue text box. Press the Alt+Enter keyboard combination to display the Properties dialog box.

15. Within the Format tab, change the **Format** property to Currency, the **Left** property to 7.3132", the **Top** property to 0.1979", the **Width** property to 1.0833", and the **Height** property to 0.1979".

16. Change the **Font Name** property to Arial, the **Font Size** property to 8, and the **Font Italic** property to Yes.

17. Within the Data tab, change the **Control Source** property to the following:

```
=Sum([MarketValuePerBottle]*[Quantity])
```

18. Click on the Label control icon in the toolbox. When you move the cursor back over the report, Access 2000 displays the label-creation cursor.

19. Click anywhere within the WineType Footer section, hold down the mouse button, and drag the mouse down and to the right to create a new label. The size of the label is not particularly important; you'll set its properties momentarily from the Properties dialog box. Enter the caption as "Sum".

20. Within the WineType Footer area of the designer, click on the Sum label. Press the Alt+Enter keyboard combination to display the Properties dialog box.

21. Within the Format tab, change the **Left** property to 0.05", the **Top** property to 0.1979", the **Width** property to 0.3229", and the **Height** property to 0.1979".

22. Change the **Font Name** property to Times New Roman, the **Font Size** property to 10, and the **Font Weight** property to Bold.

Now that the layout of the WineType Footer section is complete, you'll design the Page Footer section of the report.

Laying Out The Page Footer Section Of The Report

The Page Footer section of the report will contain two text boxes—one to display the report time and one to display the current page number in the report. To place the text boxes in the Page Footer section, perform the following steps:

1. If the toolbox is not currently displayed, click on the Toolbox icon on the toolbar. Within the toolbox, click on the Text Box control icon. When you move the cursor back over the report, Access 2000 displays the text box-creation cursor.

2. Click anywhere within the Page Footer section, hold down the mouse button, and drag the mouse down and to the right to create a new text box. Enter the name as "Time".

3. Within the Page Footer area of the designer, click on the Time text box. Press the Alt+Enter keyboard combination to display the Properties dialog box.

4. Within the Format tab, change the **Format** property to Long Date, the **Left** property to 0.05", the **Top** property to 0.1667", the **Width** property to 3.5", and the **Height** property to 0.2083".

5. Change the **Fore Color** property to 8388608, the **Font Name** property to Times New Roman, the **Font Size** property to 9, the **Font Weight** property to Bold, and the **Font Italic** property to Yes.

6. Switch to the Data tab, and change the **Control Source** property to the following:

```
=Now()
```

7. Click anywhere within the Page Footer section, hold down the mouse button, and drag the mouse down and to the right to create a new text box. The size of the text box is not particularly important; you'll set its properties momentarily from the Properties dialog box. Enter the name as "PageNum".

8. Within the Page Footer area of the designer, click on the PageNum text box. Press the Alt+Enter keyboard combination to display the Properties dialog box.

9. Within the Format tab, change the **Left** property to 5.45", the **Top** property to 0.1667", the **Width** property to 3.5", and the **Height** property to 0.2083".

10. Change the **Fore Color** property to 8388608, the **Font Name** property to Times New Roman, the **Font Size** property to 9, the **Font Weight** property to Bold, and the **Font Italic** property to Yes.

11. Switch to the Data tab, and change the **Control Source** property to the following:

```
="Page " & [Page] & " of " & [Pages]
```

12. Select the Page Footer section (by clicking on the Page Footer gray bar), and change the **Height** property to 0.375".

Now that the layout of the Page Footer section is complete, you'll design the Report Footer, the final section of the report.

Laying Out The Report Footer Section Of The Report

The Report Footer section of the report will contain a pair of text boxes and a label, indicating grand totals for the entire collection. To place the text boxes and the label in the Report Footer section, perform the following steps:

1. Select the Report Footer section (by clicking on the Report Footer gray bar), and change the **Height** property to 0.25".

2. If the toolbox is not currently displayed, click the Toolbox icon on the toolbar. Within the toolbox, click on the Text Box control icon. When you move the cursor back over the report, Access 2000 displays the text box-creation cursor.

3. Click anywhere within the Report Footer section, hold down the mouse button, and drag the mouse down and to the right to create a new text box. The size of the text box is not particularly important; you'll set its properties momentarily from the Properties dialog box. Enter the name as "Quantity Grand Total Sum".

4. Within the Report Footer area of the designer, click on the Quantity Grand Total Sum text box. Press the Alt+Enter keyboard combination to display the Properties dialog box.

5. Within the Format tab, change the **Left** property to 5.9438", the **Top** property to 0.0", the **Width** property to 1.3194", and the **Height** property to 0.2083".

6. Change the **Font Name** property to Times New Roman, the **Font Size** property to 10, and the **Font Italic** property to Yes.

7. Within the Data tab, change the **Control Source** property to the following:

```
=Sum([Quantity])
```

8. Click anywhere within the Report Footer section, hold down the mouse button, and drag the mouse down and to the right to create a new text box. The size of the text box is not particularly important; you'll set its properties momentarily from the Properties dialog box. Enter the name as "Current Value Grand Total Sum".

9. Within the Report Footer area of the designer, click on the Current Value Grand Total Sum text box. Press the Alt+Enter keyboard combination to display the Properties dialog box.

10. Within the Format tab, change the **Format** property to Currency, the **Left** property to 7.3132", the **Top** property to 0.0", the **Width** property to 1.0833", and the **Height** property to 0.2083".

11. Change the **Font Name** property to Times New Roman, the **Font Size** property to 10, and the **Font Italic** property to Yes.

12. Within the Data tab, change the **Control Source** property to the following:

```
=Sum([MarketValuePerBottle]*[Quantity])
```

13. Click on the Label control icon in the toolbox. When you move the cursor back over the report, Access 2000 displays the label creation cursor.

14. Click anywhere within the Report Footer section, hold down the mouse button, and drag the mouse down and to the right to create a new label. The size of the label is not particularly important; you'll set its properties momentarily from the Properties dialog box. Enter the caption as "Grand Total".

15. Within the WineType Footer area of the designer, click on the Grand Total label. Press the Alt+Enter keyboard combination to display the Properties dialog box.

16. Within the Format tab, change the **Left** property to 0.05", the **Top** property to 0.0", the **Width** property to 0.7604", and the **Height** property to 0.1979".

17. Change the **Font Name** property to Times New Roman, the **Font Size** property to 10, the **Font Weight** property to Bold, and the **Font Italic** property to Yes.

Now that the layout of the Report Footer section is complete, the entirety of the form's design is complete. When you finish, the report should look similar to the one shown in Figure 12.10.

When you display the report in Preview Mode, it should look similar to the report shown in Figure 12.11.

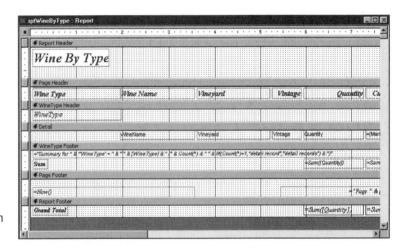

Figure 12.10
The completed report in Design View.

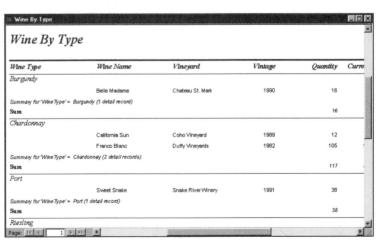

Figure 12.11
The completed report in Preview Mode.

Where To Go From Here

In this chapter, you designed, programmed, and tested a pair of reports on a sample database. Using the report design tools and the techniques you learned in this chapter, you can easily create powerful and useful reports for use within your applications. Coming up next, we'll take a closer look at the theory and application behind report design, how to determine what information you should report, and how to create parameterized reports.

Chapter 13

Understanding Access Report Design

Generating good reports from Access 2000 is simple. However, top-flight report design requires more than just the display of data—it also requires customization of events and other actions.

As you've learned, the forms you use within Access 2000 let you format the data in your database in many different fashions to make accessing the data much easier for your users. However, there are many cases where you need to generate output—either hardcopy reports or onscreen reports—in which you'll often find that such data cannot be easily reflected in a form. In such cases, you'll probably want to generate a report to display the information. In Chapter 12, you learned some of the important techniques for creating reports and methods for formatting the reports in the best manner possible. In this chapter, we'll consider some more advanced information about reports, including the types of reports available and the use of events to customize your report output.

Types Of Reports Available

The reporting engine of Microsoft Access 2000 is very powerful and includes a wealth of features. Many types of reports are available in Access 2000, several of which are detailed in the following list:

- Detail reports

- Summary reports

- Cross-tabulation reports

- Reports containing graphics and charts

▶Tip

Although there are many different types of reports, most of them will share one or more characteristics of the different types discussed in this section. These generalized types aren't constraining, but are instead intended to provide you with guidelines from which to work.

- Reports containing forms
- Reports containing labels
- Reports including any combination of the above

Detail Reports

A *detail report* provides an entry for each record included in the report. You can then group the detail within the report. You can also provide subtotals, grand totals, and summaries within detail reports. The reports you created in Chapter 12 were both detail reports, with the second example including summary information as well as the underlying recordset data.

Summary Reports

A *summary report* provides summary data for all the records included in the report. For example, you might print a report that displays only total sales by quarter and by year. The underlying detail records that compose the summary data aren't displayed within the report. A summary report itself contains no controls in its Detail section. All controls are placed in report group headers and footers, which are grouped on the quarter and year of the ship date. Because no controls are found in the Detail section of the report, Access 2000 prints summary information only.

Cross-Tabulation Reports

Cross-tabulation reports display summarized data grouped by one set of information on the left side of the report and by another set across the top of the report. For example, you might create a report that displays total sales by product name and employee. Cross-tabulation reports are always based on a crosstab query and generally require a fair amount of VBA code, because each time the report is run, a different number of employees might need to be displayed in the columns of the report. In other words, the number of columns needed might be different each time the report is run.

Working With Other Types Of Reports

In addition to the three basic report types that you can take advantage of, Access 2000 provides you with the necessary tools to create other types of reports, including reports that embed other objects. Most often, you would use such reports as part of a presentation or other common activity.

Reports Containing Graphics And Charts

Research proves that people more successfully retain data displayed as pictures rather than numbers. Fortunately, Access makes the process of including graphics and charts in your reports quite easy. You can effortlessly design reports that include a combination of numbers and charts.

Reports Containing Or Emulating Forms

A report that emulates a printed form is a common need. The Access Report Builder, with its many graphical tools, enables you to quickly produce reports that emulate the most elegant of data-entry forms. The use of graphics, color, fonts, shading, and other special effects give the form a professional look and feel.

Reports Containing Labels

Creating mailing labels in Access 2000 is easy. Mailing labels are simply a special type of report with a page setup indicating the number of labels across the page and the size of each label. You can also create your labels in another product, such as Microsoft Word, and then simply import data from your Access 2000 database.

Understanding The Sections Of A Report

Reports can contain many parts (referred to as the *sections* of the report). You were exposed to working with sections in the last chapter. A new report is automatically made up of three sections:

- Page header
- Detail section
- Page footer

The Detail section of a report is the main section used to display the detailed data of the table or query underlying the report. Certain reports, such as summary reports, contain nothing in the Detail section but rather contain data only in the group headers and footers (which you'll learn more about later in this chapter).

The page header of a report is the portion that automatically prints at the top of every page. It often includes information such as the title of the report. The page footer automatically prints at the bottom of every page, and it often contains information such as the page number and date. Each report can contain only a single page header and a single page footer.

In addition to the three sections that are automatically added to every report, a report can contain the following sections:

- Report header
- Report footer
- Group headers
- Group footers

In a given report, you can add one, some, or all of the additional sections. Figure 13.1 shows a report in Design View with each of the sections, excepting the group footer, displayed.

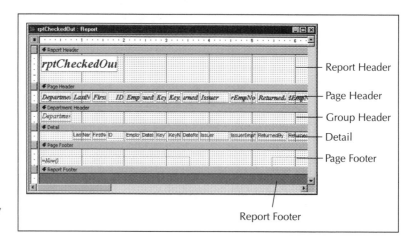

Figure 13.1
A report in Design View showing six sections.

A report header prints once at the beginning of the report, while the report footer prints once at the end of the report. Each Access report can contain only a single report header and a single report footer. The report header is often used to create a cover sheet for the report. It can contain graphics and other fancy effects to give a professional look to a report containing important information. The most common use of the report footer is for grand totals. It can also include any other summary information for the report.

In addition to report and page headers and footers, an Access 2000 report can contain up to 10 group headers and footers. Report groupings separate data both logically and physically. A group header prints before the detail for the group, and the group footer prints after the detail for the group. For example, you can group customer sales by country and city, printing the name of the country each time the country changes and the name of the city each time the city changes. You can total the sales for each country and city. The country and city names are placed in the Country and City group headers. The totals are placed in the Country and City group footers.

Moving Objects Around In The Report

If you want to move a single control along with its attached label, click on the object and drag it to a new location. The object and the attached label move as a unit. To move multiple objects, use one of the many cut-and-paste methods available to you—lassoing, multiple selection with the Shift or Ctrl key, and so on. After the objects are selected, click and drag any of them. The selected objects and their attached labels move as a unit.

Moving an object without its attached label is a trickier process. When placed over the center or border of a selected object (not on a sizing handle), the mouse pointer appears as a hand with all five fingers pointing upward. When the mouse pointer appears as a hand, the selected object and its attached label move as a unit, maintaining their relationship to one another. By placing your mouse pointer directly over the selection handle that appears in the upper-left corner of the object, the mouse pointer appears as a hand with the index finger pointing upward. If you click and drag with the mouse pointer in this format, the object and the attached label move independently of one another, so you can alter the distance between them.

Aligning Objects To One Another On The Report

To align objects to one another, you first need to select the objects you want to align. Next, select the Format menu's Align option and then select Left, Right, Top, Bottom, or To Grid. The selected objects will then align with each other.

During the alignment process, Access 2000 never overlaps objects. For this reason, if the objects you're aligning don't fit, Access 2000 is unable to align them. For example, if you attempt to align the bottom of several objects horizontally and they don't fit across the report, Access 2000 aligns only the objects that fit on the line. You can also use tools such as Snap To Grid, just as you did with forms, when you design your reports.

Although it's easy to create most reports, as you mature as an Access 2000 developer, you'll probably want to learn the intricacies of Access 2000 report design. The remainder of this chapter covers event handling with reports and some advanced report design techniques.

Events Available With Reports

Although the events that reports have are not as plentiful as the events that forms have, the report events you can trap for enable you to control what happens as your report runs. This section discusses report events. In later sections of this chapter, you will learn about events that are specific to report sections. Although determining what event to use will often take some time, as you

▶Tip

It's easy to see the huge need in many enterprises for sophisticated reporting tools for IT people as well as end users. Although you may find that the Access report writer isn't a sufficiently complex tool for your enterprise's needs, the report writer provides many powerful tools that are often underutilized. We've provided a good overview of report design, but spend some time really working with all the properties and events that the report writer provides for specialization—you and your organization will reap the benefits.

get more comfortable with report events you will be able to more easily determine whether to use a report event or a report section event.

The Open Event

The **Open** event is the first event that occurs for a report. It occurs before the report begins printing or displaying. In fact, it occurs before the query underlying the report is run. Here's an example of the use of the **Open** event:

```
Private Sub Report_Open(Cancel As Integer)
  DoCmd.OpenForm "frmReportDateRange", , , , , _
    acDialog,  "Wine Acquisitions By Date"
  If Not IsLoaded("frmReportDateRange") Then _
    Cancel = True
End Sub
```

This code can be found in the report rptWineAcquisitionsByDate in Chap13.mdb on this book's CD-ROM. In the second line, the code attempts to open the form frmReportDateRange. This is the criteria form that's used to supply the parameters for the query underlying the report. Within the form, the user supplies the date range to check. After he or she enters data within the form, Access 2000 goes ahead and displays the report for the selected range. If the form cannot be loaded, the report is canceled, which occurs in the fourth and fifth lines.

The Close Event

The **Close** event occurs as the report is closing, before the **Deactivate** event occurs. The following example illustrates the use of the **Close** event:

```
Private Sub Report_Close()
  DoCmd.Close acForm, "frmReportDateRange"
End Sub
```

This code is found in the report rptWineAcquisitionsByDate in Chap13.mdb on the book's companion CD-ROM. It closes the criteria form frmReportDateRange when the report is closing.

The Activate Event

The **Activate** event of a report occurs when the report becomes the active window. It occurs after the **Open** event and before the report starts printing. It's often used to display a custom toolbar that's visible whenever the report is active. Here's an example:

```
Private Sub Report_Activate()
   ' Hide built-in Print Preview toolbar.
   ' Show Custom Print Preview toolbar.

   DoCmd.ShowToolbar "Print Preview", acToolbarNo
   DoCmd.ShowToolbar "Custom Print Preview", _
      acToolbarYes
End Sub
```

This code hides the Print Preview toolbar and shows the custom toolbar called Custom Print Preview. As you'll see in the next section, this event works along with the **Deactivate** event to show and hide the custom report toolbars when the report becomes the active window and the user moves the focus to another window.

The Deactivate Event

The **Deactivate** event occurs when the user moves to another Access 2000 window or closes the report. The **Deactivate** event does *not* occur when focus is moved to another application. Here's an example of how the **Deactivate** event is used:

```
Private Sub Report_Deactivate()
   ' Hide Custom Print Preview toolbar.
   ' Show built-in Print Preview toolbar.

   DoCmd.ShowToolbar "Custom Print Preview", acToolbarNo
   DoCmd.ShowToolbar "Print Preview", _
      acToolbarWhereApprop
End Sub
```

This routine hides the custom toolbar that was displayed during the **Activate** event and indicates that the Print Preview toolbar should once again display where appropriate. You do not want to show the Print Preview toolbar here. Instead, you just "reset" it to display whatever Access 2000's default behavior tells it to display.

The NoData Event

If no records meet the criteria of the recordset underlying a report's **RecordSource** property, the report prints without any data. The report displays the string **#Error** in the Detail section of the report. To eliminate this problem, you can write code within the **NoData** event of the report. Here's an example:

```
Private Sub Report_NoData(Cancel As Integer)
  MsgBox "There is no data for this report. " & _
    "Canceling report... "
  Cancel = -1
End Sub
```

This code is found in the **NoData** event of the report rptWine-AcquisitionsByDate in Chap13.mdb on the companion CD-ROM. In case no data is returned by the report's underlying recordset, a message is displayed to the user, and **Cancel** is set equal to True. This exits the report without running it.

The Page Event

The **Page** event gives you the opportunity to perform an action immediately before the formatted page is sent to the printer. For example, it enables you to place a border around a page. The following code shows something you might do inside the **Report_Page** event:

```
Private Sub Report_Page()
  'Draw a page border around this report.
  Me.Line (0, 0)-(Me.LogicalPageWidth, _
    Me.LogicalPageHeight), , B
End Sub
```

This code draws a line on the report, starting in the upper-left corner of the report and going to the lower-right corner of the report. It uses the **LogicalPageWidth** and **LogicalPageHeight** properties of the **Report** object (referenced with a call to **Me** in this case) to determine where the lower-right corner of the printable area of the report is.

The Error Event

If a Jet engine error occurs when the report is formatting or printing, the **Error** event is triggered. This error usually occurs if the **RecordSource** property for the report does not exist or if someone else has exclusive use of the report's recordsource—that is, the underlying table or query is locked. Here's an example of how you might place code within the **Error** event to handle such a situation:

```
Private Sub Report_Error(DataErr As Integer, _
    Response As Integer)
  If DataErr = 2580 Then
    MsgBox "Record Source Not Available for This Report"
    Response = acDataErrContinue
  End If
End Sub
```

This code responds to a **DataErr** of **2580**. This error code means that the recordsource for the report is not available. A custom message is displayed to the user, and the Access 2000 error is suppressed.

Order Of Events For Reports

Just as it's important to understand the order of events for forms, it's also important that you understand the order of events for reports. When the user opens a report, previews it, and then closes it, the following sequence of events occurs:

```
Open-Activate-Close-Deactivate
```

When the user switches to another report *or* to a form, the following sequence occurs:

```
Deactivate(Current Report)-Activate(Form or Report)
```

NOTE

*The **Deactivate** event does not occur when the user switches to a dialog box, to a form whose **PopUp** property is set to Yes, or to a window of another application.*

Report Section Events

Just as the report itself has events, so too does each section of the report. The three section events are **Format**, **Print**, and **Retreat**. These events are covered in this section.

The Format Event

The **Format** event occurs after Access 2000 has selected the data to be included in a report section, but before it formats or prints the data. The **Format** event enables you to affect the layout of the section or to calculate the results of data within the section before the section actually prints. Here's an example:

```
Private Sub Detail2_Format(Cancel As Integer, _
    FormatCount As Integer)
  '  Determine whether to print
  '  detail record or "Continued."
  '  Show Continued text box if at maximum number of
  '  detail records for page.
  If (Me.Row = Me.OrderPage * (Me.RowsPerPage - 1) + 1) _
    And Me.Row <> Me.RowCount Then
    Me.Continued.Visible = True
  End If

  ' Show page break and hide controls in detail record.
  If Me.Continued.Visible Then
    Me.DetailPageBreak.Visible = True
    Me.ProductID.Visible = False
    Me.ProductName.Visible = False
    Me.Quantity.Visible = False
    Me.UnitPrice.Visible = False
    Me.Discount.Visible = False
    Me.ExtendedPrice.Visible = False

    ' Increase value in Order Page.
    Me.NextRecord = False
    Me.OrderPage = Me.OrderPage + 1
    ' Increase row count if detail record is printed.
  Else
    Me.Row = Me.Row + 1
  End If
End Sub
```

NOTE

*By placing logic in the **Format** event of the Detail section of a report, you're able to control what happens as each line of the Detail section is printed.*

In this case, the report must contain controls that track how many rows of detail records should be printed on each page. If the maximum number of rows has been reached, a control containing the text "Continued on Next Page..." will become visible. If the control is visible, the Page Break control is also made visible, and all the controls that display the detail for the report are hidden. The report is kept from advancing to the next record.

The Print Event

The code within the **Print** event is executed when the data has been formatted to print in the section, but before it's actually printed. The **Print** event occurs at the following times for the various sections of the report:

- *Detail section*—Just before the data is printed.

- *Group headers*—Just before the group header is printed. The **Print** event of the group header has access to both the group header and to the first row of data in the group.

- *Group footers*—Just before the group footer is printed. The **Print** event of the group detail has access to both the group footer and to the last row of data in the group.

For example, consider the following code for the **Print** event:

```
Private Sub Detail_Print(Cancel As Integer, _
    PrintCount As Integer)
  Dim intX As Integer
  Dim lngRowTotal As Long

  '  If PrintCount is 1, initialize rowTotal variable.
  '  Add to column totals.

  If Me.PrintCount = 1 Then
    lngRowTotal = 0
    For intX = 2 To intColumnCount
      '  Starting at column 2 (first text box with
      '  crosstab value), compute total for current
      '  row in detail section.

      lngRowTotal = lngRowTotal + _
          Me("Col" + Format$(intX))
      '  Add crosstab value to total for current column.

      lngRgColumnTotal(intX) = lngRgColumnTotal(intX) _
          + Me("Col" +  Format$(intX))
    Next intX

    '  Place row total in text box in detail section.
    Me("Col" + Format$(intColumnCount + 1)) = _
        lngRowTotal

    '  Add row total for current row to grand total.
    lngReportTotal = lngReportTotal + lngRowTotal
  End If
End Sub
```

The code begins by evaluating the **PrintCount** property. If the **PrintCount** property is equal to 1, indicating that this is the first time the **Print** event has occurred for the Detail section, the row total is set equal to 0. The code then loops through each control in the section, accumulating both totals for each column of the report and a total for the row. After the loop has been exited, the routine places the row total into the appropriate control and adds the row total to the grand total for the report. The Detail section of the report is now ready to be printed.

The Retreat Event

Sometimes Access 2000 needs to move back to a previous section when printing. This occurs, for example, when a group's **Keep Together** property is set to With First Detail or Whole. Access 2000 needs to format the group header and the first detail record or, in the case of Whole, the entire group. It then determines whether it can fit the section on the current page. It retreats from the two sections, formats them, and prints them. A **Retreat** event occurs for each section in such an environment. Here's an example of the **Retreat** event for a report Detail section:

```
Private Sub Detail1_Retreat()
  ' Always back up to previous record when
  ' detail section retreats.
  rstReport.MovePrevious
End Sub
```

This particular code would go inside of an unbound report. Because the report is an unbound report, it needs to return to the previous record in the recordset whenever the **Retreat** event occurs.

Order Of Section Events

Just as report events have an order, report sections also have an order of events. All the **Format** and **Print** events for each section occur after the **Open** and **Activate** events of the report, but before the **Close** and **Deactivate** events for the report. The sequence looks like this:

```
Open(Report)-Activate(Report)-Format(Report Section)-
   Print(Report Section)-
   Close(Report)-Deactivate(Report)
```

Special Report Properties

Several report properties are available only at runtime. They enable you to refine the processing of your report significantly. The following sections describe some of those report properties:

- **MoveLayout**—The **MoveLayout** property is used to indicate to Access 2000 whether it should move to the next printing location on the page. By setting the property to False, the printing position is not advanced.

- **NextRecord**—The **NextRecord** property is used to specify whether a section should advance to the next record. By setting this property to False, you suppress advancement to the next record.

- **PrintSection**—The **PrintSection** property is used to indicate whether the section is printed. By setting this property to False, you can suppress the printing of the section.

- **FormatCount**—The **FormatCount** property is used to evaluate the number of times the **Format** event has occurred for the current section of the report. The **Format** event occurs more than once whenever the **Retreat** event occurs. By checking the **FormatCount** property, you can ensure that complex code placed within the **Format** event is executed only once.

- **PrintCount**—The **PrintCount** property is used to identify the number of times the **Print** event occurs for the current section of the report. The **Print** event occurs more than once whenever the **Retreat** event occurs. By checking the value of the **PrintCount** property, you can ensure that logic within the **Print** event is executed only once.

- **HasContinued**—The **HasContinued** property is used to determine whether part of the current section is printed on a previous page. You can use this property to hide or show certain report controls (for example, Continued From...), depending on whether the section is continued.

- **WillContinue**—The **WillContinue** property is used to determine whether the current section continues on another page. As with the **HasContinued** property, you can use this property to hide or display certain controls when a section continues on another page.

Interaction Of MoveLayout, NextRecord, And PrintSection

By using the **MoveLayout**, **NextRecord**, and **PrintSection** properties in combination, you can determine exactly where, how, and whether data is printed. Table 13.1 illustrates this point.

Table 13.1   Interaction of MoveLayout, NextRecord, and PrintSection.

MoveLayout	NextRecord	PrintSection	Effect
True	True	True	Move to the next position, get the next record, and print the data.
True	False	True	Move to the next position, remain on the same record, and print the data.
True	True	False	Move to the next position, get the next record, and don't print the data. This has the effect of skipping a record and leaving a blank space.
True	False	False	Move to the next position, remain on the same record, and don't print. This causes a blank space to appear without moving to the next record.
False	True	True	Remain in the same position, get the next record, and print the data. This has the effect of overlaying one record on another.
False	False	True	Not allowed.
False	True	False	Remain in the same position, get the next record, and refrain from printing. This has the effect of skipping a record without leaving a blank space.
False	False	False	Not allowed.

Some Practical Applications Of Report Events And Properties

In developing reports, you should ensure that the report can be used in as many situations as might be reasonably good fits for the report. This means that you should build as much flexibility into the report as possible. By using the events and properties that have been covered in this chapter, you can build flexibility into your reports. This might involve changing the report's recordsource at runtime, using the same report to print summary data, detail data, or both, changing the print position, or even running a report based on a crosstab query with unbound controls. All these aspects of report design are covered in this section.

Changing A Report's Recordsource

There are many times when you might want to change a report's recordsource at runtime. By doing this, you can allow your users to alter the conditions for a report and transparently modify the query on which the report is based. The rptVineyardListing report, contained in Chap13.mdb, has the following code in its **Open** event:

```
Private Sub Report_Open(Cancel As Integer)
  DoCmd.OpenForm "frmVineyardListingCriteria", _
      WindowMode:=acDialog
  If Not IsLoaded("frmVineyardListingCriteria") Then
    Cancel = True
  Else
    With Forms!frmVineyardListingCriteria
      Select Case!optCriteria.Value
        Case 1
          Me.RecordSource = "qryVineyardListingCity"
        Case 2
          Me.RecordSource = _
              "qryVineyardListingStateProv"
        Case 3
          Me.RecordSource = "qryVineyardListing"
      End Select
    End With
  End If
End Sub
```

This code begins by opening the frmVineyardListingCriteria form if it's not already loaded. It loads the form modally and waits for the user to select the report criteria (see Figure 13.2). Once the user clicks to preview the report, the form sets its own **Visible** property to False. This causes execution to continue within the report, but leaves the form in memory so that its controls can be accessed using VBA code. The value of the form's optCriteria option button is evaluated. Depending on which option button is selected, the report's **RecordSource** property is set to the appropriate query. The following code is placed in the **Close** event of the report:

```
Private Sub Report_Close()
  DoCmd.Close acForm, "frmVineyardListingCriteria"
End Sub
```

This code closes the criteria form as the report is closing. The frmVineyardListingCriteria form contains some code that's important to the processing of the report. It's found in the **AfterUpdate** event of the **optCriteria** option group:

```
Private Sub optCriteria_AfterUpdate()
  Select Case optCriteria.Value
    Case 1
      Me!cboCity.Visible = True
      Me!cboStateProv.Visible = False
    Case 2
      Me!cboStateProv.Visible = True
      Me!cboCity.Visible = False
    Case 3
      Me!cboCity.Visible = False
      Me!cboStateProv.Visible = False
  End Select
End Sub
```

Figure 13.2
The criteria selection used to determine the recordsource.

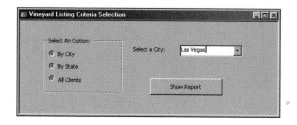

This code evaluates the value of the option group. It hides and shows the visibility of the cboCity and cboState combo boxes, depending on which option button is selected. The cboCity and cboState combo boxes are then used as appropriate criteria for the queries that underlie the rptVineyardListing report.

Using The Same Report To Display Summary, Detail, Or Both Types Of Information

Many programmers create three reports for their users: one that displays summary information only, one that displays information detail only, and another that displays both types. This repetitiveness is not only totally unnecessary, but it consumes a lot of time and space. Because report sections can be optionally hidden or displayed at runtime, you can create *one* report that meets all three needs. The rptBottlesByVineyard report included in the Chap13.mdb database illustrates this point. Place the following code in the **Open** event of the report:

```
Private Sub Report_Open(Cancel As Integer)
  DoCmd.OpenForm "frmReportDateRange", _
      WindowMode:=acDialog, OpenArgs:= _
      "rptBottlesByVineyard"
  If Not IsLoaded("frmReportDateRange") Then
    Cancel = True
  Else
    With Forms!frmReportDateRange
      Select Case!optDetailLevel.Value
        Case 1
          Me.Caption = Me.Caption & " - Summary Only"
          Me!lblTitle.Caption = Me.lblTitle.Caption _
            & " - Summary Only"
          Me.Detail.Visible = False
        Case 2
          Me.Caption = Me.Caption & " - Detail Only"
          Me!lblTitle.Caption = Me.lblTitle.Caption _
            & " - Detail Only"
          Me.GroupHeader0.Visible = False
          Me.GroupFooter1.Visible = False
          Me!CompanyNameDet.Visible = True
        Case 3
          Me.Caption = Me.Caption & _
            " - Summary and Detail"
```

```
                Me!lblTitle.Caption = Me.lblTitle.Caption & _
                    " - Summary and Detail"
                Me!CompanyNameDet.Visible = False
            End Select
        End With
    End If
End Sub
```

The code begins by opening frmReportDateRange (see Figure 13.3), which is included in Chap13.mdb. The form contains an option group that asks users whether they want a summary report, a detail report, or a report that contains both summary and detail information. If Summary is selected, the captions of the report window and the lblTitle label are modified, and the **Visible** property of the Detail section is set to False. If the user selects Detail, the captions of the report window and the lblTitle label are modified, and the **Visible** properties of the Group Header and Footer sections are set to False. A control in the Detail section containing the company name is made visible. The Vineyard-Name control is visible in the Detail section when the detail-only report is printed, but it's invisible when the summary and detail report is printed. When the Both option is selected, no sections are hidden. The **Caption** properties of the report window and the lblTitle label are modified, and the VineyardName control is hidden.

The code behind the Preview button of the form looks like this:

```
Private Sub Preview_Click()
    If IsNull([BeginDate]) Or IsNull([EndDate]) Then
        MsgBox "You must enter both beginning " & _
            "and ending dates."
        DoCmd.GoToControl "BeginDate"
    Else
        If [BeginDate] > [EndDate] Then
            MsgBox "Ending date must be greater " & _
                "than Beginning date."
            DoCmd.GoToControl "BeginDate"
        Else
            Me.Visible = False
        End If
    End If
End Sub
```

▶**Tip**

Be careful that you don't generate too much complexity when creating combined reports—you will often find that a front-end selection form, with a variety of different back-end reports, may be a better solution. The difference is invisible to the user, but maintenance issues can become significant if you try to pack too many different types and styles of information into a single report.

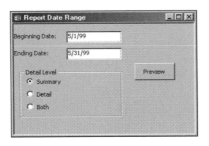

Figure 13.3
The criteria selection used to determine detail level.

This code ensures that both the beginning date and the ending date are filled in, and that the beginning date is before the ending date. If both of these rules are fulfilled, the **Visible** property of the form is set to False. Otherwise, an appropriate error message displays.

Printing Multiple Labels

Many times, users want to print multiple copies of the same label. This can be accomplished by using the **MoveLayout**, **NextRecord**, **PrintSection**, and **PrintCount** properties of a report. The form shown in Figure 13.4 is named frmVineyardLabelCriteria and is found in Chap13.mdb. It asks that users select a client and the number of labels they want to print for that client. The code under the Print Labels command button looks like this:

```
Sub cmdPrintLabels_Click()
  On Error GoTo Err_cmdPrintLabels_Click

  Dim stDocName As String
  stDocName = "lblVineyardMailingLabels"
  DoCmd.OpenReport stDocName, acPreview, , _
      "VineyardName = '" _
      & Me!cboVineyardName.Value & "'"

Exit_cmdPrintLabels_Click:
  Exit Sub

Err_cmdPrintLabels_Click:
  MsgBox Err.Description
  Resume Exit_cmdPrintLabels_Click
End Sub
```

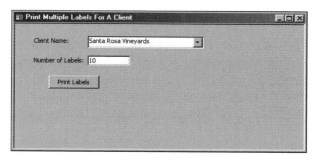

Figure 13.4
The criteria selection used to specify vineyard name and the number of labels to print.

Tip

This type of processing is often very useful in a shipping department application—a situation where one or a dozen different boxes might go to the same client. When combined with intelligent processing—for example, 12 bottles of wine to a shipping case, the customer ordered 144 bottles of wine, therefore the application should print 12 labels automatically—can provide significant productivity benefits to your organization or client.

Notice that the routine uses the company name selected from the combo box as criteria to run the lblVineyardMailingLabels report. The **Open** event of lblVineyardMailingLabels looks like this:

```
Private Sub Report_Open(Cancel As Integer)
  If Not IsLoaded("frmVineyardLabelCriteria") Then
    MsgBox "You Must Run This Report From The " & _
        "Label Criteria Form"
    Cancel = True
  End If
End Sub
```

This code tests to ensure that the frmVineyardLabelCriteria form is open. If it's not open, a message is displayed and the report is canceled. The key to the whole process is found in the **Print** event of the Detail section. It looks like this:

```
Private Sub Detail_Print(Cancel As Integer, _
    PrintCount As Integer)
  With Forms!frmVineyardLabelCriteria
    If PrintCount <!txtNumberOfLabels Then
      Me.NextRecord = False
    End If
  End With
End Sub
```

This code compares the **PrintCount** property to the number of labels that the user wants to print. As long as the **PrintCount** is less than the number of labels requested, the record pointer is not advanced. This causes multiple labels to be printed for the *same* record.

Determining Where A Label Prints

One problem facing users is that they might want to print multiple copies of the same label—another common problem is that users might want to print mailing labels in a specific position on the page. This is done so that users can begin the print process on the first unused label. The frmVineyardLabelPosition form found in Chap13.mdb is shown in Figure 13.5. It requests that the user specify the first label location on which to print by designating the number of labels that need to be skipped. The **Open** event of lblVineyardMailLabelsSkip looks like this:

```
Private Sub Report_Open(Cancel As Integer)
  If Not IsLoaded("frmVineyardLabelPosition") Then
    MsgBox "You Must Run This Report From The " & _
        "Label Criteria Form"
    Cancel = True
  Else
    mfFirstLabel = True
  End If
End Sub
```

The code tests to ensure that the frmVineyardLabelPosition form is loaded. It also sets a private variable, **mfFirstLabel**, equal to True. The Detail section's **Print** event then looks like this:

```
Private Sub Detail_Print(Cancel As Integer, _
    PrintCount As Integer)
  With Forms!frmVineyardLabelPosition
    If PrintCount <=!txtLabelsToSkip _
        And mfFirstLabel = True Then
      Me.NextRecord = False
      Me.PrintSection = False
    Else
      mfFirstLabel = False
    End If
  End With
End Sub
```

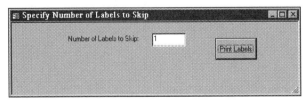

Figure 13.5
The criteria selection used to indicate the number of labels to skip.

This routine checks to see whether the **PrintCount** property of the report is less than or equal to the number of labels to skip. It also checks to ensure that the **mfFirstLabel** variable is equal to True. If both these conditions are true, the report does not move to the next record and does not print anything. The print position is advanced. Once **PrintCount** becomes greater than the number of labels to skip, the **mfFirstLabel** variable is set to False and printing proceeds as usual. One additional event makes all this work—the **Print** event of the report header:

```
Private Sub ReportHeader_Format(Cancel As Integer, _
    FormatCount As Integer)
  mfFirstLabel = True
End Sub
```

The report header section's **Format** event sets **mfFirstLabel** back to True. This is a necessary step in case the user previews and then prints the labels. If the **mfFirstLabel** variable is not reset to True, the selected number of labels is not skipped on the printout, because the condition that skips the labels is never met.

▶Tip

You would generally use this type of printing control with any program that generates its own labels. However, you might also find that you use a variant of this code hand-in-hand with any other printing routine—you may want your programs to be "smart" enough to determine where they should start printing automatically, without input from the user.

NOTE

*If **mfFirstLabel** is not set to False, the designated number of labels are skipped between each record.*

Building A Report From A Crosstab Query

It's very difficult to base a report on the results of a crosstab query, because the number of columns in a crosstab query generally varies. Consider the example shown in Figure 13.6. Notice that the employee names appear across the top of the report as column headings, and the products appear down the side of the report. This report is based on a crosstab query called EmployeeSales

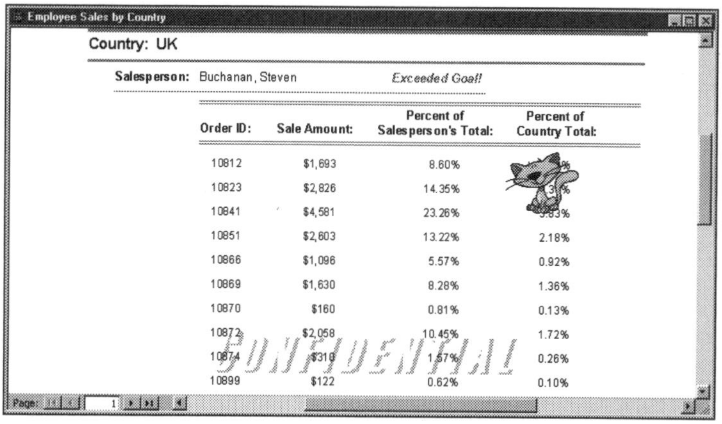

Figure 13.6
A report based on a crosstab query.

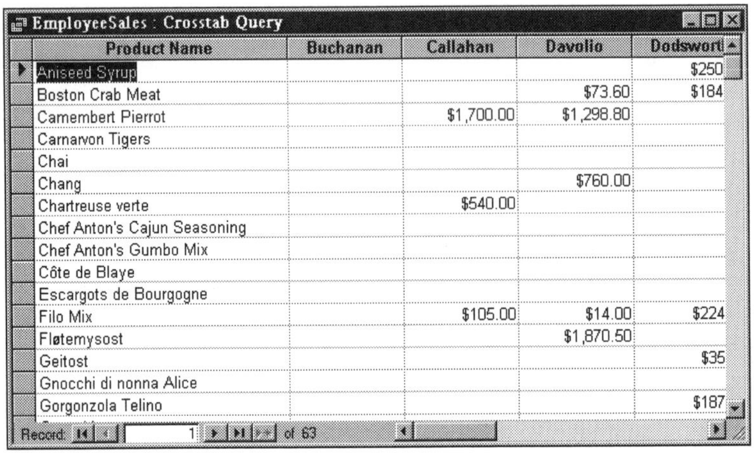

Product Name	Buchanan	Callahan	Davolio	Dodswort
Aniseed Syrup				$250
Boston Crab Meat			$73.60	$184
Camembert Pierrot		$1,700.00	$1,298.80	
Carnarvon Tigers				
Chai				
Chang			$760.00	
Chartreuse verte		$540.00		
Chef Anton's Cajun Seasoning				
Chef Anton's Gumbo Mix				
Côte de Blaye				
Escargots de Bourgogne				
Filo Mix		$105.00	$14.00	$224
Fløtemysost			$1,870.50	
Geitost				$35
Gnocchi di nonna Alice				
Gorgonzola Telino				$187

Figure 13.7
The crosstab query underlying the report.

(see Figure 13.7). The problem is that the number of employees, and therefore the number of column headings, can vary. This report is coded to handle such an eventuality.

When the report runs, the **Open** event of the report is executed:

```
Private Sub Report_Open(Cancel As Integer)
  '  Create underlying recordset for report using
  '  criteria entered in EmployeeSalesDialogBox form.

  Dim intX As Integer
  Dim qdf As QueryDef
  '  Don't open report if EmployeeSalesDialogBox
  '  form isn't loaded.

  If Not (IsLoaded("EmployeeSalesDialogBox")) Then
    Cancel = True
    MsgBox "To preview or print this report, _
       you must open the Employee _
       Sales Dialog Box in Form view.", 48, _
       "Must Open Dialog Box"
  Exit Sub
End If

  '  Set database variable to current database.
  Set dbsReport = CurrentDb()

  '  Open QueryDef.
  Set qdf = dbsReport.QueryDefs("EmployeeSales")
```

```
'  Set parameters for query based on values entered
'  in EmployeeSalesDialogBox form.
qdf.Parameters("Forms!EmployeeSalesDialogBox! _
    BeginningDate") = _
    Forms!EmployeeSalesDialogBox!BeginningDate
qdf.Parameters("Forms!EmployeeSalesDialogBox! _
    EndingDate") = _
    Forms!EmployeeSalesDialogBox!EndingDate

'  Open Recordset.
Set rstReport = qdf.OpenRecordset()

'  Set a variable to hold number of columns
'  in crosstab query.
intColumnCount = rstReport.Fields.Count
End Sub
```

The code first checks to ensure that the criteria form, Employee-
SalesDialogBox, is open. This form supplies the criteria for the
EmployeeSales query that underlies the report. The **Open** event
then sets a database object variable to the current database. It
opens the EmployeeSales query definition and passes it the
parameters from the EmployeeSalesDialogBox criteria form. Next,
it opens a recordset based on the query definition, using the
criteria found on the EmployeeSalesDialogBox form. The number
of columns returned from the crosstab query is very important. It's
stored in a **Private** variable called **intColumnCount** and is used
throughout the remaining functions to determine how many
columns to fill with data.

After the **Open** event, the **Activate** event occurs. This event
displays the Custom Print Preview toolbar that appears whenever
the report is the active object:

```
Private Sub Report_Activate()
    '  Used to show toolbar that includes
    '  Show Me button.
    '  Hide built-in Print Preview toolbar.
    '  Show Custom Print Preview toolbar.

    DoCmd.ShowToolbar "Print Preview", acToolbarNo
    DoCmd.ShowToolbar "Custom Print Preview", acToolbarYes
End Sub
```

Next, the report header's **Format** event occurs. It moves to the first record in the recordset created during the **Open** event. It also calls the **InitVariables** routine:

```
Private Sub ReportHeader3_Format(Cancel As Integer, _
    FormatCount As Integer)
  '  Move to first record in recordset at
  '  beginning of report
  '  or when report is restarted.
  '  (A report is restarted when you print a report
  '  from Print Preview window, or when you return
  '  to a previous page while previewing.)
  rstReport.MoveFirst

  'Initialize variables.
  InitVariables
End Sub
```

The **InitVariables** routine initializes some variables used within the report:

```
Private Sub InitVariables()
  Dim intX As Integer

  ' Initialize lngReportTotal variable.
  lngReportTotal = 0

  ' Initialize array that stores column totals.
  For intX = 1 To conTotalColumns
    lngRgColumnTotal(intX) = 0
  Next intX
End Sub
```

The **lngReportTotal** variable is used for the report grand total (all products and all salespeople), and the **lngRgColumnTotal** array contains the total for each salesperson. After the report header's **Format** event occurs, the page header's **Format** event takes place. The code within the event looks like this:

```
Private Sub PageHeader0_Format(Cancel As Integer, _
    FormatCount As Integer)
  Dim intX As Integer

  ' Put column headings into text boxes in page header.
  For intX = 1 To intColumnCount
    Me("Head" + Format$(intX)) = rstReport(intX - 1).Name
  Next intX
```

```
    '  Make next available text box Totals heading.
    Me("Head" + Format$(intColumnCount + 1)) = "Totals"

    '  Hide unused text boxes in page header.
    For intX = (intColumnCount + 2) To conTotalColumns
      Me("Head" + Format$(intX)).Visible = False
    Next intX
End Sub
```

The page header's **Format** event has the important responsibility of using the names of the fields in the query results as column headings for the report. It's a smart routine because, after it fills in all the column headings, it hides all the extra controls on the report.

Next, the Detail section's **Format** event occurs. The code within it looks like this:

```
Private Sub Detail_Format(Cancel As Integer, _
    FormatCount As Integer)
  '  Place values in text boxes and hide
  '  unused text boxes.
  Dim intX As Integer

  '  Verify that not at end of recordset.
  If Not rstReport.EOF Then
    '  If FormatCount is 1, place values from recordset
    '  into text boxes in detail section.
    If Me.FormatCount = 1 Then
      For intX = 1 To intColumnCount
        '  Convert null values to 0.
        Me("Col" + Format$(intX)) = _
            xtabCnulls(rstReport(intX - 1))
      Next intX

      '  Hide unused text boxes in detail section.
      For intX = intColumnCount + 2 To conTotalColumns
        Me("Col" + Format$(intX)).Visible = False
      Next intX

      '  Move to next record in recordset.
      rstReport.MoveNext
    End If
  End If
End Sub
```

The Detail section's **Format** event checks the **EOF** property of the recordset to determine whether the last record in the query has already been read. If not, the **FormatCount** property of the section is tested to see whether it is equal to 1. If so, each column in the current record of the recordset is read. Each control in the Detail section is filled with data from a column in the recordset, and any unused text boxes in the Report Detail section are hidden. Finally, the code moves to the next record in the recordset, readying the report to print the next line of detail. The **xtabCnulls** function, which converts Null values into zeros, is called each time the recordset underlying the report is read:

```
Private Function xtabCnulls(varX As Variant)
  ' Test if a value is null.
  If IsNull(varX) Then
    ' If varX is null, set varX to 0.
    xtabCnulls = 0
  Else
    ' Otherwise, return varX.
    xtabCnulls = varX
  End If
End Function
```

The **xtabCnulls** function evaluates each value it's sent to determine whether the value is Null. If so, 0 is returned from the function. Otherwise, the value that the function was passed is returned. After the Detail section's **Format** event is executed, the Detail section's **Print** event occurs:

```
Private Sub Detail_Print(Cancel As Integer, _
    PrintCount As Integer)
  Dim intX As Integer
  Dim lngRowTotal As Long
  '  If PrintCount is 1, initialize rowTotal variable.
  '  Add to column totals.

  If Me.PrintCount = 1 Then
    lngRowTotal = 0
    For intX = 2 To intColumnCount
      '  Starting at column 2 (first text box with
      '  crosstab value), compute
      '  total for current row in detail section.
      lngRowTotal = lngRowTotal + _
        Me("Col" + Format$(intX))
```

```
      '  Add crosstab value to total for current column.
      lngRgColumnTotal(intX) = _
          lngRgColumnTotal(intX) + Me("Col" + _
          Format$(intX))
    Next intX

      '  Place row total in text box in detail section.
      Me("Col" + Format$(intColumnCount + 1)) = _
          lngRowTotal

      '  Add row total for current row to grand total.
      lngReportTotal = lngReportTotal + lngRowTotal
   End If
End Sub
```

The Detail section's **Print** event is responsible for generating the row total value, placing it in the last column of the report, accumulating column totals, and accumulating the **lngReportTotal** value, which is the grand total for all columns and rows. It accomplishes this by ensuring that the **PrintCount** property of the section is 1. If so, it resets the **lngRowTotal** variable to 0. Starting at column 2 (column 1 contains the product name), the **Print** event begins accumulating a row total. It does this by looking at each control in the row and adding its value to **lngRowTotal**. As it traverses each column in the row, it also adds the value in each column to the appropriate element of a private array called **lngRgColumnTotal**, which maintains all the column totals for the report. It prints the row total and then adds the row total to the report's grand total.

When the **Retreat** event occurs, the following code executes:

```
Private Sub Detail_Retreat()
   ' Always back up to previous record when
   ' detail section retreats.
   rstReport.MovePrevious
End Sub
```

This code forces the record pointer to be moved back to the previous record in the recordset. Finally, the report footer prints. This causes the report footer's **Print** event to execute:

```
Private Sub ReportFooter_Print(Cancel As Integer, _
    PrintCount As Integer)
  Dim intX As Integer

    ' Place column totals in text boxes in report footer.
    ' Start at Column 2 (first text box
    ' with crosstab value).
    For intX = 2 To intColumnCount
      Me("Tot" + Format$(intX)) = lngRgColumnTotal(intX)
    Next intX

    ' Place grand total in text box in report footer.
    Me("Tot" + Format$(intColumnCount + 1)) = _
        lngReportTotal

    ' Hide unused text boxes in report footer.
    For intX = intColumnCount + 2 To conTotalColumns
      Me("Tot" + Format$(intX)).Visible = False
    Next intX
End Sub
```

The report footer's **Print** event loops through each control in the footer, populating each one with the appropriate element of the **lngRgColumnTotal** array. This provides the column totals for the report. Finally, the grand total is printed in the next available column. Any extra text boxes are hidden from display.

Where To Go From Here

In order to take full advantage of what the Access 2000 report writer has to offer, you must understand—and be able to work with—report and section events. This chapter went through the report and section events, providing detailed examples of when to employ each event.

In addition to the report events, several special properties are available to you only at runtime. By manipulating these properties, you can greatly control the behavior of your reports. After covering the report and section events, the chapter covered the properties you can manipulate only at runtime. Examples were provided to highlight the appropriate use of each property.

Many tips and tricks of the trade can help you to accomplish tasks that you might otherwise think are impossible to accomplish. This chapter concluded by providing several practical examples of these tips and tricks, making it easy for you to employ them in your own application development.

In Chapter 14, you'll learn about a new feature in Access 2000—data access pages—and how you can use them to help you move data to the Web.

Chapter 14

Introducing Data Access Pages

These days, most information technology is Web-directed in some way. Access 2000 extends its desktop capabilities to the Web by using data access pages.

What Are Data Access Pages?

Data access pages are HTML documents that can be directly bound to table data in a database. You'll find that data access pages are like Access forms except that they're designed to run in a Web browser—specifically Internet Explorer 5.0. In this chapter, you'll get your feet wet with data access pages by building a couple of working examples. We'll get into some data access page enhancement techniques a little later in this chapter. But now, let's get started creating a basic data access page.

Project Creating A Simple Data Access Page

Let's begin this look at data access pages by building a simple data entry form. This will be a painless process, as you're already familiar with a few of the mechanics involved. You'll see what I mean as you execute the following steps:

1. Launch Access 2000, and open the FirstDatabase database.

2. Select the Pages button under the Objects frame of the Access 2000 database window. Then double-click on Create Data Access Page In Design View to enter the data access page development area (see Figure 14.1).

3. Click once on the line that says "Click here and type title text," and at the blinking cursor, enter the words "My First Data Access Page".

NOTE

Access 2000's data access page capability requires Internet Explorer 5.0.

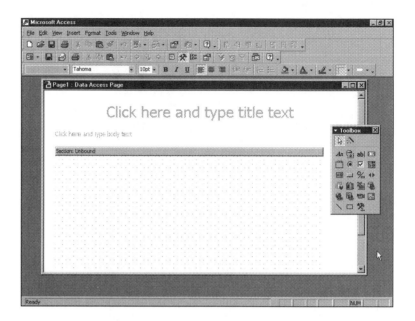

Figure 14.1
The data access page development area.

4. Click once on the line that says "Click here and type body text," and at the blinking cursor, enter the words "Sample Data Entry Page".

5. Place the mouse cursor just before the "S" in "Sample," and then hold down the left mouse button and drag the mouse from left to right highlighting the words "Sample Data Entry Page."

6. Select the Center button on the Access 2000 Formatting toolbar to center the body text line, and then select File|Save. When prompted, save the current page as "FirstDAP". Your page should appear as shown in Figure 14.2.

Adding Fields To A Data Access Page

With your page header completed, it's time to add data. You'll place data fields on your data access page by performing the following steps:

1. Select View|Field List from the Access 2000 menu bar to open the Field List dialog box, and then click the plus sign next to the Tables folder to expand the folder view into a list of tables available for you to use (see Figure 14.3).

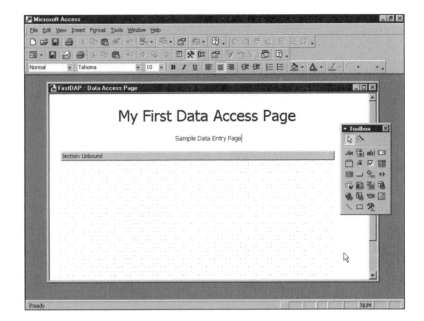

Figure 14.2
The FirstDAP data access page with text headers.

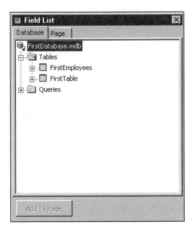

Figure 14.3
The Field List dialog box.

2. In the Field List dialog box, click the plus sign next to the FirstEmployees table to display the table's fields.

3. Click the field name FirstEmployeesID, and then click the Add To Page button on the Field List dialog box. This action places the selected field on the data access page grid.

4. Repeat Step 3 for each of the remaining fields in the FirstEmployees table, and then select File|Save from the Access 2000 menu bar.

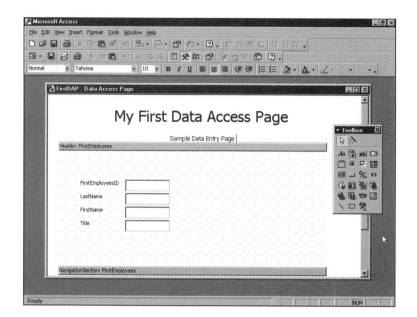

Figure 14.4
The FirstDAP data access page with text headers and fields.

5. Close the Field List dialog box by clicking the Close button in the dialog box's upper right corner. Your screen should appear as shown in Figure 14.4.

Viewing Your New Data Access Page

Congratulations, you've built your first data access page. Now it's time to give it a test drive by performing the following steps:

1. Maximize the data access page window by selecting the window's maximize button.

2. Select View|Page View from the Access 2000 menu bar to see a standard Page View of the completed page (see Figure 14.5).

3. Select File|Web Page Preview from the Access 2000 menu bar to launch Internet Explorer 5.0 so you can see the Browser View of the completed page (see Figure 14.6).

4. Use the Record Navigation toolbar to review each record in the FirstEmployees table (see Figure 14.7). Table 14.1 provides a key to the Record Navigation toolbar buttons.

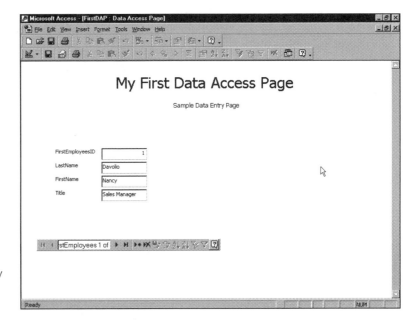

Figure 14.5
The standard Page View of the FirstDAP data access page.

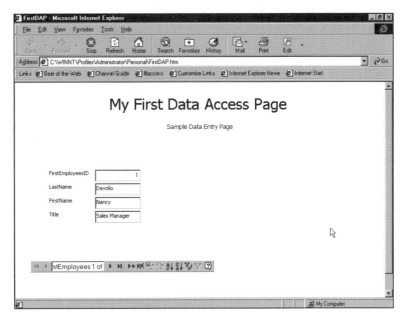

Figure 14.6
The Web Browser View of the FirstDAP data access page.

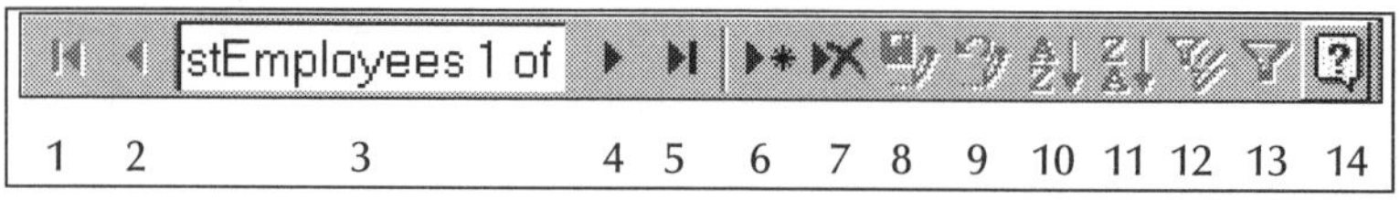

Figure 14.7
The Record Navigation
toolbar.

Table 14.1   Key to the Record Navigation toolbar.

Button Number	Description
1	Go to first record
2	Go to previous record
3	Position in the record
4	Go to next record
5	Go to last record
6	Add new record
7	Delete record
8	Save record
9	Undo record
10	Sort records in ascending order
11	Sort records in descending order
12	Filter by selection
13	Apply filter
14	Data access pages Help

Adjusting Object Sizes On Data Access Pages

As you may have noticed when reviewing the records from the
FirstEmployees table in your data access page, some of the values
are truncated. You can correct this by adjusting the size of the
objects residing on the data access page. Adjust the size of the
Title field and the Record Navigation toolbar by completing the
following steps:

1. Select View|Design View from the Access 2000 menu bar.

2. On the FirstDAP data access page design grid, click once on
   the Title field to expose the field's sizing handles.

3. Place the mouse cursor over a field-sizing handle.

4. When the mouse cursor changes to crossed arrows, hold down
   the left mouse button and drag the field to the left to extend it.

5. Release the left mouse button.

6. Repeat Steps 2 through 5 to resize the Record Navigation toolbar.

7. Select File|Save from the Access 2000 menu bar.

8. Select File|Web Page Preview from the Access 2000 menu bar to launch Internet Explorer 5.0 so you can see the revised Browser View of the completed page (see Figure 14.8).

Adding New Records Using Data Access Pages

Now that things look pretty good, let's add a new record to the FirstEmployees table using the FirstDAP data access page. You can accomplish this by completing the following steps:

1. With the FirstDAP data access page showing in your Web browser, click the Add A New Record button on the Record Navigation toolbar.

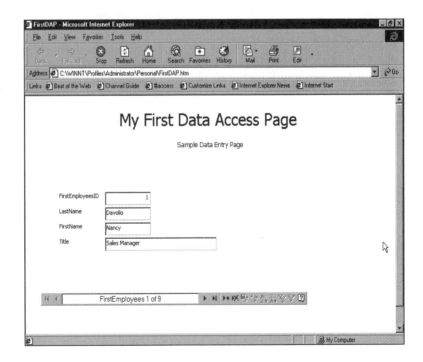

Figure 14.8
The FirstDAP data access page with resized Page objects.

2. Enter the following data into the fields listed below, pressing the Tab key to move between fields:

LastName   Doe

FirstName   John

Title   President, John Doe Company

3. When you're done, click the Save A Record icon on the Record Navigation toolbar to save the record, and the FirstEmployeesID field is filled in automatically.

Deleting Records Using Data Access Pages

Perhaps you've decided that you need to delete the record for employee Doe from the FirstEmployees table. Complete the following steps to accomplish this:

1. Select the Go To Last Record icon on the Record Navigation toolbar.

2. When the record of choice appears, click the Delete Record icon on the Record Navigation toolbar.

Creating Write-Only Data Access Pages

With data access pages, you have the option of creating read/write pages and write-only pages. In case you want to create the latter, here's what you'd do, making use of the FirstEmployees table:

1. With the FirstDAP data access page open in Page View mode, use the Record Navigation toolbar to advance through each table record, then select the Go To First Record icon. You'll notice that each field on the page displays data.

2. Select View|Design View to return FirstDAP to Design View mode.

3. Select Edit|Select Page, and then select View|Properties from the Access 2000 menu bar to launch the Page property sheet.

4. On the FirstDAP Page property sheet, select the Data tab.

5. On the Data tab, locate the DataEntry property and change it to True by selecting the True option from the property's drop-down menu (see Figure 14.9).

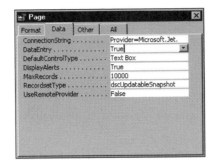

Figure 14.9
Change the Page
DataEntry property
to True to make it
write-only.

6. Close the Page property sheet, and then select File | Save from the Access 2000 menu bar.

7. Select View|Page View to browse the changed page, and notice that no data appears in the fields on the page.

Listing 14.1 presents a sample of the HTML code that supports the FirstDAP data access page. Don't worry if all of it doesn't make sense yet; I'll cover HTML code in more detail in Chapter 15.

Listing 14.1   Sample HTML for FirstDAP.

```
<!DOCTYPE HTML PUBLIC "-//W3C//DTD W3 HTML//EN">
<HTML><HEAD><TITLE>FirstDAP</TITLE>
<META content=Access.Application name=ProgId>
<META name=VBSForEventHandlers VALUE = TRUE>
<META content="text/html;
charset=windows-1252" http-equiv=Content-Type>
<STYLE id=MSODAPDEFAULTS
type=text/css rel = stylesheet>.mstheme-label {
    FONT-FAMILY: Tahoma; FONT-SIZE: 8pt
}
TEXTAREA {
    FONT-FAMILY: Tahoma; FONT-SIZE: 8pt
}
.msoboundhtml {
    FONT-FAMILY: Tahoma; FONT-SIZE: 8pt
}
HR {
    COLOR: black
}
SELECT {
    FONT-FAMILY: Tahoma; FONT-SIZE: 8pt
}
```

```
INPUT {
   FONT-FAMILY: Tahoma; FONT-SIZE: 8pt
}
BODY {
   FONT-FAMILY: Tahoma; FONT-SIZE: 10pt
}
MARQUEE {
   FONT-FAMILY: Tahoma; FONT-SIZE: 8pt
}
LEGEND {
   FONT-FAMILY: Tahoma; FONT-SIZE: 8pt
}
.msoHyperlinkDisplayText {
   FONT-FAMILY: Tahoma; FONT-SIZE: 8pt
}
BODY {
   FONT-FAMILY: Tahoma; FONT-SIZE: 10pt
}
.MsoShowDesignGrid {
   BEHAVIOR: url(#DEFAULT#MsoShowDesignGrid)
}
</STYLE>

<OBJECT
classid=CLSID:0002E530-0000-0000-C000-000000000046
codeBase="" id=MSODSC>
<PARAM NAME="XMLData"
VALUE="<?xml:namespace ns=&quot;
urn:schemas-microsoft-com:office:access&quot;
prefix=&quot;a&quot;?>&#13;&#10;<xml>&#13;&#10;
<a:DataSourceControl>&#13;&#10;
<a:OWCVersion>9.0.0.2209</a:OWCVersion>&#13;&#10;
<a:ConnectionString>
Provider=Microsoft.Jet.OLEDB.4.0;
Persist Security Info=False; User ID=Admin;
Data Source=C:\WINNT\Profiles\Administrator
\Personal\FirstDatabase.mdb;
Mode=Share Deny None;
Extended Properties=&amp;quot;&amp;quot;

Locale Identifier=1033;
Jet OLEDB:System database=&amp;quot;&amp;quot;
Jet OLEDB:Registry Path=&amp;quot;&amp;quot;
Jet OLEDB:Database Password=&amp;quot;&amp;quot;
Jet OLEDB:Engine Type=5;
Jet OLEDB:Database Locking Mode=0;
Jet OLEDB:Global Partial Bulk Ops=2;
```

```
Jet OLEDB:Global Bulk Transactions=1;
Jet OLEDB:New Database Password=&amp;quot;&amp;quot;
Jet OLEDB:Create System Database=False;
Jet OLEDB:Encrypt Database=False;
Jet OLEDB:Don't Copy Locale on Compact=False;
Jet OLEDB:Compact Without
Replica Repair=False;Jet
OLEDB:SFP=False</a:ConnectionString>&#13;&#10;
<a:MaxRecords>10000</a:MaxRecords>&#13;&#10;
<a:GridX>12</a:GridX>&#13;&#10;
<a:GridY>12</a:GridY>&#13;&#10;
<a:ElementExtension>&#13;&#10;
<a:ElementID>FirstEmployeesNavigation
</a:ElementID>&#13;&#10;
<a:ConsumesRecordset/>&#13;&#10;
</a:ElementExtension>&#13;&#10;
<a:ElementExtension>&#13;&#10;
<a:ElementID>FirstEmployeesID
</a:ElementID>&#13;&#10;
<a:ControlSource>FirstEmployeesID
</a:ControlSource>&#13;&#10;
<a:ChildLabel>FirstEmployeesID_Label
</a:ChildLabel>&#13;&#10;
</a:ElementExtension>&#13;&#10;
<a:ElementExtension>&#13;&#10;
<a:ElementID>LastName
</a:ElementID>&#13;&#10;
<a:ControlSource>LastName
</a:ControlSource>&#13;&#10;
<a:ChildLabel>LastName_Label
</a:ChildLabel>&#13;&#10;
</a:ElementExtension>&#13;&#10;
<a:ElementExtension>&#13;&#10;
<a:ElementID>FirstName
</a:ElementID>&#13;&#10;
<a:ControlSource>FirstName
</a:ControlSource>&#13;&#10;
<a:ChildLabel>FirstName_Label
</a:ChildLabel>&#13;&#10;
</a:ElementExtension>&#13;&#10;
<a:ElementExtension>&#13;&#10;
<a:ElementID>Title</a:ElementID>&#13;&#10;
<a:ControlSource>Title
</a:ControlSource>&#13;&#10;
<a:ChildLabel>Title_Label
</a:ChildLabel>&#13;&#10;
</a:ElementExtension>&#13;&#10;
```

```
<a:GroupLevel>&#13;&#10;
<a:RecordSource>FirstEmployees
</a:RecordSource>&#13;&#10;
<a:DefaultSort>
</a:DefaultSort>&#13;&#10;
<a:HeaderElementId>HeaderFirstEmployees
</a:HeaderElementId>&#13;&#10;
<a:FooterElementId>
</a:FooterElementId>&#13;&#10;
<a:CaptionElementId>
</a:CaptionElementId>&#13;&#10;
<a:RecordNavigationElementId>
NavigationSectionFirstEmployees
</a:RecordNavigationElementId>&#13;&#10;
<a:DataPageSize>1
</a:DataPageSize>&#13;&#10;
</a:GroupLevel>&#13;&#10;
<a:Datamodel version=&quot;0816&quot;>&#13;&#10;
<a:SchemaRowsource id=&quot;FirstEmployees&quot;
type=&quot; dscTable&quot;>&#13;&#10;
<a:SchemaField id=&quot;FirstEmployeesID&quot;
datatype=&quot;3&quot;
size=&quot;0&quot; iskey=&quot;1&quot;/>&#13;&#10;
<a:SchemaField id=&quot;
LastName&quot; datatype=&quot;130&quot;
size=&quot;50&quot;/>&#13;&#10;
<a:SchemaField id=&quot;FirstName&quot;
datatype=&quot;130&quot;
size=&quot;50&quot;/>&#13;&#10;
<a:SchemaField id=&quot;Title&quot;
datatype=&quot;130&quot;
size=&quot;50&quot;/>&#13;&#10;
</a:SchemaRowsource>&#13;&#10;
<a:RecordsetDef id=&quot;
FirstEmployees&quot;
uniquetable=&quot;
FirstEmployees&quot;>&#13;&#10;
<a:PageField id=&quot;
FirstEmployeesID&quot;/>&#13;&#10;
<a:PageField id=&quot;LastName&quot;/>&#13;&#10;
<a:PageField id=&quot;FirstName&quot;/>&#13;&#10;
<a:PageField id=&quot;Title&quot;/>&#13;&#10;
</a:RecordsetDef>&#13;&#10;
</a:Datamodel>&#13;&#10;
</a:DataSourceControl>&#13;&#10;</xml>'&quot;">
</OBJECT>
...
```

Creating An Enhanced Data Access Page

Now that you have somewhat of a feel for what data access pages are and how they're put together, let's get a little creative. Remember the survey tool that you built in Chapter 6? Well, let's improve on it a bit using data access pages. In the next exercise, we'll build a data access page that pulls data from the Responses table in Chapter 6 to generate a bar chart representing average responses to the five survey questions. Pay particular attention to the seamless interaction of the code. If you need a refresher on the survey tool that serves as the basis for this exercise, revisit Chapter 6.

.*Project* Updating Your Data Source

Before you build your next data access page, you'll need to be sure that the data required to support the page is complete and accessible. For this reason, the first thing you'll need to do is to update the Responses table in the FirstDatabase database by completing the following steps:

1. Launch Access 2000, and open the FirstDatabase database.

2. Select the Tables button under the Objects frame of the Access 2000 database window, and then double-click on the Responses table to open it.

3. Make sure that the Responses table looks like Table 14.2.

4. After making your revisions to the Responses table, select File|Save and then choose File|Close.

5. Select the Queries button under the Objects frame of the Access 2000 database window, and then double-click the item Create Query In Design View.

6. On the Show Table dialog box, select Responses, click Add, and then select the Close button.

7. Select View|SQL View, and then replace **SELECT FROM Responses** with the following code:

Table 14.2   The Responses data table.

RespondentID	Q1	Q2	Q3	Q4	Q5
1		2	1	3	1
2		3	2	2	2
3		1	3	1	-3
4		2	3	-1	1
5		3	1	2	1
6		-2	2	3	2
7	2	1	1	2	-3
8	2	2	3	-1	1
9	2	2	1	2	-3
10	2	2	3	-1	1

```
SELECT DISTINCTROW Avg([Responses].[Q1])
AS [Avg Of Q1], Avg([Responses].[Q2])
AS [Avg Of Q2], Avg([Responses].[Q3])
AS [Avg Of Q3], Avg([Responses].[Q4])
AS [Avg Of Q4], Avg([Responses].[Q5])
AS [Avg Of Q5]
FROM Responses;
```

8. Select File|Save. In the Save As dialog box, name the query "FirstResponses Query", and then click OK.

9. Select Query|Run from the Access 2000 menu bar. Your query results should appear as shown in Figure 14.10.

10. Close all open windows except the Access 2000 database window.

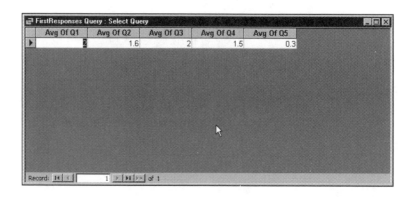

Figure 14.10
FirstResponses query results.

.*Project*   Creating An Enhanced Data Access Page

Now that you've updated your data and built a query, it's time to build an enhanced data access page to use the data you've prepared. You may proceed with this activity by performing the following steps:

1. Select the Pages button under the Objects frame of the Access 2000 database window. Then double-click Create Data Access Page In Design view.

2. Click once on the line that says "Click here and type title text," and, at the blinking cursor, enter the words "Average Survey Responses".

3. Click once on the line that says "Click here and type body text," and, at the blinking cursor, enter the words "An Enhanced Data Access Page".

4. Place the mouse cursor just before the "A" in An, and then hold down the left mouse button and drag the mouse from left to right, highlighting the words "An Enhanced Data Access Page".

5. Select the Center button on the Access 2000 Formatting toolbar to center the body text line, and then select File|Save. When prompted, save the current page as "EnhancedDAP".

6. Select View|Field List from the Access 2000 menu bar to open the Field List dialog box. Then click the plus sign next to the Tables folder to expand the folder view.

7. In the Field List dialog box, click the plus sign next to the Responses table to display the table's fields.

8. Click the RespondentID field name, and then click the Add To Page button on the Field List dialog box.

9. Repeat Step 8 for each of the remaining fields in the Responses table, and then select File|Save from the Access 2000 menu bar.

Figure 14.11
The Office Chart icon.

Adding A Chart

Next, you'll enhance the page by adding a chart object. Accomplish this task by performing these steps:

1. On the floating toolbox, select the Office Chart icon (see Figure 14.11).

2. With the Office Chart icon selected, place the mouse cursor to the right of the RespondentID field, hold down the left mouse button, and then drag down and to the right.

3. Release the left mouse button to open Step 1 of the Microsoft Office Chart Wizard (see Figure 14.12).

4. On the Office Chart Wizard, accept the Column chart default, and then click Next.

5. In Step 2 of the Chart Wizard, select FirstResponses Query, and then click Next.

6. In Step 3a of the Chart Wizard, select the Entries For The Legend Are In Multiple Columns radio button, and then click Next.

7. In Step 3b of the Chart Wizard, construct your chart by clicking the Add button, and then replace the word "Series" in the Series Names field with "Q1". Select Avg Of Q1 from the Values drop-down menu, and then select Avg Of Q1 from the Category (X) Axis Labels drop-down menu.

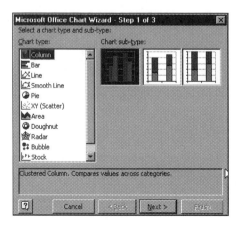

Figure 14.12
Step 1 of the Microsoft Office Chart Wizard.

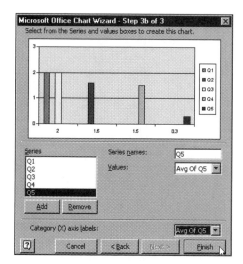

Figure 14.13
Your final panel should display five entries.

8. Repeat Step 7 for fields Q2 through Q5. When you're done, Step 3b of the Chart Wizard appears as shown in Figure 14.13.

9. Click the Finish button.

10. Resize the Record Navigation toolbar so that it appears on the page immediately beneath the last field and the chart, and then select File|Save from the Access 2000 menu bar.

Using Your Enhanced Page

Now it's time to view your work and do a little data manipulation. Perform the following steps to view and manipulate data on your enhanced data access page:

1. Select File|Web Page Preview from the Access 2000 menu bar to view the finished product. The page in your browser should appear as shown in Figure 14.14.

2. From your browser, change all Q1 values for RespondentIDs 1 through 10 as shown in Table 14.3.

3. Once you've changed all the Q1 values, select the Save Record icon on the Record Navigation toolbar, and then select the Refresh button on your browser. You should notice that the chart data is updated dynamically and appears as shown in Figure 14.15.

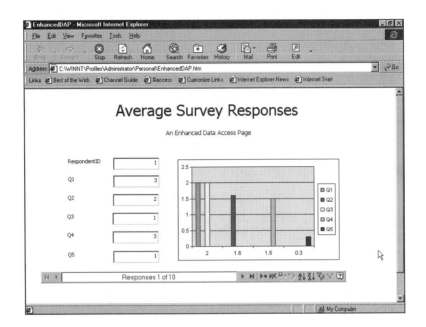

Figure 14.14
The enhanced data access page.

Table 14.3 Q1 values by RespondentID.

RespondentID	Q1
1	1
2	1
3	1
4	3
5	1
6	2
7	3
8	-1
9	-2
10	-1

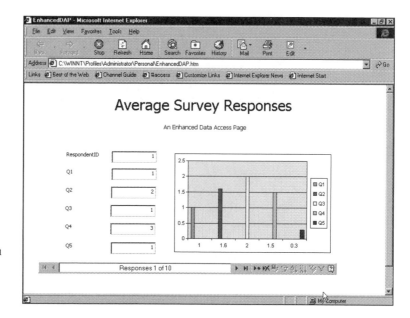

Figure 14.15
Use the enhanced data
access page to
dynamically update
chart data.

Listing 14.2 presents some of the HTML code that supports the
EnhancedDAP data access page.

Listing 14.2   Sample HTML for EnhancedDAP.

```
<!DOCTYPE HTML PUBLIC "-//W3C//DTD W3 HTML//EN">
<HTML><HEAD><TITLE>EnhancedDAP</TITLE>
<META content=Access.Application name=ProgId>
<META name=VBSForEventHandlers VALUE = TRUE>
<META content="text/html;
charset=windows-1252"
http-equiv=Content-Type>
<STYLE id=MSODAPDEFAULTS
type=text/css rel = stylesheet>.mstheme-label {

    FONT-FAMILY: Tahoma; FONT-SIZE: 8pt
}
TEXTAREA {
    FONT-FAMILY: Tahoma; FONT-SIZE: 8pt
}
.msoboundhtml {
    FONT-FAMILY: Tahoma; FONT-SIZE: 8pt
}
HR {
    COLOR: black
}
```

```
SELECT {
    FONT-FAMILY: Tahoma; FONT-SIZE: 8pt
}
INPUT {
    FONT-FAMILY: Tahoma; FONT-SIZE: 8pt
}
BODY {
    FONT-FAMILY: Tahoma; FONT-SIZE: 10pt
}
MARQUEE {
    FONT-FAMILY: Tahoma; FONT-SIZE: 8pt
}
LEGEND {
    FONT-FAMILY: Tahoma; FONT-SIZE: 8pt
}
.msoHyperlinkDisplayText {
    FONT-FAMILY: Tahoma; FONT-SIZE: 8pt
}
BODY {
    FONT-FAMILY: Tahoma; FONT-SIZE: 10pt
}
.MsoShowDesignGrid {
    BEHAVIOR: url(#DEFAULT#MsoShowDesignGrid)
}
</STYLE>

<OBJECT
classid=CLSID:0002E530-0000-0000-C000-000000000046
codeBase=file:F:\msowc.cab id=MSODSC>
<PARAM NAME="XMLData" VALUE="
<?xml:namespace ns=&quot;
urn:schemas-microsoft-com:
office:access&quot;
prefix=&quot;a&quot;?>&#13;&#10;
<xml>&#13;&#10;
<a:DataSourceControl>&#13;&#10;
<a:OWCVersion>9.0.0.2209
</a:OWCVersion>&#13;&#10;
<a:ConnectionString>
Provider=Microsoft.Jet.OLEDB.4.0;
Persist Security Info=False;
User ID=Admin;Data Source=C:\WINNT\Profiles\
Administrator\Personal\FirstDatabase.mdb;
Mode=Share Deny None;
Extended Properties=&amp;quot;
&amp;quot;;;Locale Identifier=1033;Jet OLEDB:System
atabase=&amp;quot;&amp;quot;;
Jet OLEDB:Registry Path=&amp;quot;&amp;quot;;
```

```
Jet OLEDB:Database Password=&amp;quot;&amp;quot;
Jet OLEDB:Engine Type=5;
Jet OLEDB:Database Locking Mode=0;
Jet OLEDB:Global Partial Bulk Ops=2;
Jet OLEDB:Global Bulk Transactions=1;
Jet OLEDB:New Database Password=&amp;quot;
&amp;quot;;Jet OLEDB:Create System Database=False;
Jet OLEDB:Encrypt Database=False;
Jet OLEDB:Don't Copy Locale on Compact=False;
Jet OLEDB:Compact Without Replica Repair=False;Jet
OLEDB:SFP=False</a:ConnectionString>&#13;&#10;
<a:MaxRecords>10000</a:MaxRecords>&#13;&#10;
<a:GridX>12</a:GridX>&#13;&#10;
<a:GridY>12</a:GridY>&#13;&#10;
<a:ElementExtension>&#13;&#10;
<a:ElementID>ResponsesNavigation
</a:ElementID>&#13;&#10;
<a:ConsumesRecordset/>&#13;&#10;
</a:ElementExtension>&#13;&#10;
<a:ElementExtension>&#13;&#10;
<a:ElementID>RespondentID
</a:ElementID>&#13;&#10;
<a:ControlSource>RespondentID
</a:ControlSource>&#13;&#10;
<a:ChildLabel>RespondentID_Label
</a:ChildLabel>&#13;&#10;
</a:ElementExtension>&#13;&#10;
<a:ElementExtension>&#13;&#10;
<a:ElementID>Q1</a:ElementID>&#13;&#10;
a:ControlSource>Q1</a:ControlSource>&#13;&#10;
<a:ChildLabel>Q1_Label</a:ChildLabel>&#13;&#10;
</a:ElementExtension>&#13;&#10;
<a:ElementExtension>&#13;&#10;
<a:ElementID>Q2</a:ElementID>&#13;&#10;
<a:ControlSource>Q2</a:ControlSource>&#13;&#10;
<a:ChildLabel>Q2_Label</a:ChildLabel>&#13;&#10;
</a:ElementExtension>&#13;&#10;
<a:ElementExtension>&#13;&#10;
<a:ElementID>Q3</a:ElementID>&#13;&#10;
<a:ControlSource>Q3</a:ControlSource>&#13;&#10;
<a:ChildLabel>Q3_Label</a:ChildLabel>&#13;&#10;
</a:ElementExtension>&#13;&#10;
<a:ElementExtension>&#13;&#10;
<a:ElementID>Q4</a:ElementID>&#13;&#10;
<a:ControlSource>Q4</a:ControlSource>&#13;&#10;
<a:ChildLabel>Q4_Label</a:ChildLabel>&#13;&#10;
</a:ElementExtension>&#13;&#10;
<a:ElementExtension>&#13;&#10;
```

```
<a:ElementID>Q5</a:ElementID>&#13;&#10;
<a:ControlSource>Q5</a:ControlSource>&#13;&#10;
<a:ChildLabel>Q5_Label</a:ChildLabel>&#13;&#10;
</a:ElementExtension>&#13;&#10;
<a:ElementExtension>&#13;&#10;
<a:ElementID>Chart1</a:ElementID>&#13;&#10;
<a:ConsumesRecordset/>&#13;&#10;
</a:ElementExtension>&#13;&#10;
<a:GroupLevel>&#13;&#10;
<a:RecordSource>Responses</a:RecordSource>&#13;&#10;
<a:DefaultSort></a:DefaultSort>&#13;&#10;
<a:HeaderElementId>HeaderResponses
</a:HeaderElementId>&#13;&#10; <a:FooterElementId></
a:FooterElementId>&#13;&#10;
<a:CaptionElementId></a:CaptionElementId>&#13;&#10;
<a:RecordNavigationElementId>NavigationSectionResponses
</a:RecordNavigationElementId>&#13;&#10;
<a:DataPageSize>1</a:DataPageSize>&#13;&#10;
</a:GroupLevel>&#13;&#10;

...
```

Where To Go From Here

In this chapter, you were introduced to one of the new features of Access 2000: data access pages. You created a couple of sample data access pages and discovered how to add, edit, and delete data. You also learned to add charts to data access pages and then manipulate the chart data dynamically. Coming up next, we'll take a look at what this all means and how data access pages work in conjunction with other Web technologies.

Chapter 15

Understanding Data Access Pages And The Web

Now that you've had the chance to gain some first-hand experience with data access pages, let's take a look at what's going on "behind the screens." In the process, you'll even learn a little about Internet technologies.

Behind The Screens Of FirstDAP And EnhancedDAP

As you discovered in the previous chapter, data access pages are HTML documents used to view and manipulate data over the Internet or a corporate intranet. This data may be stored in either Access 2000 or Microsoft SQL Server, but it may also reside outside of a database in applications such as Excel 2000 and Word 2000. However, as you'll soon discover, there's a bit more to data access pages than meets the eye. Now, before we dive into the underbelly of data access pages, let's first take another look at how you created FirstDAP and EnhancedDAP.

Understanding FirstDAP And EnhancedDAP

You began creating the FirstDAP data access page by opening the Data Access Page development area from the Access 2000 Database window. When you selected the Pages button under the Database window's Objects pane, you may have noticed that Access 2000 provides the following three options for producing data access pages (see Figure 15.1):

- Create Data Access Page In Design View
- Create Data Access Page By Using Wizard
- Edit Web Page That Already Exists

Because the intent was for you to get your hands dirty by building from scratch, the first option, Create Data Access Page In Design View, was the one chosen for building both FirstDAP and EnhancedDAP.

After selecting Create Data Access Page In Design View, you were presented with a standard Web page containing a one-dimensional (1D) section having no positioning control and a two-dimensional (2D) grid labeled Section: Unbound (see Figure 15.2). The Section: Unbound area of the page allowed you to control how objects were positioned on the page.

Figure 15.1
Access 2000 offers three options for creating data access pages.

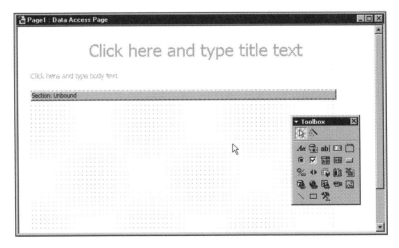

Figure 15.2
Data access pages in Design view have a 1D section and a 2D section.

After adding a title and subtitle to the 1D section of the page, you began to add data fields to the page's 2D section from the Field List dialog box. The Field List dialog box provides a hierarchical view of the active database, including tables, queries, and stored procedures, depending on the database's composition. Similar in function to Windows Explorer, clicking the + sign next to a view category such as Tables expands the category name to reveal additional subcategories by table name, which further expand to reveal named fields. By making field selections from the Field List dialog box using the drag-and-drop method or by clicking the dialog box Add button, you made the fields added to the data access page data bound. In other words, the fields added to the data access page have an automatic association with a given table and the data stored in that table.

After you added your data fields, your first data access page was complete and ready for use. Typically, you'll use data access pages for data entry, as was the case with FirstDAP. However, data access pages can also be used for interactive reporting and data analysis. Consequently, your next task was directed at extending the capabilities of FirstDAP beyond simple data entry. You accomplished this by creating a new data access page (EnhancedDAP) that took advantage of Access 2000's close-knit integration with Microsoft Office 2000. By using Microsoft Office Chart, a Microsoft Office Web Component, you were able to embed a Web-compatible bar chart in your data access page to support dynamic data reporting based on query results. But enough about the functional aspects of data access pages. What really makes them work? You'll gain some insights into answering this question in the next section.

What's Behind Data Access Pages?

If you refer to the source code listings for FirstDAP and EnhancedDAP, it should come as no surprise that what you'll find is HTML, also known as *Hypertext Markup Language*. You find HTML as source code because data access pages are really just

NOTE

If you aren't using Internet Explorer 5 or better, then you should forget about data access pages technology because the objects won't appear in lower versions of Internet Explorer, or in other browsers.

hypertext documents designed to extend the capabilities of Access forms and reports to the World Wide Web. However, data access page technology doesn't stop with HTML. Data access pages have been designed to support an integrated technical foundation consisting of a scripting language, a host environment, and controls and component objects. Understanding this foundation will help you move between Access 2000 programming for the desktop and Access 2000 programming for the Web.

The Technology Of Data Access Pages

Adding programming logic to data access pages is called *scripting*. You'll also hear the term *client-side scripting* from time to time, because your Web browser, as opposed to the Web server, processes data access page scripts. Three primary elements comprise the client-side scripting model:

- A scripting language such as VBScript, JScript, JavaScript, or Perl

- A scripting language-compatible host such as Internet Explorer 5 (IE5)

- Controls and other component objects

Scripting languages require a host environment that can translate scripting language into machine code. With Access 2000, VBScript is the default scripting language, and the integrated Internet Explorer 5 is your host environment. Using these tools, you can undertake development of procedures and functions for Access controls, HTML controls, and other component objects comprising the Internet Explorer object hierarchy, as shown in Figure 15.3.

The Internet Explorer Object Reference

NOTE

Server-side scripting supports another Microsoft Web development technology known as Active Server Pages.

When you begin to program data access pages, which you'll do a little later, you'll want to have some idea of the impact of your object references. Just like the Access 2000 object model and object collections that you learned about in Chapters 3 and 11,

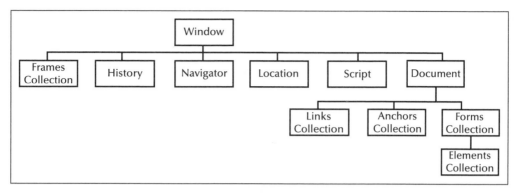

Figure 15.3   VBScript references objects by their IE5 object hierarchy position.

the Internet Explorer object model and the objects that comprise it are characterized by distinct properties, methods, and events. The following sections describe the objects you're likely to encounter in your data access page development, along with their respective properties, methods, and events.

The Window Object

The **Window** object is the parent of all other objects in the IE object hierarchy. In other words, the **Window** object is the container in which all other objects reside. It can hold a single **Document** object; however, that **Document** object can contain **Frame** objects that are capable of storing other **Document** objects. The properties of the **Window** object include:

- *defaultStatus*—Gets or sets the default status text in the status bar

- *frames*—Returns the array of frames for the current window

- *history*—Returns the **History** object of the current window

- *location*—Returns the **Location** object for the current window (read-only)

- *name*—Returns the name of the current window (read-only)

- *navigator*—Returns the **Navigator** object of the current window

- *parent*—Returns the **Window** object that evaluates to the parent window

NOTE

Don't confuse objects with the <OBJECT> tag. The <OBJECT> tag is used to add binary objects to HTML code.

- *self*—Returns the **Window** object of the current window

- *status*—Gets or sets the status text in the status bar

- *top*—Returns the **Window** object of the topmost window (the containing window of all the frames in the current browser instance)

The methods of the **Window** object include:

- *alert*—Displays an alert message box

- *clearTimeout*—Clears a timer set with the **setTimeout** method

- *close*—Closes the window

- *confirm*—Displays a message box that allows the user to click on OK or Cancel and returns either True or False

- *navigate*—Navigates the window to a new URL

- *open*—Opens a new window

- *prompt*—Prompts the user for input

- *setTimeout*—Sets a timer to execute a procedure after a specified number of milliseconds

The events include:

- *onLoad*—Triggered when the contents of the window are loaded

- *onUnload*—Triggered when the contents of the window are unloaded

The History Object

The **History** object provides the capability to programmatically navigate previously viewed pages. The Web browser gives you a little help here, in that you can use its Forward and Back buttons. However, because you're quickly becoming a knowledgeable programmer, I'm sure you'll want to use code to navigate page history under your own steam.

There's only one property for the **History** object:

- *length*—Returns the length of the history list

Methods for the **History** object include:

- *back*—Jumps back in the history a specified number of steps

- *forward*—Jumps forward in the history a specified number of steps

- *go*—Goes to a particular item in the history

There are no events for the **History** object.

The Location Object

The **Location** object provides specific technical information about the URL of the active document. Properties of the **Location** object include:

- *host*—Gets or sets both the host and port portion of the URL (*hostname:port*)

- *hostname*—Gets or sets the host portion of the URL—either a name or an IP address

- *href*—Gets or sets the complete URL for the location

- *pathname*—Gets or sets the path name in the URL

- *port*—Gets or sets the port of the URL

- *protocol*—Gets or sets the protocol portion of the URL (for example, HTTP)

- *search*—Gets or sets the search portion of the URL, if specified

There are no methods or events for the **Location** object.

The Script Object

The **Script** object is a code block stored in the active document between a **<SCRIPT></SCRIPT>** tag pair.

The Document Object

This is the object the user sees when the Web browser is opened and a page is loaded. The **Document** object can reside below the **Window** object in the IE hierarchy, as well as below a **Frame** object.

The properties of the **Document** object include:

- *aLinkColor*—Gets or sets the current color of the active link in a document
- *anchors*—Returns the array of anchors in a document
- *bgcolor*—Gets or sets the background color of a document
- *cookie*—Gets or sets the cookie for the current document
- *fgcolor*—Gets or sets the foreground color of a document
- *forms*—Returns the array of forms in a document
- *LastModified*—Returns the date the document was last modified
- *LinkColor*—Gets or sets the current color of the links in a document (cannot be changed after the document loads)
- *links*—Returns the array of links for the current document
- *referrer*—Gets the URL of the referring document
- *title*—Returns the document's title (read-only)
- *vLinkColor*—Gets or sets the current color of the visited links in a document (cannot be changed after the document loads)

The methods for the **Document** object include:

- *clear*—Updates the screen to display all the strings written after the last open method call
- *close*—Closes the document output stream and writes data to the screen
- *open*—Opens the document stream for output
- *write*—Inserts a string at the end of a document
- *writeLn*—Inserts a string at the end of a document (with a new-line character appended to the end)

There are no events for the **Document** object.

The Links Collection

Objects belonging to the **Links** collection represent hyperlinks in a **Document** object. Properties of the **Links** collection include:

- *host*—Returns both the host and port portion of the URL (*hostname:port*) for the link

- *hostname*—Returns the host portion of the URL for the link—either a name or an IP address

- *href*—Returns the complete URL for the link

- *pathname*—Returns the path name of the URL for the link

- *port*—Returns the port of the URL for the link

- *protocol*—Returns the protocol portion of the URL for the link

- *search*—Returns the search portion of the URL for the link

- *target*—Returns the target of the link

There are no methods for this collection. Events for the **Links** collection include:

- *onClick*—Fires an event any time the link is clicked

- *onMouseMove*—Fires an event any time the pointer moves over a link

- *onMouseOver*—Fires an event any time the pointer moves over a link

The Forms Collection

Objects belonging to the **Forms** collection are forms contained in a **Document** object. Properties include:

- *action*—Gets or sets the URL to be used to carry out the action of the form

- *elements*—Returns the array of elements contained in the form

- *encoding*—Gets or sets the encoding for the form

- *method*—Specifies how the form data should be sent to the server

- *target*—Specifies the name of the target window in which to display the form results

The one method for this collection is:

- *submit*—Submits form data

There is also only one event:

- *onSubmit*—Triggered when the form is submitted

The Elements Collection

Objects in the **Elements** collection are items displayed in a **Document** object by the HTML **<INPUT>** tag. These elements are typically the standard HTML controls, including the Button control, Checkbox control, Radio Button control, Text control, and TextArea control:

- Button control properties:
  - *name*—The name of the button
  - *value*—The caption of the button
- Button control method:
  - *click*—Clicks the button
- Button control event:
  - *onClick*—Triggered when the button is clicked
- Checkbox control properties:
  - *checked*—True if the checkbox is checked; False otherwise
  - *defaultChecked*—True if the checkbox is checked by default; False otherwise
  - *name*—The name of the checkbox
  - *value*—A value assigned to the checkbox
- Checkbox control method:
  - *click*—Clicks the checkbox
- Checkbox control event:
  - *onClick*—Triggered when the checkbox is clicked
- Radio button control properties:
  - *checked*—Indicates True if the radio button is checked; False if not checked
  - *defaultChecked*—True if the radio button is checked by default; False otherwise
  - *length*—The number of radio buttons in the group

- *name*—The Radio button control name
- *value*—The value assigned to the Radio button control
- Radio button control method:
  - *click*—Clicks the Radio button control
- Radio button control event:
  - *onClick*—Triggered when the Radio button control is clicked
- Text control properties:
  - *defaultValue*—The default value of the Text control
  - *name*—The Text control name
  - *value*—The value of the Text control
- Text control methods:
  - *blur*—Clears the focus from the Text control
  - *focus*—Sets the focus to the Text control
  - *select*—Selects the contents of the Text control
- Text control events:
  - *onBlur*—Triggered when the Text control loses the focus
  - *onChange*—Triggered when the Text control is changed
  - *onFocus*—Triggered when the Text control gets the focus
  - *onSelect*—Triggered when the contents of the Text control are selected
- Textarea control properties:
  - *defaultValue*—The default value of the Textarea control
  - *name*—The name of the Textarea control
  - *value*—The value of the Textarea control
- Textarea control methods:
  - *blur*—Clears the focus from the Textarea control
  - *focus*—Sets the focus to the Textarea control
  - *select*—Selects the contents of the Textarea control

- Textarea control events:
  - *onBlur*—Triggered when the Textarea control loses the focus
  - *onChange*—Triggered when the Textarea control is changed
  - *onFocus*—Triggered when the Textarea control gets the focus
  - *onSelect*—Triggered when the contents of the Textarea control are selected

The Language Of Data Access Pages

Now that you understand a little about the overall technology of data access pages, let's take a closer look at the languages that power them. Effectively, you're likely to encounter three languages as you develop data access pages—Dynamic HTML, VBScript, and JavaScript.

Understanding Dynamic HTML

What is Dynamic HTML, you might ask? Well, consider this. With standard HTML, when a page is downloaded from the Web server, the contents of the page are pretty much fixed and cannot be modified without the benefit of components such as Java applets, ActiveX controls, or other third-party plug-ins. Dynamic HTML (DHTML) overcomes this limitation by extending the capabilities of an existing Web standard, namely *Cascading Style Sheets*. Cascading Style Sheets let you define and apply paragraph and character styles to an entire document or Web page. In effect, Cascading Style Sheets are a collection of styles or formatting commands that define particular paragraph or heading types, font attributes, alignment, and so on. Dynamic HTML uses the Cascading Style Sheet model of overall page effect to make every object on the page capable of interactivity and dynamic update. In addition, Dynamic HTML supports precise object positioning and three-dimensional layout. This means that Z-axis support, which allows objects to be layered over and under each other, is now possible. Table 15.1 identifies mouse events and actions supported by Dynamic HTML.

Understanding VBScript

Think of VBScript, also known as *Visual Basic Scripting Edition*, as Visual Basic for Applications Lite. It's specifically designed for Web-based application development and is supported (as of this writing) by Internet Explorer 3 or higher. VBScript on the client side is the language of ActiveX controls, and on the server-side it's the language of Active Server Pages. In practice, you embed VBScript code into your HTML documents (for our purposes, your data access pages). As you develop with VBScript, you'll find that basically two options are available to you for integrating VBScript with HTML. You can either add VBScript code to your HTML source by placing statements between a **<SCRIPT> </SCRIPT>** tag pair, or you can create a procedure.

In the former case, when Internet Explorer loads a Web page containing VBScript, it proceeds normally until it encounters the **<SCRIPT>** tag. At that point, the browser's VBScript interpreter

Table 15.1   Dynamic HTML mouse events.

Mouse Event	Action Triggered When...
OnMouseOver	Mouse cursor is placed on an object such as a link or image map.
OnMouseOut	Mouse cursor is placed outside of an object.
OnMouseDown	Mouse cursor is placed near the bottom of an object.
OnMouseUp	Mouse cursor is placed near the top of an object.
OnMouseMove	Mouse cursor passes over an object.
OnClick	Left mouse button is clicked on an object.
OnDblClick	Left mouse button is clicked twice on an object.
OnKeyPress	A keyboard key is pressed and released.
OnKeyDown	A keyboard key is pressed.
OnKeyUp	A keyboard key is released.

NOTE

*Here are some time-related VBScript expressions. Compare them with JavaScript in the next section, and note the differences: day = **Day()**, month = **Month()**, and year = **Year()**.*

kicks in and executes VBScript statements until it runs into the **</SCRIPT>** tag. When the VBScript code is finished executing, the remainder of the HTML document is displayed. In the latter case, VBScript code uses an HTML control to trigger a **click** event. This works in the same way as the VBA event procedures to which you've grown accustomed. The VBScript feature set is less robust than its more full-featured cousins; however, this is by design. Nevertheless, VBScript is a very powerful scripting language. Table 15.2 provides a short list of VBScript feature limitations.

Understanding JavaScript

JavaScript is a scripting language for the Web developed by Netscape Communications Corporation. The Microsoft incarnation of JavaScript is called JScript. The differences between the two are not really significant, because JavaScript code runs in Microsoft's JScript browser, and JScript code runs in Netscape's JavaScript browser. Now here's a bit of trivia. JavaScript was formerly called *LiveScript*; however, Netscape adopted the term *JavaScript* because of Java's growing popularity in the Web-development marketplace. As far as capability, JavaScript, like VBScript, supports the introduction of programming logic into HTML code, thereby facilitating more dynamic Web development. Also like VBScript, JavaScript has its own set of feature limitations, as listed in Table 15.3.

NOTE

*Here's a little time-related JavaScript: day = **now.getDay()**, month = **now.getMonth()**, and year is, well you guessed it, **now.getYear()**.*

Table 15.2   VBScript feature limitations.

Feature	Limitation
Array handling	Inflexible array base. All arrays must begin at 0.
Collections and classes	Does not allow the creation of user-defined classes.
Conversion	Does not support the **Format** command.
Data type	**Variant** is the only supported data type.
Dynamic Data Exchange	Not supported.
File I/O	Language features that enable local file access are not supported. This limitation was designed to enhance the language's security on the Internet and corporate intranets.
User-defined types	Not supported.

Table 15.3   JavaScript feature limitations.

Feature	Limitation
Interpreted language	Not compiled like C or compressed into byte codes like Java, consequently processing speed is slower than for a compiled language.
Pointer free	Does not support pointers like C or C++.
Constants	Does not support constants.
Functions	Variable numbers of arguments are not supported.

Programming Data Access Pages

Now it's time to have a little fun. In the tasks you're about to perform, you're going to see first hand how to add programmed functionality to a data access page. You'll do this by making some minor modifications to FirstDAP. So, let's get you started programming data access pages by performing the following steps:

1. Launch Access 2000, and open the FirstDatabase database.

2. Select the Pages button under the Objects pane of the Access 2000 Database window.

3. In the Access 2000 Database window, select FirstDAP and click the Design button on the Database window toolbar.

4. Using the Access toolbox, place a command button in the Navigation area of FirstDAP, immediately following the Navigation control, and name the button "Message" (see Figure 15.4).

5. Right-click on the Message button, and then select Microsoft Script Editor from the right-click menu.

6. In the Script Outline window of the Microsoft Script Editor, expand the folder called Client Objects & Events.

7. Locate the object named **Message**, and then click the plus sign to expand it and display the available events for the **Message** object.

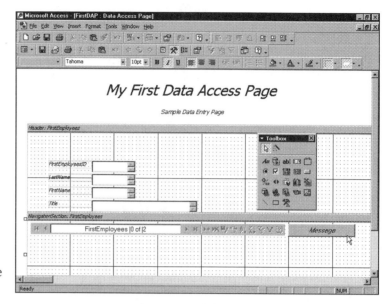

Figure 15.4
FirstDAP with a message button added.

8. Locate and double-click the event **onclick** (see Figure 15.5). Notice the placement of the cursor in the Script Editor's Output window. Clicking the **onclick** event causes the following structure, called a *script block*, to appear in the Output window:

```
<SCRIPT LANGUAGE=vbscript FOR=Message EVENT=onclick>
<!--

-->
</SCRIPT>
```

9. Place the statement **MsgBox "See how easy it is to program your Data Access Page!"** between the two opposite arrows of the code structure so that it appears as shown in the following code:

```
<SCRIPT LANGUAGE=vbscript FOR=Message EVENT=onclick>
<!--
MsgBox "See how easy it is to
        program your Data Access Page!"
-->
</SCRIPT>
```

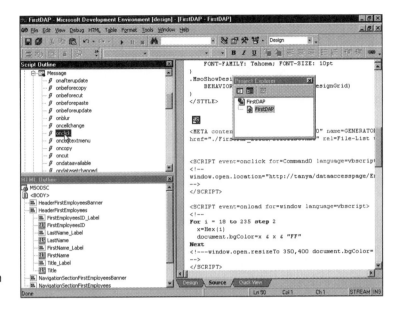

Figure 15.5
The **onclick** event creates a script block in the Output window.

10. Select File|Save from the Script Editor menu bar, and then select the Quick View tab on the Script Editor's Output window.

11. Scroll right in the Quick View window until the Message button is visible, and then click on the button. The result is shown in Figure 15.6.

Manipulating Properties

This time you're going to program FirstDAP to have a background color adjustment when it loads. You'll accomplish this by scripting an **onload** event to affect the background color property of the document FirstDAP. I think you'll be surprised with the result! Proceed by completing the following steps:

1. With the FirstDAP data access page open in Design View, select Tools|Macro|Microsoft Script Editor from the Access 2000 menu bar.

2. In the Script Outline window of the Microsoft Script Editor, look for the **Window** object in the Client Objects & Events folder and then expand the object by clicking the plus sign to reveal its available events.

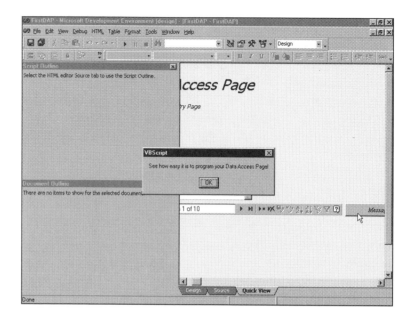

Figure 15.6
Successful coding results in a FirstDAP message box.

3. Double-click on the **onload** event, and then place the following code in the resulting script block in the Script Editor Output window:

```
For c = 18 to 235 step 2
    x=Hex(c)
    document.bgColor=x & x & "FF"
Next
```

4. Select File|Save from the Script Editor menu bar, select the Quick View tab on the Script Editor's Output window, and then watch what happens.

Controlling Windows

For your next task, you're going to open EnhancedDAP in a new browser window while FirstDAP remains open. This task demonstrates one of the more useful aspects of programming data access pages—being able to open a new browser session to display other data. Observe the behavior of your page after you complete the following steps:

1. With the FirstDAP data access page open in Design View, use the Access 2000 toolbox to place a second command button in the Navigation area of FirstDAP, just beneath the start of the navigation control. Name the button "Get Chart" (see Figure 15.7).

2. In the Script Outline window of the Microsoft Script Editor, look for the **Get Chart** object in the Client Objects & Events folder and then expand the object by clicking on the plus sign to reveal its available events.

3. Double-click on the **onclick** event, and then place the following code between the resulting script block in the Script Editor Output window:

```
window.open.location="C:\path to\EnhancedDAP.htm"
```

4. Select File|Save from the Script Editor menu bar, and then select the Quick View tab on the Script Editor's Output window.

5. Click on the Get Chart button in the Quick View window. The result is shown in Figure 15.8.

NOTE

*Note that the code between the quotes following the **window.open.location** statement should be the path on your machine where EnhancedDAP.htm is stored.*

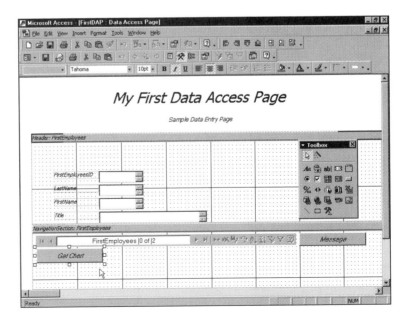

Figure 15.7
FirstDAP with the Get Chart button.

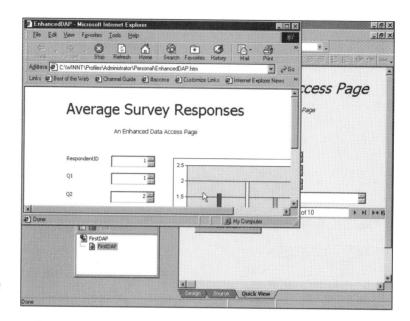

Figure 15.8
EnhancedDAP
appearing in a separate
browser window.

Publishing Data Access Pages On The Web

If you've come this far, you should now have an idea of what's going on behind the screens of data access pages. But what about making those pages available for others to view and work with on the Web? Not to worry, there's a simple solution. Publishing and viewing data access pages on the Web requires five elements—a database, data access page files, a hosting Web server, a file transfer utility, and Internet Explorer 5. Using an FTP utility such as WS-FTP or a Web publishing tool such as Microsoft FrontPage, it's an easy task to transfer your database and data access page files to either a corporate intranet or a remote Web server. Figure 15.9 presents a view of how your database and data access page files might be stored upon completion of just such a file transfer. As you can see, the files firstdap.htm and EnhancedDAP.htm are stored outside of the Access 2000 database FirstDatabase.mdb. After you've transferred all appropriate files to your Web server host, users can work with your data access pages as long as their Web browser is Internet Explorer 5.

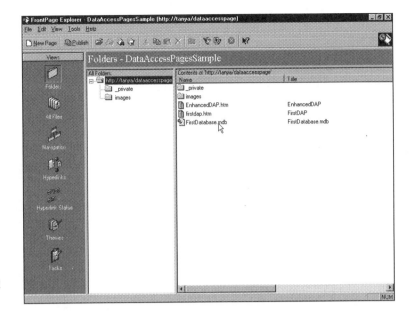

Figure 15.9
Server view of data access pages and database via Microsoft FrontPage.

Where To Go From Here

In this chapter, you took a look behind the screens of data access pages and the Web. You gained insight into the integrated foundation that supports data access pages as well as the technology and languages used to power them. You gained some hands-on experience with programming data access pages using the Microsoft Script Editor, and you discovered how to go about publishing and viewing your work on the Web. Next, you'll return to the Access 2000 desktop to begin working with form controls.

Chapter 16

Let's Work With Form Controls

Most interfaces these days provide point-and-click access to information. Consequently, your Access 2000 applications must use point-and-click to provide the type of database interaction users have come to expect.

As you've seen so far, forms are the windows through which you view and access the data stored in your database. However, the ease with which your forms allow you to interact with the data is a function of how you use form controls. In this chapter, you're going to gain some hands-on experience with programming form controls and discover how these controls add new levels of sophistication to the way that you work with Access. You'll gain this expertise by building a user interface to the now familiar FirstEmployees table, using the standard form controls the Access 2000 toolbox provides. So, let's get the show on the road.

Getting To Know The Toolbox

When you open a new form grid, Access 2000 presents you with a toolbox consisting of 20 icons. Each of the icons will help you develop either the function or the appearance of your forms. As shown in Figure 16.1, the toolbox is divided into two sections. The top section provides you with options to either select controls manually from the bottom half of the toolbox, or to use wizards that walk you through specific control creation processes. As you no doubt have surmised, we won't be using the Control Wizard.

Figure 16.1
The Access 2000 toolbox.

Building A User Interface

Let's get to know form controls by creating a user interface for the FirstEmployees table. We'll cover the details of this task in the next chapter; for now open Access 2000, if you haven't already done so, and select FirstDatabase. On the FirstDatabase database window, select the Forms option under the Objects button, and then double-click Create Form In Design View in the database window pane. Once a new form grid is open, point, click, and drag the bottom edge of the grid to make the grid size three blocks deep by five blocks wide (see Figure 16.2).

.Project ## Using The Label Control

Now, you're ready to begin adding controls to the form grid user interface for the FirstEmployees table. You'll start with one of the appearance-oriented controls Access provides, namely the Label control. Perform the following steps:

1. Select the Label control from the toolbox, and place the cursor flush against the form's first vertical gridline. Click once.

2. At the blinking cursor, type "The FirstEmployees Table User Interface", and then click outside the Label control to place sizing handles around it.

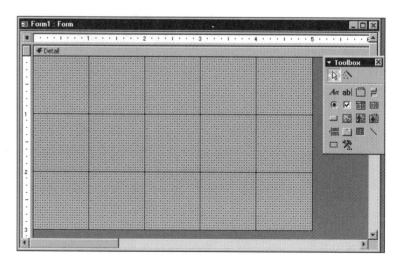

Figure 16.2
Start with a form grid three blocks deep and five blocks wide.

3. Right-click and select Properties from the control's right-click menu.

4. On the Label property sheet, select the Format tab, and then scroll to the Font Size property field.

5. Change the Font Size from 8 to 14, and close the property sheet.

6. Resize the Label control so that the entire title appears on the form, and then point, click, and drag the control to the upper edge of the form.

7. Center the Label control at the top of the form, and select File|Save to save the form as "FEInterface." Your form should appear as shown in Figure 16.3.

.Project Using The Tab Control

Next, you'll add a Tab control to the form, in preparation for the addition of data fields. Perform this task by completing the following steps:

1. Select the Tab control from the toolbox, and place the cursor in the form's grid. Then click and drag the control until it appears as shown in Figure 16.4.

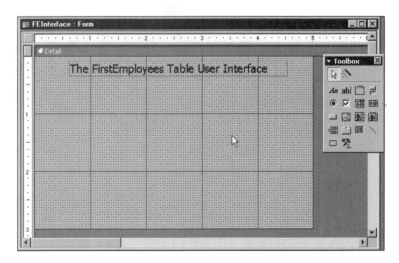

Figure 16.3
The FEInterface Form with a Label control.

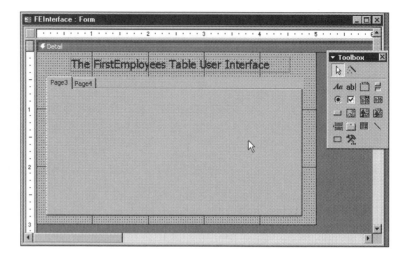

Figure 16.4
Fill the form grid with the Tab control.

2. Right-click and select Insert Page from the control's right-click menu.

3. Select the control's first tab, right-click, and select Properties.

4. Enter "Summary Data View" in the Caption field of the Format tab.

5. Select each additional tab, entering "Detailed Data View" in the first Caption field and "Interface Settings" in the second Caption field.

6. Close the property sheet, and then select File|Save. Your form should now appear as shown in Figure 16.5.

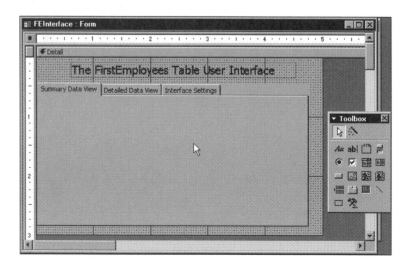

Figure 16.5
FEInterface with a Tab control.

Project Using The Text Box Control

I know you're probably itching to write some code, but just hold your horses—we'll get to that soon. For now, you need to add some Text Box controls to the form. This is where you'll get to look inside the FirstEmployees table by using the interface. This time, instead of creating Text Box controls from scratch, you'll allow Access 2000 to create them for you by following these steps:

1. Select Form from the Object drop-down menu of the Access 2000 formatting toolbar, and then right-click on the form's title bar.

2. Select Properties, and then select the Data tab on the form's property sheet.

3. Click the RecordSource property drop-down menu, select FirstEmployees, and then close the property sheet.

4. Select View|Field List from the Access 2000 menu bar.

5. From the FirstEmployees field list, click and drag each field onto the Summary Data View tab.

6. Resize and arrange the fields on the tab so that they appear as shown in Figure 16.6.

7. Select File|Save to save the form in its current state.

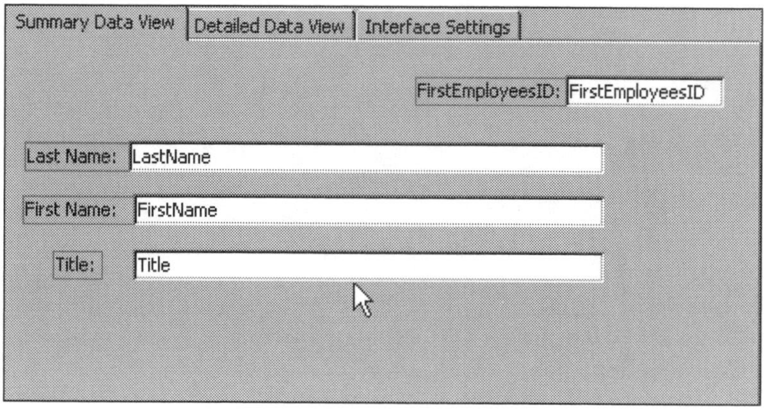

Figure 16.6
FEInterface with Text Box controls.

Project Adding Custom Navigation Buttons

Here is where the fun begins! Even though Access forms provide a set of default navigation controls, chances are you'll want your custom forms to have custom navigation controls as well. Using the Command Button control, you'll create custom navigation buttons for this form by completing the following steps:

1. Select the Command Button control from the toolbox, and place the cursor beneath the Title label. Click once to add a Button control to the form.

2. Continue to add Command Button controls until you have a row of five across the bottom of the form.

3. For each button, enter the following names in the following order in the Caption field of the property sheet's Format tab:

   - *First Button*—Go Last

   - *Second Button*—Go Back

   - *Third Button*—Go Next

   - *Fourth Button*—Go First

   - *Fifth Button*—Add Record

4. Your form should now appear as shown in Figure 16.7.

Figure 16.7
FEInterface with Custom Navigation buttons.

Coding The Navigation Buttons

You'll need to create an **OnClick** event for each of the navigation buttons you just added to the FEInterface form. As you work through the following steps, pay close attention to the techniques that you'll use to set button behavior. We'll discuss these techniques in the next chapter. For now, let's produce a little code. This may get a bit repetitive, but bear with me.

Create an **OnClick** event for the Go Last button by doing the following:

1. With the FEInterface form open in Design View, right-click on the Go Last button, and then select Properties.

2. On the property sheet, click the All tab, scroll to the top of the property sheet field list, and then enter "GoLast" in the Name property field.

3. Click the Event tab, and then double-click the **OnClick** event field.

4. When [Event Procedure] appears in the field, click the button to the right of the field to open the Visual Basic Editor.

5. Place the following lines of code between the **Sub** and **End Sub** lines:

```
DoCmd.GoToRecord Record:=acLast
Me!GoFirst.Enabled = True
DoCmd.GoToControl "GoFirst"
Me!GoLast.Enabled = False
```

6. Select Debug|Compile FirstDatabase, and then File|Save FirstDatabase. Then select File|Close And Return To Microsoft Access.

Create an **OnClick** event for the Go Back button by completing the following steps:

1. With the previous button's property sheet open, right-click on the Go Back button.

2. On the property sheet, click the All tab, scroll to the top of the property sheet field list, and then enter "GoBack" in the Name property field.

3. Click the Event tab, and then double-click the **OnClick** event field.

4. When [Event Procedure] appears in the field, click the button to the right of the field to open the Visual Basic Editor.

5. Place the following lines of code between the **Sub** and **End Sub** lines:

```
On Error GoTo ErrorHandling_Err2
DoCmd.GoToRecord Record:=acPrevious
ErrorHandling_Exit:
Exit Sub
ErrorHandling_Err2:
If Err.Number = 2105 Then
MsgBox "There are no previous records."
Resume ErrorHandling_Exit
Else
End If
```

6. Select Debug|Compile FirstDatabase, and then File|Save FirstDatabase. Then select File|Close And Return To Microsoft Access.

Create an **OnClick** event for the Go Next button by completing the following steps:

1. With the previous button's property sheet open, right-click on the Go Next button.

2. On the property sheet, click the All tab, scroll to the top of the property sheet field list, and then enter "GoNext" in the Name property field.

3. Click the Event tab, and then double-click the **OnClick** event field.

4. When [Event Procedure] appears in the field, click the button to the right of the field to open the Visual Basic Editor.

5. Place the following lines of code between the **Sub** and **End Sub** lines:

```
DoCmd.GoToRecord Record:=acNext
Me!GoLast.Enabled = True
Me!GoFirst.Enabled = True
```

6. Select Debug|Compile FirstDatabase and then File|Save FirstDatabase. Then select File|Close And Return To Microsoft Access.

Create an **OnClick** event for the Go First button by completing the following steps:

1. With the previous button's property sheet open, right-click on the Go First button.

2. On the property sheet, click the All tab, scroll to the top of the property sheet field list, and then enter "GoFirst" in the Name property field.

3. Click the Event tab, and then double-click the **OnClick** event field.

4. When [Event Procedure] appears in the field, click the button to the right of the field to open the Visual Basic Editor.

5. Place the following lines of code between the **Sub** and **End Sub** lines:

```
DoCmd.GoToRecord Record:=acFirst
Me!GoLast.Enabled = True
DoCmd.GoToControl "GoLast"
Me!GoFirst.Enabled = False
```

6. Select Debug|Compile FirstDatabase and then File|Save FirstDatabase. Then select File|Close And Return To Microsoft Access.

Create an **OnClick** event for the Add Record button by completing the following steps:

1. With the previous button's property sheet open, right-click on the Add Record button.

2. On the property sheet, click the All tab, scroll to the top of the property sheet field list, and then enter "AddRecord" in the Name property field.

3. Click the Event tab, and then double-click the **OnClick** event field.

4. When [Event Procedure] appears in the field, click the button to the right of the field to open the Visual Basic Editor.

5. Place the following line of code between the **Sub** and **End Sub** lines:

```
DoCmd.RunCommand acCmdRecordsGoToNew
```

6. Select Debug|Compile FirstDatabase and then File|Save FirstDatabase. Then select File|Close And Return To Microsoft Access.

7. Close the open property sheet.

Testing The Custom Navigation Controls

The Summary Data Panel of the FEInterface form is just about done. However, you still need to test each button to ensure that it functions properly. This means checking to see that clicking a button invokes the correct view of the data, as well as whether specific behaviors like button disabling and enabling occur.

Project ## Removing The Default Navigation Controls

Let's put some finishing touches on this form. We're not done with the other tabs yet, so the cleanup you're about to do will put you ahead of the game.

1. Resize the Form window to bind the form grid on all sides.

2. Click the Object drop-down menu on the Formatting toolbar, and then select Form.

3. Right-click on the Form title bar to open the right-click menu, and then select Properties to open the Form's property sheet.

4. On the property sheet, click the All tab, and then set the following property values:

   - *Scroll Bars*—Neither
   - *Record Selectors*—No

- *Navigation Buttons*—No
- *Dividing Lines*—No
- *Auto Resize*—No
- *Border Style*—Dialog

5. Close the Form property sheet, and then select File|Save to save the form.

6. Select View|Form View to see the finished panel. Your panel should appear as shown in Figure 16.8.

.Project Extending The FirstEmployees Table Structure

Let's continue this discovery of form controls by turning our attention to the Detailed Data View tab. Using this tab requires that we add some additional fields to the FirstEmployees table, so let's proceed:

1. Select File|Save and then File|Close to remove the FEInterface form from the work area.

2. In the FirstDatabase database window, select the Tables option under the Objects button, select FirstEmployees in the database window Table view, and then click Design on the database window toolbar.

3. Add the field names and data types shown in Table 16.1 to the FirstEmployees table design.

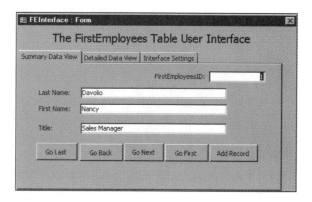

Figure 16.8
The Summary Data View tab of the FEInterface—Enhanced.

Table 16.1   Additional FirstEmployees fields.

Field Name	Data Type
City	Text
State	Text
Comments	Memo

4. Select File|Save and then File|Close to save the table structure changes and close the Design View.

5. Click the Open button on the database window toolbar, and your screen should appear similar to Figure 16.9.

6. Select File|Close from the Access menu bar to return to the database window.

Project Developing The Detailed Data View Tab

Now that you've extended the FirstEmployees table structure, you can begin work on the Detailed Data View tab of the FEInterface form. Do this by following these steps:

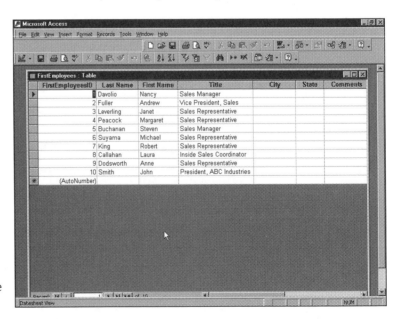

Figure 16.9
The FirstEmployees table with three added fields.

1. Open the FEInterface form in Design View.

2. Select the Detailed Data View tab on the FEInterface form, and then drag the FirstEmployeesID field from the FirstEmployees field list to the blank tab.

3. On the All tab of the Label control's property sheet, enter "EID2" in the Name property field, and "First Employees ID" in the Caption property field.

4. With the property sheet still open to the All tab, click the FirstEmployeesID Text Box control and enter "EID3" in the Name property field.

5. Select File|Save, and then close the property sheet.

6. In the Access 2000 work area, scroll the FirstEmployees table field list until the City, State, and Comments fields are visible.

7. Click and drag each of the new fields from the field list to the Detailed Data View tab, and then size and arrange the fields so that they appear as shown in Figure 16.10.

8. Select File|Save from the Access menu bar.

9. On the Detailed Data View tab, re-create the custom navigation buttons and **OnClick** events from the Summary Data View tab. Review the previous section, if you need assistance.

10. After adding the navigation buttons, the Detailed Data View tab should appear as shown in Figure 16.11.

NOTE

You can't copy and paste the navigation buttons to the new tab, as the Tab control requires you to create new controls for each new Tab control page. Also, remember to change the name of each Button control as you did for the Label and Text Box control in Steps 3 and 4, so there won't be a conflict with the pre-existing button set.

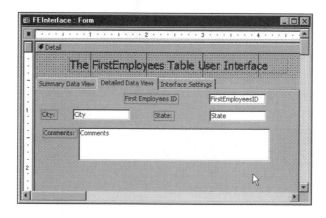

Figure 16.10
Field arrangement for the Detailed Data View tab.

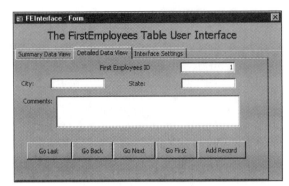

Figure 16.11
The completed Detailed Data View tab.

You can test the navigation buttons on the Detailed Data View tab by clicking each and watching what happens in the FirstEmployeesID field. In addition, add some data to each of the new fields on the tab, and then open the FirstEmployees table to see if your new data has been added.

Project Developing The Interface Settings Tab

The Interface Settings tab of the FEInterface is where you get to play around with what's on the other two tabs. You'll also get some firsthand experience with how some of the other toolbox controls can be put to use. Let's finish up the FEInterface with the following steps:

1. With the FEInterface in Design View, select the Interface Settings tab.

2. Select the Toggle Button control from the toolbox, place the cursor on the form, and then click once to add a control to the form.

3. Repeat Step 2, placing a second Toggle Button control just below the first.

4. On the All tab of the property sheet for the topmost toggle button, enter "ColorOn" in the Name property field and "Color On" in the Caption property field.

5. Create an **OnClick** event for the ColorOn toggle button by placing the following code between the **Sub** and **End Sub** lines:

```
Me!ColorOff.Enabled = True
DoCmd.GoToControl "ColorOff"
Me!ColorOff.Value = False
Me!ColorOn.Value = True
Me!ColorOn.Enabled = False
Me!FirstEmployeesID.BackColor = 16776960
Me!LastName.BackColor = 16776960
Me!FirstName.BackColor = 16776960
Me!Title.BackColor = 16776960
Me!EID3.BackColor = 16776960
Me!City.BackColor = 16776960
Me!State.BackColor = 16776960
Me!Comments.BackColor = 16776960
MsgBox "The data field colors are now light blue!"
```

NOTE

In case you haven't done so, now is a good time to compile and save your work.

6. Repeat Step 4 for the second toggle button. This time replace "ColorOn" and "Color On" with "ColorOff" and "Color Off".

7. Repeat Step 5 for the second toggle button. This time use the following code:

```
Me!ColorOn.Enabled = True
DoCmd.GoToControl "ColorOn"
Me!ColorOn.Value = False
Me!ColorOff.Value = True
Me!ColorOff.Enabled = False
Me!FirstEmployeesID.BackColor = 16777215
Me!LastName.BackColor = 16777215
Me!FirstName.BackColor = 16777215
Me!Title.BackColor = 16777215
Me!EID3.BackColor = 16777215
Me!City.BackColor = 16777215
Me!State.BackColor = 16777215
Me!Comments.BackColor = 16777215
MsgBox "The data field colors are now normal!"
```

NOTE

Again, remember to compile and save your work.

8. Select the Option Group control from the toolbox, place the cursor in the upper left corner of the tab, and then click once.

9. On the All tab of the property sheet for the Option Group control's label, enter "Color Toggle" in both the Name and Caption property fields.

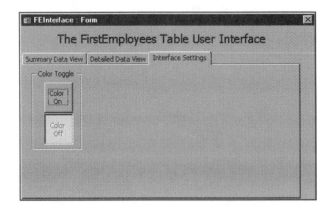

Figure 16.12
The completed Color Toggle control.

10. Click and drag both toggle buttons into the Color Toggle frame, and then click the Color Off control. Your screen should appear as shown in Figure 16.12.

Testing The Color Toggle

The Color Toggle on the FEInterface Interface Settings tab changes the field background color on the other tabs. By selecting Color On, you should get a message that all fields are now light blue. Selecting the Color Off toggle should inform you that all fields are back to normal.

Project Hiding Controls With Checkboxes

The color thing was a pretty neat trick, right? Well, let's proceed by showing you how to make form controls disappear and re-appear using checkboxes. You can make this happen by completing the following steps:

1. With the FEInterface in Design View, select the Interface Settings tab.

2. Select the Check Box Control from the Toolbox, place the cursor on the form, and then click once to add a control to the form.

3. Repeat Step 2, placing a second Check Box control just below the first.

4. On the All tab of the property sheet for the topmost checkbox, enter "ShowComments" in the Name property field and "Show Comments" in the Caption property field.

5. Select only the checkbox portion of the Check Box control.

6. On the All tab of the property sheet for the checkbox, enter "ShowIt" in the Name property field.

7. Create an **OnClick** event for the ShowIt checkbox by placing the following code between the **Sub** and **End Sub** lines:

```
Me!Comments.Visible = True
If Me!Comments.Visible = True Then
Me!HideIt.Value = Disabled
End If
```

8. Repeat Steps 4, 5, and 6 for the second checkbox, replacing "ShowComments", "Show Comments", and "ShowIt" with "HideComments", "Hide Comments", and "HideIt".

9. Create an **OnClick** event for the HideIt checkbox, by placing the following code between the **Sub** and **End Sub** lines:

```
Me!Comments.Visible = False
If Me!Comments.Visible = False Then
Me!ShowIt.Value = Disabled
End If
```

Testing The Show/Hide Checkboxes

The Show/Hide checkboxes are designed to let you hide or show the Comments field on the Detailed Data View tab. When you select the Hide Comments checkbox, the Show Comments checkbox should automatically enable, the Hide Comments checkbox should disable, and the Comments control should be hidden when you next access the Detailed Data View tab. Conversely, selecting the Show Comments checkbox should cause the Hide Comments checkbox to automatically enable and the Show Comments checkbox to disable, and of course the Comments control should re-appear. Figures 16.13 and 16.14 show you a before and after view of the Show/Hide checkbox effect.

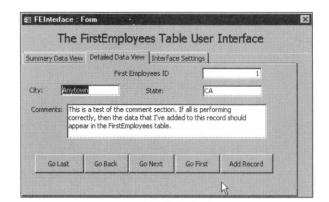

Figure 16.13
Detailed Data View
with Comments.

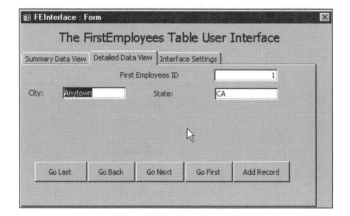

Figure 16.14
Detailed Data View
without Comments.

 ***Project*** Disabling Controls With Option Buttons

From time to time, you may find it necessary to disable your data
fields to prevent unauthorized editing (or for some other reason).
This next task shows you how to disable fields programmatically
by using Access option buttons. Access option buttons are called
radio buttons in some circles. Undertake your next programming
activity by completing the following steps:

1. With the FEInterface in Design View, select the Interface
   Settings tab.

2. Select the Option Button control from the toolbox, place the
   cursor on the form, and then click once to add a control to
   the form.

3. Repeat Step 2, placing a second Option Button control just below the first.

4. On the All tab of the property sheet for the top option button, enter "Disable" in the Name property field and "Disable All Fields" in the Caption property field.

5. Select only the option button portion of the Option Button control.

6. On the All tab of the property sheet for the option button only, enter "AllOff" in the Name property field.

7. Create an **OnClick** event for the AllOff option button by placing the following code between the **Sub** and **End Sub** lines:

```
Me!FirstEmployeesID.Enabled = False
Me!LastName.Enabled = False
Me!FirstName.Enabled = False
Me!Title.Enabled = False
Me!EID3.Enabled = False
Me!City.Enabled = False
Me!State.Enabled = False
Me!Comments.Enabled = False
If Me!FirstEmployeesID.Enabled = False Then
Me!AllOn.Value = Enabled
End If
```

8. Repeat Steps 4, 5, and 6 for the second option button by replacing "Disable", "Disable All Fields", and "AllOff" with "Enable", "Enable All Fields", and "AllOn".

9. Create an **OnClick** event for the AllOn option button by placing the following code between the **Sub** and **End Sub** lines:

```
Me!FirstEmployeesID.Enabled = True
Me!LastName.Enabled = True
Me!FirstName.Enabled = True
Me!Title.Enabled = True
Me!EID3.Enabled = True
Me!City.Enabled = True
Me!State.Enabled = True
Me!Comments.Enabled = True
If Me!FirstEmployeesID.Enabled = True Then
Me!AllOff.Value = Enabled
End If
```

Testing The Disable/Enable Option Buttons

Like the Show/Hide checkboxes, the Disable/Enable option buttons (as their names imply) are designed to give you the option of disabling and re-enabling all fields on the FEInterface form. When testing this capability, selecting Disable All Fields disables the option, disables all form fields, and enables the alternate option. This works in reverse when you select the Enable All Fields option. Figures 16.15 and 16.16 show you a before and after view of the option's effect.

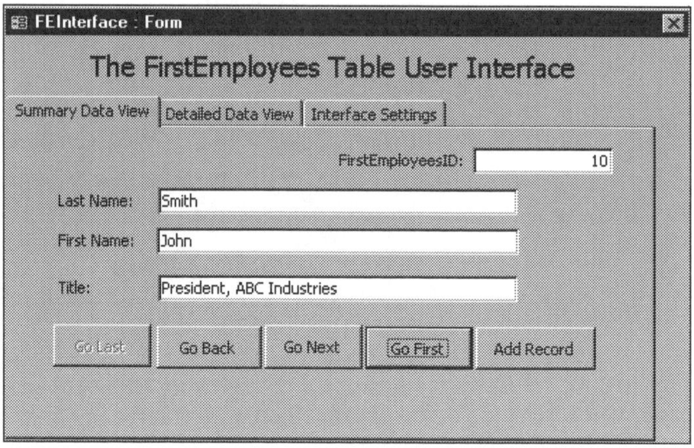

Figure 16.15
Normal Summary
Data View.

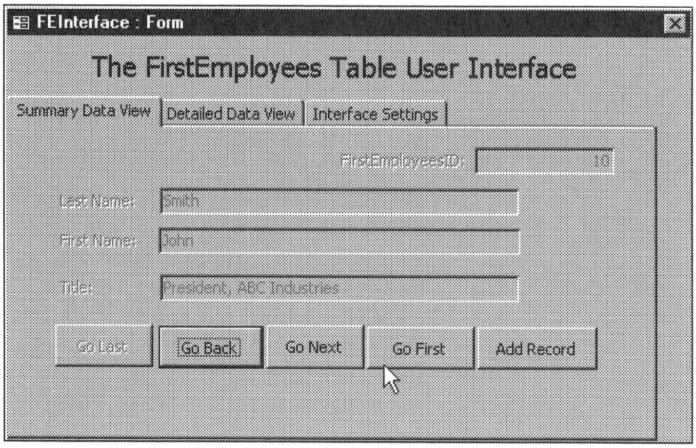

Figure 16.16
Disabled Summary
Data View.

Where To Go From Here

You've done quite a bit in this chapter! Now you should have a pretty good appreciation for how to use Form controls to extend the capabilities of Access 2000. We moved pretty fast and didn't spend much time discussing the tools and techniques used to design and program the FEInterface. But you're in luck; the next chapter will revisit the FEInterface and explain some of the points that we glided over. So take a moment to catch your breath, and I'll see you in the next chapter.

Chapter 17

Understanding Form Controls

Once you've got a handle on how to apply and program form controls, you've turned the corner from being an Access user to being an Access developer.

NOTE

You can alter the physical appearance of some form controls, such as the Label control and the Text Box control, by setting the **Special Effect** *property. Standard effects are Flat, Raised, Sunken, Etched, Shadowed, and Chiseled.*

In Chapter 16, you built a form-based front end to interact with the FirstEmployees table of FirstDatabase. The intent was to give you a little practical experience with form control programming before settling into a more definitive discussion. Now, it's time to step back and look at what you accomplished in creating the FEInterface form. In this chapter, you'll examine the FEInterface form and gain some understanding about how it was put together and how the controls are used to make it functional. You'll also be introduced to a couple of new controls—namely the combo box and the list box—and you'll get to see how to use them to add a little versatility to your form-based data collection activity.

Examining The FEInterface Form

As is the case with most of the sample forms you've built thus far, the FEInterface form is constructed from a standard Access 2000 form. By design, this form demonstrates the use of Access 2000's standard selection of control objects. We'll discuss each of these control objects in more detail later in this chapter. However, before we get to this, let's take a closer look at what was involved in putting the FEInterface form together.

Reviewing the FEInterface Development Process

In applying the PRACTICE methodology to the development of the FEInterface form, you'll notice that the *purpose* of the form, as previously mentioned, is to demonstrate the use of standard Access 2000 form control objects. In addition, you'll notice that task accomplishment is tied to the *resolution* that the program would use 9 of the 13 standard form controls found on the Access 2000 toolbox. Specifically, the controls used for this application were the Label, the Rectangle, the Tab, the Text Box, the Command Button, the Toggle Button, the Option Group, the Check Box, and the Option Button.

Because the intent of the FEInterface form was for it to be a user interface for the FirstEmployees table, your first task was to establish the form's design. In this case, you used a 3-by-5 form grid and added a Label control and a Rectangle control to the top of the form as a form identifier. The next piece of the interface design called for the creation of a Tab control containing three tabs. The first two Control tabs were used to present summary and detailed data views, whereas the third Control tab was used as a utility screen to manipulate the form's properties.

Your first task in developing the form involved adding Text Box controls to the first two tabs. Completing this task allowed the FEInterface form to display table data. The next task called for the creation of a set of custom navigation controls. The intent here was to change the default navigation controls provided by Access 2000 to something a little more user friendly. The custom navigation controls you created used VBA code to move through the FirstEmployees table and to manipulate the **Enabled** properties of the GoLast and GoFirst buttons. Consequently, clicking on the GoLast button disables it and moves you to the last record in the FirstEmployees table. Furthermore, clicking on the GoFirst button not only moves you to the first record in the First-Employees table but also results in the GoFirst button being disabled and, consequently, the GoLast button being reenabled.

NOTE

Forms and reports are both designed using controls from the Access 2000 toolbox.

After designing and coding the form's custom navigation buttons, you removed the form's default navigation controls by manually setting the form's **Navigation Buttons** property to No. After making a few additional manual property adjustments to remove items such as form scrollbars and record selectors, you modified the structure of the FirstEmployees table, adding three new data elements to support the form's Detailed Data View tab. As a result, records from the FirstEmployees table, seen on the Summary Data View tab, could be enhanced with additional detail viewable on the Detailed Data View tab.

With both the Summary Data View and Detailed Data View tabs of the FEInterface complete, your final task was to design and code the Interface Settings tab. On the Interface Settings tab, you added and programmed Toggle Button controls within an Option Group control. The result was the capability to add color to and remove color from the form's data fields. You then added Check Box controls to the tab and programmed them to hide and show the Comments field on the Detailed Data View tab. Finally, you completed work on the Interface Settings tab by adding Option Button controls, which were programmed to disable and enable the Text Box controls on both the Summary and Detailed Data View tabs. Figures 17.1 through 17.3 give you another look at the completed FEInterface form.

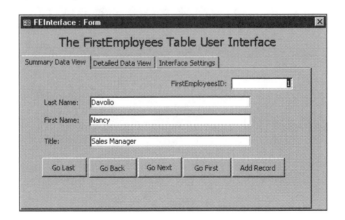

Figure 17.1
The FEInterface form's Summary Data View tab.

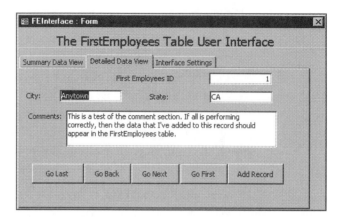

Figure 17.2
The FEInterface form's
Detailed Data View tab.

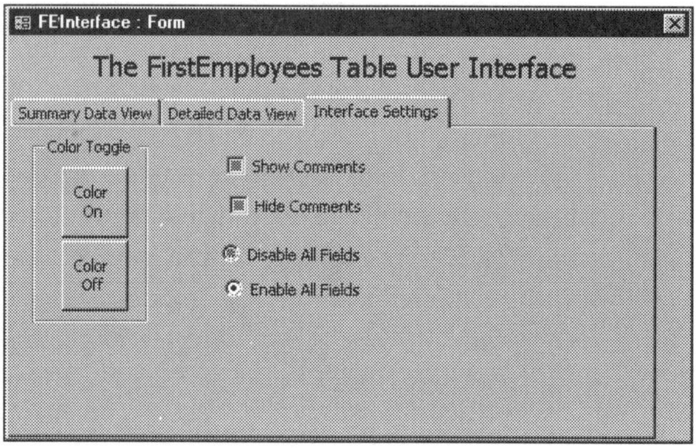

Figure 17.3
The FEInterface form's
Interface Settings tab.

About The FEInterface Form Controls

In this section, you'll get up close and personal with some of the more functional controls used to build the FEInterface form. Keep in mind that the use of form controls for the FEInterface form is but one application. By adjusting property settings either manually or programmatically, the application of form controls is limited only by your own ingenuity.

The Label Control

This control lets you add static text to a form that's editable in Design View only. Here are a couple of interesting things to consider when you use the Label control:

- Adding a text string to the ControlTip **Text** property for this control causes the string to appear when the mouse cursor is placed on the control in Form View.

- Right-clicking on the control's **Hyperlink Address** property field, located on the Format tab of the control's property sheet, and selecting Build launches the Insert Hyperlink dialog box (see Figure 17.4). Here, you can create a hyperlink to a Web address invoked by clicking on the Label control.

The Tab Control

This control is a self-contained group of pages, typically used when you want to display several screens of related data. When it's created, the Tab control contains two tabs. Additional tabbed pages are added to the control by selecting Insert|Tab Control Page from the Access 2000 menu bar or by right-clicking on the control and selecting Insert Page from the right-click menu.

The Text Box Control

The Text Box control is a text field. You use Text Box controls when you want to enter or display data on a form, report, or data access page. Text Box controls can be bound or unbound. A bound Text Box control is a text field that's specifically attached to an underlying table field based on the value stored in the

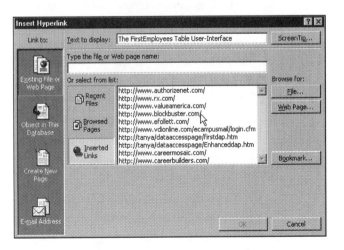

Figure 17.4
The Insert Hyperlink dialog box.

control's **ControlSource** property. An unbound Text Box control has no specific value relationship to an underlying database table.

The Command Button Control

This control is one of my favorites because of the utility it offers. The Command Button control is a pushbutton used to trigger an action. The action is driven by either a macro or an event procedure linked to the control's **onClick** property. It's capable of having either a text caption or a picture displayed on its face by setting its **Caption** or **Picture** property. A Command Button control can also be programmatically disabled or enabled.

The Toggle Button Control

The Toggle Button control is a single-state button control. In other words, it exists in either a "down" state or an "up" state. For Toggle Button controls, an up state represents a True or Yes condition, whereas a down state represents a False or No condition. Using a Toggle Button control allows only one condition to be true at any one time. Notice in the FEInterface form that when the Color On control is down, the Color Off control is up, and vice versa.

The Option Group Control

The Option Group control can be thought of as a kind of control organizer. It lets you place a set of like controls together for the purpose of selecting one member of the control set. Each control that resides within the Option Group control has its own value. Consequently, when a control within an Option Group control is selected, the value of that selection applies to the entire control group.

The Check Box Control

The Check Box control is a control that exists in two states. When not selected, the Check Box control is empty and represents a False or No condition. When selected, the Check Box control contains a small checkmark, indicating a True or Yes condition. You'll notice in the FEInterface form that the Check

NOTE

All the controls used to enable the FEInterface form could just as well have been created using the Access 2000 toolbox Control Wizard. You can enable the assistance of the Control Wizard by selecting the Magic Wand icon at the top of the Access 2000 toolbox.

Box control was used to indicate the selection of a single option. However, a more typical use of a Check Box control is to allow the selection of multiple options, such that numerous True conditions could exist simultaneously.

The Option Button Control

Like the Check Box control, the Option Button control also exists in two states. Typically used inside an Option Group control to allow the selection of a single option, the Option Button control displays a filled circle to indicate a True or Yes condition. Conversely, when not selected, the Option Button control displays an empty circle to represent a False or No condition.

Using Combo And List Boxes

Combo boxes and list boxes are controls that display multiple data selections, which allows you to pick a single item from a range of available choices. Although they share many of the same features, there are differences between them, as listed in Table 17.1

Understanding Combo And List Boxes

The FEInterface form didn't use Combo or List Box controls by design. However, in order for you to gain some practical experience with Combo and List Box controls, you need to roll up your sleeves one more time. In the paragraphs that follow, you're going to modify the FEInterface form by adding two more tabs. You'll

Table 17.1   Combo box and list box differences.

Control Feature	As Handled By Combo Box	As Handled By List Box
Available choices	You may choose from listed values or add new values to the existing list.	Lets you choose only items shown in the displayed list.
Selection options	Only one data element at a time may be selected	Multiple data elements may be selected. However, the **MultiSelect** property must be set for this to occur.
Screen usage	Consumes no more screen space than a single-line text field.	Uses as much screen space as you allow.

create one tab for a Combo Box control and another tab for a List Box control. You'll then have the chance to work with both control types to get a feel for how they're used.

.Project Expanding The FEInterface Control

Add two new tab pages to the FEInterface form by completing the following steps:

1. From the Access 2000 database window, select Forms from the window's Object pane and then double-click FEInterface from the list of available forms.

2. Select View|Design View from the Access 2000 menu bar.

3. Right-click on the FEInterface form Tab control, and select Insert Page.

4. Repeat Step 3 once again and then proceed to Step 5.

5. Select the first new tab page, right-click, and then select Properties.

6. Enter "Combo Boxes" in the Caption field of the Format tab.

7. Select the second new tab page, and enter "List Boxes" in the page's Caption field.

8. Close the property sheet, select the Combo Boxes tab, and then select File|Save from the Access 2000 menu bar.

.Project Adding Combo Boxes And List Boxes To A Form

Now that you've expanded the FEInterface form with two new tab pages, let's continue the modification of the form by adding combo and list boxes. Proceed by performing the following steps:

1. Deselect the Control Wizard on the Access 2000 toolbox, and then select the Combo Box control.

2. Place the cursor on the Combo Boxes tab page of the FEInterface form, and click once to apply the control to the form.

NOTE

When applied to a form, combo boxes and list boxes consist of two elements—the Label control and the Combo or List Box control itself. Each element has its own properties. Be careful not to give the label the same name as the combo or list box, or you'll get a naming conflict.

3. Right-click on the label of the newly applied combo box control, and then select Properties from the right-click menu.

4. On the property sheet that appears, select the All tab and enter "Combo Box Label A" in the Name property field and "Last Name" in the Caption property field.

5. Click on the Combo Box control containing the word "Unbound," and then enter "ComboBoxA" in the Name property field of the combo box property sheet.

6. Select File|Save from the Access 2000 menu bar.

Adding Data To Combo And List Boxes

Take a look at Figure 17.5. Pay particular attention to the **Row-Source** and **RowSourceType** property fields. The datasource for Combo or List Box controls are determined by how the **Row-Source** and **RowSourceType** properties are set. The **RowSource-Type** property determines the type of datasource a combo box or list box will use. The **RowSourceType** property has three built-in settings—Value List, Table/Query (the default setting, as shown in Figure 17.5), and Field List. You can also set this property to the name of a function that you can create to fill a combo box or list box. Each of the three built-in settings for the **RowSourceType** property are discussed in the following sections.

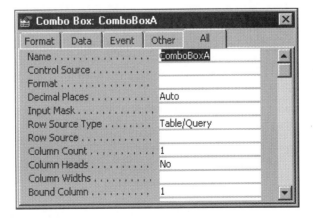

Figure 17.5
The All tab of the ComboBoxA property sheet.

Project Building A Combo Box Using A Value List

Using the Value List setting of the **RowSourceType** property, you provide the values that you want the combo box or list box to display. Generally, you'll use this setting for small value sets that won't change. When you set the **RowSourceType** property to Value List, you must provide a list of values, separated by semicolons, as the **RowSource** property setting. The values in the semicolon-separated list will fill the combo box or list box with data. You can see this in action by performing the following steps:

1. With the ComboBoxA property sheet open, select the Event tab.

2. Click on the etched square in the left corner of the FEInterface form window, just below the FEInterface form title bar.

3. On the Event tab of the form property sheet, double-click the **onLoad** property field.

4. With [Event Procedure] appearing in the **onLoad** property field, click on the button with three dots, immediately to the right of the field, to launch the Visual Basic Editor.

5. Place the following code between the **Sub** and **End Sub** statements:

```
Dim demo As ComboBox
Set demo = Me!ComboBoxA
demo.RowSourceType = "Value List"
demo.RowSource = "Washington;Lincoln;" & _
  Jefferson;Roosevelt"
```

6. Select Debug|Compile FirstDatabase from the VB Editor menu bar; then select File|Close And Return To Microsoft Access.

7. Close the form property sheet, and then select File|Save from the Access 2000 menu bar.

8. Select File|Close from the Access 2000 menu bar.

9. From the Access 2000 database window, select Forms from the window's Object pane, and then double-click on FEInterface from the list of available forms.

10. On the FEInterface form, select the Combo Boxes tab and then click the arrow on the combo box. The result is shown in Figure 17.6.

When you're ready to supply a value for the **ControlSource** property of the combo box or list box, then you want your combo or list box to be bound to a field in a table. In this case, the value that a user would select from the combo box or list box is the value stored in the field specified by the **ControlSource** property. You'll see a practical example of this in the next section.

.Project Creating A Control Based On A Table, Query, Or SQL Statement

When you set the **RowSourceType** property to Table/Query, you specify that a table, query, or SQL statement will be the data-source for the active combo box or list box. In this case, the **RowSource** property setting of the control would be the name of the table, query, or SQL statement containing the data you want the combo box or list box to display. Setting the **ControlSource** property means that you want to have the active Combo or List Box control bound to a field. Furthermore, if your datasource is a

Figure 17.6
A combo box populated by a value list.

table, query, or SQL statement specified in the **RecordSource** property of the active form, you can bind the control to a field in that table, query, or SQL statement by setting the **ControlSource** property. When the control is bound, the value selected by a user will be stored in that field, in the table where the field is defined. Let's take a practical look at this whole concept by creating a List Box control on the FEInterface form, using the following steps:

1. With the FEInterface form in Design View, select the List Boxes tab.

2. Deselect the Control Wizard on the Access 2000 toolbox; then select the List Box control.

3. Place the cursor on the List Boxes tab page of the FEInterface form, and click once to apply the control to the form.

4. Right-click on the label of the newly applied List Box control, and then select Properties from the right-click menu.

5. On the property sheet that appears, select the All tab and enter "List Box Label A" in the Name property field and "Last Name" in the Caption property field.

6. Click on the list box control containing the word "Unbound," and then enter "ListBoxA" in the Name property field of the list box property sheet.

7. Click on the drop-down menu for the ControlSource property field, and then select LastName.

8. Click on the drop-down menu for the RowSource property field, and then select FirstEmployees.

9. Select File|Save from the Access 2000 menu bar. Congratulations, you've bound your list box control to the LastName field of the FirstEmployees table.

You have two decisions to make when designing a bound combo box or list box. First, you must decide what value should be stored in the control and in the underlying table or query. Second, you must decide whether the value stored in the control is the same value to be displayed in the control, because you can either store the value that's displayed or store one value and display another.

▶**Tip**

*The **RecordSource** property setting for a Combo or List Box control can be a table name, a query name, or an SQL statement, and it can be set programmatically as well as manually.*

Binding And Displaying Columns

Once you set the **RowSource** property of a combo box or list box to a table name, query name, or SQL statement, all the fields in the specified table, query, or SQL statement are available to the control. Therefore, you can choose the field you want to be bound and the field or fields you want to display.

Combo or list boxes can contain multiple columns, and each of these columns corresponds to a table field, query field, or SQL statement specified by the **RowSource** property. However, the **Value** property of a combo box or list box can only return a single value. The column that contains the value returned by the control's **Value** property is known as the *bound column*. The **BoundColumn** property indicates which column in the datasource that the Combo or List Box control is bound to. If you've set the control's **ControlSource** property to a particular field, the setting for the **BoundColumn** property should be the number of the column that corresponds to the same field in the data table. The columns in a combo box or list box are numbered beginning with 1, in the same order as the fields in the underlying table or query. Therefore, in order to set the **BoundColumn** property to the first column, you would set it to 1, to set it to the second column you would set it to 2, and so on. For example, the FEInterface list box control's **RowSource** property is set to the FirstEmployees table and the **ControlSource** property is set to the FirstEmployeesID field. You'll find that the **BoundColumn** property is set to 1, indicating that the first column in the control is bound to the FirstEmployeesID field.

The **ColumnCount** property specifies the number of columns contained in the combo box or list box. The number of columns available is determined by the number of fields in the table, query, or SQL statement specified by the **RowSource** property. The FEInterface list box is bound to a table that returns seven fields. Specifically, these fields are FirstEmployeesID, LastName, FirstName, Title, City, State, and Comments. The **ColumnCount** property for this list box is set to 1. Because the first column, FirstEmployeesID, is the bound column, it's supplying the values displayed in the list box (see Figure 17.7).

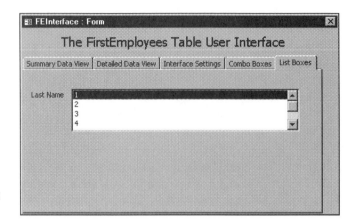

Figure 17.7
The FEInterface list box bound to Column 1.

*Any column can be the bound column, and although it's not the case in the FEInterface example, in most cases you'll want to choose a column that's either a primary key or a foreign key. In addition, for a bound control, the data type of the bound column must match the data type of the fields specified in the **ControlSource** property.*

For the FEInterface List Box control, if you set the **Bound-Column** property to 2 and the **ColumnCount** property to 3, three columns will appear in the List Box control (see Figure 17.8). If you set the **ColumnWidths** property, you can hide the First-EmployeesID column altogether and display only the LastName column. You can set the **ColumnWidths** property by specifying widths for each column, separated by semicolons. If you omit a column, the default width is used for that column. For example, to hide the FirstEmployeesID column, set the **ColumnWidths** property to "0; ;".

The settings for these three properties—**BoundColumn, ColumnCount,** and **ColumnWidths**—are summarized in Table 17.2.

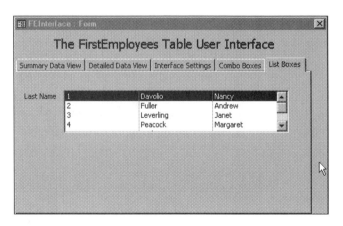

Figure 17.8
The FEInterface list box with **ColumnCount** set to 3.

Table 17.2   Combo and list box bind and display properties.

Property	Setting
BoundColumn	The number of the column that provides the value of the combo box or list box. If the control is bound to a field in an underlying table or query, the bound column corresponds to the field indicated in the **ControlSource** property.
ColumnCount	The number of columns in the combo box or list box. If the control is bound to a table, query, or SQL statement, the first field in the table, query, or SQL statement corresponds to the first column in the control, the second field corresponds to the second column, and so on. For example, if you want to display the fifth field in a table in a combo box, you need to specify 5 for the **ColumnCount** property or create a query or SQL statement that includes only this field and any others you need.
ColumnWidths	The width of each column in the combo box, separated by semicolons.

Using A Combo Or List Box With A Field List

When you set the **RowSourceType** property to Field List, the combo or list box displays a list of the fields available from the form's record source. For instance, if the form's **RecordSource** property is set to the FirstEmployees table, the control will display the names of all the fields in that table. You don't need to set the **ControlSource** property when you use this setting, because you're not binding the control to a particular field. However, you must set the **RecordSource** property for the form; otherwise, no fields will be displayed in the field list.

Adding Items To A Combo Box Programmatically

Should you decide that a Combo Box control is more your cup of tea than a List Box control, you can create one so that a user can add new data or edit existing data, or you can prevent a user from changing data. You accomplish this by using the combo box's **LimitToList** and **NotInList** properties. The **LimitToList** property determines whether a user can add a new item to the Combo Box control value list. The default setting for this property is No.

When this property is set to No, a user can type a new value in the text portion of the combo box, but the value isn't added to the combo box drop-down list. When this property is set to Yes, however, the **NotInList** event is triggered and presents a message when a user tries to enter a new combo box value. Within the **NotInList** event procedure, you can add the new item to the control's source and requery it, ignore a user's attempt to enter it, or post an error message stating that the item can't be added. The resulting action depends on the value given to the **Response** argument of the **NotInList** event procedure.

When you set the **Response** argument to **acDataErrAdded**, Access 2000 allows you to add the value of the **NewData** argument to the **RowSource** property setting. Once the value has been added, Access 2000 automatically requeries the combo box. If you set the **Response** argument to **acDataErrContinue**, Access 2000 doesn't display an error message. If you don't set the **Response** argument or set it to the default value, **acDataErrDisplay**, Access 2000 displays the default message stating that the value the user typed is not in the list. Use this value or **acDataErrContinue** if you don't want a user to add an item to the list.

Be aware that before you can use the **NotInList** event, you must set the **LimitToList** property to Yes. It's a good idea to do this when the form is loaded so that you can be sure it's set correctly. You can also set it manually on the Access 2000 property sheet.

You can also use the **LimitToList** property and the **NotInList** event procedure to add a new combo box to an underlying table or query. For example, suppose you added a LastName combo box to an Employee Password form, and you wanted to let users add new employees while adding new username/password combinations. When a user types in the name of an unlisted employee, you can automatically open the FEInterface form and enter in all the necessary information for that employee. Access 2000 automatically refreshes the combo box to show the new employee in the list after the information has been added.

Project Building A Dynamically Filled Combo Box

So you can see the practical application of this concept, let's do a little database modification. Proceed by completing the following steps:

1. With FirstDatabase open, select Tables under the Objects pane of the Access 2000 database window.

2. Open the table FirstTable in Design View, and then add the field FirstEmployeesID with the data type **Number**.

3. Select File|Save from the Access 2000 database window, and then close the FirstTable Design View.

4. Select Tools|Relationships from the Access 2000 database window.

5. Right-click inside the Relationships window, and then select Show Table from the right-click menu.

6. On the Show Table dialog box, select FirstEmployees and click on the Add button, select FirstTable and click on the Add button, and then click on the Close button.

7. Drag the field FirstEmployeesID from the FirstTable field list to the FirstEmployeesID field of the FirstEmployees field list.

8. Click on the Create button in the Edit Relationship dialog box, and then select File|Save.

9. Close the Relationships window.

Now, let's build a practical example to demonstrate how to dynamically add items to a combo box control. Proceed by performing the following steps:

1. Use the Form Wizard to create a form called Employee Passwords. The form should contain three fields—Username, Password, and FirstEmployeesID.

2. When prompted by the Form Wizard, select the option to modify design.

3. Add a Combo Box control to the form Employee Passwords.

4. Right-click on the combo box label, and then select Properties.

5. Select the All tab on the label property sheet, and then enter the following values:

   - *Name*—EmployeePasswords

   - *Caption*—Employee Name

6. Select the Combo Box control, and set the following properties:

   - *Name*—LastName

   - *RowSourceType*—Table/Query

   - *RowSource*—FirstEmployees

   - *ColumnCount*—2

   - *ColumnWidths*—"0;;"

   - *BoundColumn*—2

7. Select File|Save from the Access 2000 menu bar. Your form should now appear similar to the one shown in Figure 17.9.

8. Create an **onLoad** event procedure for the Employee Password form using the following code:

```
Private Sub Form_Load()
    Me!LastName.LimitToList = True
End Sub
Private Sub LastName_NotInList(NewData As String,
   Response As Integer)
   Dim demo As ComboBox, strMsg As String
   Set demo = Me!LastName
   strMsg = "This Employee is not in the list.
          Would you like to add it?"
   If MsgBox(strMsg, vbOKCancel) = vbOK Then
       Response = acDataErrAdded
       DoCmd.OpenForm "FEInterface"
          , , , , acFormAdd, acDialog, NewData
   Else
       LastName.Undo
       Response = acDataErrContinue
   End If
End Sub
```

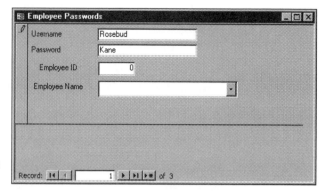

Figure 17.9
The Employee Passwords
form.

Now, perform the following steps to see your results:

1. Open the Employee Passwords form in Form View, and enter the name *Welles* in the blank combo box control, which shows a username and password combination Rosebud, Kane. The name Welles doesn't exist in the FirstEmployees table.

2. A message box appears asking whether you want to add the new employee. When you choose OK, the FEInterface form opens to a new record so that you can enter data about Welles. Note the EmployeeID number assigned by the FEInterface form—you'll need to enter this in a moment.

3. Close the FEInterface form when you're done adding the new record.

4. Use the Employee Passwords form to add the EmployeeID number for Welles to Record 1 of the table FirstTable.

5. Select File|Save and then File|Close from the Access 2000 menu bar.

6. Reopen the Employee Passwords form, and then click the Combo Box control. You'll see that Access 2000 now displays the new employee name in the control's drop-down list (see Figure 17.10).

7. Close the Employee Passwords form.

The **NotInList** event can also be used to dynamically add an item to a combo box or list box based on a value list. In this instance, you would concatenate a string containing the value to be added with the existing value of the **RowSource** property. Be aware,

NOTE

One of the neat new features in Access 2000 is the ability to access a related record in another table as a subdatasheet. This feature is invoked when the active table has a relationship to another table. The subdatasheet is accessed by selecting a plus sign to the left of a specific record (see Figure 17.11).

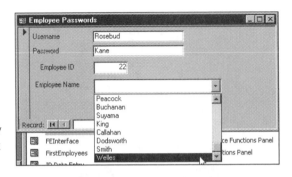

Figure 17.10
The name Welles is now listed in the Combo Box control.

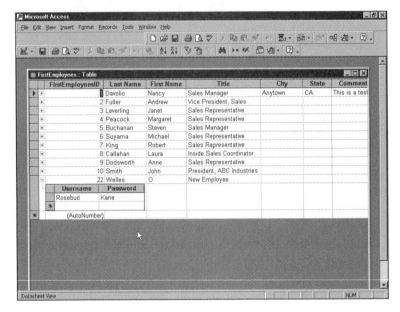

Figure 17.11
Access 2000 now features subdatasheet access by row across tables.

▶Tip

*If you change the setting of the **RowSource** property by adding an item to a combo or list box control at runtime, that change will be lost when you close and reopen the form. You need to edit the property in Design View to preserve your change.*

however, that if you change a property setting while a form is in Form View, that change is preserved only as long as that instance of the form exists. Once you close the form or switch to Design View, you lose the change.

Determining A User's Selection In A List Box

List Box controls are enabled with the **MultiSelect** property. This property determines how users are able to select list box data. You can set this property to None, which prevents users from selecting more than one item at a time; to Simple, which allows users to

NOTE

*Rows in a list box are indexed beginning with zero, so if the first row is selected, **ListIndex** returns 0; if the second row is selected, **ListIndex** returns 1, and so on.*

select multiple items by clicking them with the mouse; or to Extended, which allows users to select multiple items using the Shift and Ctrl keys.

If the **MultiSelect** property is set to None, you can determine which row a user selected by returning the value of the **ListIndex** property. This property returns the index of the selected row.

If the **MultiSelect** property is set to Simple or Extended, you can use the **Selected** property or the **ItemsSelected** collection to determine whether a particular item in the list is selected. The **Selected** property is a zero-based array that contains the selection state of each item in a list box. For example, if you want to determine that the first item in a list box is selected, you would check the value of the **Selected** property for that item. The following line of code prints the value of the **Selected** property for the first item in the list box named ListBoxA to the VB Editor's Immediate window:

```
Debug.Print Me!ListBoxA.Selected(0)
```

To return data from a row in a list box, regardless of whether that row is selected, you can use either the **ItemData** property or the **Column** property. The **ItemData** property returns data from the column specified by the **BoundColumn** property. The **Column** property returns data from a specified row and column.

The following example fills a list box with data and then checks the **Column** property for each row and column in the list box and prints it to the Debug window. To try this example, paste the following code into the **onLoad** event module for the ListBoxA list box that you created on the FEInterface list box tab and then switch to Form View. As before, you can check your results in the Immediate window of the VB Editor:

```
Private Sub Form_Load()
    Dim lst As ListBox
    Dim intI As Integer, intJ As Integer
    Set lst = Me!ListBoxA
    ' Display FirstEmployeesID, LastName, and
    ' FirstName fields in list box.
```

```
    With lst
        .RowSourceType = "Table/Query"
        .RowSource = "FirstEmployees"
        .ColumnCount = 3
    End With
    ' Print value of each column for each row.
    For intI = 0 To lst.ListCount - 1
        For intJ = 0 To lst.ColumnCount - 1
            Debug.Print lst.Column(intJ, intI)
            Debug.Print
        Next intJ
    Next intI
End Sub
```

Where To Go From Here

In this chapter, you got a pretty comprehensive look at form controls. You got the chance to gain an understanding of how the FEInterface form was put together, and you took a good look at the controls used to make it work. You were then introduced to the Combo Box and the List Box controls, and you discovered how to use them to dynamically and programmatically manipulate data. Next up, you'll get up close and personal with macros.

Chapter 18

Working With Macros In Access 2000

Macros are very useful for automating simple tasks, such as carrying out an action when the user clicks a command button. Plus, you don't need to know how to program to use macros.

Macros were first introduced in Access 1.0. At the time, they were the only automation technique at the developer's disposal when creating Access databases. In subsequent versions of the product, first Access Basic and then Visual Basic for Applications were added to the Access product, until by Access 97, macros were really only necessary for controlling custom toolbars and for performing startup actions. With the release of Access 2000 and the inclusion of the **CommandBar** object, macros are no longer necessary to even handle toolbars. Macros are still useful, however, for automating simple tasks, and they are often useful as a means of prototyping certain actions. In fact, especially as you first start working with Access 2000, you'll likely find that you create macros to handle certain tasks and then convert those macros to Visual Basic code for efficiency.

In this chapter, we'll consider how to design and use a macro, and we'll actually design some macros for use with the Chap18.mdb database. In the next chapter, we'll consider some of the issues when working with macros versus Visual Basic code, as well as more closely evaluate the situations when macros are most useful.

Working With Macros

As you might expect, you'll need to perform a variety of tasks when working with macros. The most common tasks, of course, involve creating and running the macros. In the following sections, we'll explore the steps necessary for the creation and running of macros.

Creating And Running A Macro

To create a macro, click the Macros tab and then click New. The Macro Design window will appear, as shown in Figure 18.1. This window allows you to build a macro "program" by adding macro actions, arguments, names, and conditions to the macro.

Macro *actions* are like programming commands or functions. They instruct Access to take a specific action—for example, to open a form. Macro *arguments* are like parameters to a command or function. They provide Access 2000 with specifics regarding the selected action. For example, if the macro action instructs Access 2000 to open a form, the arguments for that action tell Access 2000 which form is to be opened and how it's to be opened (for example, in Form, Design, or Datasheet View or Print Preview). Macro *names* are like subroutines. Multiple subroutines can be included within one Access macro. Each of these routines is identified by its macro name. Macro *conditions* allow you to determine when a specific macro action will execute. For example, you might want one form to open in one situation and a second form to open in another situation.

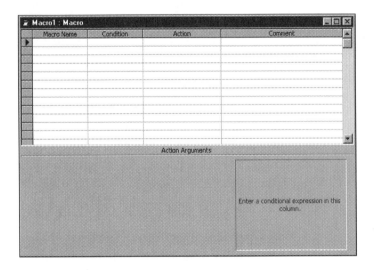

Figure 18.1
The Macro Design window within Access 2000.

.*Project* Adding Macro Actions

As mentioned, macro actions instruct Access 2000 to perform a task. You can add a macro action to the Macro Design window in several ways. One method is to click on a cell within the Macro Action column and then click to open the drop-down menu, as shown in Figure 18.2.

A list of all the macro actions appears. Select the desired action from the list to add it instantly to the macro. Use this method of selecting a macro action if you aren't sure of the name of the macro action and want to browse the available list.

After you've been working with macros for a while, you'll know which actions you want to select. Rather than opening the drop-down menu and scrolling through the entire list of actions, you can click on a cell within the Action column and begin to type the name of the macro action you want to add. Access locates the first macro action beginning with the character(s) you type.

The **OpenTable**, **OpenQuery**, **OpenForm**, **OpenReport**, and **OpenModule** actions are used to open a table, query, form, report, or module, respectively. These actions and their associated arguments can all be filled in quite easily using the drag-and-drop technique detailed in the following list:

1. Use the Window menu's Tile option to tile the Database window and the Macro Design window on the desktop.

2. Select the appropriate tab from the Database window. For example, if you want to open a form, select the Forms tab.

3. Click and drag the object you want to open to the Macro Design window. The appropriate action and arguments are automatically filled in by Access. Figure 18.3 shows an example where the frmCheckedOut form was dragged and dropped onto the Macro Design window.

Figure 18.2
The macro editor's Action drop-down menu.

The process of dragging and dropping a table, query, form, report, or module onto the Macro Design window saves you some time, because all the macro action arguments are automatically filled in for you. Notice in Figure 18.3 that six action arguments are

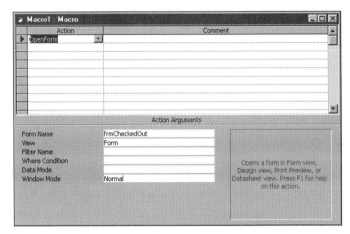

Figure 18.3
The macro editor after a form has been placed in the macro action.

associated with the **OpenForm** action: **Form Name**, **View**, **Filter Name**, **Where Condition**, **Data Mode**, and **Window Mode**. The process of dragging and dropping the frmCheckedOut form to the Macro Design window filled in three of the arguments for the **OpenForm** action. The name of the form (frmCheckedOut), the view (Form), and the window mode (Normal) were all automatically filled in. Macro action arguments are covered more thoroughly in the next section.

Setting Action Arguments

A macro action argument is like a parameter to a command or function. The macro action arguments that are available differ depending on what macro action has been selected. The macro action arguments give Access 2000 specific instructions on how to execute the selected macro action. Some macro action arguments force you to select from a drop-down menu containing appropriate choices; others allow you to enter a valid Access 2000 expression. Macro action arguments are automatically filled in when you click and drag a table, query, form, report, or module to the Macro Design window. In all other situations, you must supply Access 2000 with the arguments required to properly execute a macro action. To specify a macro action argument, perform the following five steps:

1. Select a macro action.

2. Press the F6 function key on the keyboard to jump down to the first macro action argument for the selected macro action.

3. If the macro action argument requires that you select from a list of valid choices, click to open the drop-down menu for the first macro action argument associated with the selected macro action. All the available choices will appear.

4. If the macro action argument requires that you enter a valid expression, you can type the argument into the appropriate text box, or you can solicit assistance from the Expression Builder. An example is the **Where Condition** argument of the **OpenForm** action. After you click the Where Condition text box, an ellipsis appears. If you click on the ellipsis, the Expression Builder dialog box is invoked, as shown in Figure 18.4.

5. To build an appropriate expression, select a database object from the list box on the left and then select a specific element from the center and right list boxes. Click Paste to paste the element into the text box. Click on OK to close the Expression Builder dialog box.

It's important to remember that each macro action has different macro action arguments. Some of the macro action arguments associated with a particular macro action are required, whereas others are optional. If you need help on a particular macro action argument, click on the specific argument, and Access 2000 will provide you with a short description of the selected argument. If you need additional assistance, press the F1 key, and Access 2000 will display Help for the macro action and all its arguments.

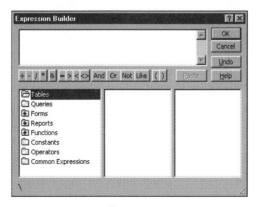

Figure 18.4
The Expression Builder dialog box.

Specifying Macro Names

Macro names are like subroutines. They allow you to place more than one routine within a macro. This means you can create many macro routines without having to create a large volume of separate macros. It's appropriate to include macros that perform related functions within one particular macro. For example, you might build a macro that contains all the routines required for form handling and another that contains all the routines required for report handling. Only two steps are needed to add macro names to a macro:

1. Click on the Macro Names button on the Macro Design toolbar. The Macro Name column will appear, as shown in Figure 18.5.

2. Add macro names to each macro subroutine.

The Macro Name column is a *toggle*—you can hide it and show it at will without losing the information within the column.

Specifying Macro Conditions

At times, you'll want a macro action to execute only when a certain condition is true. Fortunately, Access 2000 allows you to specify the conditions under which a macro action executes. To do so, perform the following steps:

1. Click the Conditions button on the Macro Design toolbar. The Condition column appears.

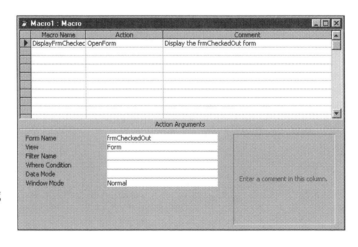

Figure 18.5
The Macro Design window after displaying the Macro Name column.

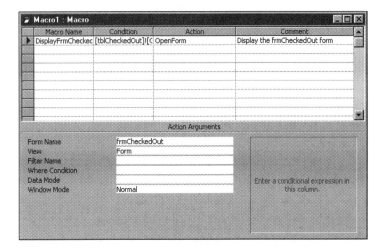

Figure 18.6
The Macro Design window after the addition of a condition to the macro.

2. Add conditions to each macro action as desired. To add conditions with the Expression Builder, right-click on the Condition column and select the Build option. Figure 18.6 shows the Macro Design window after the addition of a condition to the macro.

 # Running An Access Macro

The process of executing a macro varies depending on what you're attempting to accomplish. A macro can be run from the Macro Design window, from the Macros tab, by being triggered from a form or report event, or by selecting a menu or toolbar option.

Running A Macro From The Macro Design Window

A macro can be executed easily from the Macro Design window and can be run without subroutines. Click on Run in the Macro Design toolbar. Each line of the macro is executed unless conditions have been placed on specific macro actions.

From within the Macro Design view, you can run only the first subroutine within a macro. To run a macro containing subroutines, click on Run in the Macro Design toolbar. The first subroutine within the macro will execute. As soon as the second macro name is encountered, the macro execution will terminate.

Running A Macro From The Macros Tab

To run a macro from the Macros tab of the Database window, follow these two steps:

1. Click on the Macros tab of the Database window.

2. Double-click on the name of the macro you want to execute, or click on the name of the macro and then click on Run.

If the macro you execute contains macro names, only the macro actions within the first subroutine will be executed.

Triggering A Macro From A Form Or Report Event

Four steps are needed to associate a macro with a form or report event:

1. Select the object you want to associate the event with.

2. Open the Properties window, and click to select the event properties.

3. Click the event you want the macro to execute in response to.

4. Use the drop-down list to select the name of the macro you want to execute. If the macro contains macro names, make sure you select the correct macro name subroutine. Figure 18.7 shows a form's Properties dialog box after the selection of the mcrFrmChecked.DisplayFrmChecked macro.

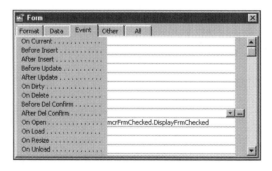

Figure 18.7
The **On Open** event after the selection of an existing macro.

Then, the macro will execute whenever the event executes—either automatically, in the case of most report events or form events, or in response to a user action, in the case of most control events.

Creating a macro is, however, as with most development tasks, just the beginning. It's rare indeed that you'll create the macro and never need to modify it afterwards. In the following sections, we'll consider how to modify a macro after its creation.

Project   Modifying An Existing Macro

So far in this chapter, in just a few pages, you've learned a lot about macros. You've learned how to create a macro, to add macro actions and their associated arguments, to create macro subroutines by adding macro names, and conditionally to execute the actions within a macro by adding macro conditions. Once a macro has been created, you can modify it. Enter Design View for the macro by performing the following steps:

1. Click on the Macros tab of the Database window.

2. Select the macro you want to modify.

3. Click Design.

The Design View of the macro will appear. You can now insert new lines, delete existing lines, move the macro actions around, or copy macro actions to the macro you're modifying or to another macro.

Inserting New Macro Actions In The Macro

To insert a macro action in an existing macro, perform the following steps from the macro editor:

1. Click on the line above which you want the macro action to be inserted.

2. Press the Insert key, click on the Insert Rows button on the toolbar, or select the Insert menu's Rows option. Access 2000 will insert a new line in the macro at the cursor.

To insert multiple macro actions, you must perform a slightly different series of steps from the macro editor, as follows:

1. Place your cursor on the line above the line where you want the new macro action lines to be inserted. Click on the macro action selector. (*Macro action selectors* are the gray boxes that appear to the left of the Macro Action column.)

2. Click and drag to select the same number of macro action selectors as the number of macro actions you want to insert.

3. Press the Insert key, click on the Insert Rows button on the toolbar, or select the Insert menu's Rows option. Access 2000 will insert all the new macro lines above the macro actions you selected.

Deleting Macro Actions

To delete a single macro action, perform the following steps:

1. Click on the macro action selector of the macro action you want to delete.

2. Press the Delete key, click on the Delete Rows button on the toolbar, or select the Edit menu's Delete Rows option.

To delete multiple macro actions, perform the following steps:

1. Click and drag to select the macro action selectors of all the macro actions you want to delete. All the macro actions should become black.

2. Press the Delete key, click on the Delete Rows button on the toolbar, or select the Edit menu's Delete Rows option.

Moving Macro Actions

You can move macro actions in a few ways, including dragging and dropping and cutting and pasting. To move macro actions by dragging and dropping, perform the following steps:

1. Click and drag to select the macro action(s) you want to move.

2. Release the mouse button.

3. Place your mouse cursor over the macro action selector of any of the selected macro actions.

▶Tip

If you accidentally drag and drop the selected macro actions to an incorrect place, use the Undo button on the Macro Design toolbar to reverse your action.

▶Tip

Don't click on the macro action selector of the row where you want to insert the cut macro actions unless you want to overwrite the macro action you've selected. If you don't click to select the macro action selectors, the cut lines are inserted into the macro without overwriting any other macro actions. If you select any of the macro action selectors, Access 2000 will overwrite the existing, selected macro actions.

4. Click and drag. A black line appears, indicating where the selected macro actions will be moved.

5. Release the mouse button when the black line is in the appropriate location.

To move macro actions by cutting and pasting, perform the following steps:

1. Click and drag to select the macro action selectors of the macro actions you want to move.

2. Click on Cut in the Macro Design toolbar (or use Ctrl+X or the Edit menu's Cut option).

3. Click within the line above which you want the cut macro actions to be inserted. Don't click on the macro action selector.

4. Click on Paste (or use one of the alternate Paste options). The macro actions are inserted at the cursor.

Copying Macro Actions

Macro actions can be copied within a macro or to another macro. To copy macro actions within a macro, follow these steps:

1. Click and drag to select the macro action selectors of the macro actions you want to copy.

2. Click on Copy in the Macro Design toolbar (or use Ctrl+C or the Edit menu's Copy option).

3. Click within the line above which you want the copied macro actions to be inserted. Don't click on any macro action selectors unless you want to overwrite existing macro actions (see the tip above).

4. Click on Paste (or use one of the alternate Paste options). Access 2000 will insert the macro actions at the cursor.

To copy macro actions to another macro, follow these steps:

1. Click and drag to select the macro action selectors of the macro actions you want to copy.

2. Click on Copy on the Macro Design toolbar (or use Ctrl+C or the Edit menu's Copy option).

3. Open the macro that will include the copied actions.

4. Click within the line above which you want the copied macro actions to be inserted.

5. Click on Paste (or use one of the alternate Paste options). Access 2000 will insert the macro actions at the cursor.

Clearly, as you can see from the previous sections, working with the Access 2000 macro Design View is a straightforward process. Most of the steps you take to create, modify, and manage macros are intuitive, or nearly so. However, there's one important consideration about macro design that we haven't discussed yet—adding comments to your macros. We'll discuss this topic in the next section.

.Project Adding Comments To Your Macros

NOTE

Macros don't provide the depth of commenting support that VBA does, which is one of the many reasons why VBA is a better choice.

Just as it's useful to document any program, it's useful to document what you're trying to accomplish within your macro. Comments can be used when you or others are attempting to modify your macro at a later time. They can also be used as documentation, because they print when you print the macro. To add a comment to a macro, click on the Comment column of the macro and begin to type. In general, your comments for macros are limited to one line (256 characters).

.Project Testing Your Macros

Access 2000 doesn't provide very sophisticated tools for testing and debugging your macros. However, it does provide a method by which you can step through each line of a macro. To do so, perform the following steps:

1. Open the macro in Design View.

2. Click on Single Step in the toolbar.

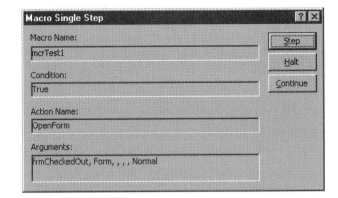

Figure 18.8
The Macro Single Step
dialog box.

3. To execute the macro, click on Run (the exclamation point) in the toolbar. Access 2000 will execute the first line of the macro. The Macro Single Step dialog box then appears, as shown in Figure 18.8.

   This dialog box shows you the macro name, condition, action name, and arguments. In the figure, the macro name is mcrTest1, the condition evaluates to True, and the action name is **OpenForm**. The **OpenForm** arguments are **frmCheckedOut**, **Form**, and **Normal**.

4. To continue stepping through the macro, click on Step. If you want to halt execution of the macro without proceeding, click on Halt. To continue normal execution of the macro without stepping, click on Continue.

.Project Finding And Changing A Customer Address In The Chap18.mdb Database

Suppose you want to add a command button to an Orders form that allows the user to search the customer records and change a particular customer's address. To do this through macros, you need to create a custom dialog box and two macros. The custom dialog box, which we'll name frmCustomerAddress, contains two text fields: txtCustomerName and txtNewAddress. It also has an OK button. Additionally, the already-existing frmCustomerInfo form contains a Change button, which actually invokes the frmCustomerAddress form.

Designing The Dialog Box

To design the dialog box, perform the following steps:

1. From within the Database window, click on the Forms tab. Next, click on the New button to display the New Form dialog box.

2. Within the New Form dialog box, choose Design View and click on OK. Access 2000 opens the new blank form in the form designer.

3. Click on the Save button on the toolbar, and name the form frmCustomerAddress.

4. If the toolbox is not currently displayed, click on the Toolbox icon on the toolbar. Within the toolbox, click on the Text Box control icon. When you move the cursor back over the form, Access 2000 displays the text box-creation cursor.

5. Click anywhere within the form designer, hold down the mouse button, and drag the mouse down and to the right to create a new text box. The size of the text box is not particularly important; you'll set its properties momentarily from the Properties dialog box. Enter the name as "txtCustomerName".

6. Within the form designer, click on the txtCustomerName text box. Open the Properties dialog box, and change the properties as detailed in the following steps.

7. Within the Format tab, change the **Left** property to 1.0833", the **Top** property to 0.0833", the **Width** property to 2.0", and the **Height** property to 0.25".

8. Change the **Font Name** property to Arial and the **Font Size** property to 8.

9. Click within the label associated with the text box, and change its caption to "Customer Name:". Next, within the

Format tab, change the **Left** property to 0.1" and the **Top** property to 0.0833".

10. Within the toolbox, click on the Text Box control icon. When you move the cursor back over the report, Access 2000 displays the text box-creation cursor.

11. Click anywhere within the form designer, hold down the mouse button, and drag the mouse down and to the right to create a new text box. The size of the text box is not particularly important; you'll set its properties momentarily from the Properties dialog box. Enter the name as "txtNewAddress".

12. Within the form designer, click on the txtNewAddress text box. Open the Properties dialog box, and change the properties as detailed in the following steps.

13. Within the Format tab, change the **Left** property to 1.0833", the **Top** property to 0.4583", the **Width** property to 2.0", and the **Height** property to 0.25".

14. Change the **Font Name** property to Arial and the **Font Size** property to 8.

15. Click within the label associated with the text box, and change its caption to "New Address:". Next, within the Format tab, change the **Left** property to 0.1", the **Top** property to 0.4583", and the **Width** property to 0.8847".

Creating The Macros

Next, you'll want to add an OK button to invoke the first macro. The second macro is actually invoked from the frmCustomerInfo form. You must first, however, create the macros. To create the macros, perform the following steps:

1. From within the Database window, click on the Macros tab. Next, click on the New button to display the Macro Design window.

2. Use the right mouse button to display the Macro Name column within the designer.

3. Enter the first macro name as "Hide Form". Design the macro using the actions and conditions detailed in Table 18.1.

Table 18.1 The actions, conditions, and comments for the Hide Form macro.

Condition	Action	Action Arguments	Comment
Forms![New Customer Address]!Customer Name Is Null Or Forms! [New Customer Address] !NewAddress Is Null	MsgBox	**Message:** You must enter a valid company name and a new address.	This macro is attached to the OK button on the New Customer Address form.
		Beep: Yes	
		Type: None	If the user doesn't enter a valid company name or a new address, the macro shouldn't run.
...	StopMacro		The ellipsis (...) in the Condition column applies the condition to this action row as well (in other words, if the condition is true, the macro stops executing).
	SetValue	**Item:** Forms![New Customer Address].Visible	
		Expression: False	Hides the New Customer Address form to allow the **ChangeAddress** macro to resume execution.

4. Move down two lines, and enter the second macro name as "FindCustomerRecord". Design the macro using the actions and conditions detailed in Table 18.2.

5. Save the macro set as "FormMacros" and close the Macro Designer window.

Adding A Button To The Form

Now, you'll add the button to the form. From the OK button, you'll want to run the Hide Form macro, which hides the New Customer Address dialog box by setting the **Visible** property of the dialog box form to False. You'll run the ChangeAddress macro from the frmCustomerInfo form. This macro finds the customer whose address you want to change and then changes the address.

Table 18.2 **The actions, arguments, and comments for the FindCustomerRecord macro.**

Action	Action Arguments	Comment
OpenForm	**Form Name:** New Customer Address	This macro is attached to the cmdChangeAddress button on the frmCustomerInfo form.
	View: Form	
	Window Mode: Dialog	You want to set **Window Mode** to Dialog so that the macro suspends execution until the user enters the requested data in the New Customer Address dialog box. When the user clicks on the OK button, the dialog box is hidden. This allows the FindCustomerRecord macro to resume execution while still making the data in the dialog box available.
FindRecord	**Find What:** =Forms! [frmCustomerAddress] !CustomerName	Finds the first record for the company name that the user entered in the dialog box. Note the equal sign in front of the expression.
	Match: Whole Field	
	Match Case: No	
	Search: All	
	Search As Formatted: Yes	
	Only Current Field: No	
	Find First: Yes	
SetValue	**Item:** Address	Changes the address.
	Expression: Forms! [frmCustomerAddress] !NewAddress	
Close	**Object Type:** Form	Closes the dialog box.
	Object Name: New Customer Address	
	Save: Prompt	

To create the new button on the frmCustomerAddress form, perform the following steps:

1. Change back to Design View for the frmCustomerAddress form.

2. If the toolbox is not currently displayed, click on the Toolbox icon on the toolbar. Make sure the Wizard icon is selected. Within the toolbox, click on the Command Button control icon. When you move the cursor back over the form, Access 2000 displays the command button-creation cursor.

3. Click anywhere within the form designer, hold down the mouse button, and drag the mouse down and to the right to create a new command button. The size of the command button is not particularly important; you'll set its properties momentarily from the Properties dialog box. When you finish drawing the command button, Access 2000 invokes the Command Button Wizard, as shown in Figure 18.9.

4. Within the Command Button Wizard, select the Miscellaneous option from the list on the left. Within the list on the right, click on Run Macro. Click on the Next button at the bottom of the wizard's dialog box after you make your selections.

5. Access 2000 moves to the second dialog box in the Command Button Wizard, where you can select a macro to execute when the user clicks on the button. In this case, select the FormMacros.HideForm macro. After you make your selection, click on Next to move to the next dialog box in the wizard. Figure 18.10 shows the second dialog box in the Command Button Wizard.

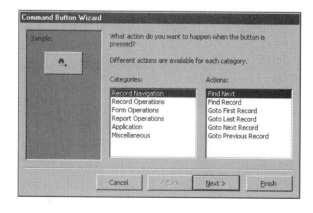

Figure 18.9
The first dialog box in the Command Button Wizard.

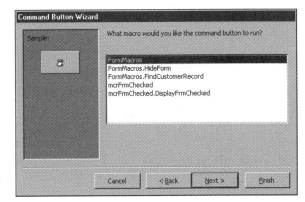

Figure 18.10
The second dialog box in the Command Button Wizard.

6. The third dialog box lets you select either text or a picture to place on the command button. Select the Text option and change the text to "OK". After you make your selection, click on Next to move to the last dialog box in the wizard.

7. Within the last dialog box of the wizard, you can assign a meaningful name to the command button. Name the command button "cmdOK". Click on Finish to exit the wizard.

8. Within the form designer, click on the cmdOK command button. Open the Properties dialog box, and change the properties as detailed in the following steps.

9. Within the Format tab, change the **Left** property to 0.2917", the **Top** property to 0.8333", the **Width** property to 2.667", and the **Height** property to 0.2813".

10. Change the **Font Name** property to Arial and the **Font Size** property to 8.

When you finish, your form will look similar to the one shown in Figure 18.11.

You can now load and execute the form frmCustomerInfo, and when you click on the Change Address button (after entering a value for the customer's name and a new value for the address), the macro will display the frmCustomerAddress form and perform the replacement operation for you.

These macros work for the task you had in mind. However, they can be hard to keep track of because there are two macros. Also,

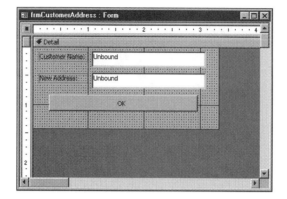

Figure 18.11
The form after you complete its design.

only simple error handling is performed in these macros. Note that if you enter an invalid or misspelled company name in the dialog box, the macro will change the address of the current record in the form without catching the error. It's much easier to catch these sorts of errors in VBA, which you'll learn more about in other chapters.

.Project   Converting A Macro To VBA Code

Now that you've discovered some of the power and many of the limitations of macros, you might be thinking about all the macros you've already written that you wish you'd developed using VBA code. Or, after seeing how easy it is to accomplish certain tasks using macros, you might be disappointed to learn how limited macros are. Fortunately, Access 2000 comes to the rescue—it's easy to convert an Access 2000 macro to VBA code. Once the macro has been converted to VBA code, the code can be modified just like any VBA module. The process of converting an Access 2000 macro to VBA code consists of six steps:

1. Open the macro you want to convert in Design View.

2. Select the File menu's Save As option. Access 2000 will display the Save As dialog box.

3. Within the As drop-down list, change the selection from "Macro" to "Module".

4. Change the name of the macro—at the very least, be sure to precede the macro name with *mdl* rather than *mcr*. After you change the selection and the module name, the Save As dialog box will look similar to what's shown in Figure 18.12.

5. Click on the OK button. The Convert Macro dialog box will appear. Within the dialog box, you can indicate whether you want to add error handling to the generated code and whether the code should include your original macro comments. After making your choices, click on the Convert button.

6. If the conversion is successful, you'll receive an indication from Access 2000 that the conversion completed. Click on the OK button.

The converted macro appears under the list of modules with "Converted Macro-" followed by the name of the macro. Click on Design to view the results of the conversion process. Figure 18.13 shows the results of a sample conversion process.

The macro is converted into distinct subroutines, one for each macro name. Note that VBA doesn't assign the same name to each subroutine, but rather it leaves a placeholder for you to assign the name you want to the subroutine. The macro is complete with logic, comments, and error handling. All macro conditions are converted into **If...Else...End If** statements. All macro comments are converted into VBA comments. Basic error-handling routines are automatically added to the code.

When you convert a macro to a VBA module, the original macro remains untouched. Furthermore, all the objects in your application will still call the macro. It's important that you realize that to effectively utilize the macro conversion options, you must find all places where the macro is called and replace these macro references with calls to the VBA function.

Figure 18.12
The Save As dialog box from the macro editor.

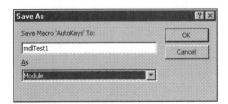

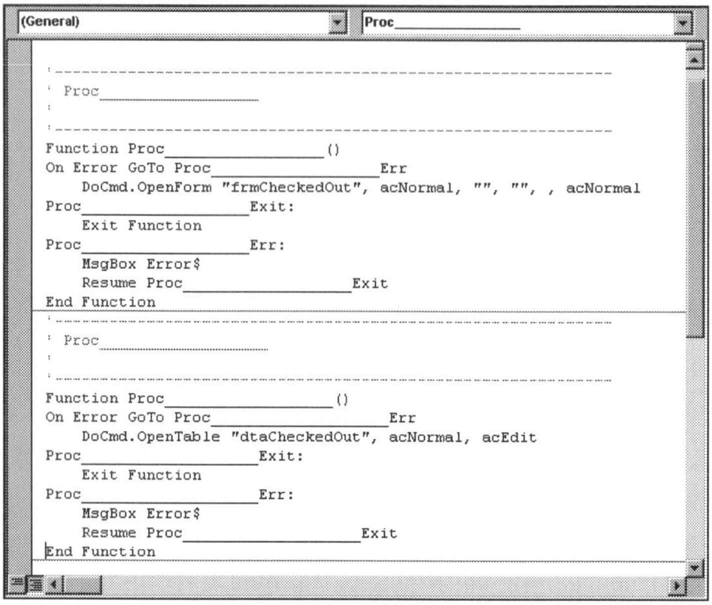


```
'------------------------------------------------------------
' Proc____
'
'------------------------------------------------------------
Function Proc____()
On Error GoTo Proc____Err
    DoCmd.OpenForm "frmCheckedOut", acNormal, "", "", , acNormal
Proc____Exit:
    Exit Function
Proc____Err:
    MsgBox Error$
    Resume Proc____Exit
End Function
'------------------------------------------------------------
' Proc____
'
'------------------------------------------------------------
Function Proc____()
On Error GoTo Proc____Err
    DoCmd.OpenTable "dtaCheckedOut", acNormal, acEdit
Proc____Exit:
    Exit Function
Proc____Err:
    MsgBox Error$
    Resume Proc____Exit
End Function
```

Figure 18.13
The converted macro within the VBA editor.

Creating An AutoExec Macro

In Chapter 19, you will learn more about some specific uses for macros that Access has built-in support for. During the course of that chapter, you'll learn about several different methods at your disposal to control what occurs when a database is opened. In many such cases, you can use an AutoExec macro.

Many developers, because they prefer to include as few macros in their applications as possible, tend to designate a startup form for their application. The startup form calls a custom AutoExec-style routine when it's opened.

The process of creating an AutoExec macro is quite simple. It's just a normal macro saved with the name *AutoExec*. An AutoExec macro usually performs tasks such as hiding or minimizing the Database window and opening a Startup form or switchboard, or directly invoking VBA code to perform complex processing.

When you're opening your own database to make changes or additions to the application, you probably won't want the AutoExec macro to execute. Remember, you can prevent the

AutoExec macro from executing by holding down the Shift key as you open the database.

Creating An AutoKeys Macro

In Chapter 19, you will learn more about AutoKeys macros. For now, it is enough to understand that an AutoKeys macro lets you redefine keystrokes within your database. You can map selected keystrokes to a single command or to a series of commands. Follow these steps to build an AutoKeys macro:

1. Open a new macro in Design View.

2. Make sure the Macro Name column is visible.

3. Enter a key name in the Macro Name column. Allowable key names are defined in Chapter 19 in Table 19.3 and can also be found within the Access Help file.

4. Select the macro action you want to associate with the key name. You can apply conditions and arguments just as in a normal macro. You can have Access 2000 execute multiple commands in one of three ways: associate multiple macro actions with a key name, perform a **RunCode** action, or perform a **RunMacro** action.

5. Continue adding key names and macro actions to the macro as desired. Separate each key name by one blank line to improve readability.

6. Save the macro as "AutoKeys". The moment you save the macro, the key names are in effect, and the keystrokes are remapped. The AutoKeys macro comes into effect automatically each time you open the database.

It's generally not a good idea to remap common Windows or Access keystrokes. Your users become accustomed to certain keystrokes having certain meanings in all Windows applications. If you attempt to alter the definition of these common keystrokes, your users will become confused and frustrated. Therefore, you should use keystroke combinations that are rarely, if ever, used within Windows.

Where To Go From Here

In this chapter, you learned the basics of working with macros in Access 2000. You also designed several different types of macros to handle different types of situations. In the next chapter, you'll look more at some of the general theory behind macro design and at some of the most common situations in which you'll use macros. You'll also take a closer look at the Hide Form macro and the FindCustomerRecord macro.

Chapter 19

Further Examining Macros

Although macros provide a useful means for you to automate and handle simple tasks within your Access 2000 applications, they do have significant limitations. In this chapter, you'll analyze some of the pros and cons of working with macros.

Although macros shouldn't be used to develop the routines that control your applications—a task better left to modules and Visual Basic for Applications (VBA) program code—a few, specific application-development tasks can be accomplished only by using macros. Therefore, you need to understand at least the basics of how macros work. Furthermore, using Access 2000 macros can often help you get started with the application-development process, because Access 2000 macros can be converted to VBA code. This means you can develop part of your application using macros, convert the macros to VBA code, and proceed with the development process. Although it's not recommended that you use this approach if you're a serious developer, it does provide a great jumpstart for those new to Access or Windows development in general.

Before we get into a more general discussion of macros, however, let's consider the actions performed by some of the macros discussed in the last chapter. Let's first consider the Hide Form macro, after which we'll look at the FindCustomerRecord macro.

Evaluating The Macros In The Chap18.mdb Database

As you saw in Chapter 18, you can create macros to automate common tasks relatively easily. We also indicated that there are many situations in which a macro is not an appropriate solution, but rather program code is called for. As the introduction to the two macros in Chapter 18 indicated, implementing the macros in the manner discussed might not be the best solution—instead, using VBA code would be a better answer. In the following sections, we'll discuss the components of the two macros and how they perform their processing. Then, we'll look at some VBA code that performs similar processing and evaluate some of the benefits of using the VBA code over using a comparable macro.

Evaluating The Hide Form Macro

As discussed previously, the Hide Form macro is attached to the OK button on the frmNewCustomerAddress form. Its purpose is to hide the form from the user when he or she clicks on the OK button. After the form is hidden, the program code within the FindCustomerRecord macro will resume its processing. The form can then be shown again at any later point in the program's processing by either a reinvocation of the form or the use of the VBA **Show** method. Table 19.1 details the actions specified in the Hide Form macro.

The first line in the Hide Form macro makes sure the user has entered a non-**NULL** value for both the txtCustomerName and txtNewAddress fields. If the user has not, the macro will display a

Table 19.1 The actions, arguments, and conditions for the Hide Form macro.

Condition	Action	Action Arguments
Forms![New Customer Address]!CustomerName Is Null Or Forms![New Customer Address]!NewAddress Is Null	MsgBox	**Message:** You must enter a valid company name and a new address.
		Beep: Yes
		Type: None
...	StopMacro	
	SetValue	**Item:** Forms![New Customer Address].Visible
		Expression: False

NOTE

The macro code does not check the value of either field for its validity—that is, it doesn't make sure that the values are in the correct format, that the customer name equals an existing name in the database, and so on. Rather, the condition merely ensures that the user has entered some value in each field. As you'll note later in this chapter, this inability to evaluate or verify complex conditions simply and efficiently is one of the largest limitations when using macros for program design.

message box to alert the user to the problem. The condition, then, for the first line in the macro is as follows:

```
Forms![frmNewCustomerAddress]!txtCustomerName Is Null _
  Or Forms![frmNewCustomerAddress]!txtNewAddress Is Null
```

The processing performed by the condition is pretty straightforward—it checks to make sure that neither text box contains a **NULL** value.

When the macro executes, the first thing it does is evaluate the condition discussed previously. In the event the condition evaluates to True—that is, in the event that either text box contains a **NULL** value—the macro code then moves on to execute the first statement, which is a call to the macro **MsgBox** function. The **Message** property specifies the message to display within the box—in this case, a warning to the user that the macros cannot continue execution until the user enters a value in both fields. Valid values for the **Message** property include any string value less than 255 characters long. The **Beep** property specifies that the computer should issue an audible warning when it displays the message box. The **Beep** property is a Yes or No value, indicating either that an audible warning should be issued or that an audible warning should not be issued. The **Type** property specifies that there's no type to the message box—that is, the message box has no special properties. Other valid values for the **Type** property include **Critical, Warning?, Warning!,** and **Information**.

The **Critical** type indicates a system- or program-critical failure and should only be used in situations where something catastrophic has occurred (see Figure 19.1). The **Warning?** message box type indicates a warning message to the user, which is displayed with a question mark (see Figure 19.2).

Figure 19.1
The **Critical** message box.

Figure 19.2
The **Warning?** message box.

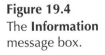

Whichever macro-created message box you choose, it will only display a single option—OK. Message boxes you create from VBA will, instead, provide you with many construction choices for your message boxes—both in appearance and in options offered to the user.

The **Warning!** message box type also indicates a warning message—this one with an exclamation point rather than a question (see Figure 19.3). The second type of warning should be used in situations where the problem is more significant than a basic warning but is not yet critical. The **Information** message box type displays with a blue "i" inside of a voice bubble and indicates that the program is providing additional information to the user (see Figure 19.4).

In the next line of the macro definition, the Condition column contains an ellipsis (...). This ellipsis tells the macro interpreter that the condition from the previous row also applies to the current row. In this case, if the condition is again True (that is, there's a **NULL** value in either of the textboxes), the interpreter will cease the execution of the macro by invocation of the **StopMacro** action. As with the previous line, if the condition is False, the interpreter will go ahead and fall through to the next line in the macro.

In the next line of the macro, the macro interpreter encounters the **SetValue** action, which you can use to assign a value to any assignable object property. In this particular case, the statement

Figure 19.3
The **Warning!** message box.

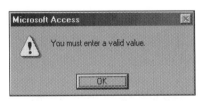

Figure 19.4
The **Information** message box.

sets the **Visible** property of the frmNewCustomerAddress form (which is part of the **Forms** collection) to False—this has the result of hiding the frmNewCustomerAddress form from the user.

Therefore, as indicated previously, the frmNewCustomerAddress form is opened from elsewhere and then, when it closes, the execution at the other location continues. Specifically, the FindCustomerRecord macro opens the frmNewCustomerAddress form, pauses its execution while the form is open, and then resumes its execution after the form closes. In the next section, we'll look more closely at the FindCustomerRecord macro and what actions it performs over the course of its execution.

Evaluating the FindCustomerRecord Macro

So, as you saw in the previous section, the Hide Form macro is pretty simple. Aside from the key condition that it has to evaluate, the macro really only performs a single action. The FindCustomerRecord macro, on the other hand, performs some more complex processing. Before we start to discuss some of the specifics of the macro, let's look again at the statements that make up the macro (see Table 19.2).

The first action with the macro opens the frmNewCustomer-Address form, providing the user with the opportunity to enter customer and address information. The **OpenForm** action, as discussed in the previous chapter, opens a single form. The **Form Name** argument specifies the name of the form to open. The **View** argument specifies that the form should be opened in Form View—that is, user interface view. You can also specify Design View, Print Preview, or Datasheet View. The **Window Mode** argument, in this particular macro, specifies that the window should be opened as a dialog box. If you set the **Window Mode** argument to **Normal**, the macro will open the window to its default size, as specified within the form's design. If you select the **Hidden** argument, the macro will open the window but hide it from display. If you select the **Icon** argument, the macro will open the window but minimize it and display its icon in the toolbar (or

Table 19.2 **The conditions, actions, and arguments for the FindCustomerRecord macro.**

Conditions	Action	Action Arguments
	OpenForm	**Form Name:** frmNewCustomerAddress
		View: Form
		Window Mode: Dialog
	FindRecord	**Find What:** =Forms![frmNewCustomerAddress]! CustomerName
		Match: Whole Field
		Match Case: No
		Search: All
		Search As Formatted: Yes
		Only Current Field: No
		Find First: Yes
	SetValue	**Item:** Address
		Expression: Forms![frmNewCustomerAddress]!NewAddress
	Close	**Object Type:** Form
		Object Name: frmNewCustomerAddress
		Save: Prompt

▶**Tip**

*You want to set the **Window Mode** argument of the **OpenForm** action to **Dialog** so that the macro suspends execution until the user enters the requested data in the New Customer Address dialog box. When the user clicks on the OK button, the dialog box is hidden. This allows the FindCustomerRecord macro to resume execution while still making the data in the dialog box available.*

within the parent window if the window is a child window). Finally, if you select the **Dialog** argument, the macro interpreter will open the window as a dialog box, assigning it the properties **PopUp** and **Modal**.

After the dialog box closes (which is driven by the previously discussed macro), the macro resumes its execution with the **FindRecord** action. **FindRecord** locates a record within the underlying table or database. It has a series of options that let you define how the engine should perform the search. The first option is **Find What**, which specifies the search string the action should use. In this case, it looks for the string in the CustomerName text box. In general, for a construction of this type, you'll want to look at some control that receives user input. However, the control in question might be a combo box, a text box, some information from a series of text boxes (such as date range information), and so on.

The next several options instruct the action on how to perform the search. For the **Match** option, you can specify **Whole Field**, **Any Part Of Field**, or **Start Of Field**. These control what criteria the engine uses in the search. How you've constructed your search information will determine which of these options you use. The next option, **Match Case**, tells the engine whether it should perform a case-sensitive search. The **Search** option lets you specify whether the search should go through the entirety of the recordset, no matter where the record pointer is currently (the **All** option), from the current record pointer in the table to the end (the **Down** option), or from the current record pointer in the table to the beginning (the **Up** option).

The next option, **Search As Formatted**, lets you specify whether the engine should search the formatted data to find a match or whether it should work against the raw data. The option is important when searching Date fields, for instance, which are stored as integer variants but are formatted as human-readable dates. In general, the value you specify here will be dependent on the type of data you're searching.

The **Only Current Field** option lets you tell the engine to search only a single field for the data—presuming you've set a current field already. Searching only a single field will speed your searches but may cause unpredictable effects if you're not sure what the current field is. The **Find First** option also lets you specify how to search the database—if you set this option to Yes, the engine will always start searching from the first record in the recordset, no matter what the current record pointer is.

▶Tip

*If you do not specify an expression with the **SetValue** action, Access 2000 attempts to clear the field entirely. Depending on your macro and the nature of the field, such actions may cause an error—setting a value that cannot be **NULL** to empty, for example, is a common mistake.*

The next action is the **SetValue** action. This action lets you change the value of a specific item. In this case, you're changing the value of the Address field in the record located by the **FindRecord** action to the new address value specified in the NewAddress box on the frmNewCustomerAddress form. The **Expression** option lets you specify the expression to use when setting the value. Depending on what type of value you're setting, this option can even let you set new values based on computations—multiplying some field by a third value or even some set of fields by other values, and so on.

After the macro changes the address, it should go ahead and clean up after itself—specifically, by closing the frmNewCustomer-Address form. It does so by invoking the **Close** action. The **Object Type** option lets you specify additional information about what to close. It might be any of the Access-supported objects—from a table to a data access page. The **Object Name** option, as you might expect, is required—otherwise, the macro will not know which object to close. The **Save** option lets you specify how the engine should close the object—whether it should prompt the user to save information (in this case, the underlying table) or whether it should abort the action.

A Visual Basic Example Of Finding And Changing A Customer Address

Instead of using a macro, you can attach the following Visual Basic code to the frmNewCustomerAddress button on the Orders form. Chapter 21 discusses the Visual Basic code in this example in more detail; it's reprinted here for you solely as a reference:

```
Function ChangeCustomerAddress() As Boolean
    Dim dbs As Database
    Dim rst As Recordset
    Dim strCustomerName As String
    Dim strNewAddress As String
    Dim strCriteria As String

    On Error GoTo ChangeCustomerAddress_Err

    Set dbs = CurrentDb()
    Set rst = dbs.OpenRecordset("Customers", _
        dbOpenDynaset)
    strCustomerName = _
        InputBox("Enter the company name", _
        "Company Name")
    If Len(strCustomerName) = 0 Then _
        Exit Function
    strNewAddress = InputBox("Enter the new address", _
        "New Address")
    If Len(strNewAddress) = 0 Then _
        Exit Function
    strCriteria ="[CompanyName] = " & """" & _
        strCustomerName & """"
```

Tip

As mentioned previously, one of the most compelling reasons to use VBA is its ability to handle errors efficiently. We'll consider this issue more in later chapters.

```
With rst
  .MoveFirst
  .FindFirst strCriteria
  If .NoMatch Then
    MsgBox("The company name you entered " & _
        "isn't valid.")
    Exit Function
  End If
  ' Set the Address field to strNewAddress.
  .Edit
    !Address = strNewAddress
  .Update
End With
MsgBox("The address has been changed.")
ChangeCustomerAddress = True

ChangeCustomerAddress_Bye:
  Exit Function

ChangeCustomerAddress_Err:
  MsgBox Err.Description, vbOKOnly, "Error = " & _
      Err.Number
  ChangeCustomerAddress = False
  Resume ChangeCustomerAddress_Bye
End Function
```

In addition to performing the same processing as the macro pair we analyzed earlier in the chapter, the VBA code also includes error processing and additional feedback information for the user.

Understanding Macros

A macro is a set of one or more actions that each perform a particular operation, such as opening a form or printing a report. Macros can help you automate common tasks. For example, you can run a macro that prints a report when a user clicks a command button.

A macro can be one macro composed of a sequence of actions, or it can be a macro group. You can also use a conditional expression to determine whether in some cases an action will be carried out when a macro runs.

If you have numerous macros, grouping related macros in macro groups can help you to manage your database more easily. To display the names of macros for a macro group, click Macro Names on the View menu in the Macro window.

Understanding Modules

Whereas a macro is a specific task set that performs a sequence of actions, a module contains a collection of VBA declarations and procedures that are stored together as a unit. Two types of modules are available—modules associated with a specific form or report and modules that are standalone, known as *class modules*.

Modules differ from macros primarily in two ways. First, as you have already seen, macros perform a prespecified series of steps, or actions, that take advantage of built-in Microsoft Access features. Second, macros provide only a limited set of actions for you to take advantage of and do not directly allow for the creation of your own functions, unlike VBA. Macros are useful for performing certain specific tasks but are limited in scope. Modules, on the other hand, expose the entire VBA model, providing you with a broad set of functions, including calls to the Windows application programming interface (API), to truly make your applications highly functional.

Considering Macros Vs. Modules

Clearly, using macros in certain cases makes sense, and in other cases, using modules makes more sense. Some general rules govern when you should use each. Typically, choose macros if your design requirements meet most or all of the following:

- *You need to prototype your application quickly*. Macros make it simple to open, close, and manipulate forms and reports, which makes it easier for you to rapidly mock up the application's flow.

- *You're really not concerned about bulletproofing your application*. Because macros can't trap for errors, Access 2000 handles any runtime errors that occur while your application is running. If

NOTE

*In the Access 2000 VBA implementation, you can create menus and toolbars directly from code, using the **CommandBars** collection and the **CommandBar** object. You can also use the **KeyDown** and **KeyPress** events from within form modules to capture keystrokes, although you're still better served using macros for global keystroke interception.*

you're providing an application for your own purposes or for in-house use, it may not be worth your while to trap for errors.

- *You need to trap keystrokes or provide a macro that runs automatically without any command-line interference.* Each of these actions requires a macro (although you can trap keystrokes from VBA, it's a little more difficult).

On the other hand, you should use VBA for most of the other tasks you want to perform. It should be your programming model of choice for larger applications, because you can easily document, comment, and control VBA code. Additionally, you must use VBA code if you need to perform any of the following tasks:

- Call functions in dynamic link libraries (DLL), including any and all Windows API functions.

- Control transaction processing—specifically, rollbacks and commitments of partially completed sets of actions.

- Use scoped variables (variables that are visible to program code only in certain parts of your application).

- Provide commented printouts of your application. (In fact, you can print out macros, but it's much more difficult to document them in depth than it is to document VBA code.)

Using Macros Within Your Access Applications

In general, as detailed previously, you'll use macros within your applications for three specific situations: trapping keystrokes globally, providing user-defined menus, and executing a macro from the command line or automatically at startup.

Using The AutoKeys Macro

By default, Access 2000 looks for a macro named AutoKeys to control the global key mappings for an application. When you specify a value within the macro, you assign it to a specific key set. The syntax for the macro names you can use is shown in Table 19.3.

Table 19.3 The macro syntax for the AutoKeys macro group.

Syntax	Key Combinations
^A or ^2	Ctrl+any letter or number
{Fn}	Any function key (1 through 12)
^{Fn}	Ctrl+any function key (1 through 12)
+{Fn}	Shift+any function key (1 through 12)
^+{Fn}	Ctrl+Shift+any function key (1 through 12)
{Insert}	Insert key
^{Insert}	Ctrl+Insert key
+{Insert}	Shift+Insert key
^+{Insert}	Ctrl+Shift+Insert key
{Delete}	Delete key
^{Delete}	Ctrl+Delete key
+{Delete}	Shift+Delete key
^+{Delete}	Ctrl+Shift+Delete key

Just as with any other macro you create, the Action column of the macro can contain any of the standard macro actions and can use the **RunCode** action to invoke VBA code from the given keystroke.

To separate the key mapping, simply place a new macro name (actually, the keystroke set to map) on a new row. Access 2000 will stop playing back each macro when it runs across a new name in the macro group. You can also separate each macro from the next with a blank line and, perhaps, some comments.

Figure 19.5 shows the macro editor after a pair of macros have been added to the file. In this case, if the user presses the Ctrl+F1 key combination, the application will display a simple message box and beep at the user. If the user presses the Ctrl+P key combination, the application will print the currently open object.

Limitations Of The AutoKeys Macro

As you can see in Table 19.3, a lot of key combinations are noticeably absent from the keys you can map within the

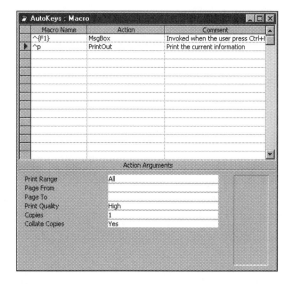

Figure 19.5
The macro editor after a pair of keystroke combinations have been created.

AutoKeys macro. Specifically, you can't trap the following key combinations from within the AutoKeys macro:

- Alt+function keys
- Alt+Insert key
- Alt+Delete key
- The Esc key
- Cursor movement keys (alone or in combination with Ctrl, Shift, or Alt)
- Alt+A through Alt+Z (which Access 2000 reserves for hot key use)

You can trap these keys, but only from within your VBA code for the application.

Restricting Key Playback To Specific Situations

Although keys you assign to the AutoKeys macro will normally take effect anywhere in the Access 2000 environment, you can limit the situations where the macro will take effect. If you set a condition in the macro sheet's Condition column, the macro attached to the particular keystroke will be invoked only if the

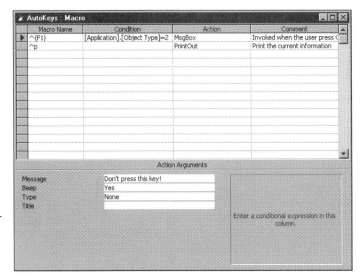

Figure 19.6
The Macro window after a condition has been added to the Ctrl+F1 macro.

▶Tip

*You'll learn more about using command constants such as **RunCode** in Chapters 20 and 21.*

condition is met. For example, in Figure 19.6, the Ctrl+F1 macro you saw previously has been modified to limit its execution to only occur if the user is viewing a form when the macro is invoked.

You can also use the **RunCode** action and invoke VBA code that determines whether to perform the action. For example, you can use the **RunCode** action's **DoMsgBox** invocation within the macro and include the following code within a module:

```
Function DoMsgBox()
  If Application.CurrentObjectType = A_FORM Then
    MsgBox "Invoke the VBA Code", vbOKOnly, "Test Box"
    Beep
  End If
End Function
```

Running A Macro Automatically

For many applications, you'll want Access 2000 to take a specific action or series of actions automatically every time the user loads the application. Although Access 2000 lets you use the Tools|Startup menu option to load forms at startup, you need to use a macro to perform more complex processing. The macro that you'll use must be named AutoExec, and after you create it, Access 2000 will automatically execute the macro each time the database loads.

NOTE

If your application uses an AutoExec macro and you also specify a macro to execute at startup, Access 2000 will first run the AutoExec macro and then run the specified macro.

Loading Other Macros At Startup

In addition to specifying the AutoExec macro, you can also manually instruct an application to load and execute a specific macro at startup by including the macro's name in the command-line invocation of the application, as shown here:

```
MSACCESS AppName.mdb /xMacroName
```

Access 2000 will run the macro name that follows the **/x** switch as soon as it loads the application. You might, for example, create a series of shortcuts on the desktop that load different parts of an application as the startup screen and use a custom macro to open that portion of the application.

Bypassing The AutoExec Macro

If you create a macro that runs automatically every time you load an application, it's almost inevitable that a time will come when you'll want to run the application without running the macro. To bypass the AutoExec macro, for example, simply press and hold the Shift key while the application loads. Access 2000 will load the application but will bypass the macro.

If your application is running in the Access 2000 runtime environment (rather than the development environment), the runtime engine will ignore the Shift key and will execute the AutoExec macro normally. In other words, there's no way for users not using the development environment to bypass the macro.

Using The DoCmd Object

Most macro commands can be performed in VBA code using the **DoCmd** object. The macro action becomes a method of the **DoCmd** object; the arguments associated with each macro action become the arguments of the method. For example, the following method of the **DoCmd** object is used to open a form:

```
DoCmd.OpenForm "frmCheckedOut", acNormal, "", _
    "[tblCheckedOut]![OutDate]>Date() -30", _
    acEdit, acNormal
```

NOTE

*The **openargs** argument is available only in VBA; you cannot use it if you create the macro solely from the Macro window.*

The **OpenForm** method of the **DoCmd** object opens the form that appears as the first argument to the method. The second argument indicates the view in which the form will be opened. The third and fourth arguments are used to specify a filter and **Where** condition, respectively. The fifth argument of the **OpenForm** method is used to specify the data mode for the form (Add, Edit, or Read Only). The sixth argument is used to indicate the window mode (Normal, Hidden, Minimized, or Dialog).

Finally, VBA makes available an additional seventh argument you can use within your program—the optional **openargs** argument. You can use this string expression to set the form's **OpenArgs** property. This setting can then be used by code in a form module, such as the **Open** event procedure. You can also refer to the **OpenArgs** property in macros and expressions.

For example, suppose the form you open is a continuous form list of clients. If you want the focus to move to a specific client record when the form opens, you can specify the client name with the **openargs** argument and then use the **FindRecord** method to move the focus to the record for the client with the specified name.

Notice the intrinsic constants that are used for the **OpenForm** arguments; these greatly aid in the readability of the code. You can find the arguments for each **DoCmd** method in the Access 2000 online Help.

Understanding The Methods Of The DoCmd Object

In short, almost every action you can perform from within a macro—from applying a filter to transferring text—can be done using the **DoCmd** object. Most of the methods you'll use have a list of parameters that correspond exactly with the action arguments for the method's action equivalent.

However, there are some actions that don't have an equivalent **DoCmd** method, as shown in the following list:

- **AddMenu**—You should use the VBA methods of adding menus to your applications.

- **MsgBox**—Use the VBA **MsgBox** function instead.

- **RunApp**—Use the VBA **Shell** function instead to run another application.

- **RunCode**—Run the target function directly in VBA instead.

- **SendKeys**—Use the VBA **SendKeys** statement instead.

- **SetValue**—Set the value directly in VBA instead.

- **StopAllMacros**—There's no VBA equivalent to this action.

- **StopMacro**—There's no VBA equivalent to this action.

Going Straight To The Code

Most Microsoft Access 2000 developers who've made the leap from writing macros to using VBA code rarely go back to using the Expression Builder or the Macro Builder. And yet, every time you click the build button (...) on a property sheet, the Choose Builder dialog box pops up, asking you which builder you want to use.

If, for the most part, you want to control events by writing Visual Basic for Applications code (using the Code Builder) rather than Access 2000 macros and would prefer to bypass this dialog box, you can use the following procedure to accomplish this goal:

1. In Access 2000, open any existing database.

2. In the Database window, click on a table, form, or report on the appropriate tab, and then click on the Design button on the toolbar. The database object you selected will now be open in Design View.

3. Select Tools|Options. Access 2000 displays the Options dialog box.

4. On the Forms/Reports tab, make sure the Always Use Event Procedures checkbox is selected. Click on OK to close the dialog box.

Tip

You can always create macros using the Macros tab in the Database window, and then associate those macros with whatever object you need to. Suppressing the Choose Builder dialog box has no impact on your ability to continue using macros within your applications.

Where To Go From Here

In this chapter, you've learned more about working with macros in Access 2000. You've also learned about several of the different types of macros you can use to resolve specific issues within your applications. In the next chapter, we'll move on to a discussion of command constants in Access 2000 and how you can use them with and in the place of macros to accomplish many of the same goals as macros. Because command constants are used entirely from VBA, we'll also be doing some more extended VBA programming with the constants. Then, in Chapter 21, we'll look more closely at the VBA code introduced here as a potential replacement for the macro pair we designed and analyzed in Chapter 18 and in this chapter.

Chapter 20

Working With Command Constants And Common Dialogs

Access 2000 provides you with many different tools you can use to effectively manage the interface you provide your users.

In the previous chapters, you worked extensively with Access 2000 macros and learned a lot about the functionality those macros expose to you. You also learned that macros are not necessarily the best way to accomplish certain tasks—but that they may be applicable in some cases.

In this chapter, we'll focus on the use of the command constants (sometimes called *action constants*) and the Windows Common Dialog control, as well as how you can use these objects to simplify your programming efforts. We'll also design some code and place it in several event handlers, which will help show common uses of these objects. We'll analyze the code in more depth in Chapter 21.

.Project   Working With The DoCmd Action

Nearly any macro action command can be invoked using the **DoCmd** action from VBA code. Although the number of examples is as large as the number of different macro actions, the following three sections discuss how to work with the **DoCmd** action using the three Transfer macro items.

Importing Database Data Using Code

The **TransferDatabase** method of the **DoCmd** object is used to import data from a database such as Visual FoxPro, dBASE, Paradox, or another Access database. It looks like this:

```
Sub ImportDatabase()
  DoCmd.TransferDatabase _
      TransferType:=acImport, _
      DatabaseType:="Microsoft Access", _
      DatabaseName:="Chap19.mdb",
      ObjectType:=acTable, _
      Source:="Customers", _
      Destination:="tblCustomers", _
      StructureOnly:=False
End Sub
```

To execute this code, make sure you add the correct path to the Chap19.mdb database in the **DatabaseName** argument. The performance of this code will be explained in detail in Chapter 21.

Importing Text Data Using Code

The **TransferText** method of the **DoCmd** object is used to import text from a text file. Here's an example:

```
Sub ImportText()
  DoCmd.TransferText _
      TransferType:=acImportDelim, _
      TableName:="tblCustomerText", _
      FileName:="Customer.Txt"
End Sub
```

Importing Spreadsheet Data Using Code

The **TransferSpreadsheet** method of the **DoCmd** object is used to import data from a spreadsheet file. Here's an example:

```
Sub ImportSpreadsheet()
  DoCmd.TransferSpreadsheet _
      TransferType:=acImport, _
      SpreadsheetType:=5, _
      TableName:="tblCustomerSpread", _
      FileName:="Customer.Xls",
      HasFieldNames:=True
End Sub
```

Project Working With The RunCommand Action

You can use the **RunCommand** action to run a built-in Microsoft Access command. The command may appear on a Microsoft Access menu bar, toolbar, or shortcut menu.

The following example uses the **RunCommand** method to open the Options dialog box (available by selecting Tools|Options):

```
Function DisplayOptions() As Boolean
  On Error GoTo Error_DisplayOptions
  DoCmd.RunCommand acCmdOptions
  DisplayOptions = True

Exit_DisplayOptions:
  Exit Function

Error_DisplayOptions:
  MsgBox Err & ": " & Err.Description
  DisplayOptions = False
  Resume Exit_DisplayOptions
End Function
```

NOTE

Although you haven't worked with error-handling routines in any depth at this point, this code includes error-handling capabilities. You'll learn more about error handling in Chapters 26 and 27.

Project Working With The Common Dialog Control

Now that you've worked with some of the built-in Access 2000 intrinsic objects, it's worthwhile to work with another example of an object that's closely managed by constants. Over the next several sections, you'll add such a control—in this case, the Common Dialog control—to your Access form and then write VBA code to manage the control so that you can see how it works.

NOTE

Depending on what other Microsoft components you have on your system—for example, perhaps you allowed the Office Installer to install Internet Explorer 5 on your computer—you may have an earlier version of the Common Dialog control or none at all. Additionally, if you use Visual Basic 5 or some other edition before the version 6 release, you may have an early version of the control. For the purposes of this chapter, the earlier version will work fine, but you may want to consider upgrading your other components so that everything is fully compatible with Office 2000, which requires version 6.

Adding The Common Dialog Control To A Form

The first thing you must do—as you might expect—is to create a form and then to add the Common Dialog control to the form. To do so, perform the following steps:

1. From within the Database window, change to the Forms object. Next, double-click on the Create New Form In Design View icon. Access 2000 will open a blank form (Form1) in Design View.

2. If the toolbox is not currently displayed, click on the Toolbox icon on the toolbar. Within the toolbox, click on the More Controls icon, as shown in Figure 20.1. When clicked, this icon displays a list of available ActiveX controls that are registered on the system, as shown in Figure 20.2.

3. Within the list, use the arrow at the list's bottom to scroll down until you're presented with the Microsoft Common Dialog Control, Version 6.0 option. Select the option. Access 2000 will close the list and display a generic drawing tool icon on the form.

4. On the form, draw the common dialog near the top-left corner. Access 2000 will display a small icon that looks like a dialog box. (You'll see this later in the chapter in Figure 20.3.)

5. Open the Properties dialog box for the Common Dialog control, and change its name to cdlChap20.

Now that you've added the Common Dialog control, it's time to add the other controls to the form. You'll do this in the next two sections.

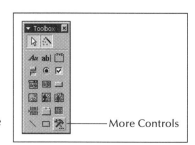

Figure 20.1
The toolbox includes the More Controls icon.

More Controls

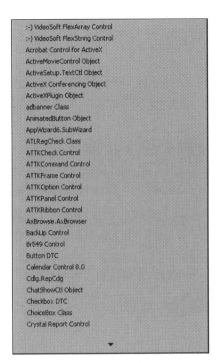

Figure 20.2
The list of additional controls displayed by the toolbox (yours will vary).

Project Adding A Rich Text Box Control To The Form

Since the Common Dialog control is generally used to help you more easily manage tasks such as saving files, opening files, and generating print information, you need to add something to the form that you can then use as the source of the information to manage. One of the best controls for such a task is the Rich Text Box control. To add a Rich Text Box control to your form, perform the following steps:

1. Within the toolbox, click on the More Controls icon. When clicked, this icon displays a list of available ActiveX controls that are registered on the system.

2. Within the list, use the arrow at the list's bottom to scroll down until you're presented with the Microsoft Rich Text

Box Control, Version 6.0 option. Select the option. Access 2000 will close the list and display a generic drawing tool icon on the form.

3. Draw the Rich Text Box control so that it fills the majority of the form, leaving space for six command buttons across the bottom (you'll draw these buttons in the next section).

4. Open the Properties dialog box for the Rich Text Box control, and change its **Name** property to rtbChap20. Additionally, change the **Text** property to nothing (delete its contents).

In the next section, you'll add the various command buttons that we'll use to write code to manage the Common Dialog control. After that, you'll begin adding code to the buttons, as well as to some of the events exposed by the Rich Text Box control.

Saving The Form

Now that you have some components in place on the form, you should go ahead and save the form so that, in the event of a catastrophe, you don't lose your work. Save the form as frmCommonDialog.

Adding Command Buttons To The Form

Now, you'll add the buttons to the form. From each button, you'll want to run VBA code, so you should turn off the Wizards button in the toolbox before you start to draw. To create the new buttons on the frmCommonDialog form, perform the following steps:

1. If the toolbox is not currently displayed, click on the Toolbox icon on the toolbar. Within the toolbox, click on the Command Button control icon. When you move the cursor back over the form, Access 2000 will display the command button-creation cursor.

2. Click anywhere within the free space of the form designer, hold down the mouse button, and drag it down and to the right to create a new command button. The size of the command button is not particularly important; you'll set its properties momentarily from the Properties dialog box.

▶**Tip**

If the Wizard icon is selected, Access 2000 will try to make you associate the button with some specific task using the Command Button Wizard, which you saw in Chapter 18. Turning the wizard off will make your development process go more quickly, because you can work directly with the control without completing all the steps in the wizard.

3. If the Properties dialog box is not displayed, press Alt+Enter to display the dialog box. Change the button's properties as detailed in the following steps.

4. Within the Format tab, change the **Caption** property to Show Open. Change the **Left** property to 0.125", the **Top** property to 1.625", the **Width** property to 0.75", and the **Height** property to 0.2917".

5. Within the Other tab, change the **Name** property to cmdShowOpen.

6. Within the toolbox, click on the Command Button control icon. When you move the cursor back over the form, Access 2000 will display the command button-creation cursor.

7. Click anywhere within the free space of the form designer, hold down the mouse button, and drag it down and to the right to create a new command button. The size of the command button is not particularly important; you'll set its properties momentarily from the Properties dialog box. Change the button's properties as detailed in the following steps.

8. Within the Format tab, change the **Caption** property to Save As. Change the **Left** property to 0.975", the **Top** property to 1.625", the **Width** property to 0.75", and the **Height** property to 0.2917".

9. Within the Other tab, change the **Name** property to cmdShowSaveAs.

10. Within the toolbox, click on the Command Button control icon.

11. Click anywhere within the free space of the form designer, hold down the mouse button, and drag it down and to the right to create a new command button. The size of the command button is not particularly important; you'll set its properties momentarily from the Properties dialog box. Change the button's properties as detailed in the following steps.

12. Within the Format tab, change the **Caption** property to Fonts. Change the **Left** property to 1.825", the **Top** property to 1.625", the **Width** property to 0.75", and the **Height** property to 0.2917".

13. Within the Other tab, change the **Name** property to cmdShowFont.

14. Within the toolbox, click on the Command Button control icon.

15. Click anywhere within the free space of the form designer, hold down the mouse button, and drag it down and to the right to create a new command button. The size of the command button is not particularly important; you'll set its properties momentarily from the Properties dialog box. Change the button's properties as detailed in the following steps.

16. Within the Format tab, change the **Caption** property to Colors. Change the **Left** property to 2.675", the **Top** property to 1.625", the **Width** property to 0.75", and the **Height** property to 0.2917".

17. Within the Other tab, change the **Name** property to cmdShowColors.

18. Within the toolbox, click on the Command Button control icon.

19. Click anywhere within the free space of the form designer, hold down the mouse button, and drag it down and to the right to create a new command button. The size of the command button is not particularly important; you'll set its properties momentarily from the Properties dialog box. Change the button's properties as detailed in the following steps.

20. Within the Format tab, change the **Caption** property to Print. Change the **Left** property to 3.525", the **Top** property to 1.625", the **Width** property to 0.75", and the **Height** property to 0.2917".

21. Within the Other tab, change the **Name** property to cmdShowPrinter.

22. Within the toolbox, click on the Command Button control icon.

23. Click anywhere within the free space of the form designer, hold down the mouse button, and drag it down and to the right to create a new command button. The size of the command button is not particularly important; you'll set its properties momentarily from the Properties dialog box. Change the button's properties as detailed in the following steps.

24. Within the Format tab, change the **Caption** property to Help. Change the **Left** property to 4.375", the **Top** property to 1.625", the **Width** property to 0.75", and the **Height** property to 0.2917".

25. Within the Other tab, change the **Name** property to cmdShowHelp.

When you finish constructing the form, it should look similar to the one shown in Figure 20.3.

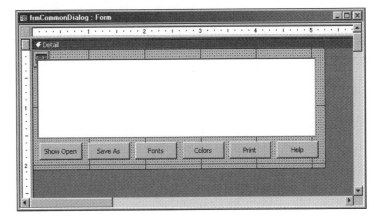

Figure 20.3
The frmCommonDialog form after you finish its design.

Project Adding Code To The Form's Stubs

Now that you've designed the interface, you need to add VBA code to the form. In the following sections, we'll look at the various events you need to add code to so that the application runs correctly. You'll learn more about the code in Chapter 21, as well as what other techniques you can use when manipulating the Common Dialog control.

Adding Code To The cmdShowOpen Button

As you might expect with command buttons, the only event you need to code is the **Click** event. Open the VBA interface (by choosing the **Click** event from the Properties dialog box or by whatever other means you prefer), and move to the **Click** event for the cmdShowOpen button. Within this event, enter the following code:

```
Private Sub cmdShowOpen_Click()
  cdlChap20.FileName = ""
  cdlChap20.Filter = "RTF Files (*.rtf)|*.rtf"
  cdlChap20.InitDir = CurDir
  cdlChap20.ShowOpen
  If cdlChap20.FileName = "" Then
    MsgBox "You Must Specify a File Name", _
      vbExclamation, "File Cannot Be Opened!"
  Else
    rtbChap20.LoadFile cdlChap20.FileName
    cmdShowSaveAs.Enabled = True
  End If
End Sub
```

You'll look more closely at this code in Chapter 21. However, even the most cursory examination should show you that the code uses the Common Dialog control and the Rich Text Box control. What it does with these controls is discussed later. For now, it's enough to know that when the user clicks on the Show Open button, the application will display the dialog box shown in Figure 20.4.

Adding Code To The cmdShowSaveAs Button

As was the case in the previous section, the only event you need to code for the cmdShowSaveAs button is the **Click** event. Open

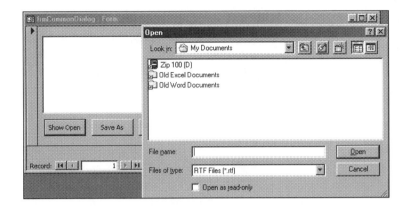

Figure 20.4
The File Open
dialog box.

the VBA interface and move to the **Click** event for the cmdShow-SaveAs button. Within this event, enter the following code:

```
Private Sub cmdShowSaveAs_Click()
  cdlChap20.Filter = "RTF Files (*.rtf)|*.rtf"
  cdlChap20.ShowSave
  If cdlChap20.FileName = "" Then
    MsgBox "You Must Specify a File Name", _
        vbExclamation, "File NOT Saved!"
  Else
    rtbChap20.SaveFile cdlChap20.FileName
  End If
End Sub
```

You'll look more closely at this code in Chapter 21. However, you should notice that the code uses the Common Dialog control and the Rich Text Box control. What it does with these controls is discussed later. For now, it's enough to know that when the user clicks on the Save As button, the application will display the dialog box shown in Figure 20.5.

Adding Code To The cmdShowFont Button

We'll add code to the cmdShowFont button that's similar to the code you've seen so far. This button's code will display the Font dialog box. Open the VBA interface, and move to the **Click** event for the cmdShowFont button. Within this event, enter the following code:

```
Private Sub cmdShowFont_Click()
  Dim ctl As Control
```

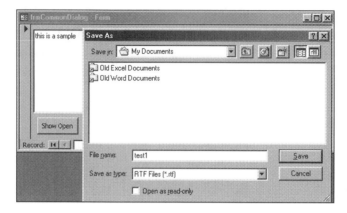

Figure 20.5
The Save As dialog box.

```
cdlChap20.Flags = 1
cdlChap20.ShowFont
For Each ctl In Controls
   If TypeOf ctl Is CommandButton Then
     With ctl
       .FontName = cdlChap20.FontName
       .FontBold = cdlChap20.FontBold
       .FontItalic = cdlChap20.FontItalic
       .FontSize = cdlChap20.FontSize
     End With
   End If
 Next ctl
End Sub
```

You'll look more closely at this code in Chapter 21. However, note that this code uses the Common Dialog control and a loop that iterates through all the other controls on the form. When the user clicks on the Fonts button, the application will display the dialog box shown in Figure 20.6.

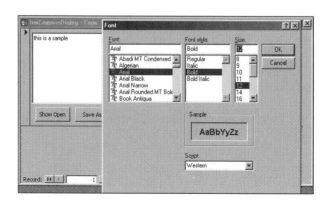

Figure 20.6
The Font dialog box displayed by the Common Dialog control.

Adding Code To The cmdShowColors Button

Changing the colors of text or items within the interface is a common task for any application. You can make such changes easier for your users to accomplish via the Common Dialog control. In our simple application, you'll write code for the cmdShowColors button's **Click** event. Open the VBA interface, and move to the **Click** event for the cmdShowColors button. Within this event, enter the following code:

```
Private Sub cmdShowColors_Click()
  cdlChap20.Flags = 2
  cdlChap20.ShowColor
  rtbChap20.SelColor = cdlChap20.Color
End Sub
```

You'll look more closely at this code in Chapter 21. However, even the most cursory examination should show you that the code uses the Common Dialog control and the Rich Text Box control. What it does with these controls is discussed later. For now, it's enough to know that when the user clicks on the Colors button, the application will display the dialog box shown in Figure 20.7.

Adding Code To The cmdShowPrinter Button

Often, you'll want to let your users print information from within your application without them necessarily having to generate a report or other preformatted Access object. You can use the Common Dialog control to speed that process. To set up the

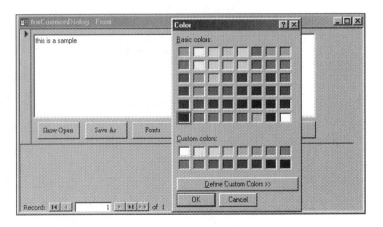

Figure 20.7
The Color dialog box.

cmdShowPrinter button to display the Print dialog box, open the VBA interface and move to the **Click** event. Within this event, enter the following code:

```
Private Sub cmdShowPrinter_Click()
  cdlChap20.Flags = 0
  cdlChap20.ShowPrinter
  rtbChap20.SelPrint cdlChap20.hDC
End Sub
```

You'll look more closely at this code in Chapter 21. However, even the most cursory examination should show you that the code uses the Common Dialog control and the Rich Text Box control. What it does with these controls is discussed later. For now, it's enough to know that when the user clicks on the Print button, the application will display the dialog box shown in Figure 20.8.

Adding Code To The cmdShowHelp Button

Open the VBA interface, and move to the **Click** event for the cmdShowHelp button. Within this event, enter the following code:

```
Private Sub cmdShowHelp_Click()
  ' Set the name of the help file
  cdlChap20.HelpFile = "c:\windows\help\dao35.HLP"
  cdlChap20.HelpCommand = cdlHelpContents
  ' Display Data Access Objects Help contents topic.
  cdlChap20.ShowHelp
End Sub
```

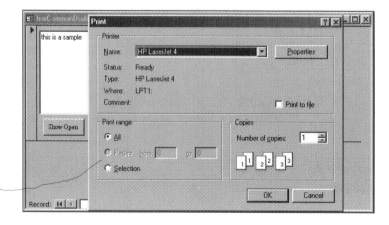

Figure 20.8
The Print dialog box.

You'll look more closely at this code in Chapter 21. However, you should notice that, unlike the other examples, the code uses the Common Dialog control and the Rich Text Box control. What it does with the Common Dialog control is discussed later. For now, it's enough to know that when the user clicks on the Help button, the application will display the Help dialog box shown in Figure 20.9.

Writing Code For The Form_Load Event

Depending on what it is you're trying to accomplish with the management of the Rich Text Box control, you could probably get by without doing any initialization work against the form and the controls that compose it. However, for most applications, you'll likely want to perform certain actions to initialize the controls. For example, perhaps you want to disable the Print button until the control contains some text. You'll probably also want to disable the Save As button until the user has typed in something worth saving. The following code disables these two buttons from within the **Form_Load** event:

```
Private Sub Form_Load()
  cmdShowSaveAs.Enabled = False
  cmdShowPrinter.Enabled = False
End Sub
```

Figure 20.9
The Help dialog box displaying information about DAO.

Writing Code For The Rich Text Box's Change Event

Just as you'll want to disable certain code due to a lack of content within the Rich Text Box control, you'll also want to enable that code when content actually appears within the text box. The following code enables the command buttons:

```
Private Sub rtbChap20_Change()
  cmdShowSaveAs.Enabled = True
  cmdShowPrinter.Enabled = True
End Sub
```

Where To Go From Here

Throughout this chapter, you worked with command constants, the **DoCmd** action, the **RunCommand** action, and the Common Dialog control. You also worked briefly with the Rich Text Box ActiveX control. You've seen the ways in which you can integrate these tools into your application to make the interface more accessible to your users and to provide your users with additional functionality. The additional functionality you have seen can be used either together with or in addition to the database connection and management functionality that Access 2000 is designed for.

In Chapter 21, you'll look more closely at the code you must use to manage these different activities, and you'll learn more about some of the underlying constants and methods you'll use to more effectively manage these events.

Chapter 21

Talking About Command Constants And Common Dialogs

Using command constants with built-in Access 2000 objects and control constants with ActiveX controls lets you modify and specify the performance of certain actions and interface elements in Access 2000.

As you saw in Chapter 20, you can use the Access 2000 built-in constants together with the **DoCmd** and **RunCommand** actions to perform specific processing within Access 2000. Most notably, you saw how the command constants can work together within your macros (and VBA code that references macros) to open up a large number of performance areas that macros would not allow you access to otherwise.

You also saw, briefly, how you can use the Windows Common Dialog ActiveX control to add significant additional functionality to your application, and you saw how the use of VBA-defined constants can help you with the management of the Common Dialog control. In this chapter, you will also work briefly with the Rich Text Box control and some of the VBA-defined constants that it requires.

Working With Command Constants

As you've seen in previous chapters, macros provide you with a significant amount of functionality. You can use the **DoCmd** action to execute macro actions from your VBA code. In Chapter 20, you used the **DoCmd** action to execute three types of data transfers. In the following sections, we'll look more closely at those transfers.

Importing Database Data Using Code

The **TransferDatabase** method of the **DoCmd** object is used to import data from a database such as FoxPro, dBASE, Paradox, or another Access database. It looks like this:

```
Sub ImportDatabase()
  DoCmd.TransferDatabase _
      TransferType:=acImport, _
      DatabaseType:="Microsoft Access", _
      DatabaseName:="Chap19.mdb", _
      ObjectType:=acTable, _
      Source:="Customers", _
      Destination:="tblCustomers", _
      StructureOnly:=False
End Sub
```

Basically, this action imports an existing table in another database (the Customers table in the Chap19.mdb database) into a new table in the current database (in this case, tblCustomers). Then, the **TransferDatabase** method accepts a series of arguments that let you control how the method executes when performing a transfer. Here's a description of each argument:

- **TransferType**—The **TransferType** argument lets you specify the type of transfer being performed. Valid values are **acImport** (which makes a new copy of the original data within the target table), **acExport** (which you use to send data from a table in the current database to some other database), and **acLink** (which lets you link from the current database to an external table). With linking, the original table maintains the values, and your database simply references that data. The default value is **acImport**.

- **DatabaseType**—The **DatabaseType** argument lets you specify the type of database being imported. The acceptable values for this argument are numerous, and they're actually controlled by Registry entries on your computer. However, default values include Paradox 3.x to 7.x, dBASE databases, Microsoft Access, and ODBC databases. If you do not specify a type, **TransferDatabase** will assume you're transferring from or to an Access datasource.

NOTE

*Do not include the file extension with the **Source** argument.*

- **DataBaseName**—The **DataBaseName** argument lets you specify the name of the database. If the table is a separate file—as is the case with dBASE, Paradox, and earlier versions of FoxPro—the database name is the name of the directory containing the table file. Do *not* include a backslash after the name of the directory.

- **ObjectType**—The **ObjectType** argument lets you specify the type of object to import. This argument is ignored for all but Access databases. However, when importing from or to Access databases, you can specify any valid Access object for importing—from a table to a data access page.

- **Source**—The **Source** argument corresponds to the name of the object you're importing. In the previous example, the **Source** argument refers to the Customers table within the Chap19.mdb database.

- **Destination**—The **Destination** argument specifies the name of the imported object—that is, where the object should be imported into the current database or exported to a foreign database if you chose the **acExport** value for the **TransferType** argument.

- **StructureOnly**—The **StructureOnly** argument specifies whether you want the method to import the structure of the table only or both the structure and the data.

Obviously, the **TransferDatabase** method is very useful when you're working with foreign data stores that are already in the form of a database. However, you'll often need to import data from a foreign source that's a text file. To manage such actions, you need to use the **TransferText** method, as described in the next section.

NOTE

If you link to data in a text file or an HTML file, the data is read-only in Microsoft Access 2000.

Importing Text Data Using Code

As indicated in the previous section, your applications can use the **TransferText** method of the **DoCmd** object to import text from a text file. In other words, the datasource should be a formatted, text-only file, with some type of delimiter to indicate to the Jet

NOTE

*Only **Import Delimited**, **Import Fixed Width**, **Export Delimited**, **Export Fixed Width**, and **Export Word for Windows Merge** transfer types are supported in an Access Data Project (ADP). You'll learn more about Access Data Projects in Chapters 24 and 25.*

▶Tip

You can go to File|Get External Data or File|Export and use the Import or Link Tables subcommands to create a specification for a particular type of text file (for example, a delimited text file that uses tabs to separate fields and has an MDY format for dates). When you click on one of these commands and select a type of text file to import, export, or link, the Import Text Wizard, Export Text Wizard, or Link Text Wizard runs. You can click the Advanced button in the wizard to define and save a specification. You can then type the specification name in this argument whenever you want to import or export the same type of text file.

engine where the fields break. You can also link the data in a text file to the current Access database. With a linked text file, you can view the text data with Microsoft Access while still allowing complete access to the data from your word processing program. You can also import from, export to, and link to a table or list in an HTML file (*.HTML). The code you saw in Chapter 20 is reprinted here for clarity:

```
Sub ImportText()
  DoCmd.TransferText _
      TransferType:=acImportDelim, _
      TableName:="tblCustomerText", _
      FileName:="Customer.Txt"
End Sub
```

Like the **TransferDatabase** method, the **TransferText** method accepts several incoming parameters. The following are the arguments for the **TransferText** method:

- **TransferType**—The **TransferType** argument specifies the type of transfer you want to make. You can import data from, export data to, or link to data in delimited or fixed-width text files, or HTML files. You can also export data to a Word mail merge data file to create merged documents such as form letters and mailing labels. The possible options for the argument are **Import Delimited, Import Fixed Width, Import HTML, Export Delimited, Export Fixed Width, Export HTML, Export Word for Windows Merge, Link Delimited, Link Fixed Width,** and **Link HTML**. The default is **Import Delimited**.

- **SpecificationName**—The **SpecificationName** argument specifies the set of options that determines how a text file is imported, exported, or linked. For a fixed-width text file, you must either specify an argument or use a schema file, which must be stored in the same folder as the imported, linked, or exported text file.

- **TableName**—The **TableName** argument specifies the name of the Microsoft Access table to import text data to, to export text data from, or to link text data to. You can also type the name of the Microsoft Access query you want to export data from. This is a required argument. If you specify the **Import**

Tip

*You can't use a SQL statement for the **TableName** argument to specify data to export when you're using the **TransferText** or **TransferSpreadsheet** action. Instead of using a SQL statement, you must first create a query and then specify the name of the query in the **TableName** argument.*

Delimited, **Import Fixed Width**, or **Import HTML** values for the **TransferType** argument, Microsoft Access appends the text data to this table if the table already exists. Otherwise, Microsoft Access creates a new table containing the text data.

- **FileName**—The **FileName** argument contains the name of the text file to import from, to export to, or to link to. This required argument *must* include the full path to the file. Access creates a new text file when you export data. If the file name is the same as the name of an existing text file, Access will replace the existing text file. If you want to import or link a particular table or list in an HTML file, you can use the **HTMLTableName** argument.

- **HasFieldNames**—The **HasFieldNames** argument specifies whether the first row of the text file contains the names of the fields. If you specify that the argument is True, Access uses the names in this row as field names in the table when you import or link the text data. If you specify False, Access treats the first row as a normal row of data. The default is False.

- **HTMLTableName**—The **HTMLTableName** argument specifies the name of the table or list in the HTML file that you want to import or link. This argument is ignored unless the **TransferType** argument is **Import HTML** or **Link HTML**. If you leave this argument blank, the first table or list in the HTML file is imported or linked.

You can export the data in Access **SELECT** queries to text files. Access 2000 exports the results of the query, treating the entire resultset as if it were a table. Text data that you append to an existing Microsoft Access table must be compatible with the table's structure. Specifically, the following rules must be met:

- Each field in the text must be of the same data type as the corresponding field in the table—that is, you cannot try to import text into a numeric field.

- The fields must be in the same order (unless you set the **HasFieldNames** argument to True, in which case the field names in the text must match the field names in the table).

Tip

If you query or filter a linked text file, the query or filter is case sensitive.

NOTE

Access 2000 creates a new spreadsheet when you export Access data. If the file name is the same as the name of an existing spreadsheet, Access replaces the existing spreadsheet, unless you're exporting to an Excel version 5, 7, 8, or 2000 workbook. In that case, Access copies the exported data to the next available new worksheet in the workbook.

Importing Spreadsheet Data Using Code

The **TransferSpreadsheet** method of the **DoCmd** object is used to import data from a spreadsheet file. It works in a manner similar to the previous two methods discussed. The code from Chapter 20 is reprinted here as an example:

```
Sub ImportSpreadsheet()
  DoCmd.TransferSpreadsheet _
    TransferType:=acImport, _
    SpreadsheetType:=5, _
    TableName:="tblCustomerSpread", _
    FileName:="Customer.xls",
    HasFieldNames:=True
End Sub
```

You can use the **TransferSpreadsheet** action to import or export data between the current database or data project and a spreadsheet file. You can also link the data in an Excel 2000 spreadsheet to the current Access 2000 database. With a linked spreadsheet, you can view and edit the spreadsheet data with Access while still allowing complete access to the data from your Excel spreadsheet program. You can also link to data in a Lotus 1-2-3 spreadsheet file (any version), but this data is read-only in Access.

The **TransferSpreadsheet** method of the **DoCmd** action has the following arguments:

- **TransferType**—The **TransferType** argument specifies the type of transfer you want to make. Valid values are **acImport** (which makes a new copy of the original data within the target table), **acExport** (which you use to send data from a table in the current database to some other database), and **acLink** (which lets you link from the current database to an external table). With linking, the original table maintains the values and your database simply references that data. The default value is **acImport**.

NOTE

*As with **TransferDatabase**, the **acLink TransferType** is not supported for Access Data Projects (ADPs).*

- **SpreadsheetType**—The **SpreadsheetType** argument specifies the type of spreadsheet to import from, export to, or link to. You can select one of a number of spreadsheets—again, these types are defined by Registry entries and by Access itself. For

NOTE

You can import from and link (read-only) to Lotus WK4 files, but you can't export Access 2000 data to this spreadsheet format. Access also no longer supports (and hasn't since Access 97) importing, exporting, or linking data to or from Lotus WKS or Excel version 2 spreadsheets. If you want to import from or link to spreadsheet data in Excel version 2 or Lotus WKS format, convert the spreadsheet data to a later version of Excel or Lotus 1-2-3 before importing or linking the data into Access.

NOTE

*If you're importing from or linking to a Microsoft Excel spreadsheet, you can specify a particular worksheet by using the **Range** argument. However, when you export to any other type of spreadsheet, you must leave this argument blank. If you enter a range, the export operation will fail.*

more information on types supported on your system, you're best served by creating a macro that uses **TransferSpreadsheet** and observing the types in the **SpreadsheetType** argument for the **macro** action. The default value for **SpreadsheetType** is **Excel 2000**.

- **TableName**—The **TableName** argument specifies the name of the Access table to import spreadsheet data from, to export spreadsheet data to, or to link spreadsheet data to (depending on the value specified within the **TransferType** argument). You can also type the name of the Access **SELECT** query you want to export data from. This is a required argument. If you specify **acImport** in the **TransferType** argument, Access will append the spreadsheet data to this table if the table already exists. Otherwise, Access will create a new table containing the spreadsheet data.

- **FileName**—The **FileName** argument corresponds to the name of the spreadsheet file to import from, to export to, or to link to. Again, as with previous transfer methods, be sure to include the full path. This is a required argument.

- **HasFieldNames**—The **HasFieldNames** argument specifies whether the first row of the spreadsheet contains the names of the fields. If you set this value to True, Access will use the names in the first row as field names in the Access table when you import or link the spreadsheet data. If you set this value to False, Access will treat the first row as a normal row of data. The default is False.

- **Range**—The **Range** argument specifies the range of cells to import or link. Leave this argument blank to import or link the entire spreadsheet. You can type the name of a range in the spreadsheet or specify the range of cells to import or link.

If you link to an Excel 2000 spreadsheet open in Edit Mode, Access 2000 will wait until the Excel spreadsheet is out of Edit Mode before completing the link—that is, there's no time-out enforced.

Project ·:::::·

Working With The RunCommand Action

You can use the **RunCommand** action to run a Microsoft Access command from a custom menu bar, custom shortcut menu, global menu bar, or global shortcut menu. However, it's normally easier to use the Customize dialog box (accessed from the View|Toolbars| Customize menu) to add Access commands to custom menus and shortcut menus. The Commands tab on the Customize dialog box lists the built-in Access commands that appear on the Access toolbars and menus. However, there will, occasionally, be times when using the **RunCommand** action is appropriate.

You can use the **RunCommand** action in a macro with conditional expressions to run a command, depending on certain conditions. However, be warned—when you convert an Access database from a previous version of Access, some commands may no longer be available. A command may have been renamed, moved to a different menu, or may no longer be available in Access 2000. The **DoMenuItem** actions for such commands can't be converted to **RunCommand** actions. When you open the macro, Access will display a **RunCommand** action with a blank **Command** argument for such commands. You must edit the macro and enter a valid command argument or delete the **RunCommand** action.

The following example uses the **RunCommand** method to open the Options dialog box (available by selecting Tools|Options):

```
Function DisplayOptions() As Boolean
  On Error GoTo Error_ DisplayOptions
  DoCmd.RunCommand acCmdOptions
  ' Alternately, invoke App.RunCommand acCmdOptions
  DisplayOptions = True

Exit_DisplayOptions:
  Exit Function

Error_DisplayOptions:
  MsgBox Err & ": " & Err.Description
  DisplayOptions = False
  Resume Exit_DisplayOptions
End Function
```

▶Tip

*In Access 97, the **RunCommand** action replaced the **DoMenuItem** action. When you open and save a macro from a previous version of Microsoft Access that contains a **DoMenuItem** action, the action and its action arguments will automatically be converted to the equivalent **RunCommand** action. The **DoMenuItem** action no longer appears in the list of actions in the Macro window.*

As you can see, the **acCmdOptions** constant specifies that the action should run the Tools|Options menu code. In fact, the **RunCommand** action provides more than 300 separate constants that refer to objects you can invoke from the action. The Access 2000 Help file details all these constants under the **RunCommand** method section.

Working With The Rich Text Box Control

The Rich Text Box control enables you to design a text box that allows you to write code that affects the selected text. Properties that can be specified for the selected text include the Font, Font Size, Bold, and Italic properties. You can even add bullet points to the selected text. Furthermore, you can save the contents of the Rich Text Box control in a rich text format (RTF) file and later retrieve it back into the control.

A text file is different than a rich text file. Rich text files include advanced formatting, such as different font size, color, and type within the same document. To display, edit, format, and save text—beyond the most basic of uses—in Access and VBA, you need a Rich Text Box control. The Rich Text Box control will let you enter text, edit text, and format text in a more advanced way than simply using a Text Box control.

The Rich Text Box control supports almost all the Text Box control's properties, methods, and events, such as **MaxLength**, **MultiLine**, **ScrollBars**, **SelLength**, **SelStart**, and **SelText**. Your Access database projects that already use Text Box controls can be easily adapted to make use of Rich Text Box controls. The Text Box control has a character capacity of about 2^{32} characters.

The Rich Text Box Control's Properties

The Rich Text Box control provides properties that let you apply formatting to any portion of text within the Rich Text Box control. To format text, you must first select (or highlight) it.

Using the Rich Text Box control's properties, you can make text bold or italic, change the text color, create superscripts and subscripts, and so on. In addition, you can adjust a paragraph's formatting by setting both left and right indents and hanging indents. Table 21.1 lists some of the Rich Text Box control's properties.

The Rich Text Box Control's Methods

The Rich Text Box control provides methods that let you display and save files in both RTF format and regular ASCII text format. You can load files using the **LoadFile** method, save files using the **SaveFile** method, and so on. Table 21.2 lists some of the Rich Text Box control's methods and provides a description for each.

Table 21.1   Some of the properties of the Rich Text Box control.

Property	Description
ScrollBars	Returns or sets a value indicating whether the control contains vertical or horizontal scrollbars
SelAlignment	Returns or sets a value that controls the alignment of a paragraph in the control
SelBold	Returns or sets a bold format for the currently selected text
SelBullet	Returns or sets a value that determines whether a paragraph in the control has a bullet style
SelCharOffset	Returns or sets a value that determines whether text in the control appears on the baseline (normal), as a superscript above the baseline, or as a subscript below the baseline
SelColor	Returns or sets a value that determines the color of the text in the control
SelFontName	Returns or sets the font used to display the currently selected (highlighted) text in the control
SelFontSize	Returns or sets a value that specifies the size of the font used to display text in the control
SelIndent	Returns or sets the distance between the left edge of the control and the left edge of the selected or added text at the current insertion point
SelItalic	Returns or sets the italic format of the currently selected text
SelLength	Returns or sets the number of characters selected
SelUnderline	Returns or sets the underline format of the currently selected text

Table 21.2   Some of the methods of the Rich Text Box control.

Method	Description
Find	Searches the text in the control for a given string.
GetLineFromChar	Returns a line number in the control that contains a specified character position. The **Find** method is used for this.
LoadFile	Loads an RTF or TXT file into the control.
SaveFile	Saves the contents of the control to an RTF or TXT file.
SelPrint	Sends formatted text in the control to a printer device for printing.
Span	Selects text in the control based on a set of specified characters.

Understanding The Rich Text Box Control's Object Embedding

The Rich Text Box control supports *object embedding*. This means you can create documents in a Rich Text Box control that contain other documents or objects. For example, you can create a document that has an embedded Microsoft Excel spreadsheet or a Microsoft Word document in it. To insert an object into a Rich Text Box control, you use your mouse to drag a file icon (from Windows Explorer, for instance) and drop it into the Rich Text Box control.

In addition, you can add data or objects from the Clipboard. When you paste an object from the Clipboard into the Rich Text Box control, the control will place the object at the current insertion point, or where your cursor is in the control. When you drag and drop an object into the Rich Text Box control, the control will track the mouse movement until the mouse button is released within the control and then insert the object at that point.

Finally, the Rich Text Box control can be bound to a Binary or Memo field in an Access 2000 database or a similar large-capacity field in other databases, such as the **TEXT** data type field in a SQL server.

Working With The Common Dialog Control

▶**Tip**

If you plan to distribute your application, you'll have to ensure that both Commdlg.dll and Comdlg32.ocx are distributed with the application, and that your setup program registers the correct version of the Common Dialog control in the target user's Registry.

The Common Dialog control provides a standard set of dialog boxes for operations such as opening and saving files, setting print options, and selecting colors and fonts. The control also has the ability to display help by running the Windows Help engine.

The Common Dialog control provides an interface between VBA/Access and the routines in the Microsoft Windows dynamic link library Commdlg.dll. To create a dialog box using this control, Commdlg.dll must be in your Microsoft Windows System directory, and you must be sure to add the Common Dialog ActiveX control to your project using the techniques described in Chapter 20.

You use the Common Dialog control in your application by adding it to a form and setting its properties. The dialog box displayed by the control is determined by the control's methods. At runtime, a dialog box is displayed or the Help engine is executed when the appropriate method is invoked; at design time, the Common Dialog control is displayed as an icon on a form. This icon can't be sized.

The Common Dialog control automatically provides context-sensitive help on the interface of the dialog boxes—using automatically displayed tooltips. The operating system provides the text shown in the Windows 95 Help pop-up menu. You can also display a Help button on the dialog boxes with the Common Dialog control by setting the **Flags** property; however, you must provide the Help topics in this situation.

NOTE

There's no way to specify where a common dialog box is displayed.

The Common Dialog control is actually like many controls in one. It's used to display the standard Windows File Open, File Save As, Font, Color, and Print dialog boxes. It's a hidden control that does not appear at runtime but whose properties and methods can be manipulated using VBA code. You saw the use of the Common Dialog control in Chapter 20, as shown in the form called frmCommonDialog. This form illustrates the use of several of the common dialog boxes as well as the Rich Text Box control, which we also looked at earlier in this chapter. Over the next several sections, we'll consider each of the implementations shown in the previous chapter.

Using The ShowOpen Method Of The Common Dialog Control

If you embed a Rich Text Box control into your application, you'll want to provide the user with some means of placing data into that control other than typing in the data at the keyboard. In addition to cut-and-paste support, you can add support for file activities to your application with the Common Dialog control. Part of that support will likely be to let the user retrieve the contents of an RTF or ASCII file into the control. To let the user open and retrieve a target file, you should use the **ShowOpen** method of the Common Dialog control. The code for displaying the Open dialog box and loading the selected file's contents into the Rich Text Box control looks like this:

```
Private Sub cmdOpen_Click()
    cdlChap20.FileName = ""
    cdlChap20.Filter = "RTF Files (*.rtf)|*.rtf"
    cdlChap20.InitDir = CurDir
    cdlChap20.ShowOpen
    If cdlChap20.FileName = "" Then
        MsgBox "You Must Specify a File Name", _
            vbExclamation, "File Cannot Be Opened!"
    Else
        rtbChap20.LoadFile cdlChap20.FileName
    End If
End Sub
```

NOTE

Although there are other methods at your disposal for granting the user access to the file system—for example, the Windows API combined with a series of list boxes—you're generally best served to use the Common Dialog control, because the interface it provides is familiar to the user.

The **Click** event of the cmdShowOpen command button uses the **ShowOpen** method to invoke the File Open common dialog box. If the user selects a file, the **LoadFile** method of the Rich Text Box control uses the **FileName** property of the Common Dialog control as the name of the file to open.

Typically, you'll use the Open dialog box to retrieve a file of a type that's not directly associated with your database application—however, you could also use it, for example, to let the user select

NOTE

The "&H" in front of each value indicates that the value is a hexadecimal (base 16) value. For further explanation of hexadecimal values, see the VBA Help file or any good mathematical text.

an exterior datasource to connect to. You'll learn more about working with exterior datasources in Chapter 25.

The **ShowOpen** method and the resulting Open dialog box support several specific flags you can use to modify and control the performance of the dialog box. Many of these flags are also shared with the Save As dialog box (explained in the next section). Table 21.3 lists the flags and their usage.

You set these flags by adding them together (or by using the **Or** keyword) and then assigning them to the **Flags** property. For example, if you want to allow multiple selections and ignore sharing errors, you would set the **Flag** property, as shown here, before opening the dialog box:

```
cdlChap21.Flags = CdlOFNAllowMultiselect Or _
    cdlOFNShareAware

' Or like this
cdlChap21.Flags = CdlOFNAllowMultiselect + _
    cdlOFNShareAware
```

Table 21.3   The flags for use with the Open and Save As dialog boxes.

Constant	Value	Description
cdlOFNAllowMultiselect	&H200	Specifies that the File Name list box allows multiple selections. The user can select more than one file at runtime by pressing the Shift key and using the up-arrow or down-arrow key to select the desired files (alternatively, the user can use the mouse together with the Shift or Ctrl key). When this is done, the **FileName** property returns a string containing the names of all selected files. The names in the string are delimited by null characters.
cdlOFNCreatePrompt	&H2000	Specifies that the dialog box prompts the user to create a file that doesn't currently exist. This flag automatically sets the **cdlOFNPathMustExist** and **cdlOFNFileMustExist** flags.
cdlOFNExplorer	&H80000	Uses the Explorer-like Open File dialog box template. Common dialog boxes that use this flag do not work under Windows NT using the Windows 95 shell.

(continued)

Table 21.3 The flags for use with the Open and Save As dialog boxes *(continued).*

Constant	Value	Description
cdlOFNExtensionDifferent	&H400	Indicates that the extension of the returned file name is different than the extension specified by the **DefaultExt** property. This flag isn't set if the **DefaultExt** property is null, if the extensions match, or if the file has no extension. This flag value can be checked upon closing the dialog box.
cdlOFNFileMustExist	&H1000	Specifies that the user can enter only names of existing files in the File Name text box. If this flag is set and the user enters an invalid file name, a warning is displayed. This flag automatically sets the **cdlOFNPathMustExist** flag.
cdlOFNHelpButton	&H10	Causes the dialog box to display the Help button.
cdlOFNHideReadOnly	&H4	Hides the Read Only checkbox.
cdlOFNLongNames	&H200000	Use long file names.
cdlOFNNoChangeDir	&H8	Forces the dialog box to set the current directory to what it was when the dialog box was opened.
cdlOFNNoReadOnlyReturn	&H8000	Specifies that the returned file won't have the Read Only attribute set and won't be in a write-protected directory.
cdlOFNNoValidate	&H100	Specifies that the common dialog box allows invalid characters in the returned file name.
cdlOFNOverwritePrompt	&H2	Causes the Save As dialog box to generate a message box if the selected file already exists. The user must confirm whether to overwrite the file.
cdlOFNPathMustExist	&H800	Specifies that the user can enter only valid paths. If this flag is set and the user enters an invalid path, a warning message is displayed.
cdlOFNReadOnly	&H1	Causes the Read Only checkbox to be initially checked when the dialog box is created. This flag also indicates the state of the Read Only checkbox when the dialog box is closed.
cdlOFNShareAware	&H4000	Specifies that sharing violation errors will be ignored.
cdlOFNNoDereferenceLinks	&H100000	Specifies that shell links (also known as shortcuts) are not to be dereferenced. By default, choosing a shell link causes it to be dereferenced by the shell.
cdlOFNNoLongNames	&H40000	Specifies that long file names cannot be used.

NOTE

Under previous versions of Windows NT (that is, 3.51 or earlier) without the Windows 95 shell, the multiselect common dialog boxes use spaces for delimiters (therefore, there's no support for long file names).

NOTE

These constants are listed in the Microsoft Common Dialog control (MSComDlg) object library in the Object Browser. You'll learn more about the Object Browser later in this chapter.

The **cdlOFNExplorer** and **cdlOFNNoDereferenceLinks** flags work only under Windows 9x and Windows NT 4. Multiselect common dialog boxes under Windows 9x using **cdlOFNExplorer** use null characters for delimiters.

Under both Windows NT 4 and Windows 9x, if you don't choose the **cdlOFNAllowMultiselect** flag, then both the **cdlOFN-Explorer** and **cdlOFNLongNames** flags have no effect and are essentially the default setting.

If you use the **cdlOFNAllowMultiselect** flag by itself under both Windows NT 4 and Windows 9x, you won't have support for long file names because the multiple file names come back space-delimited, and long file names could include spaces. You cannot avoid this behavior if you have Windows NT 3.5x.

If you use **cdlOFNAllowMultiselect**, you cannot see long file names. If you add the **cdlOFNExplorer** flag under Windows 9x, you'll be able to both select multiple files and see long file names. However, the file names come back delimited with null characters, not space characters. Therefore, using **cdlOFNAllow-Multiselect** with **cdlOFNExplorer** requires different parsing of the file name result under Windows 9x and Windows NT 4.

Using The ShowSave Method Of The Common Dialog Control

Just as you'll often want the user to be able to open files and place them into a Rich Text Box control, you'll also want the user to be able to save files to permanent storage. The Rich Text Box control contains a method called **ShowSave** that allows the user to save the contents of the Rich Text Box control to an RTF file. When used in conjunction with the Common Dialog control's **ShowSave** method, the code looks like this:

```
Private Sub cmdShowSaveAs_Click()
    cdlChap20.Filter = "RTF Files (*.rtf)|*.rtf"
    cdlChap20.ShowSave
```

```
    If cdlChap20.FileName = "" Then
      MsgBox "You Must Specify a File Name", _
          vbExclamation, "File NOT Saved!"
    Else
      rtbChap20.SaveFile cdlChap20.FileName
    End If
End Sub
```

The code begins by setting the **Filter** property of the Common Dialog control. This filters the file names that are displayed in the File Save common dialog box. The **ShowSave** method is used to invoke the Save common dialog box. After the user types in or selects a file name, the **FileName** property of the Common Dialog control is filled in with the name of the file the user specified. If the user clicks on Cancel, the **FileName** property contains a zero-length string, and the user is warned that the file was not saved.

Using The ShowFont Method Of The Common Dialog Control

Just as you'll often want to provide the user with a means of saving or retrieving information from the computer's hard drive (or a floppy, for that matter), you'll also want to let the user customize the appearance of either the program or the contents within it. There are two dialog boxes supported by the Common Dialog control that can help you and your users perform such customization. The first, the Font dialog box, lets the user select any of the fonts, formats, and styles available on the system. Your applications can then take that information and use it to perform the appropriate formatting. For example, the following code lets the user select a new font and then assigns that font information to every Command Button control on the current form. It first displays the Font dialog box (using the **ShowFont** method) and then assigns the returned characteristics to the command buttons. The following code performs the processing:

```
Private Sub cmdShowFont_Click()
    Dim ctl As Control

    cdlChap20.Flags = cdlCFScreenFonts
    cdlChap20.ShowFont
```

```
    For Each ctl In Controls
        If TypeOf ctl Is CommandButton Then
            With ctl
                .FontName = cdlChap20.FontName
                .FontBold = cdlChap20.FontBold
                .FontItalic = cdlChap20.FontItalic
                .FontSize = cdlChap20.FontSize
            End With
        End If
    Next ctl
End Sub
```

If the user clicks on the Fonts button and then changes the font to another one—for example, Verdana 14 point Bold and Italic—the application will then change the appearance of all of the command buttons on the form, as shown in Figure 21.1.

The **Click** event of cmdShowFont first sets the **Flags** property of the common dialog control to the constant **cdlCFScreenFonts** (which has a value of 1). For the Font common dialog box, the value 1 causes it to list only the screen fonts supported by the user's system. The **ShowFont** method is used to invoke the actual dialog box. Using a **With...End With** construct, the code takes each property set in the common dialog box and uses it to loop through the **Controls** collection of the form, modifying the font attributes of each command button.

Like the file management dialog boxes, the Font dialog box supports a number of unique constants that control its display and performance. Table 21.4 lists the constants and their descriptions.

Needless to say, there are quite a few situations where the Font dialog box can be very useful. For example, you might rewrite the

Figure 21.1
The frmCommonDialog form after the font on all the command buttons has been changed.

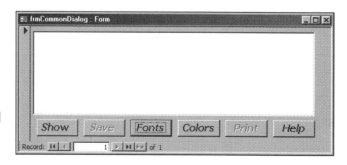

Table 21.4   The Font dialog box control constants.

Constant	Value	Description
cdlCFANSIOnly	&H400	Specifies that the dialog box allows only a selection of the fonts that use the Windows character set. If this flag is set, the user won't be able to select a font that contains only symbols.
cdlCFApply	&H200	Enables the Apply button on the dialog box.
cdlCFBoth	&H3	Causes the dialog box to list the available printer and screen fonts. The **hDC** property identifies the device context associated with the printer.
cdlCFEffects	&H100	Specifies that the dialog box enables strikethrough, underline, and color effects.
cdlCFFixedPitchOnly	&H4000	Specifies that the dialog box selects only fixed-pitch fonts.
cdlCFForceFontExist	&H10000	Specifies that an error message box is displayed if the user attempts to select a font or style that doesn't exist.
cdlCFHelpButton	&H4	Causes the dialog box to display a Help button.
cdlCFLimitSize	&H2000	Specifies that the dialog box selects only font sizes within the range specified by the **Min** and **Max** properties.
cdlCFNoFaceSel	&H80000	No font name selected.
cdlCFNoSimulations	&H1000	Specifies that the dialog box doesn't allow graphic device interface (GDI) font simulations.
cdlCFNoSizeSel	&H200000	No font size selected.
cdlCFNoStyleSel	&H100000	No font style selected.
cdlCFNoVectorFonts	&H800	Specifies that the dialog box doesn't allow vector-font selections.
cdlCFPrinterFonts	&H2	Causes the dialog box to list only the fonts supported by the printer, as specified by the **hDC** property.
cdlCFScalableOnly	&H20000	Specifies that the dialog box allows only the selection of fonts that can be scaled.
cdlCFScreenFonts	&H1	Causes the dialog box to list only the screen fonts supported by the system.
cdlCFTTOnly	&H40000	Specifies that the dialog box allows only the selection of TrueType fonts.
cdlCFWYSIWYG	&H8000	Specifies that the dialog box allows only the selection of fonts that are available on both the printer and onscreen. If this flag is set, the **cdlCFBoth** and **cdlCFScalableOnly** flags should also be set.

code within the cmdShowFont button's **Click** event to specify the font style for a given selection of text within the Rich Text Box. As in the previous code example, you would first invoke the **ShowFonts** method and then set the affected properties within the Rich Text Box control, as shown in the following code:

```
Private Sub cmdShowFont_Click()
  cdlChap20.Flags = cdlCFScreenFonts
  cdlChap20.ShowFont
  With rtbChap20
    .SelFontName = cdlChap20.FontName
    .SelBold = cdlChap20.FontBold
    .SelItalic = cdlChap20.FontItalic
    .SelFontSize = cdlChap20.FontSize
  End With
End Sub
```

The **Click** event of the cmdShowFont command button sets the **SelFontName**, **SelBold**, **SelItalic**, and **SelFontSize** properties of the Rich Text Box control to the font, style, and size selected in the Font common dialog box. The selected attributes are applied only to the selected text—in other words, you have to code the event slightly differently if you want to change all text to those attributes, or only text about to be typed, and so on.

Using the ShowColor Method Of The Common Dialog Control

The Colors command button illustrates the use of the Common Dialog control. The button invokes the Color common dialog box. The code under the **Click** event of the cmdShowColor command button looks like this:

```
Private Sub cmdColor_Click()
  cdlChap20.Flags = cdlCCFullOpen
  cdlChap20.ShowColor
  rtbChap20.SelColor = cdlChap20.Color
End Sub
```

The code begins by setting the **Flags** property of the Common Dialog control, which specifies the control's attributes. The value of **cdlCCFullOpen** (a system constant that equates to 2) for the

Color common dialog box indicates that the entire Color dialog box, including the portion that enables the user to create custom colors, will be displayed. The **ShowColor** method, when applied to the Common Dialog control, invokes the Color common dialog box. The color that the user selects is filled into the **Color** property of the Common Dialog control. This color is then used by the code to modify the **SelColor** property of selected text within the Rich Text Box control, thus changing the selected text to whatever color the user has indicated as his or her selection within the Color dialog box.

When you want to display the Color dialog box, you'll use constants together with the **Flags** property to control the display of the dialog box. Table 21.5 lists the constants that you can use with the Color dialog box and describes the effects of using the constants on the dialog box.

You can use the Common Dialog control's Color dialog box in any situation where you want to retrieve a color value. For example, you might want to let the user customize the appearance of the background on your forms. The following code does just that:

```
Private Sub cmdSetBackColor_Click()
    cdlChap20.ShowColor
    Me.BackColor = cdlChap20.Color
End Sub
```

This code uses the Color common dialog box to set the **BackColor** property of the current form to a user-selected color. The form's background appears in whatever color the user selects from the common dialog box.

Table 21.5   The constants and their descriptions for managing the Color dialog box.

Constant	Value	Description
cdlCCFullOpen	&H2	The entire dialog box is displayed, including the Define Custom Colors section
cdlCCPreventFullOpen	&H4	Disables the Define Custom Colors command button and prevents the user from defining custom colors
cdlCCRGBInit	&H1	Sets the initial color value for the dialog box
cdlCCShowHelp	&H8	Causes the dialog box to display a Help button

Using The ShowPrinter Method Of The Common Dialog Control

As you've seen before, Access 2000 includes powerful built-in printing support for certain types of native objects, such as reports. However, you may find that you want to let your users print information not directly derived from an Access object (such as some combination of information from the fields on a form) or information that cannot be easily formatted. For example, in addition to being able to open and save the contents of a Rich Text Box control, you can print the contents of the control. The **ShowPrinter** method of the Common Dialog control displays the Print common dialog box, which your applications can use to start a print job:

```
Private Sub cmdShowPrinter_Click()
  cdlChap20.CancelError = True
  cdlChap20.Flags = 0
  On Error Resume Next
  cdlChap20.ShowPrinter
  If Err.Number <> 0 Then
    rtbChap20.SelPrint cdlChap20.hDC
  Else
    ' User clicked cancel
  End If
End Sub
```

The **Click** event of the cmdShowPrint command button sets the **Flags** property of the Common Dialog control to 0. This selects the All option button in the Print dialog box (and deselects the Pages and Selection option buttons). Note, as well, the use of the Common Dialog control's **CancelError** property, which tells the dialog box to return an error if the user clicks on the Cancel button. In the case of this particular code, it checks to make sure the user didn't click on Cancel before it tells the **SelPrint** method of the Rich Text Box control to print the selected text with the default printer—that is, the currently active printer—as shown in the Print common dialog box. If the code doesn't do this, it will crash with an error because the user has not selected a printer to send the information to.

In addition to the simple constant shown here, the **ShowPrinter** method also supports a number of additional common dialog constants, as shown in Table 21.6.

Managing printers is a difficult task that's made slightly easier by the use of the VBA **Printer** object and **Printers** collection. For more information on printer management with these objects, see the VBA Help file.

Table 21.6   The constants for use with the ShowPrinter method.

Constant	Value	Description
cdlPDAllPages	&H0	Returns or sets the state of the All Pages option button.
cdlPDCollate	&H10	Returns or sets the state of the Collate checkbox.
cdlPDDisablePrintToFile	&H80000	Disables the Print To File checkbox.
cdlPDHelpButton	&H800	Causes the dialog box to display the Help button.
cdlPDHidePrintToFile	&H100000	Hides the Print To File checkbox.
cdlPDNoPageNums	&H8	Disables the Pages option button and the associated edit control.
cdlPDNoSelection	&H4	Disables the Selection option button.
cdlPDNoWarning	&H80	Prevents a warning message from being displayed when there's no default printer.
cdlPDPageNums	&H2	Returns or sets the state of the Pages option button.
cdlPDPrintSetup	&H40	Causes the system to display the Print Setup dialog box rather than the Print dialog box.
cdlPDPrintToFile	&H20	Returns or sets the state of the Print To File checkbox.
cdlPDReturnDC	&H100	Returns a device context for the printer selection made in the dialog box. The device context is returned in the dialog box's **hDC** property.
cdlPDReturnDefault	&H400	Returns the default printer name.
cdlPDReturnIC	&H200	Returns an information context for the printer selection made in the dialog box. An information context provides a fast way to get information about the device without creating a device context. The information context is returned in the dialog box's **hDC** property.

(continued)

Table 21.6   The constants for use with the ShowPrinter method *(continued)*.

Constant	Value	Description
cdlPDSelection	&H1	Returns or sets the state of the Selection option button. If neither **cdlPDPageNums** nor **cdlPDSelection** is specified, the All option button is in the "selected" state.
cdlPDUseDevModeCopies	&H40000	If a printer driver doesn't support multiple copies, setting this flag disables the Copies Edit control on the dialog box. If a driver does support multiple copies, setting this flag indicates that the dialog box stores the requested number of copies in the **Copies** property.

Using The ShowHelp Method Of The Common Dialog Control

In your Access applications are many customizable features you can use to provide the user with realtime help on a specific programming topic. In addition to these features (such as tooltips), you can use the **ShowHelp** method of the Common Dialog control to run the Windows Help engine (winhlp32.exe) and display a Help file that's set by the **HelpFile** property.

By setting the **HelpCommand** property, you can tell the Help engine what type of online help you want, such as context-sensitive help, help on a particular keyword, and so on. In the application you built in the last chapter, the cmdShowHelp button invokes the Help engine, which applications can use to display a custom Help file for the application, as shown in the following code:

```
Private Sub cmdShowHelp_Click()
  ' Set the name of the help file
  cdlChap20.HelpFile = "c:\windows\help\dao35.HLP"
  cdlChap20.HelpCommand = cdlHelpContents
  ' Display DAO 3.5 Help contents topic.
  cdlChap20.ShowHelp
End Sub
```

The code within the event is straightforward—it simply sets **HelpFile**, initializes the type of Help display, and then displays

NOTE

For more information on creating and working with Help files, you can look to the Access 2000 Developer's Black Book (ISBN: 1-57610-349-8), which discusses Help files in more detail.

the Help file. Help is unique in that the resulting dialog box is not modal. In addition to the simple constant shown here, the **ShowHelp** method also supports a number of additional Common Dialog control flags, as shown in Table 21.7.

Error Codes Returned By The Common Dialog Boxes

As you might imagine, with all the possible activities the user can perform with the common dialog boxes, the possibility for errors at any level, whether created by the user or the operating system, is significant. Clearly, it's helpful to have a series of constant representations of those error codes so that your applications can more easily respond to the possible errors a common dialog box might return. Luckily, the developers at Microsoft included just such a set of constants, together with the common dialog box, to make your development simpler. The set of constants is detailed in Table 21.8.

Table 21.7   The constants for use with the ShowHelp method.

Constant	Value	Description
cdlHelpCommandHelp	&H102	Displays help for a particular command
cdlHelpContents	&H3	Displays the contents topic in the current Help file
cdlHelpContext	&H1	Displays help for a particular topic
cdlHelpContextPopup	&H8	Displays a topic identified by a context number
cdlHelpForceFile	&H9	Creates a Help file that displays text in only one font
cdlHelpHelpOnHelp	&H4	Displays help for using the Help application itself
cdlHelpIndex	&H3	Displays the index of the specified Help file
cdlHelpKey	&H101	Displays help for a particular keyword
cdlHelpPartialKey	&H105	Calls the search engine in Windows Help
cdlHelpQuit	&H2	Notifies the Help application that the specified Help file is no longer in use
cdlHelpSetContents	&H5	Designates a specific topic as the contents topic
cdlHelpSetIndex	&H5	Sets the current index for multi-index Help

Table 21.8 The error codes returned by the common control dialog boxes.

Constant	Value	Description
cdlAlloc	&H7FF0	Couldn't allocate memory for either the **FileName** or **Filter** property (or both).
cdlBufferTooSmall	&H4FFC	The buffer to which the member **lpstrFile** points is too small.
cdlCancel	&H7FF3	Cancel was selected.
cdlCreateICFailure	&H6FF5	The **PrintDlg** function failed when it attempted to create an information context.
cdlDialogFailure	&H8000	The function failed to load the dialog box.
cdlDndmMismatch	&H6FF6	Data in the **DevMode** and **DevNames** data structures describe two different printers.
cdlFindResFailure	&H7FF9	The function failed to load a specified resource.
cdlGetDevModeFail	&H6FFA	The printer device driver failed to initialize a **DevMode** data structure.
cdlHelp	&H7FEF	A call to Windows Help failed.
cdlInitFailure	&H6FF9	The **PrintDlg** function failed during initialization.
cdlInitialization	&H7FFD	The function failed during initialization.
cdlInvalidFileName	&H4FFD	The file name is invalid.
cdlLoadDrvFailure	&H6FFB	The **PrintDlg** function failed to load the specified printer's device driver.
cdlLoadResFailure	&H7FF8	The function failed to load a specified resource.
cdlLoadStrFailure	&H7FFA	The function failed to load a specified string.
cdlLockResFailure	&H7FF7	The function failed to lock a specified resource.
cdlMemAllocFailure	&H7FF6	The function was unable to allocate memory for the internal data structures.
cdlMemLockFailure	&H7FF5	The function was unable to lock the memory associated with a handle.
cdlNoDefaultPrn	&H6FF7	A default printer doesn't exist.
cdlNoDevices	&H6FF8	No printer device drivers were found.
cdlNoFonts	&H5FFE	No fonts exist.
cdlParseFailure	&H6FFD	The **CommonDialog** function failed to parse the strings in the **[devices]** section of Win.ini.
cdlPrinterCodes	&H6FFF	The **PDReturnDefault** flag was set, but either the **hDevMode** or **hDevNames** field was nonzero.

(continued)

Table 21.8   The error codes returned by the common control dialog boxes *(continued)*.

Constant	Value	Description
cdlPrinterNotFound	&H6FF4	The **[devices]** section of Win.ini doesn't contain an entry for the requested printer.
cdlRetDefFailure	&H6FFC	The **PDReturnDefault** flag was set, but either the **hDevMode** or **hDevNames** field was nonzero.
cdlSetupFailure	&H6FFE	Failed to load required resources.
cdlSubclassFailure	&H4FFE	An attempt to subclass a list box failed due to insufficient memory.

As you can see, most of the error values revolve around printing, but it's possible (and in fact, quite common) to encounter errors in other areas, as well. For example, it's quite common to encounter the **cdlInvalidFileName** constant when working with the Save As dialog box—a user typing a file name that contains forbidden characters is the most common example.

Now that you have a more complete overview of the workings of the Common Dialog control, let's take a quick look at the Object Browser and the functionality it provides before we move on to the next chapter.

Using The Object Browser

As you learned in other chapters, the DAO Object Library contains the **Connection**, **Database**, and **Recordset** objects. It also contains properties for each of these objects, as well as methods and events. Any other object you might include in your applications will have similar effects—the Common Dialog control, for example, exposes all those properties, methods, and events. It also has support for all the predefined constants you've seen throughout this chapter for working with the control. In general, working with objects—of any type—can often be made simpler by working with the Visual Basic Object Browser, which you can invoke from within the VBA IDE you use to write program code.

The Object Browser will show classes and class functions for each object referenced within a given project. Programmers generally refer to the objects as *classes* and the class functions as *members*.

NOTE

In Access 2000, the default database library supported within the VBA IDE is the ActiveX Data Objects Library. If you want to work with the DAO Library, you must load a reference to the library into the Visual Basic project you're working with.

To view the members of the ADODB Object Library, for example, perform the following steps:

1. Within the VBA IDE, select View|Object Browser. VBA will open the Object Browser window.

2. Within the Object Browser window, select the Connection listing below the Classes heading. VBA will list the members of the **Connection** class within the area below the Members of 'Connection' heading.

3. Next, select the Recordset listing below the Classes heading. VBA will list the members of the **Recordset** class within the area below the Members of 'Recordset' heading.

4. Select the Command listing below the Classes heading. VBA will list the members of the **Command** class within the area below the Members of 'Command' heading.

5. Within the Object Browser's Members of 'Command' heading, click on the Execute member. VBA will display information about **Execute** at the bottom of the Object Browser window. Note that the Execute member is a method of the ADO **Command** object, as shown in Figure 21.2.

Almost every Access control—and certainly almost every ActiveX control—has at least one method. Before you use a method for a control, it's always helpful to understand what the method does. Access and VBA both include large help files you

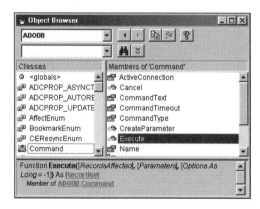

Figure 21.2
The Object Browser showing the **Execute** method of **Command**, a member of the ADO classes.

can use to find information on most controls. When you find a control and VBA displays a help file on it, you can study each method the control includes. In addition to studying control methods from the VBA help files, you can view descriptions about control methods in the Object Browser. The Object Browser is a window that VBA uses to display a control's properties, methods, and events. The Object Browser will display controls, as well as any other class items and hierarchies—including classes and hierarchies you create yourself with class modules.

As you've learned, one of the ActiveX controls you'll commonly use is the Common Dialog control. One of the Common Dialog control's methods is **ShowOpen**, which lets you display an Open dialog box. The **ShowOpen** method consists of the keyword **ShowOpen** and no parameters.

You can use the Object Browser to view the Common Dialog control's properties and methods. To display the Object Browser, select View|Object Browser. The VBA IDE will display the Object Browser. Select the MSComDlg library and the underlying **CommonDialog** class. Next, on the right-hand side of the browser, select the control's **ShowOpen** method, which the Object Browser will display, as Figure 21.3 shows.

As you can see in Figure 21.3, after you select a control's property, method, or event, the VBA IDE will display a short description at the bottom of the Object Browser. In addition, the Object Browser lists the Classes field, which is a listing of controls or classes.

▶**Tip**

You can review information about any class or object from the Object Browser—making it a very effective tool for learning about new controls, ActiveX controls that the Access IDE does not support natively, and third-party classes and libraries you reference from within your project.

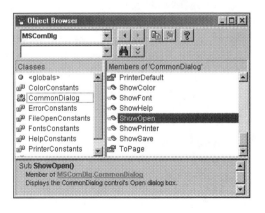

Figure 21.3
The Object Browser showing the Common Dialog control's **ShowOpen** method.

Reviewing The Macro Replacement Code

In Chapter 19, we promised that we would review the VBA code that would take the place of the pair of complex macros you designed in Chapter 18 and reviewed in Chapter 19. Now that you have reviewed some of the many tools at your disposal to assist you in programming macros—and using macros from your programs—let's go ahead and take a brief look at the code so we can evaluate exactly what it does:

```
Function ChangeCustomerAddress() As Boolean
    Dim dbs As Database
    Dim rst As Recordset
    Dim strCustomerName As String
    Dim strNewAddress As String
    Dim strCriteria As String
```

The code in the function starts off by declaring some variables that it will use to manage the changes in the name. It also declares a database and a recordset variable, to use for stepping through all the records in the retrieved recordset. In the next section, the code declares an error handler and then opens the database and the recordset:

```
On Error GoTo ChangeCustomerAddress_Err

Set dbs = CurrentDb()
Set rst = dbs.OpenRecordset("Customers", _
    dbOpenDynaset)
```

The **On Error** statement specifies an error handler that the code will invoke if there is an error in execution—for example, if the code can't open the recordset or can't find a match in the recordset. You will learn more about the use of the **On Error** statement for error management in later chapters.

```
strCustomerName = _
    InputBox("Enter the company name", _
    "Company Name")
If Len(strCustomerName) = 0 Then _
    Exit Function
```

Rather than using a custom form like the macros did, this code uses a pair of input boxes for simplicity, though you would likely use a custom dialog box with the form code just as you did with the macro code. In any event, the program code uses the **InputBox** function to retrieve the company name, then checks the length of the returned string to make sure the user has made an entry. If the user has not, the program exits the function.

Then, the code uses the **InputBox** function—this time to retrieve the address information. It also checks to make sure that the user has entered a string with some length before it continues the execution of the function:

```
strNewAddress = InputBox("Enter the new address", _
    "New Address")
If Len(strNewAddress) = 0 Then _
    Exit Function
```

The next statement constructs the **strCriteria** variable, setting it up for the **Recordset** object's **FindFirst** method:

```
strCriteria ="[CompanyName] = " & """" & _
    strCustomerName & """"
```

The code then uses a **With...End With** block to perform its processing on the **rst** object, as shown in the following code:

```
With rst
  .MoveFirst
  .FindFirst strCriteria
  If .NoMatch Then
    MsgBox("The company name you entered " & _
        "isn't valid.")
    Exit Function
  End If
  ' Set the Address field to strNewAddress.
  .Edit
    !Address = strNewAddress
  .Update
End With
```

The code within the block first tries to locate a company match. If it's not successful, it alerts the user and exits the function. If successful, it goes on to process the **Address** information. The program code uses the **Edit** and **Update** methods to change the value, as shown in the grayed code in the listing. The final part of the normally executing code alerts the user to the change, sets the function's result to **True**, and exits the function.

```
MsgBox("The address has been changed.")
ChangeCustomerAddress = True

ChangeCustomerAddress_Bye:
Exit Function
```

As mentioned previously, the use of the **On Error** construct tells the code that, should an error occur within the function, the compiler should move to the subroutine named in the statement and begin executing that code. In this case, the code to execute is after the **ChangeCustomerAddress_Err** label, as shown here:

```
ChangeCustomerAddress_Err:
  MsgBox Err.Description, vbOKOnly, "Error = " & _
    Err.Number
  ChangeCustomerAddress = False
  Resume ChangeCustomerAddress_Bye
End Function
```

The code after the label simply displays a message box detailing information about the error. It then sets the function's return value to **False** and calls the **ChangeCustomerAddress_Bye** label, which is followed immediately by the **Exit Function** statement, and so the function exits with a negative return value.

Needless to say, the invoking location should evaluate the return value—and respond appropriately. It is crucial that your code closely evaluate function return values in a situation like this—otherwise, your application will not be as responsive to problems as it should be.

Where To Go From Here

In this chapter, we discussed in greater depth the specifics of working with the command constants, the **DoCmd** and **RunCommand** actions, and the Common Dialog control. You also learned more about the Rich Text Box control. You saw how you can use the Object Browser to obtain additional information about the classes, controls, and object libraries your application contains.

You saw how you can use all these objects and actions to make your applications more efficient, as well as to provide additional types of processing power and strategies to your users. You also saw how you can use these tools to provide your users with additional functionality in a more intuitive and accessible way. In Chapter 22, we'll move on to a discussion of built-in functions within VBA. We'll also consider how you can use the built-in functions to improve the processing of your applications.

Chapter 22

Working With Functions In Access 2000

By now, you should be pretty comfortable with using subroutines in your programming. In this chapter, you'll enhance your subroutines using functions.

et's begin our examination of functions by creating an application called the Function Palette. The Function Palette is a utility that demonstrates six primary function categories available to you in VBA. These six categories extend your subroutines by supporting date and time, data conversion, math, string, variant, and user interface tasks. In addition to the built-in VBA functions, we'll also take a look at how you can write functions of your own. As defined in Chapter 7, a *function* is a type of VBA procedure that works like a subroutine, except it returns a value to the code block that invokes it. You'll get the idea as the Function Palette application evolves.

Project Designing And Building The Master Control

This first piece of the Function Palette consists of a master control palette for launching the form associated with each function category. Begin by performing the following steps:

1. Under Objects on the FirstDatabase database window, select the Forms button and then double-click on the option Create Form In Design View.

2. Resize the Detail section of the form grid by clicking on the right edge of the grid and dragging it to the left until it's two squares wide.

3. Repeat the resizing process on the bottom edge of the grid—drag the edge down until it's three squares deep. The Detail section of your form grid should appear as shown in Figure 22.1.

4. On the floating toolbox, click on the Command Button control.

5. Place the cursor in the upper-left square of the Detail section of the form grid, and then click once to place a Command Button control on the form.

6. Repeat Step 5 until you have placed a Command Button control in each remaining form grid square.

7. On the floating toolbox, click on the Label control.

8. Place the cursor above the first two form buttons, and then click once to place a Label control on the form.

9. At the blinking cursor, enter "Function Palette Master Control" and then click outside the form grid to deselect the control.

10. Right-click on the first button to open the right-click menu; then select Properties to open the button's property sheet.

11. On the property sheet, click on the Format tab and then enter "Date and Time" in the Caption property field.

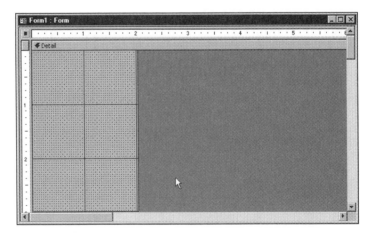

Figure 22.1
The resized form grid.

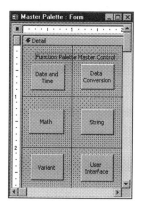

Figure 22.2
Bind the form grid on all sides with the form window.

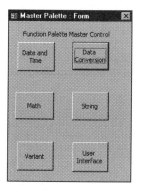

Figure 22.3
The finished Master Control.

12. Repeat Steps 10 and 11 for each of the remaining buttons, naming the buttons in succession from left to right "Data Conversion," "Math," "String," "Variant," and "User Interface."

13. Resize the form window to bind the form grid on all sides, as shown in Figure 22.2.

14. Click on the Object drop-down menu on the Formatting toolbar, and then select Form.

15. Right-click on the Form title bar to open the right-click menu; then select Properties to open the Form's property sheet.

16. On the property sheet, click on the All tab and then set the following property values:

    • *Scroll Bars*—Neither

    • *Record Selectors*—No

    • *Navigation Buttons*—No

    • *Dividing Lines*—No

    • *Auto Resize*—No

    • *Border Style*—Dialog

17. Close the Form property sheet, and then select File|Save to save the form with the name "Master Palette."

18. Select View|Form View to see the finished panel. Your panel should appear as shown in Figure 22.3.

Project Coding With A Macro

Now that the Master Control Palette is designed, let's start making it work by activating the Date and Time button. You'll accomplish this by performing the following steps:

1. Select View|Design View to reopen the finished panel for modification.

2. Open the property sheet for the Date and Time button by right-clicking on the button and selecting Properties from the right-click menu.

3. Select the Event tab, and then click once in the **OnClick** event property field.

4. Select the button to the right of the field drop-down menu, select Macro Builder from the Choose Builder dialog box, and then click on OK.

5. Enter "DT Button" in the Save As dialog box, and then click on OK.

6. In the Macro dialog box, click on the Action field, scroll the drop-down menu, and select Close.

7. Under the Action Arguments section of the Macro dialog box, click on the Object Type field and select Form from the drop-down menu.

8. Again, under the Action Arguments section, click on Object Name and then select Master Palette.

9. Moving to the next Action field, scroll the drop-down menu and select OpenForm.

10. Under the Action Arguments section of the Macro dialog box, click on the Form Name field and select Class Module Panel from the drop-down menu.

11. Select File|Save and then File|Close to close the Macro dialog box. Don't forget to close the property sheet, too.

12. Select View|Form View, and then click on the Date and Time button. Clicking this button should launch the Class Module Panel you created in Chapter 10. (See Figure 22.4.)

13. Close the Class Module Panel.

 ## Converting A Macro To VBA Code

Macros are cool for doing routine actions such as opening a form; however, VBA code is the endgame for doing more sophisticated tasks. Access 2000 allows you to convert your macros to VBA event procedures. Convert the DTButton macro to VBA code by performing the following steps:

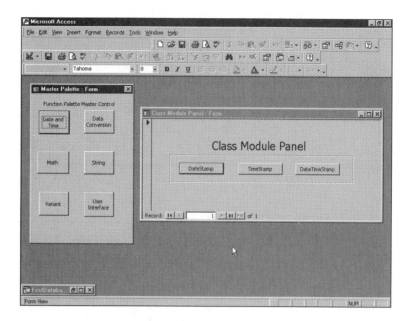

Figure 22.4
The macro you created
launches the Class
Module Panel.

1. With the Master Palette as the active form, select
   View|Design View from the Access 2000 menu bar.

2. On the menu bar Select Tools|Macros|Convert Form's Macros
   To Visual Basic to open the Convert Form Macros dialog box.
   (See Figure 22.5.)

3. Click on the Convert button, making sure that the features
   for error handling and macro comments are checked.

4. Click on OK when the Conversion Finished message appears.
   The completed macro conversion results in the following code:

```
'------------------------------------------------
' Command1_Click
'
'------------------------------------------------
Private Sub Command1_Click()
On Error GoTo Command1_Click_Err
    DoCmd.Close acForm, "Master Palette"
    DoCmd.OpenForm
"Class Module Panel", acNormal, "", "", , acNormal
    Command1_Click_Exit:
    Exit Sub
Command1_Click_Err:
    MsgBox Error$
    Resume Command1_Click_Exit
End Sub
```

NOTE

*Code in this book is
broken because of space
limitations. Do not break
the code in your routines.*

Figure 22.5
Access 2000 allows you
to convert macros to
VBA code.

By selecting View|Form View and then clicking on the Date and
Time button on the Function Palette, you'll see that the response
is exactly the same as before.

Project Using User-Defined Functions

Because the Function Palette application is meant to showcase
VBA's built-in functions in six categories, it's not designed to
demonstrate user-defined functions specifically. Therefore, let's
take a moment to add a couple of user-defined functions to the
Function Palette application, just to give you a feel for their use.
Don't worry, you'll be getting lots of practice. User-defined
functions, as you may have surmised, are code blocks you create
to return a value. Begin by performing the following steps:

1. With the form Master Palette open in Design View, right-
    click on the Form window's title bar and then select
    Properties.

2. On the Form property sheet, click on the Event tab and then
    double-click on the **OnLoad** event field.

3. When [Event Procedure] appears in the field, click on the
    button to the right of the field to open the Visual Basic Editor.

4. Place the following line of code between the **Sub** and **End
    Sub** lines:

    ```
    MsgBox Example()
    ```

5. After the **End Sub** line, place the following lines of code:

    ```
    Function Example()
        Example = "Thank you for using the
                    Function Palette Master Control!"
    End Function
    ```

NOTE

*You can view the form's
code in Design View by
selecting View|Code
from the Access 2000
menu bar.*

```
Function DoingFine()
   DoingFine = "Looks like you're
                getting the hang of this!"
End Function
```

6. Select Debug|Compile FirstDatabase, select File|Close And Return To Microsoft Access, and then close the properties sheet.

7. Right-click on the Date and Time button on the Function Palette, and then select Properties from the button's right-click menu.

8. In the button's property sheet, click on the Event tab and then double-click on the **OnClick** event field.

9. When [Event Procedure] appears in the field, click on the button to the right of the field to open the Visual Basic Editor.

10. Place the following line of code between the **Sub** and **End Sub** lines:

```
MsgBox DoingFine()
```

11. Select Debug|Compile FirstDatabase, and then select File|Close And Return To Microsoft Access.

12. Select View|Form View from the Access 2000 menu bar; your result should look similar to what's shown in Figure 22.6.

13. Click on the Date and Time button; the result is shown in Figure 22.7.

14. Close all open form and property windows.

Project Enhancing The Class Module Panel

Let's finish the coding for the Date and Time button by making some enhancements to the Class Module Control Panel. You'll complete these enhancements by performing the following steps:

1. Double-click on Master Palette in the FirstDatabase database window.

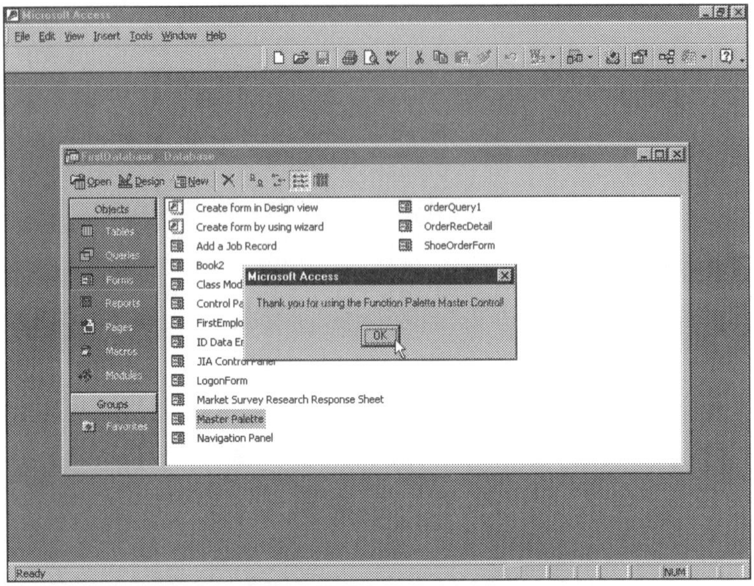

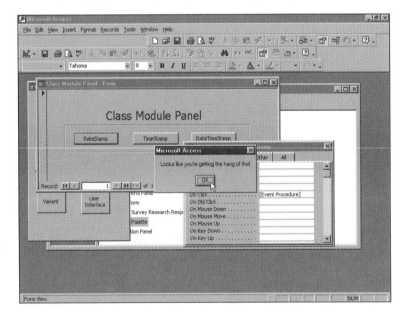

Figure 22.6
The **Example** function thanks you for opening the form.

Figure 22.7
The **DoingFine** function is called by the Date and Time button's click event.

2. After responding to the thank-you message, select the Date and Time button when the Master Control Palette opens.

3. After responding to the message box, select View|Design View from the Access 2000 menu bar.

4. Place a second row of three command buttons beneath the existing three form buttons; then center a fourth button beneath the second button row.

5. Name the buttons "Date Function," "Time Function," "Now Function," and "Exit." You make these name changes in the Caption field of the Format tab on each button's Property sheet.

6. Select Form from the Object drop-down menu on the Access 2000 Formatting toolbar, and then right-click on the Form window title bar.

7. Select Properties from the right-click menu.

8. In the Form property sheet, click on the Event tab and then double-click on the **OnLoad** event field.

9. When [Event Procedure] appears in the field, click on the button to the right of the field to open the Visual Basic Editor.

10. Place the following user-defined functions between the **Sub** and **End Sub** lines, and then delete the **Sub** and **End Sub** lines:

```
Function MyDate()
 Dim DS As New DateStamp
 TheDate = DS.DateStamp
End Function

Function MyTime()
 Dim TS As New TimeStamp
 TheTime = TS.TimeStamp
End Function

Function RightNow()
 Dim DTS As New DateTimeStamp
 ItsNow = DTS.DateTimeStamp
End Function
```

11. Create an **OnClick** event for the Date Function button by placing the following line of code between the button's **Sub** and **End Sub** lines:

```
MsgBox TheDate()
```

12. Create an **OnClick** event for the Time Function button by placing the following line of code between the button's **Sub** and **End Sub** lines:

```
MsgBox TheTime()
```

13. Create an **OnClick** event for the Now Function button by placing the following line of code between the button's **Sub** and **End Sub** lines:

```
MsgBox ItsNow()
```

14. Create an **OnClick** event for the Exit button by placing the following lines of code between the button's **Sub** and **End Sub** lines:

```
DoCmd.Close acForm, "Class Module Panel"
DoCmd.OpenForm "Master Palette", acNormal
```

15. Your enhanced Class Module Panel should appear as shown in Figure 22.8.

Now you're ready to test how the first button on the Function Palette Control Panel performs. Close all open forms in Access 2000, and then double-click on Master Palette in the FirstDatabase database window. Check out your handy work by clicking the Date and Time button to launch the enhanced Class Module Panel, and then click on each of the new buttons on the panel.

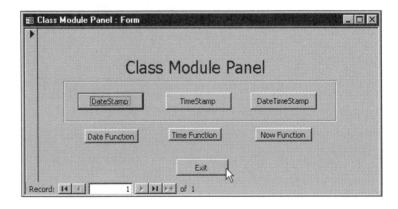

Figure 22.8
The enhanced Class Module Panel.

**Project** Designing And Programming For The Data Conversion Button

One button down and five to go! Now that the Date and Time button is completed, and it demonstrates the use of date and time functions, let's turn our attention to the data conversion category of functions. I'm sure you have the hang of panel creation by now, so have a go at building the Data Conversion Functions Panel shown in Figure 22.9; we'll add the code when you're done.

Using The Chr Function

Now you're ready to code the first panel button. This button will demonstrate how to use the **Chr** function. Create an **OnClick** event for the Chr Function button, and then place the following code between the **Sub** and **End Sub** lines:

```
Dim NewString As String
Dim JumbledString As String

NewString = InputBox("Enter your name:")
JumbledString = ""
For i = 1 To Len(NewString)
    JumbledString = JumbledString &
    Chr(Asc(Mid(NewString, i, 1)) + 1)
Next
MsgBox JumbledString, 13, "Here's your Ascii name
  converted to character codes!"
```

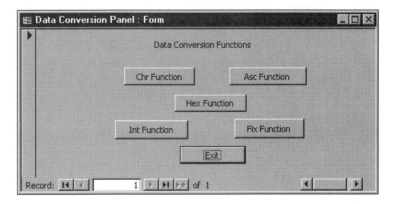

Figure 22.9
The Data Conversion
Functions Panel.

Using The Asc Function

Let's keep going by creating an **OnClick** event for the Asc Function button. This button will demonstrate how the **Asc** function differs from the **Chr** function. Place the following code between the Asc Function button's **Sub** and **End Sub** lines:

```
Dim ChrString As String
Dim UnjumbledString As String
ChrString = InputBox("Enter your jumbled name:")
UnjumbledString = ""
For i = 1 To Len(ChrString)
    UnjumbledString = UnjumbledString &
    Chr(Asc(Mid(ChrString, i, 1)) - 1)
Next
MsgBox UnjumbledString, 13, "Here's your
    character coded name converted to Ascii!"
```

Using The Hex Function

You're doing just fine. Next, repeat the previous process by creating an **OnClick** event for the Hex Function button using the following code between that button's **Sub** and **End Sub** lines:

```
Dim NumToConvert
Dim ConvertIt
NumToConvert = InputBox("Enter a number
    to convert to Hex.")
ConvertIt = Hex(NumToConvert)
MsgBox ConvertIt, 13, "Here's the number
    you entered as Hexadecimal!"
```

Using The Int Function

Between the **Sub** and **End Sub** lines, use the following code to program the Int Function button on the Data Conversion Functions Panel:

```
Dim NumToConvert2
Dim ConvertIt2
NumToConvert2 = InputBox("Enter a decimal number
    to convert using Int.")
ConvertIt2 = Int(NumToConvert2)
MsgBox ConvertIt2, 13, "Here's the number as
    affected by the Int function!"
```

Using The Fix Function

You're almost home now! Add the code below between the button's **Sub** and **End Sub** lines to produce the **OnClick** event for the Fix Function button:

```
Dim NumToConvert3
Dim ConvertIt3
NumToConvert3 = InputBox("Enter a whole number
    to convert using Fix.")
ConvertIt3 = Fix(NumToConvert3)
MsgBox ConvertIt3, 13, "Here's the number
    as affected by the Fix function!"
```

Programming The Panel Exit Button

Here's an easy one you should remember from earlier. Your final step for the Data Conversion Panel is to create the **OnClick** event that closes the panel and reopens the Master Palette. Place the following code between the **Sub** and **End Sub** lines to complete the task:

```
DoCmd.Close acForm, "Data Conversion Panel"
DoCmd.OpenForm "Master Palette", acNormal
```

Congratulations on completing the second panel's buttons. As always, test each button on the completed panel. Also, make sure the Master Palette reappears when you exit the function panel you're working with.

.Project Designing And Programming For The Math Button

The next function category you'll work with is math. The Math Functions Panel demonstrates the use of the functions **Abs, Sgn, Sqr, Rnd**, as well as the trigonometric functions **Sin, Cos, Tan**, and **Atn**. As you may have guessed, your first task is to create a Math Functions Panel like the one shown in Figure 22.10.

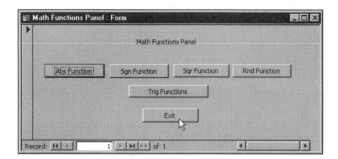

Figure 22.10
The Math Functions Panel.

Using The Abs Function

The **Abs** function returns the positive value of the argument associated with it. Create an **OnClick** event for the Abs Function button, place the following code between the **Sub** and **End Sub** lines, and then test the button:

```
Dim NumToConvert
Dim ConvertIt
NumToConvert = InputBox("Enter a number for
    the Abs function.")
ConvertIt = Abs(NumToConvert)
MsgBox ConvertIt, 13, "Here's the Abs value
    for the number you entered!"
```

Using The Sgn Function

Let's keep going by creating an **OnClick** event for the Sgn Function button. This function returns information about whether a number is positive or negative. Place the following code between the Sgn Function button's **Sub** and **End Sub** lines, and then test the button:

```
Private Sub Sgn_Function_Click()
Dim NumToConvert
Dim ConvertIt
NumToConvert = InputBox("Enter a negative number
    for the Sgn function.")
ConvertIt = Sgn(NumToConvert)
If ConvertIt = -1 Then
MsgBox "The Sgn value for the number you
    entered is less than 0"
ElseIf ConvertIt = 1 Then
MsgBox "The Sgn value for the number you
    entered is greater than 0"
ElseIf ConvertIt = 0 Then
```

```
MsgBox "The Sgn value for the number you
    entered equals 0"
Else
MsgBox "Please enter a numeric value!"
End If
End Sub
```

Using The Sqr Function

The **Sqr** function returns the square root of a number. Repeat the previous process by creating an **OnClick** event for the Sqr Function button using the following code:

```
Private Sub Sqr_Function_Click()
Dim NumToConvert
Dim ConvertIt
NumToConvert = InputBox("Enter a number to
    find the square root for.")
ConvertIt = Sqr(NumToConvert)
MsgBox ConvertIt, 13, "The square root of
    your number is..."
End Sub
```

Using The Rnd Function

The **Rnd** function returns a different number at random based on the numeric argument that's passed. Between the **Sub** and **End Sub** lines, use the following code to program the Rnd Function button:

```
Private Sub Rnd_Function_Click()
Dim RandNum
RandNum = InputBox("Enter a number to be randomized.")
Randomize
RandNum = Rnd
MsgBox RandNum
End Sub
```

Using Trig Functions

Remember high school trigonometry? These are the functions that return values for the sine, cosine, tangent, and arctangent items. Add the following code between the **Sub** and **End Sub** lines to produce the **OnClick** event for the Trig Functions button.

```
Private Sub Trig_Functions_Click()
Dim NumToConvert
Dim TheSin
```

```
Dim TheCos
Dim TheTan
Dim TheAtn
NumToConvert = InputBox("Enter a number to
    perform Trig functions on.")
TheSin = Sin(NumToConvert)
TheCos = Cos(NumToConvert)
TheTan = Tan(NumToConvert)
TheAtn = Atn(NumToConvert)
MsgBox "the Sine is " & TheSin, 13,
    "Your results are that..."
MsgBox "the Cosine is " & TheCos, 13,
    "Your results are that..."
MsgBox "the Tangent is " & TheTan, 13,
    "Your results are that..."
MsgBox "the Arctangent is " & TheAtn, 13,
    "Your results are that..."
End Sub
```

Programming The Exit Button

You can probably program this one in your sleep by now; however, here it is anyway:

```
DoCmd.Close acForm, "Math Functions Panel"
DoCmd.OpenForm "Master Palette", acNormal
```

Project Designing And Programming For The String Functions Button

Let's now take a look at functions that comprise the string category. Begin again by building your function panel (see Figure 22.11). We'll add the code as we go.

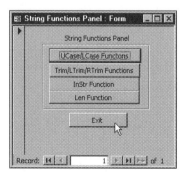

Figure 22.11
The String Functions Panel.

Using The UCase And LCase Functions

These functions let you programmatically set the case for a text string. Create an **OnClick** event for the UCase/LCase Function button, and then place the following code between the **Sub** and **End Sub** lines:

```
Private Sub UCase_LCase__Function_Click()
Dim TriggerString As String
TriggerString = InputBox("Enter a sentence
   to be cased.")
MsgBox UCase(TriggerString)
MsgBox LCase(TriggerString)
End Sub
```

Using The Trim, LTrim, And RTrim Functions

Next, create an **OnClick** event for the button that demonstrates the use of **Trim** functions. **Trim** functions are used to truncate leading and trailing spaces. Complete the **OnClick** event by placing the following code between the button's **Sub** and **End Sub** lines:

```
Private Sub Trim_LTrim_RTrim_Click()
Dim TriggerString0 As String
Dim TriggerString1 As String
Dim TriggerString2 As String
Dim TriggerString3 As String
TriggerString0 = InputBox("Enter a string with
   3 leading and 3 trailing spaces.")
MsgBox TriggerString0
TriggerString1 = InputBox("Enter a string with
   3 leading and 3 trailing spaces.")
MsgBox Trim(TriggerString1)
TriggerString2 = InputBox("Enter a string with
   3 leading spaces.")
MsgBox LTrim(TriggerString2)
TriggerString3 = InputBox("Enter a string with
   3 trailing spaces.")
MsgBox RTrim(TriggerString3)
End Sub
```

Using The InStr Function

The **InStr** function is up next. Use the following code to program the InStr Function button:

```
Private Sub InStr_Function_Click()
Dim MyString As String
MyString = InputBox("Enter either Larry, Moe,
   Curly, Joe, or Shemp")
MsgBox InStr("Larry Moe Curly Joe Shemp", MyString),
   13, "The start of the string is character..."
End Sub
```

Using The Len Function

Add the following code between the Len Function button's **Sub** and **End Sub** lines to produce its **OnClick** event:

```
Private Sub Len_Function_Click()
Dim MyString
MyString = InputBox("Enter a string to
   find the length for.")
MsgBox Len(MyString), 13, "The length of this
   string is..."
End Sub
```

Programming The Exit Button

Here's an easy one you should remember from earlier. Your final step for the String Function Panel is to create the **OnClick** event that closes the panel and reopens the Master Palette. Place the following code between the **Sub** and **End Sub** lines to complete the task:

```
Private Sub Exit_Click()
    DoCmd.Close acForm, "String Functions Panel"
    DoCmd.OpenForm "Master Palette", acNormal
End Sub
```

Project Designing And Programming For The Variant Button

The variant function category consists of two primary functions: **IsDate** and **IsNumeric**. Build the panel shown in Figure 22.12 for the Variant Function Panel, and then use the code provided to create the **OnClick** events for each panel button.

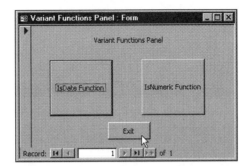

Figure 22.12
The Variant Functions Panel.

Using The IsDate Function

Place the following code in the **OnClick** event for the IsDate Function button. The **IsDate** function returns True if the value passed to it is a valid date:

```
Private Sub IsDate_Function_Click()
Dim TriggerString
Dim BadMessage
TriggerString = InputBox("Enter today's date.")
BadMessage = "This is not a Date value. Try Again!"
If IsDate(TriggerString) Then
MsgBox "The value that you've entered
    is indeed a Date value."
Else
MsgBox BadMessage
End If
End Sub
```

Using The IsNumeric Function

The **IsNumeric** function, like **IsDate**, returns True if the passed value is valid. In this case, the value must be numeric. Add the following code in the **OnClick** event for the IsNumeric Function button:

```
Private Sub IsNumeric_Function_Click()
Dim TriggerString
Dim BadMessage
TriggerString = InputBox("Enter a numeric value.")
BadMessage = "This is not a numeric value. Try Again!"
If IsNumeric(TriggerString) Then
MsgBox "The value that you've entered
    is indeed a numeric value."
```

```
Else
MsgBox BadMessage
End If
End Sub
```

Programming The Exit Button

I'm sure you already know what to do here.

Project Designing And Programming For The User Interface Button

You've been using user interface functions throughout this entire book, so, after you build the panel shown in Figure 22.13, you have the option of using the code I've supplied or creating your own to demonstrate how the functions are used.

Using The MsgBox Function

This one's a no-brainer. Creating an **OnClick** event for this button should be a piece of cake, wouldn't you say?

```
Private Sub MsgBox_Function_Click()
MsgBox "The MsgBox function is an Access 2000
    programming workhorse!"
End Sub
```

Using The InputBox Function

This one's another no-brainer. Build the **OnClick** event for this button as you wish or use the following code:

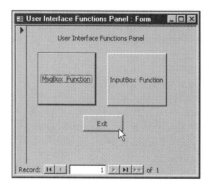

Figure 22.13
The User Interface Functions Panel.

```
Private Sub InputBox_Function_Click()
Dim TriggerString
TriggerString = InputBox("Enter any one line
    comment you choose!")
MsgBox TriggerString, 13, "Your comment was..."
End Sub
```

The User Interface Function Panel Exit Button

Don't forget your Exit button. Here's the code:

```
DoCmd.Close acForm, "User Interface Functions Panel"
DoCmd.OpenForm "Master Palette", acNormal
```

Congratulations! You've completed the Function Palette application. Now, take a moment and click through the palette and all the functions that it allows you to see. We'll discuss what you've done here and discover more about functions in the next chapter.

Where To Go From Here

In this chapter, you designed, programmed, and tested an application that allows you to see firsthand how six different categories of VBA functions can be put to use with Access 2000. This experience will serve you well because there's more programming ahead! In the next chapter, you'll get a chance to take a breather and learn a little more about the functions and techniques that you've seen in action here.

Chapter 23

Let's Talk About Functions

It's been said that we live in a world of cause and effect—an action will produce some associated result. Such is the nature of programming functions in Access 2000.

I n the last chapter, you got a firsthand look at how functions can enhance the capabilities of your Access 2000 programs. By building a utility called the Master Control Palette, you gained insight into how data can be programmatically manipulated in a variety of ways. In this chapter, you'll explore the underpinnings of the Master Control Palette utility, the basis of its development, and the functions that make it work.

Getting Acquainted With The Master Control Palette

The Master Control Palette is yet another standard Access 2000 form. Designed to demonstrate the six categories of non-user-defined functions available via VBA, the Master Control Palette provides individual working examples of each VBA built-in function available in Access 2000. You'll get detailed information on each of the Palette's individual functions in a moment. In the meantime, let's examine some of the techniques brought to bear in building the Palette utility.

NOTE

The primary difference between functions and subroutines is the fact that functions return or result in a value when processing is complete and subroutines do not.

Revisiting The Master Control Palette Development Process

Again, by applying the PRACTICE methodology to your development activity, you'll find that the purpose of the Master Control Palette form is to demonstrate the six categories of non-user-defined functions available via VBA. For this reason, it was resolved that the program should allow the user to select a function category at the click of a button, which would in turn launch a function-specific button palette. Upon selection of a button from the function-specific palette, the user would then see a message box presenting the value returned by the selected function. The six categories demonstrated by the Master Control Palette include date and time, data conversion, math, string, variant, and user interface functions.

As is usually the case, your first task was to design the form. For the Master Control Palette, you used a 2-by-3 form grid and added a label control containing the text "Function Palette Master Control." Your next task involved adding six Command Button controls to the form grid. Each of the Command Button controls were given individual captions corresponding to six respective function categories. After placing the six captioned command buttons on the form grid, you established property settings for the form that removed default scroll bars, record selectors, navigation buttons, and dividing lines. You also set the form border style to be that of a dialog box, and you disabled the capability to resize the form. You then saved your work and turned your attention to the Date and Time Button control.

Behind The Master Control Palette Buttons

When you began to activate the Master Control Palette buttons, you used macros to close the Palette when a button was selected and to open new category-specific forms, such as the Class Module Panel you created back in Chapter 10. In performing these button activation tasks, you were guided through the process of converting macro instructions to Visual Basic code using Access 2000's built-in conversion feature. In addition, you created a Master Control Palette **onLoad** event to demonstrate how user-defined functions could enhance program interactivity. Completing this event resulted in the presentation of a thank-you message with each launch of the Master Control Palette. With the exception of the Date and Time button, overall design and coding for the Master Control Palette buttons were based on a model supporting multiple function-specific forms, input boxes to collect user input, and message boxes to display results.

Function Types

Access 2000 and Visual Basic for Applications support two primary function types—user-defined functions and built-in functions. In the discussion that follows, you'll gain some additional insight into what functions are, what they do, how they do it, and how they're used. Along the way, you'll even find a few more examples to add to your Access 2000 programming bag of tricks.

User-Defined Functions

User-defined functions are small programs written by you, the developer, to return a value, to modify a value, or to test for some condition. Like user-defined procedures, user-defined functions let you keep and reuse common code blocks. This allows you to call a specific function from any point in your application whenever it's needed. Consequently, your code becomes much easier to read and maintain because you can modify the function, rather than making multiple changes to your application code. User-defined functions are typically constructed using some variation of the following syntax:

```
Function name [(list of arguments)]
    statements to execute
    [name=expression]
    [Exit Function]
    statements to execute
End Function
```

Assigning a value to the function name in the function body sets the function's return value. In cases where you don't assign a function value, zero is returned.

▶Tip

The list of arguments for functions is generally optional. However, a set of parentheses must follow the function name even if an argument list isn't applicable.

Creating A User-Defined Function To Fill A Combo Box Or List Box

In Chapter 17, you logged a little time working with Combo Box and List Box controls. Well, now you're about to learn of a little user-defined function that lets you fill a combo box or list box with an array of values or with information about the current state of a database. In practice, this function lets you create a multicolumn combo box or list box without storing values in a table or query. For instance, you could use this function to create a list box that displays the names of all open forms in one column and additional information about each form in another column. This function works as a *callback function*, which means that Access 2000 calls the function you write and uses the information you supply to fill the control. Because this user-defined "fill" function is a callback function, it must adhere to a strict format. In other words, you must use a function definition with specific arguments and specific constants. You'll find these listed in Table 23.1.

Once you've created the function, you set the **RowSourceType** property of the combo box or list box to the name of the function, without including an equal sign (=) or parentheses. Access 2000 repeatedly calls the function, starting when the form loads and ending when the combo box or list box has been filled as required. Each time Access 2000 calls the function, the function returns a value that instructs Access 2000 on how to fill the control.

Have a go at creating a fill function, using the following function definition. Remember, you must include all five arguments. The first argument must be of type **Control**, the second of type **Variant**, the third and fourth of type **Long**, and the last of type **Integer**. The function must return a variant:

Table 23.1   Arguments for the user-defined fill function.

Argument	Description
ctrl	Variable of type **Control** that refers to the combo box or list box being filled.
VrntID	Unique value that identifies the control being filled. You can also check the value of a control's **Name** property if you need to distinguish between two controls being filled by the same function.
longRw	The row currently being filled. Rows are numbered beginning with zero.
longClmn	The column currently being filled. Columns are numbered beginning with zero.
ItgrCode	A value that indicates which action Access 2000 should take on this iteration of the function.

Breaks in the code are for editorial purposes only. Do not break your code as shown in the example.

```
Function functionname(ctrl As Control,
vrntID As Variant, longRw As Long, _
    longClmn As Long,
itgrCode As Integer) As Variant
```

Whenever Access 2000 calls your fill function, a constant for the **itgrCode** argument is passed. The constant passed depends on the number of times the function has already been called. Functionally (no pun intended), the constant indicates what Access 2000 should do on a particular iteration of the function. Table 23.2 describes the constants passed for the **itgrCode** argument. This table also shows the value returned by the function when Access 2000 calls it with each particular constant.

Table 23.2   Constants passed for the ItgrCode argument.

Constant	Value	Meaning	Return Value
acLBInitialize	0	Initialize	Nonzero if the function can fill the list; False (0) or Null otherwise.
acLBOpen	1	Open	Nonzero ID value if the function can fill the list; False or Null otherwise. You can use the **Timer** function to generate a unique nonzero value.
acLBGetRowCount	3	Number	Number of rows in the list (can be zero); True (-1) if unknown.
acLBGetColumnCount	4	Number	Number of columns in the list of columns (can't be zero); must match the property sheet value.
acLBGetColumnWidth	5	Column width	Width of the column specified by the **IntCol** argument; True (-1) to use the default width.
acLBGetValue	6	List entry	List entry to be displayed in the row and column specified by the **intRow** and **intCol** arguments.
acLBGetFormat	7	Format string	Format string to be used to format the list entry displayed in the row and column specified by the **intRow** and **intCol** arguments; True (-1) to use the default format.
acLBClose	8	Not used	Not used.
acLBEnd	9	End nothing	Use this iteration of the function to free memory.

You can determine which constant has been passed on the current function call by using a **Select Case** statement. Within each case, you should include the code you want to execute when Access 2000 calls the function with the specific constant. For instance, when Access 2000 calls the function with the **acLBInitialize** constant, you may want to fill an array with values that are used to fill the combo box or list box. Each time the function runs, you assign it a return value. The return value indicates whether that iteration has been successful. For instance, if a nonzero value is returned when Access 2000 calls your function with the **acLBInitialize** constant, Access 2000 assumes that the function can fill the list and calls the function again with **acLBOpen**. If the value returned with **acLBInitialize** is False or Null, Access 2000 does not call the function again.

If a variable can be used in more than one iteration of the function, you should declare the variable as **Static** so that it preserves its value from one call to the next. For instance, if you fill the combo box or list box with an array, more than likely you'll refer to the array variable when the function is called with **acLB-Initialize** and also when it's called with **acLBGetValue**. If you declare the array variable as **Static**, the values in the array will be preserved from one function call to the next.

Access 2000 calls your function once for **acLBInitialize**, **acLBOpen**, **acLBGetRowCount**, and **acLBGetColumnCount**. With these iterations, it initializes a user-defined function, determines whether the function can fill the list, and determines the number of rows and columns in the control. Access 2000 then calls your function twice for **acLBGetColumnWidth**—once to determine the total width of the control and a second time to set the column width.

Access 2000 calls your function with the **acLBGetValue** constant to fill the list and with the **acLBGetFormat** constant to format strings in the list. Access 2000 may call your function multiple times with these constants, depending on the data with which you're filling the list. Access 2000 calls a user-defined function for **acLBEnd** when the form is closed or each time the list box or combo box is queried.

Listing 23.1 fills a combo box on a form with the list of all currently open forms. Have a go at this example by entering it into a standard module. Create a form with a combo box, and then set the control's **RowSourceType** property to **ListOpenForms**. Switch to Form View, and click on the combo box to see a list of all currently open forms:

Listing 23.1   All currently opened forms.

```
Function ListOpenForms(fld As Control, _
    id As Variant, row As Variant, _
    col As Variant, code As Variant) As Variant
    Static varReturn As Variant
    Static intCount As Integer
    Static strF() As String
    Dim intX As Integer
    ' Initialize return variable.
    varReturn = Null
    Select Case code
        ' Initialize combo box.
        Case acLBInitialize
            intCount = Forms.Count
            ' Redimension array.
            ReDim strF(intCount)
            ' Populate array with form names.
            For intX = 0 To intCount - 1
                strF(intX) = Forms(intX).Name
            Next intX
            varReturn = intX
        ' Return unique value.
        Case acLBOpen
            varReturn = Timer
        ' Indicate number of rows.
        Case acLBGetRowCount
            varReturn = intCount
        ' Indicate number of columns.
        Case acLBGetColumnCount
            varReturn = 1
        ' Specify column width.
        Case acLBGetColumnWidth
            varReturn = True
        ' Fill list with values.
        Case acLBGetValue
            varReturn = strF(row)
        ' Free memory used by array.
        Case acLBEnd
            Erase strF
```

```
        End Select
        ' Return value for each iteration of function.
        FillComboBox = varReturn
End Function
```

Built-In Functions

Access 2000 and Visual Basic for Applications provide more than 150 built-in functions to support your application development needs. Discussing each of these is beyond the scope of this book. However, so you aren't completely disappointed, I've included a rundown on the functions used to support the Master Control Palette. These functions are arranged by category, and include a brief explanation of what each function does and source code you can cut and paste to see the function's practical application.

Date And Time Functions

The functions under this category are some of the simplest you'll encounter. Their sole purpose is to tell you the current date and time using a character string. Figure 23.1 illustrates how these functions work when entered directly into the VB Editor.

![NOTE]

At this writing, certain date and time functions present a runtime error when the date input contains "00" (for example, 2/1/00, representing February 1, 2000). This is likely a Y2K glitch in the beta version of the software.

The Date Function

The **Date** function returns the current system date:

```
? Date()
```

The Time Function

The **Time** function returns the current system time:

```
? Time()
```

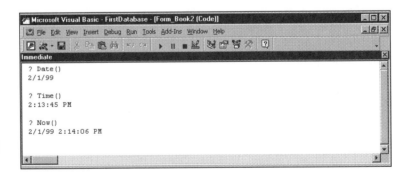

Figure 23.1
The VB Editor's Immediate window displays three date and time functions.

The Now Function

This function returns a date specifying the current date and time according to your computer's system date and time:

```
? Now()
```

Data Conversion Functions

Although data conversion functions operate to change the data from one form to another, technically, they could also qualify as string functions.

The Chr Function

The **Chr** function returns a string containing the character associated with the specified character code:

```
Dim NewString As String
Dim JumbledString As String
NewString = InputBox("Enter your name:")
JumbledString = ""
For i = 1 To Len(NewString)
    JumbledString = JumbledString &
    Chr(Asc(Mid(NewString, i, 1)) + 1)
Next
MsgBox JumbledString, 13, "Here's your Ascii name
    converted to character codes!"
```

The Asc Function

This function returns a number representing the character code corresponding to the first letter in a string:

```
Dim ChrString As String
Dim UnjumbledString As String
ChrString = InputBox("Enter your jumbled name:")
UnjumbledString = ""
For i = 1 To Len(ChrString)
    UnjumbledString = UnjumbledString &
Chr(Asc(Mid(ChrString, i, 1)) - 1)
Next
MsgBox UnjumbledString, 13, "Here's your
character coded name converted to Ascii!"
```

The Hex Function

The **Hex** function returns a string representing the hexadecimal (base 16) value of a number:

```
Dim NumToConvert
Dim ConvertIt
NumToConvert = InputBox("Enter a number
to convert to Hex.")
ConvertIt = Hex(NumToConvert)
MsgBox ConvertIt, 13, "Here's the number
you entered as Hexadecimal!"
```

The Int And Fix Functions

The **Int** function returns a value of the type passed to it containing the integer portion of a number. If the number is negative, **Int** returns the first negative integer less than or equal to the number. The **Fix** function works like the **Int** function; however, if the number is negative, **Fix** returns the first negative integer greater than or equal to the number value:

```
Private Sub Command0_Click()
Dim strComments
Dim Value
Value = InputBox("Enter a positive number with
 one decimal like 42.5")
strComments = "Value = " & Value & Chr(13) & vbCrLf
strComments = strComments & "Int(Value) = "
 & Int(Value) & Chr(13)
strComments = strComments & "Fix(Value) = "
 & Fix(Value) & Chr(13) & vbCrLf & vbCrLf
Value = InputBox("Enter a negative number
 with one decimal like -36.5")
strComments = strComments & "Value = "
 & Value & Chr(13) & vbCrLf
strComments = strComments & "Int(Value) = "
 & Int(Value) & Chr(13)
strComments = strComments & "Fix(Value) = "
 & Fix(Value) & Chr(13) & vbCrLf & vbCrLf
Value = InputBox("Enter a negative
 number with 3 decimals like -7.613")
strComments = strComments & "Value = "
 & Value & Chr(13) & vbCrLf
strComments = strComments & "Int(Value) = "
 & Int(Value) & Chr(13)
strComments = strComments & "Fix(Value) = "
 & Fix(Value) & Chr(13) & vbCrLf & vbCrLf
MsgBox strComments, 0, "The Int and Fix Functions"
End Sub
```

NOTE

Breaks in the code are for editorial purposes only. Do not break your code as shown in the example.

Math Functions

These are the functions that let you perform such exciting tasks as number randomizing and trigonometry. Great fun! Nevertheless, you'll find the functions listed here to be quite useful when you begin playing with numbers.

The Abs Function

The **Abs** function returns a value of the same type that's passed to it, specifying the absolute value of a number:

```
Dim NumToConvert
Dim ConvertIt
NumToConvert = InputBox("Enter a number for
the Abs function.")
ConvertIt = Abs(NumToConvert)
MsgBox ConvertIt, 13, "Here's the Abs value
for the number you entered!"
```

The Sgn Function

The **Sgn** function returns an integer (-1, 0, or 1), indicating the sign of a number:

```
Private Sub Sgn_Function_Click()
Dim NumToConvert
Dim ConvertIt
NumToConvert = InputBox("Enter a negative number
 for the Sgn function.")
ConvertIt = Sgn(NumToConvert)
If ConvertIt = -1 Then
MsgBox "The Sgn value for the number you
 entered is less than 0"
ElseIf ConvertIt = 1 Then
MsgBox "The Sgn value for the number you
 entered is greater than 0"
ElseIf ConvertIt = 0 Then
MsgBox "The Sgn value for the number you
 entered equals 0"
Else
MsgBox "Please enter a numeric value!"
End If
End Sub
```

The Sqr Function

As if you didn't know, this function returns the square root of a number:

NOTE

Breaks in the code are for editorial purposes only. Do not break your code as shown in the example.

```
Private Sub Sqr_Function_Click()
Dim NumToConvert
Dim ConvertIt
NumToConvert = InputBox("Enter a number to
find the square root for.")
ConvertIt = Sqr(NumToConvert)
MsgBox ConvertIt, 13, "The square root of
your number is..."
End Sub
```

The Rnd Function

This function returns a random number between 0 and 1, inclusive.

```
Private Sub Rnd_Function_Click()
Dim RandNum
RandNum = InputBox("Enter a number to be randomized.")
Randomize
RandNum = Rnd
MsgBox RandNum
End Sub
```

The Sin Function

The **Sin** function takes an angle parameter and returns its sine. The *sine* of an angle is the ratio of the side opposite the angle being evaluated, divided by the hypotenuse length:

```
Private Sub Sin_Function_Click()
Dim NumToConvert
Dim TheSin
NumToConvert = InputBox("Enter an angle
 value to return its sine.")
TheSin = Sin(NumToConvert)
MsgBox "the sine is "
 & TheSin, 13, "Your results are that..."
End Sub
```

The Cos Function

The **Cos** function takes an angle parameter and returns its cosine. The *cosine* of an angle is the ratio of the length of the side adjacent to the angle, divided by the hypotenuse length:

```
Private Sub Cos_Function_Click()
Dim TheCos
NumToConvert = InputBox("Enter an angle value to
 return its cosine.")
```

```
TheCos = Cos(NumToConvert)
MsgBox "the cosine is " & TheCos, 13,
 "Your results are that..."
End Sub
```

The Tan Function

This function returns the tangent of an angle. When you supply an angle value as a parameter, the length of the side opposite the angle is divided by the length of the side adjacent to the angle to determine the ratio value to return:

```
Private Sub Tan_Function_Click()
Dim TheTan
NumToConvert = InputBox("Enter an angle value to
 return its tangent.")
TheTan = Tan(NumToConvert)
MsgBox "the tangent is " & TheTan, 13,
 "Your results are that..."
End Sub
```

The Atn Function

The **Atn** function returns the arctangent for a given ratio. The supplied ratio represents the side opposite the angle, divided by the side adjacent to the angle:

```
Private Sub Tan_Function_Click()
Dim TheAtn
NumToConvert = InputBox("Enter a ratio value to
 return its arctangent.")
TheAtn = Atn(NumToConvert)
MsgBox "the arctangent is "
 & TheAtn, 13, "Your results are that..."
End Sub
```

String Functions

Functions in this category let you manipulate text strings. These functions could be used to change the character of the data that gets stored in your database tables.

The UCase Function

This function returns a string converted to uppercase letters:

```
Private Sub UCase_Function_Click( )
Dim TriggerString As String
```

```
TriggerString = InputBox("Enter a sentence
  to convert to uppercase.")
MsgBox UCase(TriggerString)
End Sub
```

The LCase Function

The **LCase** function returns a string converted to lowercase letters:

```
Private Sub LCase_Function_Click()
Dim TriggerString As String
TriggerString = InputBox("Enter a sentence
  to convert to lowercase.")
MsgBox LCase(TriggerString)
End Sub
```

The Trim Function

This function returns a string containing a copy of a specified string without leading and trailing spaces:

```
Private Sub Trim_Function_Click()
Dim TriggerString1 As String
TriggerString1 = InputBox("Enter a string with
  3 leading and 3 trailing spaces.")
MsgBox Trim(TriggerString1)
End Sub
```

The LTrim Function

The **LTrim** function returns a string containing a copy of a specified string without leading spaces:

```
Private Sub LTrim_Function_Click()
Dim TriggerString2 As String
TriggerString2 = InputBox("Enter a string with
  3 leading spaces.")
MsgBox LTrim(TriggerString2)
End Sub
```

The RTrim Function

The **RTrim** function returns a string containing a copy of a specified string without trailing spaces:

```
Private Sub RTrim_Function_Click()
Dim TriggerString3 As String
```

```
TriggerString3 = InputBox("Enter a string with
  3 trailing spaces.")
MsgBox RTrim(TriggerString3)
End Sub
```

The InStr Function

The **InStr** function returns a number specifying the position of the first occurrence of one string (**string2**) within another (**string1**):

```
Private Sub YourButton_Click()
    Dim strShoes, strComments
    strShoes = "dress casual running athletic"
    ' Check string for exact case
    If InStr(strShoes, "ATHLETIC") > 0 Then
      strComments = "ATHLETIC is in " &
      strShoes & vbCrLf
    Else
      strComments = "ATHLETIC is not in " &
      strShoes & vbCrLf
    End If
    ' Check string regardless of case
    If InStr(1, strShoes, "ATHLETIC", 1) > 0 Then
      strComments = strComments & "ATHLETIC is in " &
      strShoes & " but isn't case-sensitive." & vbCrLf
    Else
      strComments = strComments & "ATHLETIC is not in " &
      strShoes & " but isn't case-sensitive." & vbCrLf
    End If
msgbox strComments,0, "The InStr Function"
End Sub
```

The Len Function

The **Len** function returns the number of characters in a string:

```
Private Sub Len_Function_Click()
Dim MyString
MyString = InputBox("Enter a string to
 find the length for.")
MsgBox Len(MyString), 13, "The length of this
 string is..."
End Sub
```

Variant Functions

This category of functions lets you test for certain data types and can prove quite useful when you're trying to validate user input.

The IsDate Function

The **IsDate** function requires a variable as an argument and returns True if the variable is a date. This function comes in handy when you want to verify that a valid date has been entered. The source code that follows performs a check to see whether the date contained in the code is valid. When the program encounters a valid date, a message box will appear confirming that fact. When an invalid date is found, you'll get another message, and when a string is found instead of a date, you'll also be alerted. Create a form that contains a single command button, and then create an event procedure that uses this code:

```
Private Sub YourButton_Click()
    Dim DateCheck
    DateCheck = "2/1/99"
    If IsDate(DateCheck) = True Then
    MsgBox DateCheck & " is a valid date", 0, "Date Test"
    Else
    MsgBox DateCheck & " is not a valid date.",
     0, "Date Test"
    End If
    DateCheck = "9/37/00"
    If IsDate(DateCheck) = True Then
    MsgBox DateCheck & " is a valid date", 0, "Date Test"
    Else
    MsgBox DateCheck & " is not a valid date.",
     0, "Date Test"
    End If
    DateCheck = "You've got to be kidding!"
    If IsDate(DateCheck) = True Then
    MsgBox DateCheck & " is a valid date", 0, "Date Test"
    Else
    MsgBox DateCheck & " is not a valid date.",
     0, "Date Test"
    End If
End Sub
```

The IsNumeric Function

This function returns True if the variable is storing a number. Otherwise, it returns False. Generally, you'll want to use this function to make sure a user has entered a valid number when numeric data is the required input. Create an event procedure and try out the following code:

```
Private Sub YourButton_Click()
Dim Number
    Number = 2025
    If IsNumeric(Number) = True Then
        MsgBox Number & " is indeed a number."
    Else
        MsgBox Number & " is not a number."
    End If
    Number = "Twenty Twenty-Five"
    If IsNumeric(Number) = True Then
        MsgBox Number & " is indeed a number."
    Else
        MsgBox Number & " is not numeric value."
    End If
End Sub
```

User Interface Functions

These are the functions that allow you to interact with your application. You've seen quite a bit of them already, but here's a little information that's nice to know.

The MsgBox Function

You should be extremely familiar with this function by now. It displays a message in a dialog box, waits for the user to click a button, and returns an integer indicating which button the user clicked. However, you may not have known that you can customize the **MsgBox** function using a variety of numeric values. These values, listed in Table 23.3, let you determine which buttons appear, which button is the default, and whether an icon appears.

Try the following code in an event procedure (the result is shown in Figure 23.2):

```
Private Sub Command0_Click()
Dim Demo
Demo = MsgBox("Does this demonstrate how code 3
  and others are used?", vbYesNoCancel + vbQuestion +
  vbDefaultButton1, "Custom Message Box")
End Sub
```

You can also use the results returned by a custom message box to determine what action should occur next. This is accomplished by using the return codes that result when buttons on a message box are clicked. These codes are listed in Table 23.4.

Table 23.3 Customizing codes for the MsgBox function.

Code	VB Constant	Effect
0	**vbOKonly**	Displays the OK button only
1	**vbOKCancel**	Displays the OK and Cancel buttons
2	**vbAbortRetryIgnore**	Displays the Abort, Retry, and Ignore buttons
3	**vbYesNoCancel**	Displays the Yes, No, and Cancel buttons
4	**vbYesNo**	Displays the Yes and No buttons
5	**vbRetryCancel**	Displays the Retry and Cancel buttons
16	**vbCritical**	Displays the Critical Message icon
32	**vbQuestion**	Displays the Warning Query icon
48	**vbExclamation**	Displays the Warning Message icon
64	**vbInformation**	Displays the Information Message icon
128	**vbDefaultButton1**	Makes the first button the default
256	**vbDefaultButton2**	Makes the second button the default
512	**vbDefaultButton3**	Makes the third button the default

Table 23.4 Button click return codes.

Code	What Has Occurred
1	User clicked the OK button.
2	User clicked the Cancel button.
3	User clicked the Abort button.
4	User clicked the Retry button.
5	User clicked the Ignore button.
6	User clicked the Yes button.
7	User clicked the No button.

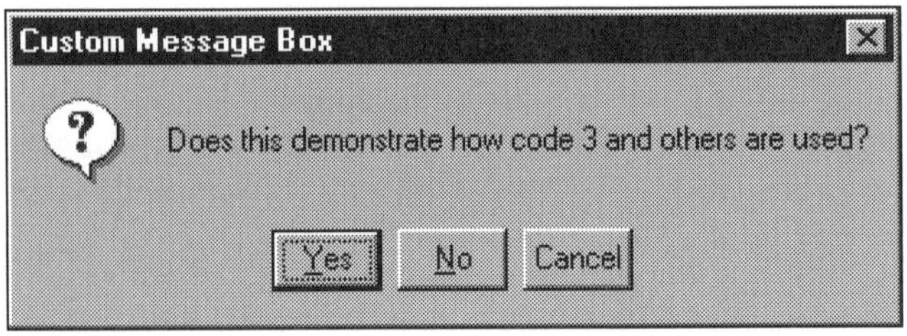

Figure 23.2
A customized message box.

Custom Message Box

Does this demonstrate how code 3 and others are used?

Yes · No · Cancel

Place the following code in an event procedure and see what happens:

```
Sub YourButton_Click
Dim Demo
Demo = MsgBox("Does this demonstrate how
 code 3 and others are used?", vbYesNoCancel +
 vbQuestion + vbDefaultButton1, "Custom Message Box")
If Demo = 6 Then
MsgBox "You're absolutely right!"
Else
MsgBox " You should have clicked Yes!"
End If
End Sub
```

The InputBox Function

This is another function with which you're intimately familiar. The **InputBox** function displays a prompt in a dialog box, waits for the user to input text or click a button, and returns a string containing the contents of the text box:

```
Private Sub InputBox_Function_Click()
Dim TriggerString
TriggerString = InputBox("Enter any one line
 comment you choose!")
MsgBox TriggerString, 13, "Your comment was..."
End Sub
```

Where To Go From Here

Hey, how about those functions! In this chapter, you took a look at user-defined and built-in functions. You learned how to build a user-defined function to populate a Combo Box or List Box control, and you even got the chance to review the work you did on the Master Control Palette form. Add to that the fact that you learned how to customize a message box and use its results, and I'd say you've covered quite a bit of ground. From here, you're going to build one final program that ties everything together.

Chapter 24

Client/Server Design With Access Technologies

Throughout this book, you've learned about developing applications for the desktop. However, Access 2000 also provides powerful client/server tools that can help you expand your data storage throughout the enterprise.

Some techniques of performing client/server programming have been in place since the introduction of Access for Windows 95, whereas others have been made available in subsequent versions. In this chapter, we'll first briefly consider some things you can do from the straight Access interface, and then we'll move on to a brief discussion of the use of Access Data Projects (ADPs) in conjunction with SQL Server to manage SQL Server databases quickly and efficiently.

Furthermore, client/server database programming creates some unique issues, including such topics as record locking, transaction processing, and more. We'll take some time to consider how to programmatically access these concerns within this chapter, leaving the more in-depth discussion of the items for Chapter 25.

Designing Client/Server Databases With MDB Files

As you'll learn in Chapter 25, you cannot design true client/server databases using only Access files—the Access database, although relational, is nevertheless a flat-file database and therefore has serious problems transitioning to a full client/server environment. However, if you're designing a database for light use by 10 people within a workgroup, you can pretty easily transition a standard desktop database to one that works in a simulated client/server environment with the Database Splitter Wizard and the use of simple table linking. The following sections discuss these methods in more detail.

Project Using The Database Splitter Wizard And Managing Links

To use the Database Splitter Wizard to split the objects within a database into two separate MDB files, perform the following steps:

1. Open the database whose objects you want to split.

2. Select Tools|Database Utilities|Database Splitter. The Database Splitter dialog box appears, as shown in Figure 24.1.

3. Click on Split Database. The Create Back-End Database dialog box will appear.

4. Enter the name for the database that will contain all the tables and click on Split. The Database Splitter Wizard creates a new database that contains all the tables. Links are created between the current database and the database containing the tables. When it finishes, the wizard will display a message indicating that the split was successful and then return you to the Database window.

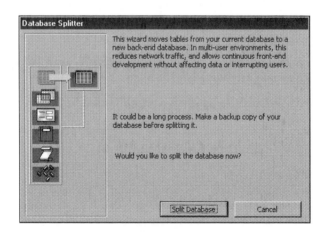

Figure 24.1
The Database Splitter dialog box.

Creating Links To Access Tables

To create a link to an Access table, perform the following steps:

1. Right-click on any tab of the Database window.

2. Select Link Tables. The Link dialog box will appear.

3. Within the Link dialog box, select the name of the database containing the table you want to link to.

4. Click on Link. The Link Tables dialog box will appear.

5. Within the Link Tables dialog box, select the tables to which you want to establish a link.

6. Click on OK. The link process finishes. Notice the arrow indicating that the tables are linked tables rather than tables whose data is stored within the current database.

Creating Links To Other Types Of Tables

The process of creating links to other types of database files is a little different. To create a link to another type of database file, perform the following steps:

1. Right-click on any tab of the Database window.

2. Select Link Tables. The Link dialog box will appear.

3. Within the Link dialog box, use the Files Of Type drop-down list to indicate the type of table you're linking to.

4. Select the external file whose data you'll be linking to.

5. Click on Link. The Select Index Files dialog box will appear. It's important that you select any index files associated with the data file. These indexes are automatically updated by Access 2000 as you add, change, and delete table data from within Access.

6. You'll receive a message indicating that the index was added successfully and that you can add other indexes if you choose. Click on OK.

7. Add any additional indexes, and click on Close when done.

8. Access 2000 displays the Select Unique Record Identifier dialog box. This dialog box enables you to select a unique identifier for each record in the table. Select a unique field and click on OK.

Notice the icon indicating the type of file you linked to.

Updating Links That Have Moved

To refresh a link using VBA code, perform the following steps:

1. Redefine the connection string.

2. Perform a **RefreshLink** method on the table definition. The code looks like this:

```
Sub RefreshLink()
  Dim db As Database

  Set db = CurrentDb
  db.TableDefs!OtherCusts.Connect = _
      "Access 9.0;DATABASE=d:\newdir"
  db.TableDefs!OtherCusts.RefreshLink
End Sub
```

This routine can be modified to prompt the user for the directory containing the data tables. The modified routine looks like this:

```
Sub RefreshLink()
  Dim db As DATABASE
  Dim tdf As TableDef
  Dim strNewLocation As String

  On Error GoTo RefreshLink_Err
  Set db = CurrentDb
  Set tdf = db.TableDefs("tblClients")
  tdf.RefreshLink
  Exit Sub

RefreshLink_Err:
  strNewLocation = InputBox("Please Enter " & _
      "Database Path and Name")
```

```
      db.TableDefs!tblClients.Connect = _
          ";DATABASE=" & strNewLocation
   Resume
End Sub
```

This routine points a **TableDef** object to the tblClients table. It then issues a **RefreshLink** method on the table definition object. The **RefreshLink** method attempts to refresh the link for the table. When an error occurs, an input box prompts the user for the new location of the database. The **Connect** property for the database is modified to incorporate the new location. The code then resumes on the offending line of code (the **RefreshLink** line). This routine should be modified to allow the user a way out, because the **Resume** routine in this code throws the user into an endless loop when the database isn't available. Modifying the code is left as an exercise for you to try on your own.

Deleting Links From Code

To remove a link using VBA code, simply execute a **Delete** method on the table definition collection of the database:

```
Sub RemoveLink()
   Dim db As Database

   Set db = CurrentDb
   db.TableDefs.Delete "OTHERCUSTS"
End Sub
```

▶**Tip**

Although Access 2000 provides legacy tools for working with true client/server databases, if you know you'll be designing only for use against an SQL Server back end, you're generally best served to use ADPs. However, if your back end is an Oracle back end, for example, you'll instead have to use an Access MDB file with VBA code to connect to the remote database.

Working With SQL Databases From Access Databases

A little later in this chapter, you'll see how to use ADPs to connect with SQL Server databases. However, Access MDB files also provide you with several tools—most notably, VBA code—that let you connect to and manage data on remote databases. In the following sections, we'll consider some of these techniques.

.*Project* Creating A Remote View From Access

To create a remote view from Access 2000, perform the following steps:

1. Create a new query.

2. When you're prompted with the Show Table dialog box, click on Close *without* selecting a table.

3. Select Query|SQL Specific|Pass-Through.

4. Type the Create View statement.

5. Click on Run.

6. Select a SQL datasource. Click on OK.

7. Supply the login information and click on OK.

Once you create a remote view, you can link to it like any other table. When you link to the view, you're prompted with the Select Unique Record Identifier dialog box. It's very important to supply Access 2000 with a unique index. Otherwise, the results of the view won't be updatable. The view can then be treated as if it were a link to a table.

.*Project* Executing A Stored Procedure With VBA Code

The following procedure executes the **sp_columns** stored procedure—a standard SQL Server system stored procedure that has analogs (that is, similar constructs) in most server-side back ends:

```
Sub StoredProcedure()
  Dim ws As Workspace
  Dim db As Database
  Dim dbAccess As Database
  Dim qdf As QueryDef
  Dim rst As Recordset

  Set dbAccess = CurrentDb
  Set ws = DBEngine(0)
```

```
    Set db = ws.OpenDatabase("", False, False, _
        "ODBC;DATABASE=Pubs;DSN=PublisherData;" &
            "UID=SA;PWD=")
    Set qdf = dbAccess.CreateQueryDef("")
    qdf.Connect = "ODBC;DATABASE=Pubs;" &
        DSN=PublisherData;UID=SA;PWD="
    qdf.SQL = "sp_columns 'sales'"
    qdf.ReturnsRecords = True
    Set rst = qdf.OpenRecordset(dbOpenSnapshot)
    Do While Not rst.EOF
      Debug.Print rst.Fields("Column_Name")
      rst.MoveNext
    Loop
End Sub
```

Here's how it works. Because you want to return records, you can't use the **Execute** method. Another way to execute a pass-through query is to first create a Data Access Object (DAO) **QueryDef** object. In this case, the **QueryDef** object is temporary (notice the quotation marks). The **Connect** property is set for the **QueryDef** object. Rather than specifying a back-end-specific SQL statement, the SQL property of the **QueryDef** object is set to the name of the stored procedure and any parameters it expects to receive. The **ReturnsRecords** property of the **QueryDef** object is set to True. The **OpenRecordset** method is then issued on the **QueryDef** object. This returns the snapshot-style **Recordset** from the stored procedure. The **Do...While** construct loops through the resulting recordset, printing the Column_Name column of each row returned from the **sp_columns** stored procedure.

NOTE

You must add the DAO library to the application to use the DAO code in this chapter.

.*Project* Using OpenDatabase To Connect To A Remote Server Database

The following subroutine shows how you can use the **OpenDatabase** function to connect to a remote server database (again, this particular block of code is designed for use with SQL Server but can be easily modified to work against any back end):

```
Sub OpenRemoteDB(strDBName As String, _
    strDataSetName As String, _
    strUserID As String, strPassWord As String)
```

► **Tip**

Preconnecting to a server is always a good idea, but it's an especially good idea when you're in environments where the server may not always be available—for example, across a WAN. Preconnecting to the server lets your program code immediately respond if there's a problem with the server, which can greatly reduce user frustration.

```
Dim ws As Workspace
Dim db As Database
Dim tdf As TableDef
Dim intCounter As Integer
Dim strConnectString As String

Set ws = DBEngine(0)
strConnectString = "ODBC;DATABASE=" & strDBName & _
    ";DSN=" & strDataSetName & ";UID=" & strUserID & _
    ";PWD=" & strPassWord
Set db = ws.OpenDatabase( "", False, False, _
    strConnectString)
For Each tdf In db.TableDefs
  Debug.Print tdf.Name
Next tdf
End Sub
```

The routine is called like this:

```
Call OpenRemoteDB("Pubs", "PublisherData", "SA", "")
```

The routine uses the **OpenDatabase** method of the **Workspace** object to open the Pubs database with the connect string specified. It then loops through the collection of table definitions, listing all the tables found within the remote server database.

.Project Preconnecting To A Server

The following code preconnects to the server. It would generally be placed in the startup form for your application:

```
Sub PreConnect(strDBName As String, _
    strDataSetName As String, _
    strUserID As String, strPassWord As String)
  Dim db As Database
  Dim strConnectString As String
  strConnectString = "ODBC;DATABASE=" & strDBName & _
      ";DSN=" & strDataSetName & ";UID=" & strUserID & _
      ";PWD=" & strPassWord
  Set db = OpenDatabase("", False, False, _
      strConnectString)
  db.Close    ' Closes database but maintains connection
End Sub
```

The trick here is that the connection and authentication information will be maintained even when the database is closed.

Using Access Data Projects For Client/Server Design

Although you have a great number of techniques at your disposal for client/server database programming—from DAO pass-through code to unbound forms with ADO objects—Access 2000 introduces a new kind of project (ADPs) that simplifies the design and management of SQL Server 6.5/7.0 databases across a network. ADPs also let you design front ends for your SQL Server databases using the more intuitive Access IDE.

Depending on your network installation, you might not currently have access to a SQL Server, or your database administrator might not want you to create a lot of tables against that server as part of your development process. Thankfully, Access 2000 includes the installation for the Microsoft Database Engine (MSDE), a local installation of SQL Server 7. In the following sections, we'll explore how to install the MSDE, as well as some of the issues involved in upsizing Access 2000 databases to SQL Server, working against the SQL Server, and more.

 ## Installing The MSDE Engine

If your network already uses SQL Server 7, you can create Access Data Projects (ADPs) directly against the SQL Server across the network. Alternatively, you can use the MSDE, installed locally, to create the connections and the SQL Server database. For simplicity's sake, in this chapter, we'll create a database with the MSDE. You must first install the MSDE onto your local, development machine (Access 2000 will not do it automatically). To install the engine, perform the following steps:

1. Insert the Office 2000 CD-ROM 1 into the CD-ROM drive. Using Windows Explorer, navigate to the \SQL\X86\Setup directory.

2. Within the directory, double-click on the file named SetupSQL.exe. Windows will start to run the MSDE installation program.

After executing the file, follow the prompts to install MSDE onto your computer. When you finish the installation, the installer will prompt you to reboot your machine. You must do so before you can use the MSDE for project design.

 ## Starting The SQL Server Service

After you install the MSDE and reboot the system, your computer will come back up with the SQL Server service icon in the system tray. However, you'll notice that the icon has a red circle over it, which indicates that the service is not currently running. To start the service (a necessary step to use the MSDE), perform the following steps:

1. Double-click on the SQL Server service icon in the system tray. Windows will display the SQL Server Service Manager.

2. The Server combo box should contain the name of the computer on which the service is running, and the dialog box should indicate that the service is stopped. Click on the Start/Continue button to start the service. Additionally, if you plan to use the MSDE regularly during development, you may want to instruct the service to start automatically when the operating system boots. If so, click on the Auto-start Service When OS Starts checkbox. When you finish, the dialog box should look similar to the one shown in Figure 24.2.

In addition, the icon in the system tray should change to a green arrow pointing right. You can either close the Service Manager dialog box entirely or minimize it, depending on whether you plan to use the Service Manager regularly.

Figure 24.2
The SQL Server Service Manager after you start the service.

 **Project** Upsizing An Existing Database To SQL Server

One of the new features of Access 2000 is its provision for easy upsizing of your databases to SQL Server 7. The easiest way to perform an upgrade of this type from within the Access IDE is through the Upsizing Wizard. To use the Upsizing Wizard on the Chap24BE.mdb database, perform the following steps:

1. Choose Open from the File menu, and open the Chap24BE.mdb database.

2. Select Tools|Database Utilities|Upsizing Wizard. Access 2000 will display the dialog box shown in Figure 24.3.

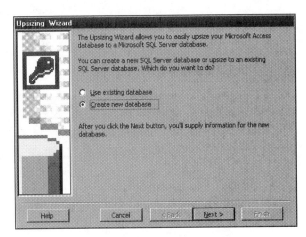

Figure 24.3
The opening dialog box of the Upsizing Wizard.

3. For this exercise, use the Create New Database option (although you can upsize into an existing database if you so choose). Click on Next to move to the next dialog box.

4. You'll be prompted to select a SQL Server to use for the database, as well as a login ID and password for a user who has Create rights on the database. Finally, it prompts you to name the new SQL Server database. After you perform these actions, click on Next to move the next dialog box.

5. You'll be prompted to select which tables to export to the SQL Server. Click on the >> button to export all the tables. Click on Next to move to the next dialog box.

6. The next dialog box lets you export table attributes in addition to data (see Figure 24.4). Accept the defaults, and click on Next to move to the next dialog box.

7. In the next dialog box, you can opt to keep your existing application as is, change the application to support links to the SQL Server tables, or create an Access Data Project (ADP) to connect to the table. Select the Create A New Access Client/Server Application option, and accept the default name. Click on Next to move to the next dialog box.

8. After you click on Finish in the last dialog box, the Upsizing Wizard will use the information you've entered to create the new SQL Server database and the ADP to access the database.

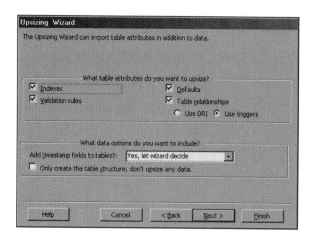

Figure 24.4
The data export selection dialog box in the Upsizing Wizard.

The new ADP maintains all your current forms and reports, but it does not maintain any data locally—instead, all data is maintained in the new SQL Server.

Working With The Access Data Project

As with standard Access 2000 databases, you must first create the data project before you can begin to work with it.

Creating An ADP

To create an ADP, perform the following steps:

1. Choose New from the File menu. Access 2000 displays the New dialog box.

2. Within the General tab of the dialog box, double-click on the Project (New Database) icon. If you're designing a project to work with an existing SQL Server 7 back end, you can choose the Project (Existing Database) icon. We'll be creating a new database as we create the project.

3. After you double-click on the Project (New Database) icon, Access 2000 displays the File New Database dialog box. Click on Create to save the new project as Chap24FE.adp. Access will display the Microsoft SQL Server Database Wizard.

4. Within the first combo box, enter the name of the server for the SQL Server database (which you can obtain from the SQL Server Service Manager or from your network administrator).

5. Enter a login ID and password of an account with Create Database privileges on the server. Finally, enter "Chap24BESQL" as the name of the new database. Click on Next to move to the last dialog box in the wizard.

6. Click on Finish. The MSDE will create the SQL Server database and return you to the Database window.

As you saw earlier in this chapter, the Database window has some additional objects that a normal MDB window doesn't have—views, database diagrams, and stored procedures. You'll learn more about these objects in Chapter 25.

Project Creating The Tables

As you saw earlier, the first step in creating a database is to create the tables that will reside in it. When you do this through an ADP, the tables are automatically created on the SQL Server, and the links to the Server data are automatically created in the project. We'll use a database example similar to others you've seen—a simple order entry database. The following sections detail how to create the tables in the database.

Creating The BillTo Table

The first table to create is the BillTo table. This table will maintain address information about the customer, which the program will (ultimately) use to maintain billing information for each customer. The design of the table is pretty straightforward—as is the design of the most of the tables in this example. To design the BillTo table, perform the following steps:

1. Double-click on the Create Table In Design View option within the Database window. When you do so, Access 2000 may display the prompt shown in Figure 24.5. If so, go ahead and install the Client Server Visual Design Tools. You'll need to insert Office 2000 CD-ROM 1 into the drive to do so.

2. After installing the design tools, Access 2000 displays the Table 1:Table Design window. It also prompts you to enter a name for the table. Enter the name as "BillTo" and click on OK.

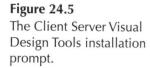

Figure 24.5
The Client Server Visual Design Tools installation prompt.

▶Tip

Depending on how many records will actually be in the table, using the uniqueidentifier field for your primary key is generally overkill—it is, after all, a 16-byte number, which means it will generate more IDs than there are computers on the Internet before it repeats. In general, you could probably get by with an autonumbered long integer as the key value. We're simply using it here to show its availability.

3. As you can see, the Design window is somewhat different than the Access 2000 Table Design window. However, most of what you know will translate; we'll explore specifics of the Design window in Chapter 25. Within the window, specify the fields in the table as shown in Table 24.1.

4. Scroll to the right, and click in the IsRowGuid checkbox for the CustomerNum field. The designer will place a checkmark in the box and set the default value for the field to **newid()**.

5. Click in the AllowNulls checkbox for the CustomerNum field. The designer will remove the checkmark from the box.

6. Click on the gray selector box to the left of the CustomerNum field. Access 2000 will highlight the entire field.

7. Click on the primary key button on the toolbar. Access 2000 will display a primary key symbol in the selector. When you finish these steps, the designer will look similar to Figure 24.6.

8. Click on the Close button on the window to close the designer. Access 2000 will prompt you to save the design changes.

Table 24.1   The fields in the BillTo table.

Field Name	Data Type	Length
CustomerNum	uniqueidentifier	16
CustomerFirst	char	25
CustomerLast	char	25
Address1	char	25
Address2	char	25
City	char	25
State	char	2
Zip	char	10
Phone	char	14
Fax	char	14

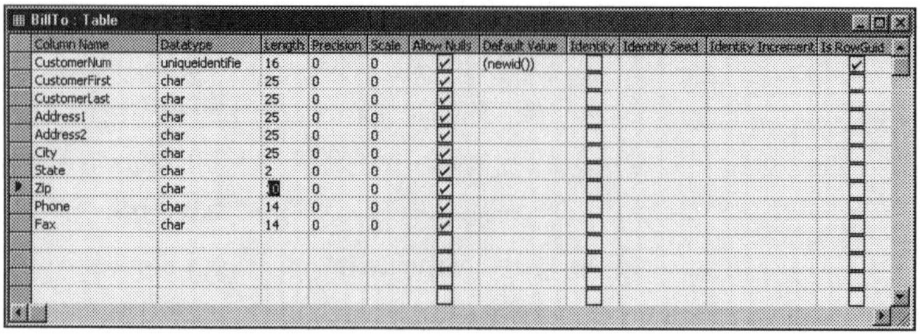

Figure 24.6
The designer after you create the BillTo table.

Creating The ShipTo Table

The second table to create is the ShipTo table. This table will maintain shipping address information about the customer, which the program will use to keep records about where orders were shipped. As with the BillTo table, the design of this table is pretty straightforward. To design the ShipTo table, perform the following steps:

1. Double-click on the Create Table In Design View option within the Database window. Access 2000 will display the Table 1 : Table Design window. It also prompts you to enter a name for the table. Enter the name as "ShipTo" and click on OK.

2. Within the window, specify the fields in the table as shown in Table 24.2.

Table 24.2   The fields in the ShipTo table.

Field Name	Data Type	Length
ShipToNum	uniqueidentifier	16
CustomerNum	uniqueidentifier	16
CustomerFirst	char	25
CustomerLast	char	25
Address1	char	25
Address2	char	25
City	char	25
State	char	2
Zip	char	10
Phone	char	14
Fax	char	14

3. Scroll to the right, and click in the IsRowGuid checkbox for the ShipToNum field. The designer will place a checkmark in the box and set the default value for the field to **newid()**.

4. Click in the AllowNulls checkbox for the ShipToNum field. The designer will remove the checkmark from the box.

5. Click on the gray selector box to the left of the ShipToNum field. Access 2000 will highlight the entire field.

6. Click on the primary key button on the toolbar. Access 2000 will display a primary key symbol in the selector.

7. Click on the Close button on the window to close the designer. Access 2000 will prompt you to save the design changes.

Creating The OrderLookup Table

The next table to create is the OrderLookup table. This table will maintain shipping address information about the customer, which the program will use to link the customer information to the order information. To design the table, perform the following steps:

1. Double-click on the Create Table In Design View option within the Database window. Access 2000 will display the Table 1 : Table Design window. It also prompts you to enter a name for the table. Enter the name as "OrderLookup" and click on OK.

2. Within the window, specify the fields in the table as shown in Table 24.3.

3. Click on the gray selector box to the left of the CustomerNum field. Hold the Shift key down, and click on the gray selector box to the left of the OrderNum field. The designer will highlight all three fields.

Table 24.3   The fields in the OrderLookup table.

Field Name	Data Type	Length	AllowNulls
CustomerNum	uniqueidentifier	16	False (unchecked)
ShipToNum	uniqueidentifier	16	False (unchecked)
OrderNum	uniqueidentifier	16	False (unchecked)

4. Click on the primary key button on the toolbar. Access 2000 will display a primary key symbol in the selector next to the three fields, indicating that the primary key will be derived from their combined values.

5. Click on the close button on the window to close the designer. Access 2000 will prompt you to save the design changes.

Creating The Orders Table

Next, we'll create the Orders table. This table will maintain order information and combine the line items from the OrderDetail table with the date and total information it contains when it displays the invoice. To design the Orders table, perform the following steps:

1. Double-click on the Create Table In Design View option within the Database window. Access 2000 will display the Table 1 : Table Design window. It also prompts you to enter a name for the table. Enter the name as "Orders" and click on OK.

2. Within the window, specify the fields in the table as shown in Table 24.4.

3. Scroll to the right, and click in the IsRowGuid checkbox for the OrderNum field. The designer will place a checkmark in the box and set the default value for the field to **newid()**.

4. Click in the AllowNulls checkbox for the OrderNum field. The designer will remove the checkmark from the box.

Table 24.4   The fields in the Orders table.

Field Name	Data Type	Length
OrderNum	uniqueidentifier	16
OrderDate	datetime	8
DeliveryDate	datetime	8
Total	money	8

5. Click on the gray selector box to the left of the OrderNum field. Access 2000 will highlight the entire field.

6. Click on the primary key button on the toolbar. Access 2000 will display a primary key symbol in the selector.

7. Click on the close button on the window to close the designer. Access 2000 will prompt you to save the design changes.

Creating The ItemInformation Table

The next table to create is the ItemInformation table. This table will maintain specific information about items. You should create this table before the OrderDetail table so that you can simply use a lookup between the tables to fill in the ItemNumber field in the OrderDetail table. To design the ItemInformation table, perform the following steps:

1. Double-click on the Create Table In Design View option within the Database window. Access 2000 will display the Table 1 : Table Design window. It also prompts you to enter a name for the table. Enter the name as "ItemInformation" and click on OK.

2. Within the window, specify the fields in the table as shown in Table 24.5.

3. Scroll to the right, and click in the IsRowGuid checkbox for the ItemNum field. The designer will place a checkmark in the box and set the default value for the field to **newid()**.

4. Click in the AllowNulls checkbox for the ItemNum field. The designer will remove the checkmark from the box.

Table 24.5   The fields in the ItemInformation table.

Field Name	Data Type	Length
ItemNum	uniqueidentifier	16
Description	varchar	50
Price	money	8

5. Click on the gray selector box to the left of the ItemNum field. Access 2000 will highlight the entire field.

6. Click on the primary key button on the toolbar. Access 2000 will display a primary key symbol in the selector.

7. Click on the close button on the window to close the designer. Access 2000 will prompt you to save the design changes.

Creating The Discount Table

Next, we'll create the Discount table (the next-to-last table in the database). This table will maintain specific information about discounts. You should create this table before the OrderDetail table so you can simply use a lookup between the tables to fill in the DiscountNum field in the OrderDetail table. To design the Discount table, perform the following steps:

1. Double-click on the Create Table In Design View option within the Database window. Access 2000 will display the Table 1 : Table Design window. It also prompts you to enter a name for the table. Enter the table's name as "Discount" and click on OK.

2. Within the window, specify the fields in the table as shown in Table 24.6.

3. Scroll to the right, and click in the IsRowGuid checkbox for the DiscountNum field. The designer will place a checkmark in the box and set the default value for the field to **newid()**.

4. Click in the AllowNulls checkbox for the DiscountNum field. The designer will remove the checkmark from the box.

5. Click on the gray selector box to the left of the DiscountNum field. Access 2000 will highlight the entire field.

Table 24.6 The fields in the Discount table.

Field Name	Data Type	Length
DiscountNum	uniqueidentifier	16
DiscountValue	decimal	9
DiscountDescription	varchar	50

6. Click on the primary key button on the toolbar. Access 2000 will display a primary key symbol in the selector.

7. Click on the close button on the window to close the designer. Access 2000 will prompt you to save the design changes.

Creating The OrderDetail Table

The last table to create is the OrderDetail table. This table will maintain specific information about discounts. To design the OrderDetail table, perform the following steps:

1. Double-click on the Create Table In Design View option within the Database window. Access 2000 will display the Table 1 : Table Design window. It also prompts you to enter a name for the table. Enter the table's name as "OrderDetail" and click on OK.

2. Within the window, specify the fields in the table as shown in Table 24.7.

3. Scroll to the right, and click in the IsRowGuid checkbox for the OrderItemID field. The designer will place a checkmark in the box and set the default value for the field to **newid()**.

4. Click in the AllowNulls checkbox for the OrderItemID field. The designer will remove the checkmark from the box.

5. Click on the gray selector box to the left of the OrderItemID field. Access 2000 will highlight the entire field.

6. Click on the primary key button on the toolbar. Access 2000 will display a primary key symbol in the selector.

7. Click on the close button on the window to close the designer. Access 2000 will prompt you to save the design changes.

Table 24.7   The fields in the OrderDetail table.

Field Name	Data Type	Length
OrderItemID	uniqueidentifier	16
OrderNum	uniqueidentifier	16
ItemNum	uniqueidentifier	16
DiscountNum	uniqueidentifier	16

NOTE

You can use transaction processing with standalone Access 2000 databases. However, transaction processing is more important with client/server databases because of the variety of issues involved in using transactions on a server—not to mention the greatly increased number of users in a client/server environment.

A Brief Discussion Of Transaction Processing

When you work with client/server environments, you'll often find that transaction processing is a particularly important part of your design considerations. Although transaction processing will be discussed in greater depth in Chapter 25, for now you can think of it as sets of processing actions. For example, if you use an **UPDATE** query, the database engine will not perform the update on *any* of the affected records until it is sure it can perform the update on *all* of the affected records. Transaction processing follows a similar principle, except you control how the transaction is processed rather than the underlying database engine.

Project Using Pessimistic Locking With Transaction Processing

Pessimistic record locking means that the database engine locks a record as soon as a user accesses the record, and it does not release the lock on the record until after the user is no longer accessing it. Consider this the opposite of *optimistic record locking*, which is explained in the next section. Transaction processing interactions with record locking are crucial, because in any large environment, it's inevitable that record locking will occur. The following VBA code provides an example of how to perform transaction processing from code with pessimistic record locking:

```
Sub PessimisticTrans(strOldCity As String, _
        strNewCity As String)
  Dim wrk As Workspace
  Dim db As Database
  Dim rst As Recordset
  Dim strCriteria As String

  Set wrk = DBEngine(0)
  Set db = CurrentDb()
  Set rst = db.OpenRecordSet("tblCustomers", _
      dbOpenDynaset)
  rst.Lockedits = True   'Pessimistic Locking
```

Tip

In general, unless a particular transaction is mission critical, you'll typically find that pessimistic record locking can cause significant performance delays on your server. As a rule, keep transaction sets that use pessimistic record locking small and try to run the transactions during low-access times to minimize the impact they will have on other users of the database.

```
   strCriteria = "[City] = '" & strOldCity & "'"
   rst.FindFirst strCriteria
   wrk.BeginTrans
   Do Until rst.NoMatch
     rst.Edit                        ' Lock occurs here
       rst.Fields("City") = strNewCity
     rst.Update
     rst.FindNext strCriteria
   Loop
   wrk.CommitTrans                    ' Lock released here
End Sub
```

Here, you can see that the lock is in place from the very first edit that occurs until **CommitTrans** is issued. This means no one can update any pages of data involving the edited records until **CommitTrans** is issued. This can be prohibitive during a long process.

Coding Around Pessimistic Locking Conflicts

It's fairly simple to write code to handle pessimistic locking conflicts. Here's an example of what your code should look like:

```
Sub PessimisticRS(strCustID As String)
  Dim db As Database
  Dim rst As Recordset
  Dim strCriteria As String
  Dim intChoice As Integer

  On Error GoTo PessimisticRS_Err
  Set db = CurrentDb()
  Set rst = db.OpenRecordSet("tblCustomers", _
    dbOpenDynaset)
  rst.LockEdits = True  'Invoke Pessimistic Locking
  strCriteria = "[CustomerID] = '" & strCustID & "'"
  rst.FindFirst strCriteria
  rst.Edit                          ' Lock occurs here
    rst.Fields("City") = "Las Vegas"
  rst.Update                        ' Lock released here
  Exit Sub

PessimisticRS_Err:
  Select Case Err.Number
    Case 3197
      rst.Move 0
      Resume
```

```
        Case 3260
          intChoice = MsgBox(Err.Description, _
              vbRetryCancel + vbCritical)
          Select Case intChoice
            Case vbRetry
              Resume
            Case Else
              MsgBox "Couldn't Lock"
          End Select
        Case 3167
          MsgBox "Record Has Been Deleted"
        Case Else
          MsgBox Err.Number & ": " & Err.Description
        End Select
End Sub
```

The error-handling code for this routine handles all the errors
that can occur with pessimistic locking. If a Data Has Changed
error occurs, the data is refreshed by the **rs.Move 0** invocation
and the code resumes on the line causing the error, thus forcing
the **Edit** method to be reissued. If a 3260 error occurs, the user is
asked whether he or she wants to try again. If the user responds
affirmatively, the **Edit** is reissued; otherwise, the user is informed
that the lock failed. If the record being edited has been deleted,
an error 3167 occurs. The user is informed that the record has
been deleted. Here's what your code should look like when
transaction processing is involved:

```
Sub PessimisticRSTrans()
  Dim wrk As Workspace
  Dim db As Database
  Dim rst As Recordset
  Dim intCounter As Integer
  Dim intTry As Integer
  Dim intChoice As Integer

  On Error GoTo PessimisticRSTrans_Err
  Set wrk = DBEngine(0)
  Set db = CurrentDb
  Set rst = db.OpenRecordSet("tblCustomers", _
      dbOpenDynaset)
  rst.LockEdits = True
  wrk.BeginTrans
```

```
         Do While Not rst.EOF
            rst.Edit
               rst.Fields("CompanyName") = _
                     rst.Fields("CompanyName") & "1"
            rst.Update
            rst.MoveNext
         Loop
         wrk.CommitTrans
         Exit Sub

PessimisticRSTrans_Err:
         Select Case Err.Number
            Case 3197
               rst.Move 0
               Resume
            Case 3260
               intCounter = intCounter + 1
               If intCounter > 2 Then
                  intChoice = MsgBox(Err.Description, _
                     vbRetryCancel + vbCritical)
                  Select Case intChoice
                     Case vbRetry
                        intCounter = 1
                     Case vbCancel
                        Resume CantLock
                  End Select
               End If
               DoEvents
               For intTry = 1 To 100: Next intTry
               Resume
            Case Else
               MsgBox "Error: " & Err.Number & _
                     ": " & Err.Description
         End Select
CantLock:
      wrk.Rollback
      Exit Sub
End Sub
```

This code attempts to lock the record. If it's unsuccessful (that is, an error 3260 is generated), it tries three times before prompting the user for a response. When the user selects Retry, the process repeats. Otherwise, a rollback occurs and the subroutine is exited. When a Data Has Changed error occurs, the subroutine refreshes the data and tries again. When any other error occurs, the **Rollback** method is issued and none of the updates are accepted.

Project Using Optimistic Locking With Transaction Processing

As you saw in the previous section, pessimistic record locking locks the record at the point it is entered and does not release the lock until after the record is exited. In the case of transaction processing, pessimistic locking can result in the locking of large numbers of records within the database. Optimistic locking, on the other hand, locks the record only during the actual update itself; with optimistic locking, the record is only locked after it is updated, and the lock is related as soon as the entire transaction is committed.

From a coding perspective, optimistic locking with transaction handling isn't much different than pessimistic locking. As the code reaches the **Update** method for each record, that record is locked. The code appears as follows:

▶Tip

Again, note that the records are locked—and will remain locked—until the transaction is completed. As a general rule, regardless of the type of locking you're using, be careful to minimize the impact of a single transaction on the database— work to make sure each transaction is truly atomic so that you don't end up crippling your database performance with long sets of transactions that don't release record locks for extended periods of time.

```
Sub OptimisticTrans(strOldCity As String, _
    strNewCity As String)
  Dim wrk As Workspace
  Dim db As Database
  Dim rst As Recordset
  Dim strCriteria As String

  Set wrk = DBEngine(0)
  Set db = CurrentDb()
  Set rst = db.OpenRecordSet("tblCustomers", _
    dbOpenDynaset)
  rst.Lockedits = False   'Optimistic Locking
  strCriteria = "[City] = '" & strOldCity & "'"
  rst.FindFirst strCriteria
  wrk.BeginTrans
  Do Until rst.NoMatch
    rst.Edit
      rst.Fields("City") = strNewCity
    rst.Update                    ' Lock occurs here
    rst.FindNext strCriteria
  Loop
  wrk.CommitTrans                 ' Lock released here
End Sub
```

Coding Around Optimistic Locking Conflicts

Remember that with optimistic locking, VBA attempts to lock the page when the **Update** method is issued. A strong chance exists that a 3197 (Data Has Changed) error could occur. This needs to be handled within your code. Let's modify the preceding subroutine for optimistic locking:

```
Sub OptimisticRS(strCustID)
  Dim db As Database
  Dim rst As Recordset
  Dim strCriteria As String
  Dim intChoice As Integer
  Set db = CurrentDb()

  On Error GoTo OptimisticRS_Err
  Set rst = db.OpenRecordSet("tblCustomers", _
    dbOpenDynaset)
  rst.Lockedits = False 'Optimistic Locking
  strCriteria = "[CustomerID] = '" & strCustID & "'"
  rst.FindFirst strCriteria
  rst.Edit
    rst.Fields("City") = "Las Vegas"
  rst.Update              ' Lock occurs and is released here
  Exit Sub

OptimisticRS_Err:
  Select Case Err.Number
    Case 3197
      If rst.EditMode = dbEditInProgress Then
        intChoice = MsgBox("Overwrite Other " &
        "User's Changes?", _
        vbYesNoCancel + vbQuestion)
        Select Case intChoice
          Case vbCancel, vbNo
            MsgBox "Update Cancelled"
          Case vbYes
            rst.Update
            Resume
        End Select
      End If
    Case 3186, 3260  'Locked or Can't Be Saved
      intChoice = MsgBox(Err.Description, _
          vbRetryCancel + vbCritical)
```

```
                    Select Case intChoice
                      Case vbRetry
                        Resume
                      Case vbCancel
                        MsgBox "Update Cancelled"
                    End Select
                Case Else
                  MsgBox "Error: " & Err.Number & _
                      ": " & Err.Description
                End Select
            End Sub
```

As with the pessimistic error handling, this routine traps for all potential errors that can occur with optimistic locking. In the case of a Data Has Changed conflict, the user is warned of the problem and asked whether he or she wants to overwrite the other user's changes or cancel his or her own changes. In the case of a locking conflict, the user is asked whether he or she wants to try again. Here's what the code looks like with transaction processing involved:

```
Sub OptimisticRSTrans()
  Dim db As Database
  Dim rs As Recordset
  Dim iCounter As Integer
  Dim iTry As Integer
  Dim iChoice As Integer

  On Error GoTo OptimisticRSTrans_Err
  Set db = CurrentDb
  Set rs = db.OpenRecordSet("tblCustBackup", _
      dbOpenDynaset)
  rs.Lockedits = False
  BeginTrans
  Do While Not rs.EOF
    rs.Edit
      rs.Fields("CompanyName") = _
          rs.Fields("CompanyName") & "1"
    rs.Update
    rs.MoveNext
  Loop
  CommitTrans
  Exit Sub
```

```
OptimisticRSTrans_Err:
  Select Case Err.Number
    Case 3197
      If rs.EditMode = dbEditInProgress Then
        iChoice = MsgBox("Overwrite Other " & _
          "User's Changes?", vbYesNoCancel + vbQuestion)
        Select Case iChoice
          Case vbCancel, vbNo
            Resume RollItBack
          Case vbYes
            'rs.Update
            Resume
        End Select
      End If
    Case 3186, 3260  'Locked or Can't Be Saved
      iCounter = iCounter + 1
      If iCounter > 2 Then
        iChoice = MsgBox(Err.Description, _
          vbRetryCancel + vbCritical)
        Select Case iChoice
          Case vbRetry
            iCounter = 1
          Case vbCancel
            Resume RollItBack
        End Select
      End If
      DoEvents
      For iTry = 1 To 100: Next iTry
      Resume
    Case Else
      MsgBox "Error: " & Err.Number & _
        ": " & Err.Description
  End Select

RollItBack:
  Rollback
  Exit Sub
End Sub
```

When a Data Has Changed conflict occurs and the user opts not to overwrite the other user's changes, the entire processing loop is canceled (a rollback occurs). When a locking error occurs, the lock is retried several times. If it's still unsuccessful, the entire transaction is rolled back.

Project Testing To See Who Has A Record Locked

Regardless of what type of error occurs with record locking, it's often useful to find out who has locked a particular record. This can be easily accomplished using VBA code. It's simply a matter of parsing the **Description** property of the **Err** object, as shown in the following code:

```
Sub WhoLockedIt()
  Dim db As Database
  Dim rst As Recordset

  On Error GoTo WhoLockedIt_Err
  Set db = CurrentDb
  Set rst = db.OpenRecordset("tblCustomers", _
      dbOpenDynaset)
  rst.Edit
    rst.Fields("CompanyName") = "Hello"
  rst.Update
  Exit Sub

WhoLockedIt_Err:
  Dim strName As String
  Dim strMachine As String
  Dim intMachineStart As Integer

  intMachineStart = InStr(43, Err.Description, _
      " on machine ") + 13
  If Err = 3260 Then
    strName = Mid(Err.Description, 44, _
        InStr(44, Err.Description, "'") - 44)
    strMachine = Mid(Err.Description, _
        intMachineStart, _
        Len(Err.Description) - intMachineStart - 1)
  End If
  MsgBox strName & " on " & strMachine & _
      " has the record locked already."
End Sub
```

The preceding routine simply parses the standard error description, pulling out the user name and machine name, and displays the information within a custom error message box.

Where To Go From Here

In this chapter, you learned the basics of working with client/ server programming and transaction processing in Access 2000. You also designed your first Access Data Project (ADP) and viewed several different sets of code to help you work with client/ server programming—whether from an ADP or from a standard Access 2000 database. You also reviewed some transaction-processing code to assist you in working with transactions on client/server databases.

In the next chapter, you'll look more at some of the general theory behind client/server design and at some of the specifics of working with ADPs. You'll also take a closer look at some of the issues surrounding transaction processing.

Chapter 25

Working Further With Client/Server Database Design

Programming for a multiuser environment— whether a pure client/server, distributed workgroup, or some other multiuser configuration— has issues of its very own. Evaluating those issues closely is part of your responsibility as a programmer.

Needless to say, whenever you introduce multiple computers into the equation, effective programming becomes more difficult. When you consider the fact that client/server today can also include Internet front ends as well as connection to a wide variety of back ends, from SQL Server to Oracle, the innate complexity of client/server programming is only increased.

This chapter will discuss some of the primary issues of client/server development, from reasons for using client/server to more specific issues such as the importance of record locking. You'll also learn more about some of the new objects specific to Access Data Projects (ADP) and how they interact with their counterparts at the SQL Server.

Uses For Databases In Client/Server Environments

The most common use, and without question the most appropriate design, for databases in the corporate environment is the client/server model. In this model, all the data is maintained in a single central location or a series of central locations. Individual users access the data by using applications specifically designed to reach it. Security is greatly improved, and client/server databases can handle many more transactions (and can handle them more

▶**Tip**

The two other common database models are the standalone model and the mainframe model. In the standalone model, all data is stored on the local machine and all processing occurs on that machine. In the mainframe model, all data is stored on the central computer and all processing occurs on that computer.

efficiently) than either of the other two common models, as noted in the Tip. In general, a client/server implementation will use SQL Server, Oracle, or some other highly scalable database product as its back end and some type of application as its front end. In this book, we'll consider Access front ends to client/server back ends. Client/server constructions should meet the following requirements:

- Data should be shared throughout the organization.

- There should be significant benefits to combining disparate pieces of data from different segments of the organization.

- The quantities of data should be enough that scalability is an issue.

- The number of users should be enough that scalability is an issue.

- Security should be a concern.

- The network backbone should be capable of handling the data passed back and forth to the server.

- The database should become large enough that different storage models are important.

- The database might accept large quantities of transactions that will succeed or fail as whole transactions, and should be able to process such transactions efficiently.

- The database should be accessed by a highly distributed client base—perhaps even from the Internet.

In general, the majority of organizations will find that their mission-critical data—whatever it may be—is best served in the client/server environment. Such databases are stable, particularly if the server platform they're on is also stable. In the vast majority of cases, client/server databases may need to handle thousands, even millions of transactions without a hiccup—a feat that most Access databases are not capable of performing.

Needless to say, you'll find some applications that fit squarely into this full client/server category. However, you may also find other applications that, although designed for multiple users, may not need the power and overhead of using a database server. The next section considers some of the things you can do to build a multiuser application without going to a database server environment.

Designing Your Application With Multiple Users In Mind

When you develop applications that will be accessed over the network by multiple users, you must ensure that these applications effectively handle the sharing of data and other application objects. Many options are available for developers when they design multiuser applications. This chapter covers the pros and cons of these options.

Multiuser issues are the issues surrounding the locking of data. These issues include deciding where to store database objects, when to lock data, and how much data to lock. In a multiuser environment, having several users simultaneously attempting to modify the same data can generate conflicts. As a developer, you need to handle these conflicts. Otherwise, your users will experience unexplainable errors.

Numerous methodologies exist for handling concurrent access to data and other application objects by multiple users. Each of these methodologies introduces solutions as well as problems. It's important that you select the best solution for your particular environment.

Strategies For The Installation Of Your Application

You can employ various strategies for the installation of your application, which may make it more compatible with a multiuser environment, such as the following:

- Install both the application and data on a file server.
- Install the data on the file server and the application on each workstation.

In other words, after you've created an application, you can place the entire application on the network, which means that all the tables, queries, forms, reports, macros, and modules that make up the system reside on the file server. Although this method of shared access keeps everything in the same place, you'll see many advantages to placing only the data tables in a database on the file server. The remainder of the objects are placed in a database on each user's machine. Each local application database is linked to the tables on the network. In this way, users share data but not the rest of the application objects.

The advantages of installing on the file server one database containing data tables and installing locally another database containing other application objects include the following:

- Because each user has a copy of the local database objects (queries, forms, reports, macros, and modules), load time and network traffic are both reduced.

- It's very easy to back up data without having to back up the rest of the application objects.

- When redistributing new versions of the application, you don't need to be concerned with overwriting the application's data.

- Multiple applications can all be designed to use the same centrally located data.

- Users can add their own objects (such as their own queries) to their local copies of the database.

In addition to storing the queries, forms, reports, macros, and modules that make up the application in a local database, most developers also recommend that you store the following objects within each local database:

- Temporary tables

- Static tables

- Semistatic tables

Temporary tables should be stored in the database that's located on each workstation, because when two users are performing operations that build the same temporary tables, you don't want one user's process to interfere with the other user's process. The potential conflict of one user's temporary tables overwriting the other's can be eliminated by storing all temporary tables in each user's local copy of the database.

You should also place static lookup tables, such as a state table, on each workstation. Because the data does not change, maintenance isn't an issue. The benefit is that Access 2000 doesn't need to pull that data over the network each time it's needed.

Semistatic tables can also be placed on the local machine. These tables are rarely updated. As with static tables, the major benefit of having these tables reside in a local database is that reduced network traffic means better performance, not only for the user requiring the data but also for anyone sharing the same network wire. Changes made to the semistatic tables can be transported to each workstation using replication.

The Basics Of Linking To External Data

Linking to external data is covered in more depth later in this chapter, beginning in the section entitled "Using Access 2000 As A Front End." However, at this point, you need to understand the three options available to you when linking to external data:

- Design the databases separately from the start.
- Include all objects in one database and split them manually when you're ready to distribute your application.
- Include all objects in one database and split them using the Database Splitter Wizard.

Be aware that when distributing an application using linked tables, you need to write code to ensure that the data tables can be located from each application database on the network. When each user has the same path to the file server, this isn't a problem. If the path to the file server varies, you need to write a routine that ensures the tables can be located. If they can't be located, the routine should prompt the user for the location of the data.

Splitting Tables And Other Objects

In a multiuser environment, it's almost imperative that the tables that make up your system be placed in one database and the rest of the system objects be placed in another database. For simplicity, this chapter refers to the database containing the tables as the *Table database* and the database containing the other objects as the *Application database*. You connect the two databases by linking the Application database to the Table database. The reasons for this strategy are:

- Maintainability

- Performance

- Scalability

Assume for a moment that you distribute your application as one Access 2000 database stored within a single MDB file. Your users work with your application for a week or two, writing down all the problems and needed changes. It's time for you to make modifications to your application. Meanwhile, live data has been entered into the application for two weeks. You make a copy of the database (which includes the live data) and make all the fixes and changes. This process takes a week. After you finish your work on the database, you're ready to install your copy of the database back to the network.

Unfortunately, the users of the application have been adding, editing, and deleting records all week. Copying your file back now will eliminate all their changes—not the best option, obviously. Data replication can help you with this problem. The simplest solution is to split the database objects so that the tables (your data) are in one MDB file, and the rest of your database objects (your application) are in a second MDB file. When you're ready to install the changes, all you need to do is to copy the Application database to the file server. The new Application database can then be installed on each client machine from the file server. In this way, users can run the new copy of the application from their machines. The database containing your data tables remains intact and is unaffected by the process.

The second benefit of splitting the database objects concerns performance. Your Table database obviously needs to reside on the network file server so the data can be shared among the users of the system. There's no good reason why the other components of the database need to be shared. Access 2000 provides optimal performance when the Application database is stored on each local machine. This method not only dramatically improves performance, but it also greatly reduces network traffic. When the Application database is stored on the file server, the application objects and code need to be sent over the network each time an object in the database is opened. If the Application database is stored on each local machine, only the data needs to be sent over the network. The only complication of this scenario is that each time the Application database is updated, it needs to be redistributed to the users—a small inconvenience relative to the performance benefits that are gained through this structural split.

The third benefit of splitting tables from the other database objects relates to scalability. Because the tables are already linked—that is, because the application and the data are already stored separately—it's easy to change from a link to a table stored in Access's own proprietary format to any Open Database Connectivity (ODBC) database, such as Microsoft SQL Server or Oracle8. This capability gives you quick-and-dirty access to client/server databases. If you've already thought through the design of your system with linked tables in mind, the transition is that much easier. Don't be fooled, though, by how easy this sounds. Many issues are associated with using Access 2000 as a front end to client/server data that go far beyond a matter of simply linking to the external tables.

A few special types of tables should be stored in the Application database rather than in the Table database. Tables that rarely change should be stored in the Application database on each user's local machine. An example would be a state table. In most situations, this table rarely, if ever, changes. On the other hand, it's continually accessed to populate combo boxes, to participate in queries, and so on. By placing the state table on each local machine, you improve performance and reduce network traffic. Temporary tables should also be placed on each local machine. This is more a necessity than an option. When two users are running the same process at the same time and that process utilizes temporary tables, a conflict occurs as one user overwrites the other's temporary tables. Placing temporary tables on each local machine improves performance and eliminates the chance of potentially disastrous conflicts.

NOTE

You saw how to use the Database Splitter Wizard in Chapter 24.

If you've already designed your application and have included all the tables in the same database as the rest of your database objects, don't despair. You can use the Database Splitter Wizard to divide up your database.

Determining When Client/Server Is Appropriate

Client/server was not as necessary when there was a clear delineation between mainframe applications and personal computer applications. Today, the line of demarcation is becoming blurry. Personal computer applications are beginning to take over many applications that had been relegated to mainframe computers in the past. The "line of demarcation" is blurred even further with the introduction of technology such as object request brokers (ORBs). The problem is that we're still very limited by the bandwidth of network communications. This is one place where client/server can really help.

Many developers are confused about what client/server really is. Access 2000 is a front-end application that can process data stored on a back end. In this scenario, the Access application runs on the client machine, accessing data stored on a database server running software such as Microsoft SQL Server. Access 2000 does an excellent job acting as the client-side, front-end software in this scenario. The confusion lies in Access 2000's capability to act as a database server.

Many people mistakenly believe that an Access MDB database file stored on a file server acts as a database server. This isn't the case. The difference lies in the way in which data is retrieved when Access 2000 is acting as the front end to a database server versus when the data is stored in an Access MDB file. Imagine the following scenario:

Assume you have a table with 500,000 records. A user runs a query that's based on the 500,000-record table stored in an Access 2000 database on a file server. The user wants to see a list of all Nevadans who make more than $75,000 per year. With the data stored on the file server in the Access MDB file format, all records are sent over the network to the workstation, and the query is performed on the workstation. This results in significant network traffic.

On the other hand, assume that these 500,000 records are stored on a database server such as Microsoft SQL Server. The user runs the same query. In this case, only the names of Nevadans who make more than $75,000 per year are sent over the network. In fact, if you request only specific fields, only the fields you request are retrieved.

Considering the implications of this for your development, why you should become concerned with client/server technology and what doing so can offer you are difficult—but important—questions. The following bulleted points briefly discuss some guidelines for why you might want to upsize:

- *Large volume of data*—As the volume of data within an Access 2000 database increases, you'll probably notice a degradation in performance. While you will typically notice this degradation at around 100MB, you might find that the need to upsize occurs when your database is significantly larger or smaller than 100MB.

- *Large number of concurrent users*—Just as a large volume of data can be a problem, so can a large number of concurrent users. In fact, more than 10 users concurrently accessing an Access 2000 database can really degrade performance.

- *Demand for faster performance*—Certain applications, by nature, demand better performance than others. An online transaction-processing (OLTP) system generally requires significantly better performance than a decision support system (DSS). Not only does the client/server architecture, itself, lead to better performance, but most back-end database servers can utilize multithreaded operating systems with multiple processors. Access 2000 can't.

- *Problems with increased network traffic*—As a file server within an organization experiences increasing demands, the Access application might simply worsen an already growing problem. By moving the application data to a database server, the reduced demands on the network overall might provide all users on the network with better performance regardless of whether they're utilizing the Access application.

- *Importance of backup and recovery*—The backup and recovery options offered with an Access MDB database stored on a file server simply don't rival the options for backup and recovery on a database server. All the available tools simply means that there's less chance of data loss or downtime. With certain applications, this type of backup and recovery is overkill. With other applications, it's imperative.

- *Importance of security*—Access 2000 offers what can be considered the best security for a desktop database. However, this security can't compare with that provided by most database servers. If security is an important consideration, you'll almost always be better served by moving to a database server environment.

- *Need to share data among multiple front-end tools*—With a back-end database server that supports ODBC, front-end applications can be written in a variety of front-end application software, all concurrently utilizing the same back-end data.

▶**Tip**

Some of what back ends have to offer in terms of backup and recovery can be mimicked by using code and replication. However, it's nearly impossible to get the same level of protection from an Access 2000 database stored on a file server that you can get from a true back-end database stored on a database server.

Using Access 2000 As A Front End

If you're planning to use Access 2000 as a front end to other databases, you need to consider a few issues. In fact, the whole design methodology of your system will differ depending on whether you plan to store your data in an Access 2000 database or on a back-end database server.

In a system where your data is stored solely in Access tables, the Jet engine part of Access 2000 provides all data retrieval and management functions. All security, data validation, and enforcement of referential integrity are handled by the Jet engine.

In a system where Access 2000 acts as a front end to client/server data, the server provides the data management functions. The server is responsible for retrieving, protecting, and updating data on the back-end database server. In a situation where Access 2000 mimics a front end, the local copy of Access 2000 is responsible only for sending requests and getting either data or pointers to data back from the database server. When you're creating an application in which Access 2000 behaves as a front end, you need to capitalize on Access's strengths as well as on the server's strengths, which can be a very challenging endeavor.

Access 2000 As The Front End And Back End

In earlier sections of this chapter, we briefly discussed some of the issues surrounding using Access 2000 as both the front end and the back end. In such cases, the Access database isn't acting as a true back end in that it's not doing any processing. The Access application resides on the workstation. Utilizing the Microsoft Jet engine, it communicates with data stored in an Access MDB database file stored on the file server. This architecture is best employed only in very small deployment environments.

▶Tip

In addition to the following suggestions for the use of Access 2000 in a client/server environment, you can, of course, choose to use an Access Data Project (ADP) as a front end. However, when you use an ADP as a front end, it's effectively a very thin client—the file uses a completely different structure than a regular MDB file does. Furthermore, ADPs can only be used with SQL Server as the database server.

Access 2000 As The Front End Using Links To Communicate To A Back End

In this scenario, back-end tables can be linked to the front-end application database. The process of linking to back-end tables is almost identical to that of linking to tables in other Access databases or to external tables stored in FoxPro, Paradox, or dBASE. After the back-end tables have been linked to the front-end application database, they can be treated like any other linked tables. Access 2000 utilizes ODBC to communicate with the back-end tables.

In use, your application sends an Access SQL statement to the Access Jet engine. Jet translates the Access SQL statement into ODBC SQL and then sends it to the ODBC Manager. The ODBC manager locates the correct ODBC driver and passes it the ODBC SQL statement. The ODBC driver, supplied by the back-end vendor, translates the ODBC SQL statement into the back end's specific dialect. The back-end-specific query is sent to the SQL server and to the appropriate database. As you might imagine, all this translation takes quite a bit of time. That's why one of the two alternatives that follow might be a better solution.

Access 2000 As The Front End Using SQL Pass-Through To Communicate To A Back End

One of the bottlenecks of linked tables is the translation of the Access SQL statement by Jet to ODBC SQL, which is translated by the ODBC driver to a generic SQL statement. Not only is the translation slow, but there might be other reasons why you'd want to bypass the translation process. Here are some examples:

- Access SQL might not support some operation that's supported by the native query language of the back end.

- Either the Jet engine or the ODBC driver produces a SQL statement that isn't optimized for the back end.

- You want a process performed in its entirety on the back end.

Let's look at what happens when a pass-through query is executed. The pass-through query is written in the syntax specific to the back-end database server. Although the query does pass through the Jet engine, Jet does not perform any translation on the query; neither does ODBC. The ODBC manager sends the query to the ODBC driver, which passes the query on to the back end without performing any translation. In other words, exactly what was sent from Access 2000 is what is received by the SQL database.

Notice that the Jet engine, the ODBC manager, and the ODBC driver aren't eliminated entirely. They're still there, but they have much less impact on the process than they do with attached tables. However, pass-through queries aren't a complete solution, although they're very useful. For example, the results of a pass-through query aren't updatable. Furthermore, because pass-through queries are written in the back end's specific SQL dialect, you need to rewrite them if you swap out your back end. For these reasons, and others, pass-through queries are usually used in combination with other solutions.

Creating A Pass-Through Query Using The User Interface

To create a pass-through query, you can build the query in the Access 2000 Query Builder. To do this, select Query|SQL Specific|Pass-Through menu. Access 2000 presents you with a

DAO Pass-Through Queries Vs. Standard DAO Queries

Ordinarily, when you store and execute a query in Access 2000, even if it's running on remote data, Access compiles and optimizes the query. In many cases, this is exactly what you want. On certain other occasions, however, it might be preferable for you to execute a pass-through query because they aren't analyzed by Access 2000's Jet engine. They're passed directly to the server, and this reduces the time it takes for Jet to analyze the query and enables you to pass server-specific syntax to the back end. Furthermore, pass-through queries can log informational messages returned by the server. Finally, bulk update, delete, and append queries are faster using pass-through queries than they are using Access 2000 action queries based on remote tables.

Negative considerations with pass-through queries include the fact that they always return a snapshot, rendering them non-updatable. You also must know the exact syntax that the server requires, and you must type the statement into the query window rather than painting it graphically. Finally, you can't parameterize a query so that it prompts the user for a value.

text-editing window in which you can enter the query statement. The SQL statement that you enter must be in the SQL flavor specific to your back end.

Access 2000 As The Front End Using ActiveX Data Objects (ADOs) To Communicate To A Back End

One additional scenario is available when working with a back-end database server. This involves using ActiveX Data Objects (ADO). Using ADO, you bypass the Jet engine entirely; SQL statements are written in ODBC SQL. ADO is a very thin wrapper on the OLE DB COM interfaces—which are themselves a wrapper of the ODBC application programming interface (API) calls. The SQL statement travels quickly through all the layers to the back-end database. From a performance standpoint, this solution puts Jet to shame. The major advantage of ADO over pass-through queries is you write the SQL statements in ODBC SQL rather than the back-end-specific SQL. This means your application is easily portable to other back-end database servers. You can swap out your back end with little modification to your application.

The major disadvantage of ADO is that it can't be used with bound forms or reports—meaning a lot more coding for you. As with pass-through queries, this option can be used in combination with the other solutions to gain required performance benefits in mission-critical parts of the application.

Things You Need To Worry About In Converting To Client/Server

The transition to client/server isn't always a smooth one. You need to consider several things when you're developing a client/server application or are planning to eventually move your application from an Access 2000 database to a back-end database:

- Not all field types supported in Access 2000 are supported in every back-end database.

- Any security that you implement in Access 2000 isn't converted to your back-end database.

- Validation rules that you set up in Access 2000 need to be reestablished on the back end.

- Referential integrity isn't supported on all back ends. If it's supported on your back end, it's not automatically carried over from Access 2000.

- Queries involving joins that were updatable within Access 2000 aren't updatable on the back-end server.

This list is just an overview of what you need to think about when you're moving an application from an Access 2000 database with attached tables to a back end, or when you're developing specifically for a back end. Many of these issues have far-reaching implications.

For example, when you set up validation rules and validation text within your application, the rules need to be rewritten as triggers on the back end. This isn't your only problem. If a validation rule is violated on the back end, you'll get a returnable error code. You have to handle this returnable error code using error handling within your application, displaying the appropriate message to your user. The **Validation Text** property can't be used.

Benefits And Costs Of Client/Server Technology

With all the issues discussed in the previous section, you might ask why you should bother with client/server technology. It does provide significant benefits but involves large costs in time and money to implement properly. In each case, you need to evaluate whether the benefits of client/server technology outweigh the costs. The major benefits to client/server technology include the following:

- Greater control over data integrity

- Increased control over data security

- Increased fault tolerance

- Reduced network traffic

- Improved performance

- Centralized control and management of data

The major costs of client/server technology include the following:

- Increased development costs

- Hardware costs for the server machine

- Setup costs for the server database

It's important to note that these costs are relatively minor when compared with the cost of a mainframe or other more traditional, large-scale implementations.

Client/Server Design Issues

So, if Access 2000 isn't really capable of true client/server design, why discuss it in a book dedicated to Access 2000 programming? With the addition of new Access Data Projects (ADPs), Access 2000 supports client/server design at a level never before possible in Access. Access projects let you actually design client/server databases directly against an SQL Server back end and maintain them from within Access 2000. Moreover, the project is essentially a very thin client against the back-end database.

The support within Access 2000 for new data access pages (DAPs) makes designing Web pages that work against an SQL Server database easier than ever before. The Access Database window even supports new objects to help you work with SQL Server databases when you create an Access Data Project, as shown in Figure 25.1.

As you can see, when you're working with an ADP, the Database window adds support for views, database diagrams, and stored procedures and removes queries from the accessible objects. The following sections briefly discuss these new objects.

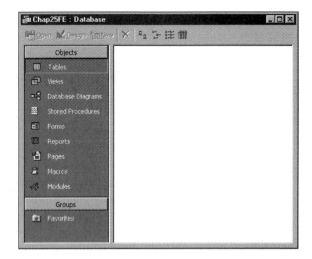

Figure 25.1
Working with an ADP within the Database window.

Creating And Manipulating Views

Views allow you to specify exactly how a user will see data. Views allow you to horizontally and vertically partition information from one or more tables in the database. In other words, with a view, you can allow the user to see only selected fields and selected rows. Views can also be created to show derived information. In addition, views have the following advantages:

- You have more control over what the user can see. This is useful for both security and ease of use. Users don't have to look at "extra" information that they don't require.

- You can simplify the user interface by creating views of often-used queries. This will allow a user to run a view with a simple statement rather than supplying parameters every time the query is run.

- You can heighten security. Users can only affect what you let them see. This may be a subset of rows or columns, statistical information, or a subset of information from another view.

Here are some rules and restrictions you should be aware of when creating views:

- When you're creating a view, any database objects that are referenced by the view are verified.

- When you're running a view, you must have SQL Server's **SELECT** permission on the objects referenced in the view definition. This means you could potentially create a view that you can't run. Permissions on views are checked each time that view is run, not when it's created.

- You can't alter a view once it has been created. To modify a view, you must drop the view and then re-create it.

- If you drop objects referenced within a view, the view still remains. You'll receive an error message the next time you attempt to run that view.

- Temporary tables can't be referenced in a view. This also means that you cannot use a **SELECT INTO** clause in a view.

- If you create a child view based on a parent view, you should be aware of what the parent view is doing. You could run into problems if the parent view is large and complex.

- Data in a view is not stored separately. This means that if you modify data in a view, you're modifying the data in the base tables.

- Triggers and indexes can't be created on a view.

Stored Procedures

Stored procedures are precompiled SQL statements that are stored at the SQL Server as a binary file—rather than being interpreted text passed across the network to the SQL Server at the time of the query's issuance. Because stored procedures are precompiled, they provide the best performance of any type of query. There are many system stored procedures defined with an **sp_** prefix that gather information from system tables and are especially useful for administration. You can create your own user-defined stored procedures as well.

Stored procedures are extremely fast database objects that are stored on the SQL Server itself. When you run a stored procedure for the first time, it is run in the following manner:

1. The procedure is parsed into its component pieces.

2. The components that reference other objects in the database (tables, views, and so on) are checked for their existence. This is also known as *resolving*.

3. Once resolving is complete, the name of the procedure will be stored in the sysobjects table and the code to create the stored procedure will be saved in syscomments.

4. Compilation continues, and, during compilation, a blueprint that defines how to run the query is created. This blueprint is often called a *normalized plan* or a *query tree*. The query tree is saved in the sysprocedures table.

5. When the stored procedure is first executed, the query plan is read and fully compiled into a procedure plan and then run. This saves you the time of reparsing, resolving, and compiling a query tree every time you run the stored procedure.

Another added benefit of using a stored procedure is that once the stored procedure is executed, the procedure plan will be stored in the procedure cache. This means that the next time you use the stored procedure, it will be read directly from the cache and run. This gives you a huge performance boost over running a standard SQL query again and again.

You can use stored procedures to encapsulate business rules. Once encapsulated, these rules can be used by multiple applications, thus giving you a consistent data interface. This is also advantageous in that, if functionality needs to change, you only need to change it in one place rather than once for each application. All in all, stored procedures can be summarized as offering the following benefits:

- Performance is boosted for all stored procedures, but even more so for stored procedures that are run more than once, because the query plan is saved in the procedure cache.

- With stored procedures, you can pass in arguments and get data returned, too.

- Stored procedures can be set up to run automatically when SQL Server starts up.

- Stored procedures can be used to extract or modify data (not at the same time).

- Stored procedures are explicitly invoked. Unlike triggers, stored procedures must be called by your application, script, batch, or task.

Working With Triggers

Triggers are a special type of stored procedure that SQL Server automatically invokes when you try to modify data that a trigger is designed to protect. Triggers help secure the integrity of your data by preventing unauthorized or inconsistent changes from being made. For example, suppose you have a customers table and an orders table. You can create a trigger that ensures that when you create a new order, it will have a valid customer ID to which it can attach. Likewise, you could create the trigger so that if you tried to delete a customer from the customers table, the trigger would check to see if there were any orders still attached to that customer and, if so, halt the delete process.

Triggers don't have parameters and can't be explicitly invoked. This means that you must attempt a data modification to fire off a trigger. Triggers can also be nested up to 16 levels. Nested triggers work like this: A trigger on your orders table might add an entry to your accounts receivable table that would, in turn, fire a trigger that checks to see whether the customer has any overdue accounts receivable and notifies you if he or she does.

As far as performance goes, triggers have a relatively low amount of overhead. Most of the time involved in running a trigger is used up by referencing other tables. The referencing can be fast if the other tables are in memory or a bit slower if they need to be read from disk.

Triggers are always considered a part of the transaction. If the trigger or any other part of the transaction fails, it's rolled back.

In the past (before SQL Server 6.5), triggers were the only means of enforcing referential integrity. However, you now have the ability to use Declarative Referential Integrity (DRI), which makes most triggers unnecessary. You can create triggers directly from the Access 2000 Interactive Development Environment (IDE) without using any of the SQL Server management tools.

Essentially, you'll use triggers, rather than the Relationships window that you use with Access-created databases, to enforce referential integrity.

Using Database Diagrams To Create Databases

You can use *database diagrams* to create, edit, or delete database objects for SQL Server or MSDE databases while you're directly connected to the database in which those objects are stored. Database diagrams graphically represent tables, the columns they contain, and the relationships between them. You can use database diagrams to do the following:

- Simply view the tables in your database and their relationships

- Perform complex operations to alter the physical structure of your database

When you modify a database object through a database diagram, the modifications you make are not saved in the database until you save the table or the database diagram. Therefore, you can experiment with "what if" scenarios on a database's design without permanently affecting its existing design or data.

In any event, when you finish working with a database diagram, you can then perform the following actions:

- Discard your changes.

- Save the changes to selected tables in the diagram or the entire database diagram and have the changes modify the server database.

- Save the Transact-SQL code that your changes to the diagram would invoke against the database in a change script. If you save a change script instead of saving your changes to the database, you then have more options as to its application. You can either apply the change script to the database at another time, using a tool such as SQL Server's wISQL command-line utility, or further edit the change script in a text editor and then apply the modified script to the database.

You control the timing, type, and extent of the changes to your database by choosing how changes to the database diagram affect the server database.

Creating And Modifying Database Objects

As noted previously, you can use a database diagram to create and modify database objects, including the following:

- Tables
- Table columns and their properties
- Indexes
- Constraints
- Table relationships

You can modify tables and their columns directly in a database diagram. You modify indexes, constraints, and relationships through the Properties window for a table in your diagram.

Understanding Access 2000's Locking Mechanisms

No matter how you design your applications, you'll always need to concern yourself with reducing network traffic and locking conflicts. In fact, locking conflicts, with the ever-increasing amounts of network bandwidth, may be a more significant consideration by far for your application. To protect shared data, Access 2000 locks a page of data as the user edits a record.

When a page of records is locked, multiple users can read the data, but only one user can make changes to the data. Data can be locked through a form and also through a recordset that isn't bound to a form. The three methods of locking for an Access application are as follows:

- Page locking
- Table and recordset locking
- Opening an entire database with exclusive access

With page locking, only the page containing the record that's being edited is locked. On the other hand, with table and recordset locking, the entire table or recordset containing the record that's being edited is locked. With database locking, the entire database is locked, unless the user opening the database has opened it for read-only access. When the user opens the database for read-only access, other users can also open the database for read-only access. The ability to obtain exclusive use of a database can be restricted through security.

It's important to note that the locking scheme to which you must adhere depends on the source of the data you're accessing. When you're accessing data on a database server using ODBC, you'll inherit the locking scheme of the particular back end you're using. When you're accessing Indexed Sequential Access Method (ISAM) data over a network, you'll get any record locking that the particular ISAM database supports. For example, if you're accessing FoxPro data, you have the capability to utilize record locking or any other locking scheme that FoxPro supports.

Recordset Locking

Recordset locking is the process of locking pages of data contained within a recordset. Using recordset locking, you can determine when and for how long the data is locked. This is different from locking data via bound forms, because with bound forms, you have little control over the specifics of the locking process.

When you're traversing through a recordset, editing and updating data, locking occurs regardless of whether you intervene. It's important for you to understand when the locking occurs and whether you need to step in to intercept the default behavior.

If you do nothing, an entire page of records will be locked each time you issue an **Edit** method from within your Visual Basic for Applications (VBA) code. This page is 2,048 bytes (2K) in size and surrounds the record being edited. When an Object Linking and Embedding (OLE) object is contained within the record being edited, it's not locked with the record because it occupies its own space.

Using Pessimistic Locking

VBA enables you to determine when and for how long a page is locked. The default behavior is called *pessimistic locking*. As you learned in Chapter 24, this means that the page is locked when the **Edit** method is issued. Here's some sample code, using DAO, that illustrates this process:

```
Sub PessimisticLock(strCustID As String)
    Dim db As Database
    Dim rst As Recordset
    Dim strCriteria As String

    Set db = CurrentDb()
    Set rst = db.OpenRecordSet("tblCustomers", _
        dbOpenDynaset)
    rst.Lockedits = True  'Invoke Pessimistic Locking
    strCriteria = "[CustomerID] = '" & strCustID & "'"
    rst.FindFirst strCriteria
    rst.Edit                        ' Lock occurs here
        rst.Fields("City") = "Las Vegas"
    rst.Update                      ' Lock released here
End Sub
```

In this scenario, although the lock occurs for a very short period of time, it's actually being issued at the invocation of the **Edit** method. It's then released upon the invocation of the **Update** method.

This method of locking is advantageous because you can ensure that no changes are made to the data between the time that the **Edit** method is issued and the time that the **Update** method is issued. Furthermore, when the **Edit** method succeeds, you're ensured write access to the record. The disadvantage is that the time between the edit and the update might force the lock to persist for a significant period of time, thus locking other users out of not only that record but the entire page of records within which the edited record is contained. This phenomenon is worsened when transaction processing is invoked. Basically, transaction processing ensures that when you make multiple changes to data, all changes complete successfully or no changes occur.

Using Optimistic Locking

Optimistic locking delays the time at which the record is locked. The lock is issued upon the **Update** call rather than the **Edit** call. The code to use optimistic locking will often look similar to the following:

```
Sub OptimisticLock(strCustID As String)
    Dim db As Database
    Dim rst As Recordset
    Dim strCriteria As String

    Set db = CurrentDb()
    Set rst = db.OpenRecordSet("tblCustomers", _
        dbOpenDynaset)
    rst.Lockedits = False 'Optimistic Locking
    strCriteria = "[CustomerID] = '" & strCustID & "'"
    rst.FindFirst strCriteria
    rst.Edit
        rst.Fields("City") = "Las Vegas"
    rst.Update 'Lock occurs and is released here
End Sub
```

As you can see, in this case, the lock doesn't happen until the **Update** method is issued. The advantage of this method is that the page is locked very briefly. The disadvantage of this method occurs when two users grab the record for editing at the same time. When one user attempts to update, no error occurs. When the other user attempts to update, he or she receives an error indicating that the data has changed since his or her edit was first issued.

Effectively Handling Locking Conflicts

When a user has a page locked and another user tries to view data on that page, no conflict occurs. On the other hand, when other users attempt to edit data on that same page, they experience an error.

You won't always want Access 2000's own error handling to take over when a locking conflict occurs. For example, rather than having Access 2000 display its generic error message indicating that a record is locked, you might want to display your own message and attempt to lock the record a couple of additional times. To do something like this, you need to learn to interpret each locking error that's generated by VBA so you can make a decision about how to respond.

Locking conflicts occur in the following situations:

- A user tries to edit or update a record that's already locked.

- A record has changed or been deleted since the user first started to edit it.

These errors can occur whether the user is editing bound data via a form or accessing the records via VBA code.

Locking Errors

To begin the discussion of locking conflicts, let's take a look at the types of errors that occur when pessimistic locking is in place. With pessimistic locking, you generally need to protect against the errors detailed in Table 25.1.

Now that you've seen what happens when a conflict occurs with pessimistic locking, let's see what happens when optimistic locking is in place or when users are adding new records. The three most common error codes generated by locking conflicts when optimistic locking is in place are detailed in Table 25.2.

Table 25.1   The errors you should generally trap for with pessimistic locking.

Error Number	Description
3260	This error occurs when the current record is locked by another user. It's generally sufficient to wait a short period of time and try the lock again.
3197	This error occurs when a record has been changed since the user last accessed it. It's best to refresh the data and attempt the **Edit** method again.
3167	This error occurs when the record has been deleted since the user last accessed it. It's best to refresh the data.

Table 25.2   The errors you should generally trap for with optimistic locking.

Error Number	Description
3186	This error occurs when the **Update** method is used to save a record on a locked page. This error generally occurs when a user tries to move off a record that he or she is adding onto a locked page or when a user tries to update a record on the same page as a record that's locked by another machine. It's generally sufficient to wait a short period of time and try the lock again.
3197	This error occurs when User 1 has updated a record in the time since User 2 first started viewing it. It can also occur when User 2 is viewing data that isn't current; the data has changed, but the changes haven't yet been reflected on User 2's screen. You have two options: You can requery the recordset, losing User 2's changes, or you can resume and issue the **Update** method again, overwriting User 1's changes.
3260	This error usually occurs when the **Edit** method is issued and the page containing the current record is locked. It's best to wait a short period of time and try the lock again.

Using Unbound Forms

One solution to locking conflicts is to use unbound forms. They allow you to greatly limit the amount of time a record is locked, and you can fully control when Access 2000 attempts to secure the lock. Unbound forms require significantly more coding than bound forms, so make sure that the benefits you receive from using unbound forms outweigh the coding and maintenance involved. With improvements to both forms and the Jet engine (as well as the introduction of ADPs), the reasons to use unbound forms with Access 2000 data are less compelling.

When And Why To Use Importing, Linking, And Opening

The process of importing data into an Access table results in the engine making a copy of the data and then placing the copy within an Access table. After data is imported, it's treated like any other native Access table. In fact, neither you nor Access has any way of knowing where the data came from. As a result, imported data offers the same performance and flexibility as any other Access table.

The process of linking to external data is quite different from the process of importing data. Linked data remains in its native format. By establishing a link to the external data, you're able to build queries, forms, and reports that use or display the data. After you've created a link to external data, the link remains permanently established, unless you explicitly remove it. The linked table appears in the database window just like any other Access table. The only difference is you can't modify its structure from within Access 2000. In fact, if the datasource permits multiuser access, the users of your application can be modifying the data along with users of the applications written in its native database format (such as FoxPro, dBASE, or Paradox).

The process of opening an external table is similar to linking to the table, except that a permanent relationship isn't created. When you link to an external table, connection information is maintained from session to session. When you open the table, you create a recordset from the table, and no permanent link is established.

Knowing Which Option To Select

It's important that you understand when to import external data, when to link to external data, and when to open an external table directly. Import external data under the following circumstances:

- When you're migrating an existing system into Access 2000.

- When you want to take advantage of and access external data, which you'll then use to run a large volume of queries and reports, but you won't be updating the data. In such cases, you'll often want the added performance that native Access data provides without converting the data between formats.

When you're migrating an existing system to Access 2000 and you're ready to permanently migrate either test or production data into your application, you should then import the tables into Access 2000. Another good reason to import external data is because data is downloaded from a mainframe into ASCII format on a regular basis, and you want to utilize the data for reports. Rather than attempting to link to the data and suffer the performance hits associated with such a link, you can import the data each time it's downloaded from the mainframe. You should link to external data under the following circumstances:

- The data is used by a legacy application requiring the native file format.

- The data resides on an ODBC-compliant database server.

- You'll access the data on a regular basis.

Often, you won't have the time or resources to rewrite an application in FoxPro, Paradox, or some other language. You might be developing additional applications that will share data with the legacy application, or you might want to utilize the strong querying and reporting capabilities of Access 2000 rather than develop queries and reports in the native environment. By linking to the external data, users of existing applications can continue to work with the applications and their data. Your Access applications can retrieve and modify data without concern for corrupting or in any other way harming the data.

When the data resides in an ODBC database such as Microsoft SQL Server, you want to reap the data-retrieval benefits provided by a database server. By linking to the ODBC datasource, you can take advantage of Access 2000's ease of use as a front-end tool while taking advantage of client/server technology at the same time. Finally, if you intend to access data on a regular basis, linking to the external table, rather than temporarily opening the table directly, provides you with ease of use and performance benefits. When you've created the link, Access 2000 treats the table just like any other Access table.

You should open an external table directly under the following circumstances:

- When you rarely need to establish a connection to the external datasource.

- When you've determined that performance actually improves by opening the datasource directly.

If you rarely need to access the external data, it might be appropriate to open it directly. Links increase the size of your MDB file. This size increase isn't necessary if you'll rarely access the data. Furthermore, in certain situations, when accessing ISAM data, you might find that opening the table directly provides better performance than linking to it.

Although importing data is an important technique, it's a one-time process. In general, you'll find much more extensive discussions about linking to data simply because linking is a more common activity and because linking creates important issues because you're working with data maintained in a different format.

Upsizing: What To Worry About

Suppose your database is using Microsoft Access 2000 as both the front end and back end. The Access tables have already been created and even contain volumes of data. Although an Access database on a file server might have been sufficient for a while, the need for better performance, enhanced security, or one of the other benefits that a back-end database provides is compelling your company (or your client's company) to upsize to a client/server architecture. *Upsizing* means moving tables from a local

Access database (or from any PC database) to a back-end database server that usually runs on Unix, Windows NT Server, OS/2 LAN Server, or as a Novell NetWare NLM.

Another reason that tables are upsized from Access 2000 to a back-end server is that many developers prefer to design their tables from within the Access environment. Access offers a more user-friendly environment for table creation than do most server applications.

Regardless of your reasons for upsizing, you need to understand several issues regarding the movement, or upsizing, of Access tables to a database server. Indeed, because of the many caveats in moving tables from Access to a back end, many people opt to design the tables directly on the back end. If you do design your tables in Access, you should export them to the back end and then link them to your local database. As you export your tables to the database server, you need to be aware of the following issues (at a bare minimum):

- *Index considerations*—When you're exporting a table to a server, no indexes are created. All indexes need to be re-created on the back-end database server.

- *Exporting autonumber fields*—Autonumber fields are exported as **Long** integers. Because most database servers don't support autonumbering, you'll generally have to create an insert trigger on the server that provides the next key value.

- *Using default values*—Default values aren't automatically moved to the server, even when the server supports default values. You can set up default values directly on the server, but these values do *not* automatically appear when new records are added to the table unless the record is saved without data being added to the field containing the default value.

- *Exporting validation rules*—Validation rules aren't exported to the server. They must be re-created using triggers on the server. No Access-defined error messages are displayed when a server

NOTE

If you use the SQL Server Upsizing Wizard, some of the issues discussed in these bullet points may not apply. For example, with the Upsizing Wizard and SQL Server 7, autonumber fields will export correctly and completely.

Tip

Although these are not all the issues you must consider when upsizing a database, they are, by far, the most important.

validation rule is violated. Your application should be coded to provide the appropriate error messages.

- *Exporting relationships*—Relationships need to be enforced using server-based triggers. Access 2000's default error messages don't appear when referential integrity is violated. You need to respond to and code for these error messages within your application.

- *Applying security to the new database*—Security features that you've set up in Access 2000 don't carry forward to the server. You need to reestablish table security on the server. When security has been set up on the server, Access 2000 becomes unaware that the security exists until the Access application attempts to violate the server's security. Then, error codes are returned to the application. You must handle these errors by using code and displaying the appropriate error message to the user.

- *Exporting table and field names*—Servers often have much more stringent rules regarding the naming of fields than Access 2000 does. When you export a table, all characters that aren't alphanumeric are converted to underscores. Most back ends don't allow spaces in field names. Furthermore, most back ends limit the length of object names to 30 characters or less. If you've already created queries, forms, reports, macros, and modules that utilize spaces and very long field and table names, these database objects might become unusable when you move your tables to a back-end database server.

Tip

As mentioned in some previous sections, Microsoft provides an Access upsizing tool that's specifically designed to take an Access application and to upsize it to Microsoft SQL Server. The Access 2000 version of this tool ships with the Microsoft Office CD-ROM.

When you set up your tables and code modules with upsizing in mind, you can eliminate many of the preceding pitfalls. Despite any of the problems that upsizing can bring, the scalability of Access 2000 is one of its stronger points. Sometimes resources aren't available to implement client/server technology in the early stages of an application. If you think through the design of the project with the possibility of upsizing in mind, you'll be pleased at how relatively easy it is to move to client/server when the time is right.

Where To Go From Here

In this chapter, you examined more information about working with client/server programming and transaction processing in Access 2000. You also considered some of the issues surrounding client/server programming and learned about some of the different objects you'll often encounter in a client/server environment. Finally, you evaluated some specific considerations for importing or linking to data and reviewed more information about the importance of record locking in application design.

In the next chapter, you'll create a final Access 2000 project that brings together many of the concepts developed throughout this book as well as introduces some important closing concepts, such as further error handling and database optimization.

Chapter 26

Let's Write One More Access Program

Programming in Access 2000 is an exercise that transforms a functional vision into an operational reality. The power of creating solutions is in your hands.

Now that your brain is teeming with knowledge about how to program with Access 2000, let's go to work one last time. In this chapter, you're going to use the knowledge you've acquired during the course of our discussions to build the prototype for a new Human Resources application. The intent here is to take you through an entire application development cycle from start to finish. To guide your activities, you'll use the PRACTICE structured development methodology that you learned in Chapter 1. To design and build the application, you'll employ concepts and techniques presented in Chapters 2 through 25. Let's get underway by again establishing a context for the application you're going to build. You may recall from Chapter 6 that you were tagged by a fictional marketing team to develop a productivity program. Well, it appears that the company liked your work so much that the Human Resources director has again engaged your services.

PRACTICE Makes Perfect

Your needs assessment meeting with the Human Resources director establishes that she wants you to develop a prototype application to help the department keep track of staff administrative data. Specifically, in addition to employee identification information, she wants to have easy access to employee contact addresses and telephone numbers, current project assignments, training classes completed, and benefit provider choices. She also wants the program to have some measure of security so that only authorized users can have access to the program's data. If the prototype meets with her approval, she'll then obtain funding to develop a production version of the program.

From Concept To Design

Given your understanding of the PRACTICE methodology and what the HR director has provided as guidance for the program's purpose, you find that resolving what the program needs to do is not difficult. In fact, you've already determined that Access 2000 is the tool for the job, and that you need to build a new relational database containing eight tables. The tables will store data for user passwords, employee identification, addresses, state of residence, contact numbers, work assignments, training classes, and benefit providers.

Project Building The HRApplication Database

You can't build a house without a foundation. Similarly, you can't build an Access program without a database. So, let's take this opportunity to create a brand new home for our Access program by completing the following steps:

1. Launch Access 2000.

2. Select the Blank Access Database radio button from the opening dialog box, and then click on OK to launch the File New Database dialog box.

3. Select the Desktop button in the Save In frame of the File New Database dialog box, and then type "HRApplication" in the File Name field and click on the Create button to open a new Access 2000 database window.

Project Importing Objects From Another Database

Because wise programmers typically reuse previously developed objects and code, you decide to make use of some of the objects you developed while working with the FirstDatabase database. Specifically, the FirstEmployee table and the FirstTable table will be of particular use because of their structure. For this reason, you decide to import these tables from FirstDatabase into the HRApplication database, rather than rebuild them from scratch. You can accomplish this task by performing the following steps:

1. Select Insert|Table from the Access 2000 menu bar, select Import Table from the New Table dialog box, and then click on OK to open the Import dialog box.

2. From the Import dialog box, locate and select FirstDatabase and then click on the Import button to open the Import Objects dialog box.

3. In the Import Objects dialog box, select FirstEmployees and FirstTable and then click on OK (see Figure 26.1). Completing this action adds the two new tables to the HRApplication database window.

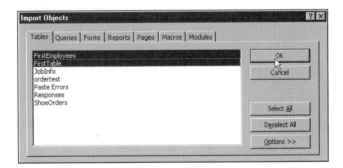

Figure 26.1
The Import Objects dialog box.

 Modifying The FirstEmployees Table

Perform the following steps to modify the table structure of the FirstEmployees table:

1. Select FirstEmployees in the HRApplication database window, and then click on Design in the database window toolbar.

2. Find the next blank row, and then enter the new field names and data types shown in Table 26.1.

3. Select File|Save and then File|Close from the Access 2000 menu bar.

 Adding New HRApplication Tables

Although being able to reuse previously built table structures helps a little, you still have a few more tables to create. With the structure information provided under each table-specific heading, perform the following steps to create the remaining tables that you'll need to populate the HRApplication databases:

1. Select New on the database window toolbar, select Design View in the New Table dialog box, and then click on OK.

2. Refer to Tables 26.2 through 26.7 for table-specific details for field names and data types.

3. Save each new table structure with its table-specific name, and then close the saved table.

Table 26.1 New FirstEmployees fields and data types.

Field Name	Data Type
Department	Text
StreetAddressHome	Text
HomePhone	Text
ProjectName	Text
ClassName	Text
HealthInsPrvdrName	Text

Table 26.2   The Addresses table structure.

Field Name	Data Type	Description
AddressID	AutoNumber	Make this field the primary key.
FirstEmployeesID	Number	
StreetAddressOffice	Text	
EmailAddress	Text	

Table 26.3   The ContactNumbers table structure.

Field Name	Data Type	Description
ContactID	AutoNumber	Make this field the primary key.
FirstEmployeesID	Number	
WorkPhone	Text	
CellPhone	Text	
FaxPhone	Text	

NOTE

The table additions shown here are to establish a context for reminding you about specific relational database design concepts. The actual application that you'll build in this chapter uses only a fraction of this data. However, should the spirit move you, once the application is complete, you can add some data to these tables, use the application, and run a few queries. You'll also get a feel for the utility of Access 2000's use of subdatasheets.

Table 26.4   The Assignments table structure.

Field Name	Data Type	Description
ProjectID	AutoNumber	Make this field the primary key.
FirstEmployeesID	Number	
ProjectDuration	Text	
ProjectChargeCode	Text	

Table 26.5   The Training table structure.

Field Name	Data Type	Description
ClassID	AutoNumber	Make this field the primary key.
FirstEmployeesID	Number	
StartMonth	Text	
EndMonth	Text	
CompletionYear	Text	

Table 26.6 The BenefitsProvider table structure.

Field Name	Data Type	Description
ProviderID	AutoNumber	Make this field the primary key.
FirstEmployeesID	Number	
DentalInsPrvdrName	Text	
VisionInsPrvdrName	Text	
LifeInsPrvdrName	Text	

Table 26.7 The StateResidency table structure.

Field Name	Data Type	Description
StateID	AutoNumber	Make this field the primary key.
FirstEmployeesID	Number	
ResidentStatus	Text	

After you've created all the new table structures for the HRApplication, the database window should appear similar to Figure 26.2.

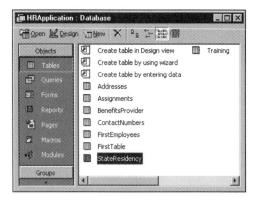

Figure 26.2
Eight tables support the HRApplication.

 ## Establishing Table Relationships

You may have noticed when creating the HRApplication table structures that the field FirstEmployeesID is a common attribute among all tables. The FirstEmployeesID field is the primary key for the FirstEmployees table, which is the parent table in the HRApplication design. When you're designing a relational database application, tables are typically identified in terms of parent and child. In this context, the parent table is capable of looking up information in a child table on the basis of the parent table's primary key field, existing in records stored in the child table. However, this look-up capability does not happen automatically. It requires you to establish the key relationship between the parent and child tables. For the purposes of the HRApplication, you'll need to create a one-to-many relationship between the FirstEmployees table and all other tables in the database, with the exception of FirstTable.

Create a one-to-many relationship between the FirstEmployees table and its child tables by performing the following steps:

1. Select Tools|Relationships from the Access 2000 menu bar to open the Relationships window. If the Show Table dialog box is not open, open it by selecting Relationships|Show Table from the Access 2000 menu bar. The relationship between FirstEmployees and FirstTable already exists.

2. In the Show Table dialog box, while holding down the Shift key, click on each entry in the dialog list box except FirstEmployees and FirstTable; then click on Add.

3. With the selected tables added to the Relationships window, select Close on the Show Table dialog box.

4. Select FirstEmployeesID in the FirstEmployees table and, while holding down the Shift key, drag the FirstEmployeesID field onto the FirstEmployeesID field of one of the unrelated tables.

5. When the Edit Relationship dialog box appears, click on the Create button to establish the relationship between the parent and child tables.

NOTE

When a single table has multiple child records, the relationship between the parent table and the child tables is called a one-to-many relationship.

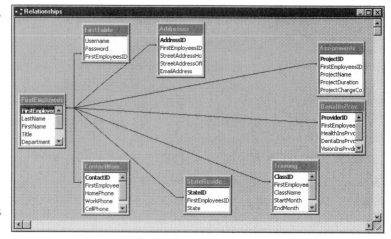

Figure 26.3
The FirstEmployees parent table related to its child tables.

6. Repeat Steps 4 and 5 for each remaining table requiring a parent/child relationship. When you're done, your Relationships window can be arranged as shown in Figure 26.3.

7. Select File|Save and then File|Close to the save the established relationships and close the Relationships window.

Designing The HRApplication User Interface

Now that the database is created and its tables are structured and related, let's turn our attention to designing the HRApplication user interface. Based on your discussions with the HR director, you've determined that the HRApplication user interface will have two primary components. The first primary component will be a logon panel like the one you built in Chapter 4. This panel addresses the HR director's requirement for the application to have some measure of security to prevent unauthorized data access. The second primary component will be a form containing a multitabbed control similar to the FEInterface form you created in Chapter 16. With this vision in mind, let's begin.

Project Exporting Objects To Another Database

Here's another case where you don't need to reinvent the wheel. The logon form you created in Chapter 4 will work just fine with some minor modification. However, this time, instead of importing the object you require, you'll export from its source. To add the FirstDatabase logon form to the HRApplication database, perform the following steps:

1. Select File|Open from the Access 2000 menu bar.

2. From the Open dialog box, locate and select FirstDatabase from your local machine and then click on the Open button. This action closes the HRApplication database and opens the FirstDatabase database.

3. Select Forms under the Objects pane of the database window, and then select LogonForm from the database window's form list.

4. Select File|Export from the Access 2000 menu bar.

5. From the Export Form 'LogonForm' To dialog box, locate and select the HRApplication database from your local machine and then click the Save button. This action opens the Export dialog box.

6. Accept the default value in the dialog box, select OK, and then select File|Close.

7. Select File on the Access 2000 menu bar, and then select the HRApplication database from the list of previously opened files.

8. Select Forms under the Objects pane of the database window, and you'll find that the form LogonForm has been added to the HRApplication database window's form list.

Project Modifying LogonForm

The design of LogonForm is intact, but let's tweak it just a bit by performing the following steps:

1. With Forms selected under the Objects pane of the database window, select LogonForm and then click on Design on the database window toolbar.

2. With LogonForm open in Design View, right-click on the form's title bar and then select Properties.

3. Select the All tab on the form's property sheet, and change the **Caption** property from "Access 2000 - Logon Program" to "HRApplication Prototype - Logon Program".

4. Select File|Save and then close the form's property sheet.

5. Select View|Code on the Access 2000 menu bar, and then modify the code as follows:

```
Private Sub Command4_Click()
On Error GoTo Command4_Click_Err (Add this line.)
'Variable Declaration Section
Dim db As Database
Dim Result
Dim SQLline As String
getpassword = "result!Password"
'Variable Definition Section
SQLline = "SELECT * FROM FirstTable
WHERE Username = [username] AND Password = [password];"
Set Result = CurrentDb.
OpenRecordset(SQLline, dbOpenDynaset)

'Processing Logic Section
Do Until Result!Password = Me!Password
  Result.MoveNext
Loop
If Result.EOF Or IsNull("password")
Or Result!Password <> Me!Password Then
    MsgBox "This ID is not on file!"
Else
    MsgBox "Your ID has been verified"
    DoCmd.Close acForm, "LogonForm"
    DoCmd.OpenForm "HRAppInterface", acNormal (Add
    this line.)
End If
Result.Close
'Call Arraytest    (Delete this line.)
Command4_Click_Exit: (Add this line.)
    Exit Sub  (Add this line.)
```

NOTE

Reminder: *Do not break your code as shown in the listing. The breaks shown in the code are for editorial purposes only.*

▶**Tip**

If you get an "object not defined" error when trying to compile, remember that Access 2000 requires that the Microsoft DAO 2.5/3.0 Compatibility Library be enabled. You can make this adjustment by selecting Tools|References on the Visual Basic Editor menu bar and then scrolling the reference listing for Microsoft DAO 2.5/3.0 Compatibility Library. When you find it, enable it by clicking on the checkbox and then clicking on OK to close the reference window. Refer to the note in Chapter 4, under "Let's Review Some Of The Code."

```
Command4_Click_Err:  (Add this line.)
    MsgBox "This ID is not on file!"
        Resume Command4_Click_Exit   (Add this line.)
End Sub
```

6. Select Debug|Compile HRApplication on the Visual Basic Editor menu bar. Then select File|Save HRApplication and then File|Close And Return To Microsoft Access. In Form View, your modified form should appear as shown in Figure 26.4.

7. Close the logon form. You'll get back to it later.

Designing The Multitabbed Interface Form

Looks like you've got some momentum, so let's keep things moving by creating the primary HRApplication interface— namely, the multitabbed form. As you may have gathered, you'll need to select the Forms option under the Objects pane and then double-click on Create Form In Design View in the database window pane. Once a new form grid is open, maximize the form window and then point, click, and drag the bottom edge of the grid to make the grid size three blocks deep. Next, point, click, and drag the right edge of the grid to make the grid size seven blocks wide.

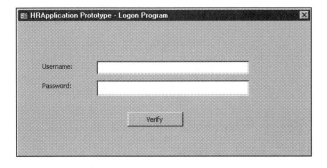

Figure 26.4
The modified LogonForm.

 **Adding The Label Control**

With your form grid sized and ready, add a custom Label control to the form by performing the following steps:

1. Select the Label control from the toolbox, and place the cursor flush against the form's first vertical gridline. Click once.

2. At the blinking cursor, type "The HRApplication Prototype Interface", and then click outside the Label control to place sizing handles around it.

3. With sizing handles around the control, right-click and select Properties from the control's right-click menu.

4. On the Label property sheet, select the Format tab and then scroll to the Font Size property field.

5. Change the font name from Tahoma to Arial, the font size from 8 to 16, and the font weight to heavy. Close the property sheet.

6. Resize the Label control so that the entire title appears on the form; then point, click, and drag the control to the upper edge of the form.

7. With the property sheet still open, click the Detail section of the form.

8. On the Format tab for the Detail section, change "-2147483633" to "16777215".

9. Center the Label control at the top of the form and then select File|Save to save the form as "HRAppInterface". Next, close the property sheet. Your form should now appear as shown in Figure 26.5.

Project **Adding The Tab Controls**

Now you're ready to add Tab controls to the form. This is where things begin to get interesting, because this task begins shaping the look and feel of the application. Perform this task by completing the following steps:

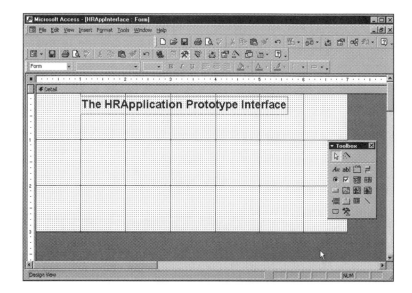

Figure 26.5
The HRAppInterface form with a Label control.

1. Select the Tab control from the toolbox and place the cursor in the form's grid, two ticks from the left edge of the form window, and then click once.

2. Right-click and select Insert Page from the control's right-click menu. Do this five times.

3. Select the control's first tab, right-click, and then select Properties.

4. Enter "Employee" in the Caption field of the Format tab.

5. Select each additional tab, entering "Addresses", "Contact Numbers", "Work Assignments", "Training", "Benefit Providers", and "Interface Control" in each tab's respective **Caption** property field.

6. Resize the Tab control to fill the form grid as shown in Figure 26.6, close the property sheet, and then select File|Save.

Project Building The Employee Tab

With the multitab control complete, it's time to start enhancing each tab page with data collection controls. Specifically, you'll use Text Box and Combo Box controls for this purpose. So, let's

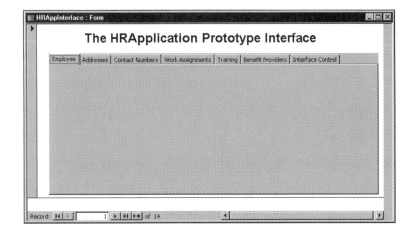

Figure 26.6
The HRAppInterface
with the multitab
control.

maintain the pace and use Access 2000 to create some data fields
for the Employee tab by completing the following steps:

1. While still in Design View, select the Employee tab on the
   HRAppInterface form, and then select Form from the Formatting toolbar's drop-down menu. You'll find this drop-down
   menu at the upper-left corner of the form, just above the
   ruler.

2. Select View|Properties from the Access 2000 menu bar, and
   then select the Data tab on the form's property sheet.

3. Click on the **RecordSource** property drop-down menu, select
   FirstEmployees, and then close the property sheet.

4. Select View|Field List from the Access 2000 menu bar.

5. From the FirstEmployees field list, click and drag the fields
   FirstEmployeesID, LastName, FirstName, Title, and Department onto the Employee tab.

6. Resize and arrange the fields on the tab so that they appear as
   shown in Figure 26.7.

7. Select File|Save to save the form in its current state.

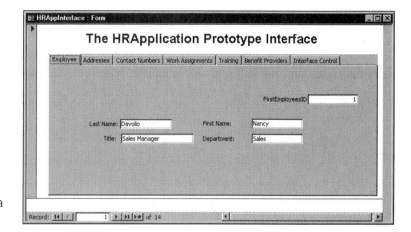

Figure 26.7
The HRAppInterface
Employee tab with data
fields.

Project Adding Custom Navigation Buttons

Because this is a custom application, you'll want to lose the
Access 2000 default navigation controls and use a custom set, as
you did in Chapter 16. Using the Command Button control,
proceed with creating custom navigation buttons for this form by
completing the following steps:

1. Select the Command Button control from the toolbox, place
   your cursor beneath the Title label, and then click once to
   add a Command Button control to the form.

2. Continue to add Command Button controls until you have a
   row of five across the bottom of the form.

3. On the All tab of the property sheet for each button, in the
   Name and Caption fields, enter the following names in order:

   - *GoLast*—First button
   - *GoBack*—Second button
   - *GoNext*—Third button
   - *GoFirst*—Fourth button
   - *Add Record*—Fifth button

NOTE

*The code for these
buttons can be lifted
straight from the
FEInterface program, so
here's an opportunity to
do a little cutting and
pasting.*

Project Cleaning Up The Form

Before you continue building the other tabs, how about getting rid of those unsightly default navigation controls and then resizing the form so that it's a bit more pleasing to the eye. In case you don't recall how to do it, simply perform the following steps.

1. Resize the Form window to bind the form grid on all sides.

2. Click the Object drop-down menu on the Formatting toolbar, and then select Form.

3. Select View|Properties from the Access 2000 menu bar, and then select the All tab on the form's property sheet.

4. On the property sheet All tab, set the following property values:

   - *Scroll Bars*—Neither

   - *Record Selectors*—No

   - *Navigation Buttons*—No

   - *Dividing Lines*—No

   - *Auto Resize*——No

   - *Border Style*—Dialog

5. Close the Form property sheet, and then select File|Save to save the form.

6. Select View|Form View to see the finished panel. Your form should now appear as shown in Figure 26.8.

Project Building The Addresses Tab

You've now made the form pretty and have completed work on the Employee tab. Your next task is to begin work on the Addresses tab. This time, you'll get to employ a Combo Box control to dynamically add data to your application table. Continue the tab page development activity by completing the following steps:

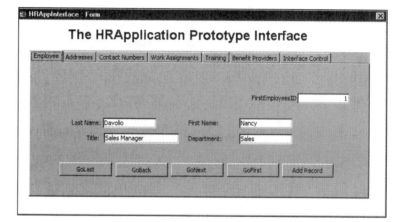

Figure 26.8
The HRAppInterface
Employee tab with only
the custom navigation
buttons.

1. Repeat Steps 1 through 7, as performed for the Employee tab. This time, however, add only two fields to the tab page—the FirstEmployeesID field and the StreetAddressHome field. Arrange the fields as shown in Figure 26.9.

2. Add a Combo Box control to the form, just below the StreetAddressHome field.

3. On the All tab for the Combo Box property sheet, set the following property values:

   - *Name*—HomeState
   - *ControlSource*—State
   - *RowSource*—FirstEmployees
   - *ColumnCount*—7

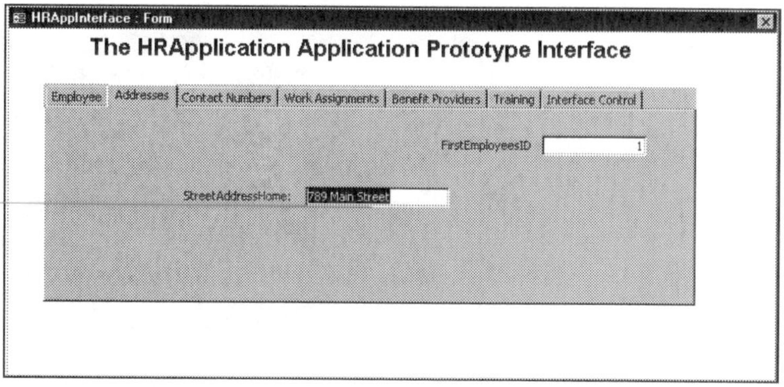

Figure 26.9
The layout shown here
will be the same for the
other tabs.

- *ColumnWidths—0;0;0;0;0;0;;*
- *BoundColumn—7*

4. Using new button-specific names with the same caption and source code as the Employee tab, add a new set of custom navigation controls to the bottom of the tab page.

5. Select File|Save and then select the Contact Numbers tab. After adding the navigation buttons, the Addresses tab should appear as shown in Figure 26.10.

Building The Other Functional Tab Pages

The next four tab pages are built with the same process used for the Addresses tab. The only differences are that each of the next four tab pages—Contact Numbers, Work Assignments, Benefit Providers, and Training—will contain its own specific data field and will not use a Combo Box control. Remember, for the sake of layout consistency, each of the next four tabs pages should look like Figure 26.9. The data fields for each of the next four tab pages are listed in Table 26.8.

Building The Interface Control Tab

The Interface Control tab page contains a few options that let the user manage the appearance of the various functional tab pages, and it also provides the capability to search for a particular employee record by last name (see Figure 26.11). The controls on

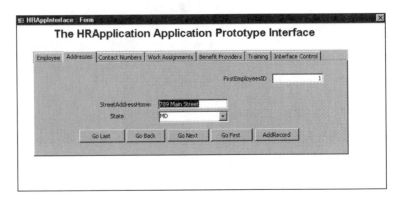

Figure 26.10
The completed Addresses tab.

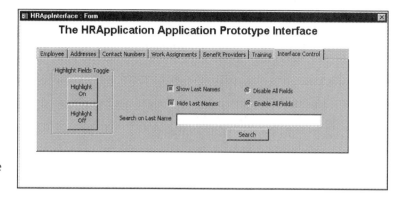

Figure 26.11
The completed Interface Control tab.

Table 26.8   Tab page data fields.

Tab Page	Items To Add
Contact Numbers	FirstEmployeesID field
	HomePhone field
	Custom navigation controls
Work Assignments	FirstEmployeesID field
	ProjectName field
	Custom navigation controls
Benefit Providers	FirstEmployeesID field
	HealthInsPrvdrName field
	Custom navigation controls
Training	FirstEmployeesID field
	ClassName field
	Custom navigation controls

the Interface Control tab page have been adapted from the FEInterface form's Interface Control page, so you can copy the controls from that page and use them here. The code in Listings 26.1, 26.2, and 26.3 indicates where modifications were made to the FEInterface code for use in this application.

Listing 26.1   Code for the Highlight Fields toggle.

```
Private Sub ColorOff_Click()
Me!ColorOn.Enabled = True
DoCmd.GoToControl "ColorOn"
Me!ColorOn.Value = False
Me!ColorOff.Value = True
```

```
Me!ColorOff.Enabled = False
Me!FirstEmployeesID.BackColor = 16777215
Me!FirstEmployeesID2.BackColor = 16777215
Me!FirstEmployeesID3.BackColor = 16777215
Me!FirstEmployeesID4.BackColor = 16777215
Me!FirstEmployeesID5.BackColor = 16777215
Me!FirstEmployeesID6.BackColor = 16777215
Me!LastName.BackColor = 16777215
Me!FirstName.BackColor = 16777215
Me!Title.BackColor = 16777215
Me!Department.BackColor = 16777215
Me!ClassName.BackColor = 16777215
Me!ProjectName.BackColor = 16777215
Me!HealthInsPrvdrName.BackColor = 16777215
Me!HomePhone.BackColor = 16777215
Me!HomeState.BackColor = 16777215
Me!StreetAddressHome.BackColor = 16777215
MsgBox "Field Highlights Are Disabled!"
End Sub

Private Sub ColorOn_Click()
Me!ColorOff.Enabled = True
DoCmd.GoToControl "ColorOff"
Me!ColorOff.Value = False
Me!ColorOn.Value = True
Me!ColorOn.Enabled = False
Me!FirstEmployeesID.BackColor = 16776960
Me!FirstEmployeesID.BackColor = 16776960
Me!FirstEmployeesID2.BackColor = 16776960
Me!FirstEmployeesID3.BackColor = 16776960
Me!FirstEmployeesID4.BackColor = 16776960
Me!FirstEmployeesID5.BackColor = 16776960
Me!FirstEmployeesID6.BackColor = 16776960
Me!LastName.BackColor = 16776960
Me!FirstName.BackColor = 16776960
Me!Title.BackColor = 16776960
Me!Department.BackColor = 16776960
Me!ClassName.BackColor = 16776960
Me!ProjectName.BackColor = 16776960
Me!HealthInsPrvdrName.BackColor = 16776960
Me!HomePhone.BackColor = 16776960
Me!HomeState.BackColor = 16776960
Me!StreetAddressHome.BackColor = 16776960
MsgBox "Field Highlights Are Enabled!"
End Sub
```

Listing 26.2   Code for the Show/Hide checkboxes.

```
Private Sub HideIt_Click()
Me!LastName.Visible = False
If Me!LastName.Visible = False Then
Me!ShowIt.Value = Disabled
End If
End Sub

Private Sub ShowIt_Click()
Me!LastName.Visible = True
If Me!LastName.Visible = True Then
Me!HideIt.Value = Disabled
End If
```

Listing 26.3   Code for the Disable/Enable All Fields option buttons.

```
Private Sub AllOff_Click()
Me!FirstEmployeesID.Enabled = False
Me!FirstEmployeesID2.Enabled = False
Me!FirstEmployeesID3.Enabled = False
Me!FirstEmployeesID4.Enabled = False
Me!FirstEmployeesID5.Enabled = False
Me!FirstEmployeesID6.Enabled = False
Me!LastName.Enabled = False
Me!FirstName.Enabled = False
Me!Title.Enabled = False
Me!Department.Enabled = False
Me!ClassName.Enabled = False
Me!ProjectName.Enabled = False
Me!HealthInsPrvdrName.Enabled = False
Me!HomePhone.Enabled = False
Me!HomeState.Enabled = False
Me!StreetAddressHome.Enabled = False
If Me!FirstEmployeesID.Enabled = False Then
Me!AllOn.Value = Enabled
End If
End Sub

Private Sub AllOn_Click()
Me!FirstEmployeesID.Enabled = True
Me!FirstEmployeesID2.Enabled = True
Me!FirstEmployeesID3.Enabled = True
Me!FirstEmployeesID4.Enabled = True
Me!FirstEmployeesID5.Enabled = True
Me!FirstEmployeesID6.Enabled = True
Me!LastName.Enabled = True
```

```
Me!FirstName.Enabled = True
Me!Title.Enabled = True
Me!Department.Enabled = True
Me!ClassName.Enabled = True
Me!ProjectName.Enabled = True
Me!HealthInsPrvdrName.Enabled = True
Me!HomePhone.Enabled = True
Me!HomeState.Enabled = True
Me!HomeState.Enabled = True
Me!StreetAddressHome.Enabled = True
If Me!FirstEmployeesID.Enabled = True Then
Me!AllOff.Value = Enabled
End If
End Sub
```

About The Employee Search Option

The employee search option is a feature that uses the **RecordsetClone** property and bookmarks to let users find an existing record and have that record displayed on the active form once it's been found. This takes a bit of explanation. When you establish the setting for a form's **RecordSource** property, by default, you're also defining the recordset for the form.

A *recordset clone*, as the term implies, is a copy of the recordset established for the active form. When you use the **RecordsetClone** property, you're able to create event procedures that can access the same recordset displayed by the active form, without affecting the form's display. With the employee search option, you're able to search the clone recordset for a record matching the name entered in the field. When you click on the Search command button, an event procedure is triggered that finds the requested record in the recordset clone and synchronizes the **Bookmark** property of the form with the current bookmark in the clone.

A recordset clone has the same set of bookmarks as the recordset from which it was cloned. The source code for the employee search option has you declare the variable **GetIt** as a **Recordset** object. It then calls for you to set the value of the **GetIt** variable to the **RecordsetClone** property for the active form. At this point, the code looks for the first instance of a record that

NOTE

If you need a refresher on the ins and outs of recordsets, revisit Chapter 8.

NOTE

You can get more details about how bookmarks work by referring to Chapter 9.

matches the value stored in the field FindIt. The bookmarks for each dataset are then synchronized, and Access 2000 displays the result in the active form. The search criteria field is then cleared, and a message box is displayed that refers you to where you can find the results of your query. The code behind the employee search option is listed here:

```
Private Sub GetIt_Click()
Dim GetIt As Recordset
Set GetIt = Me.RecordsetClone
GetIt.FindFirst "[LastName] = '" & Me![FindIt] & "'"
Me.Bookmark = GetIt.Bookmark
Me![FindIt] = Null
MsgBox "Search complete.
Click the Employee Tab for Results!"
End Sub
```

Project Testing And Integrating The Interface Components

With the last tab page complete, you're ready to bring together the LogonForm and HRAppInterface forms. The intent here, of course, is to allow access to the HRAppInterface form only with user password authorization. Check this out by performing the following steps:

1. Close all open forms in Access 2000.

2. With the Forms option selected in the database window's Object pane, select LogonForm and then click on Open in the database window toolbar.

3. Use one of the username/password combinations defined in Chapter 4 to verify your authorization to access the HRAppInterface form. In case you don't recall, you can use the username *Rosebud* and the password *Kane*. If your ID is verified, the HRAppInterface form will open and LogonForm will close. If your ID is not verified, you'll be dealt with accordingly!

Correlating And Ending With Good Documentation

With the integration and testing of the application prototype being a smashing success, PRACTICE methodology dictates that you correlate the finished product to what the customer originally asked for. Finally, you'll need to document how the prototype works so that your end user knows what to do with it. I'll leave that one up to you.

Where To Go From Here

In this chapter, you had the opportunity to build one final application to bring together many of the techniques and concepts discussed during the course of the book. Starting with the PRACTICE methodology, you had the chance to see how some of the earlier work you did applies in a practical context. Next, you'll learn a little about how to troubleshoot and optimize your programs to get the most bang for the buck.

Chapter 27

Optimizing Your Access 2000 Applications

Making something work is one thing; making something work better is quite another matter.

The Human Resources application you built in the last chapter was developed as a prototype for a fictional company. Because prototypes are typically not designed to be production version applications, they're typically not optimized for best performance and use. This chapter discusses ways to affect performance and use optimization when you're ready to turn your application prototypes into production-version applications. To set the stage for the topics discussed in the remainder of this chapter, let's begin by taking a second look at the HRApplication prototype.

The HRApplication Prototype: A Final Look

The HRApplication prototype was developed in response to a request for an automated solution that would keep track of staff administrative data for a department. You, as the developer, chose to use Access 2000 as your development tool, and you employed the PRACTICE development methodology to structure your program development activity. The prototype design, driven by database structure and code reuse, consisted of two primary user interface components—the LogonForm and the HRAppInterface forms (see Figures 27.1 and 27.2).

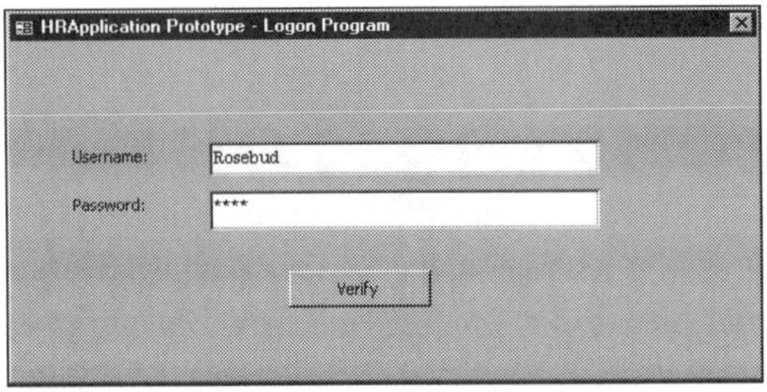

Figure 27.1
The HRApplication prototype LogonForm form.

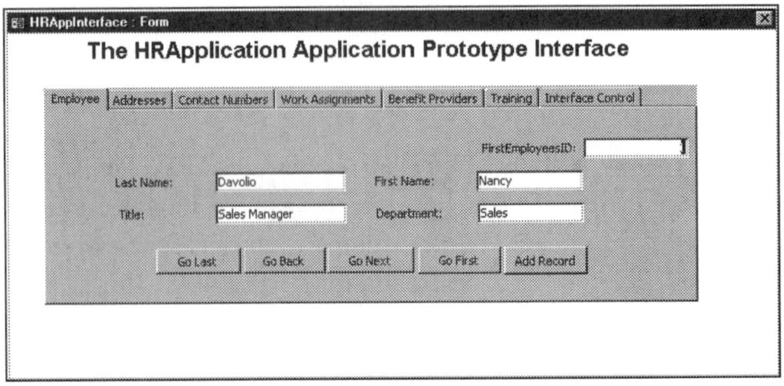

Figure 27.2
The HRApplication prototype HRAppInterface form.

Technical features highlighted by this prototype included the use of custom navigation buttons; a dynamically filled Combo Box control; controls to colorize, hide, and disable application data fields; and a search feature demonstrating the use of the **RecordsetClone** property and bookmarks. As application prototypes go, this one wasn't too bad. However, operational capability evolved from structured development methods does not an optimized application make! If you truly want to make your Access 2000 applications jump higher and run faster, you need to consider ways that improve application stability, performance, and maintainability.

Optimizing For Application Stability

Application stability has to do with how "error free" your code is and how your application reacts when errors are found. In addressing the issue of application stability, you need to understand the types of errors you're likely to encounter, how to find them, how to prevent them from occurring, and how to handle them programmatically, in case you happen to miss a few.

Understanding Program Error Types

Errors are those pesky incidents that occur when your application can't do what a statement calls for. Most of the errors you'll run across fall into one of three categories: errors in syntax, errors in execution, and errors in logic. Errors in syntax involve the language-specific aspects of your source code. Errors in execution occur while a program is running, and errors in logic have to do with the code not performing functionally as you might have expected.

Errors In Syntax

Syntax errors are the easiest to find and correct, because most programming languages and tools have built-in capabilities that detect the error, tell you the type of error found, and identify the error's location in the source code. This type of error can be anything from a misspelled VBA keyword, such as **MgsBox** for **MsgBox**, to omitting a semicolon at the end of a SQL statement. You'll likely uncover these errors when you execute the **Compile** command in the Visual Basic Editor, because VBA won't compile code that contains incorrect syntax, as shown in Listing 27.1. When this type of error is encountered, you'll get an alert message similar to the one shown in Figure 27.3.

Listing 27.1   Incorrect syntax.
```
Private Sub DateStamp_Click()
Dim DS As New DateStamp
MsgBox DS.DateStamp
```

Errors In Execution

Errors in execution, also called *runtime errors*, can significantly impact your application. You'll find execution errors when you try to run your application and it chokes. Some conditions known to cause execution errors include not having enough memory, attempting to open a nonexistent file, or having a variable with a declared data type contain data of another data type. Errors in

---

NOTE

Although you can't compile code that has syntax errors, you can save it. Therefore, it's usually a good idea to compile and save your application rather than save and close it.

Figure 27.3
Omitting an **End Sub** statement produces a compile alert.

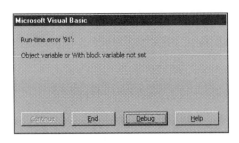

Figure 27.4
An execution error
alert message.

NOTE

*Refer to Appendix D for a
listing of Jet and Data
Access Object errors.*

execution will occur even if your source code is syntactically
correct. Figure 27.4 shows the alert displayed for the runtime error
generated by modifying the code in Listing 27.2 to the code in
Listing 27.3.

Listing 27.2   An example of error-free code.

```
Private Sub DateStamp_Click()
Dim DS As New DateStamp
MsgBox DS.DateStamp
End Sub
```

**Listing 27.3   An example of code that produces a runtime
execution error.**

```
Private Sub DateStamp_Click()
Dim DS As Criteria
MsgBox DS.DateStamp
End Sub
```

Errors In Logic

Logic errors occur when you tell your program to do something
that doesn't make sense. Logic errors are very subtle, in that you
may not realize you've introduced them. After all, the application
only does what you tell it to do. The most common logic errors
occur when your program is executing along a specific path, as
with an **If...Then** statement, or if you mistakenly perform a
calculation with a minus sign that requires a plus sign. With logic
errors, the application can be compiled, saved, and executed as if
everything is just fine. However, when your expected result
doesn't occur and you've received no alert of any kind, chances
are you need to check your program logic. Type the following line
of code in the Visual Basic Editor Immediate window to see a real
live logic error in Access 2000 related to the year 2000. Figure
27.5 shows you an unexpected alert.

NOTE

*Logic errors sometimes
manifest themselves as
runtime errors.*

Figure 27.5
A logic error related
to how the **Year**
function handles a
year 2000 date.

```
? Year(2/3/00)
```

NOTE

Debugging has its own set of terminology. For example, a breakpoint *is a location you set in your code at which VBA will temporarily halt program execution.* Watch *is an expression used to track the values during program execution.*

Understanding Debugging

Debugging is the process of finding and removing errors from your program code. Access 2000 provides two primary tools to aid you in this pursuit—the Debug menu item on the Visual Basic Editor's menu bar and the Debug menu item found on the Microsoft Script Editor's menu bar. With the options found in these menu items, you can execute your programs one line at a time and see the value of application variables during program execution. The Debug options of the VB Editor and the Microsoft Script Editor are considered an integrated debugging capability because they're built-in components of the development environment. Table 27.1 lists the Debug menu commands common to both the VB Editor and the Microsoft Script Editor.

Understanding Error Handling

Error handling is the process of managing how Access 2000 responds when it encounters some type of glitch in your program code. There may be a case when you want to display your own custom alert message, rather than having an Access 2000 alert message appear. You may also want to simply ignore an error if it doesn't significantly impact your program results. When these cases arise, you'll typically create an error-handling routine to gracefully deal with the glitch occurrence. Notice the highlighted statements in Listing 27.4 for LogonForm. The highlighted statements cause the program to display the message "This ID is not on file," when the **MoveNext** command is unable to move

Table 27.1   Debug menu commands.

Command	What It Does
Step Into	Causes VBA to begin execution of a program one line at a time
Step Over	Steps through each program line and executes a function in total before resuming line-by-line program execution
Step Out	Executes a program to the first statement after the function call
Run To Cursor	Executes the program until it reaches the insertion point
Add Watch	Lets you add a variable to the Watch window for the purpose of viewing it during a debugging session
Clear All Breakpoints	Clears all displayed breakpoints for a given program

any further. The **On Error** statement identifies a label in the code where program execution should restart. As you can see, the restart label is the same as the procedure label, except it has **_Err** at the end. The **Resume** command found in the restart code tells Access 2000 that error handling is complete and to continue execution of the main program code. The **Exit Sub** statement, as its name implies, allows you to simply exit the current subroutine without an Access message or a custom message being displayed.

Listing 27.4 Code containing error handling.

```
Private Sub Command4_Click()
On Error GoTo Command4_Click_Err
'Variable Declaration Section
Dim db As Database
Dim Result
Dim SQLline As String

getpassword = "result!Password"
'Variable Definition Section
SQLline = "SELECT * FROM FirstTable
WHERE Username = [username]
AND Password = [password];"
Set Result =
  CurrentDb.OpenRecordset(SQLline, dbOpenDynaset)
'Processing Logic Section
Do Until Result!Password = Me!Password
  Result.MoveNext
Loop
If Result.EOF Or IsNull("password")
Or Result!Password <> Me!Password Then
    MsgBox "This ID is not on file!"
Else
    MsgBox "Your ID has been verified"
    DoCmd.Close acForm, "LogonForm"
    DoCmd.OpenForm "FEInterface", acNormal
End If
Result.Close
Command4_Click_Exit:
    Exit Sub

Command4_Click_Err:
    MsgBox "This ID is not on file!"
    Resume Command4_Click_Exit
End Sub
```

NOTE

*You may be wondering why both **Command4_Click_Err** and **Command4_Click_Exit** appear in the code. I must admit that **Command4_Click_Exit** is stray code. In other words, I didn't clean up the procedure after it was complete. See! You're debugging already.*

Optimizing For Application Performance

Application performance has to do with how efficiently your code is able to execute. When it comes to Access 2000 programming, you'll find that improving performance in three significant areas will enhance your application's overall performance. These three areas include memory management, queries and recordsets, and forms.

Improving Application Performance By Managing Memory

No doubt you've heard the rule of thumb that says "You can never have enough memory." Well, although more is better when it comes to memory, *using more* is not better when it comes to your applications. In other words, the less memory required by your program, the faster it's likely to perform. Consider the following memory savers when developing your Access 2000 programs:

• Be data type aware. Different variable data types use different amounts of memory. See Table 27.2 for a listing of data type memory requirements.

• Group single procedures into functional modules so that all related procedures can be loaded into memory at once, rather than individual procedures that reside across a number of modules being loaded along with other routines belonging to the same module.

• Eliminate unused code from your procedures. (OK, I'm guilty.)

Improving Query And Recordset Performance

Consider the following performance improvement recommendations when working with queries and recordsets. These recommendations are designed to augment Access 2000's native query optimizing capabilities:

Table 27.2 Data type memory requirements.

Data Type	Memory Required
Byte	1 byte
Fixed String	1 byte per character
Boolean	2 bytes
Integer	2 bytes
Long	4 bytes
Object	4 bytes
Single	4 bytes
Currency	8 bytes
Date	8 bytes
Double	8 bytes
Decimal	14 bytes
Numeric Variant	16 bytes
String Variant	22 bytes plus string length

NOTE

See Chapter 3 for a discussion of table normalization.

- Use primary keys instead of unique indexes. Primary key indexes disallow nulls and offer the Jet query optimizer more join options.

- Normalize your tables. Breaking large tables into many smaller ones causes table scans to execute more quickly.

- Use as few columns as necessary in result sets. As may be obvious, the fewer columns that need to be returned, the faster your query will execute.

- Use the **Between** operator to restrict value ranges rather that using the >, >=, <, and <= operators. Using the **Between** operator returns fewer rows. Again, this means faster query execution.

NOTE

These recommendations are also applicable for improving the performance of reports, because the speed of a report's output is directly associated with the queries that drive it.

- For complex queries, use saved queries instead of SQL, because saved queries are optimized.

Improving Form Performance

Forms are a user's primary means of interacting with your data, so consider the following recommendations to improve their

NOTE

Refer to Chapters 16 and 24 for examples of how the Tab control reduces form complexity.

performance. Any gains you can make in speed of execution translate to a more user-friendly application.

- Reduce form complexity by making long scrollable forms into multiple forms containing unique data, or you can employ the Tab control to accomplish the same effect.

- Refrain from using overlapping controls.

- Consider using hyperlinks to move between forms.

Optimizing For Application Maintainability

Application maintainability has to do with the ease with which a third party can look at your code and repair it or enhance it. Depending on budget, schedule, ego, and prevailing attitudes, application maintainability might not be a priority. However, if you want to avoid potential long-term headaches, make the decision to have application maintainability be a priority to you. The guidelines that follow are designed to help you write better software and perform better bug prevention, as well as ease your application troubleshooting efforts.

- Design and build for functionality first. In other words, don't get so carried away about adding all the bells and whistles that you lose sight of what the program is supposed to do.

- Build and test your code in isolation. Ever heard the riddle "How do you eat a whole elephant?" Answer: one bite at a time. Well, the same holds true for programming. If you've got a large, complex application to build, break it down into small functional components and then test each component on its own before integrating it with the other components. Smaller blocks of code are easier to maintain, and they facilitate reuse.

- Don't reinvent the wheel. Write your code so that you can use it again and again with minor modifications. This is how some of the great software utilities have come into being.

- Make your code self-documenting. In other words, make use of embedded comments and procedure headers to remind yourself what you were thinking about when you revisit your code after being away from it for awhile. Commenting your code is also a great organizing technique. Refer to the highlighted lines of code in Listing 27.5.

Listing 27.5 Code containing comments.

```
Private Sub Command10_Click()
'Variable Declaration Section
Dim db As Database
Dim RecordSource
Dim Advance As Integer
'Variable Definition Section
Set db = CurrentDb
Set RecordSource = db.OpenRecordset("FirstEmployees")
Advance = InputBox("Enter the number of rows
  you wish to move ahead")
'Processing Logic Section
    If IsEmpty(Advance) Then
    MsgBox "Please enter a value!"
    Else
    RecordSource.Move Advance
    MsgBox "This record contains
      the last name " & RecordSource("LastName")
    End If
End Sub
```

- Use descriptive variable, function, and control names. Cryptic names don't help anyone. When you're looking at a piece of code nine months from now and you see an event procedure with the name **Clfmtrg**, will you remember that its intent was to close a form? How about something like **Close_Form_Trigger** instead?

- Be guided by a method. You were introduced to the PRAC-TICE methodology in this book. This is one of many structured development methods. The point here is to add some programming method to your programming madness. In case you don't recall them from Chapter 1, the eight points of the PRACTICE method are listed here:

  - **P**ose a purpose for your program.

  - **R**esolve what the program needs to do.

  - **A**llocate what the program needs to do to logical functions.

- Consider the process steps.
- Test each functional code block.
- Integrate and debug.
- Correlate to the original purpose.
- End with good documentation.

Optimizing Your Database

Optimizing your Access 2000 applications is not just a function of improving the efficiency of your code. It's also a matter of fine-tuning the database that supports the code. Access 2000 again puts capability at your fingertips by equipping you with tools such as MDE file conversion, compacting, and database repair, which are designed to optimize database performance.

Saving Your Database As An MDE File

By selecting Tools|Database Utilities|Make MDE File, you cause Access 2000 to create a new copy of the current database and to perform the following actions on it.

1. It stores to the new database copy all the database objects contained in the original, except for modules.

2. Next, it compiles the source database modules and saves them in their compiled form in the new database copy, which it then compacts.

Tip

Should you decide to create an MDE file, be aware that once the conversion is complete, you won't be able to add, modify, or delete forms, reports, controls, and modules. In addition, MDE files created in Access 97 may not be upwardly compatible with Access 2000.

When you save your database as an MDE file, database performance is optimized because modules are compiled, and your database is more secure because MDE files are limited with respect to how you can modify them.

Compacting And Repairing Your Database

When a record is deleted from an Access table, the space occupied by that record is not reused. Consequently, over time, your database performance may degrade because of the lack of contiguous space. This condition is similar to what happens to a hard drive after numerous files have been added and deleted. By

> **NOTE**
>
> *VBA does not allow you to programmatically compact and repair the current database—it only allows you to invoke the Compact and Repair capability on another database.*

selecting Tools|Database Utilities|Compact And Repair Database, you cause Access 2000 to recover all the unused space left by numerous record deletions. It does this by copying all the current database objects and writing them contiguously to a new database copy. The new database is effectively reduced in size, making data access more efficient. Again, this procedure is similar to defragmenting your hard drive. In addition to compacting the current database, Access 2000 also performs a repair routine when compacting is complete. This routine checks to determine whether the current database is corrupt and then attempts to repair any damage if necessary.

Where To Go From Here

Well, you've come to the end of the line. You've been exposed to quite a bit of information, and hopefully you've learned a few tips and techniques along the way. At this point, I'm guessing that you have a pretty good working knowledge of Access 2000 programming and the things that it makes possible. However, if you're still champing at the bit for more, then check out the appendixes. Happy programming!

Appendix A

Questions And Answers About Access 2000

W hen you've finished working your way through a book about a new or upgraded software product, it's not unusual to have lingering questions about everything that's been discussed. Because Access 2000 brings some significant enhancements to the table, there's no doubt you'll have questions about concepts, features, and techniques that were covered throughout the book. The intent of this appendix is to provide answers to some of those lingering questions, to clarify potential points of confusion, and to challenge you to continue to discover all that Access 2000 and Access 2000 programming has to offer. For easy reference, the information you find here has been arranged by chapter.

Chapter 1—Access 2000: A New Beginning

What Is Access 2000?

Access 2000 is the latest version of Microsoft's desktop relational database management system designed for Windows, and it's enhanced with integrated support for the Office 2000 application productivity suite.

What Is Access 2000 Programming?

Access 2000 programming is the use of Visual Basic for Applications to interact with and manipulate data objects.

What Is The Focus Of Access 2000 Product Enhancements?

Access 2000 differs from its predecessors as a result of enhancements in the areas of productivity, programmability, objects, client/server, and the Jet 4.0 database engine.

What Are Subdatasheets?

Subdatasheets allow users to browse table, query, form, or subform data hierarchically in the datasheet view.

What Are The Primary Programmability Enhancements Found In Access 2000?

Primary programmability enhancements include the addition of the Visual Basic Editor and the Microsoft Script Editor.

What Is The Most Significant New Object Type Introduced With Access 2000?

Chances are that the most significant new object type introduced with Access 2000 is the data access page. Data access pages are HTML documents that can be bound directly to database data like Access forms, but they're designed to run in Internet Explorer 5.

What Is PRACTICE?

PRACTICE is an acronym for eight activities used to support structured application program development using Access 2000. Specifically, PRACTICE stands for:

- Pose a purpose for your program.
- Resolve what the program needs to do.

- Allocate what the program needs to do to logical functions.

- Consider the process steps.

- Test each functional code block.

- Integrate and debug.

- Correlate to the original purpose.

- End with good documentation.

Chapter 2—Let's Write An Access Program

What Languages Are Used To Program In Access 2000?

Access 2000 supports Visual Basic for Applications, the standard programming language for all applications comprising the Microsoft Office suite, and Structured Query Language (SQL).

What Is The Significance Of The Statement Option Compare Database?

The statement **Option Compare Database** indicates that VBA will use the string comparison parameters established by the current database to support string comparisons executed within the specific program module.

What Is The Significance Of The Keywords Sub And End Sub?

The VBA keyword **Sub** indicates the start of a procedure type called a *subroutine*. A subroutine is a group of program statements that can be called from anywhere in a program to perform a specific task. The keywords **End Sub** signify the end of a subroutine.

How Are Comments Designated In Visual Basic For Applications?

In VBA, comments are designated in source code by preceding a string with a single quote (').

What Is A Variable?

A variable is a named memory location used to store information.

What Is An Operator?

An operator is a symbol that's applied to a data value that causes a specific process to be performed on the data value. There are three primary types of operators:

- *Arithmetic operators*—Include math symbols such as + and -

- *Comparison operators*—Used to check for comparison conditions using symbols such as =, >, and <

- *Logical operators*—Indicate a True or False condition using -1 and 0, respectively

Chapter 3—What Makes Access Programs Tick?

What Is The Access Development Model?

The Access Development Model is a solution-building model driven by three fundamental components: database development, object-oriented design, and event-driven programming.

What Is A Relational Database?

A relational database is an electronic container used to store multiple tables linked by common data elements for the purpose of data lookup and retrieval.

What Is A Primary Key?

A primary key is a column or set of columns containing unique values for a table.

What Is A Data Model?

A data model is a graphical depiction of all tables, fields, indexes, and rules needed to construct a relational database.

What Is Normalization?

Normalization is the process of simplifying the design of a database so that its structure is optimized.

What Are Normal Forms?

Normal forms are a progressively affective set of rules applied to achieve more efficient database design. There are three normal forms:

- *First Normal Form*—The normalization rule stating that every row-by-column position must contain one and only one value, with no columns being duplicates of other columns.

- *Second Normal Form*—The normalization rule stating that all First Normal Form criteria must be satisfied and column values should be fully identifiable by the entire primary key.

- *Third Normal Form*—The normalization rule stating that all Second Normal Form criteria must be met and all nonkey columns should not be dependent on other columns to exist.

What Is A Class?

A class is a model that describes all the attributes and behaviors of a particular data type.

What Is An Object?

An object is an instance of a class.

What Is Distinctive About An Object?

An object is characterized by its attributes (also called *properties*) and its behaviors (also called *methods*).

What Is A Macro?

A macro is a set of one or more actions, each performing a specific operation.

What Is A Standard Module?

A standard module is a standalone code block that does not depend on a specific object to work.

What Is A Class Module?

A class module is a standard module that depends on a specific object to work.

What Is A Collection?

A collection is a set of one or more objects of the same type contained within a larger object.

What Is DAO?

DAO stands for *Data Access Object*. Data Access Objects perform data management tasks such as viewing, editing, adding, and deleting fields, rows, and tables.

Chapter 4—Let's Create A Form-Based Program

What Is An Unbound Control?

An unbound control is a control object that has no association with a database field.

What Is The Significance Of The VBA Keyword Private?

The keyword **Private** indicates that the procedure in use cannot be called from outside the module where it's declared; it can only be used by other procedures residing in the same module.

How Do I Access The Microsoft DAO 2.5/3.5 Compatibility Library?

Click on References in the Tools menu of the VB Editor while in module Design View.

What Is The Code Used To Build The Form LogonForm?

The code used to create the form LogonForm is shown in Listing A.1.

Listing A.1   The form LogonForm.

```
Option Compare Database
Private Sub Command4_Click()
'Variable Declaration Section
Dim db As Database
Dim Result
Dim SQLline As String

getpassword = "result!Password"
'Variable Definition Section
SQLline = "SELECT * FROM FirstTable
WHERE Username = [username]
AND Password = [password];"
Set Result =
CurrentDb.OpenRecordset(SQLline, dbOpenDynaset)

'Processing Logic Section
Do Until Result!Password = Me!Password
  Result.MoveNext
Loop
If Result.EOF Or IsNull("password") & _
Or Result!Password <> Me!Password Then
    MsgBox "This ID is not on file!"
Else
    MsgBox "Your ID has been verified"
End If
Result.Close
End Sub
```

Chapter 5—Programming With Access SQL

What Is SQL?

SQL is an acronym for Structured Query Language. Structured Query Language is similar to a programming language; however, it's specifically designed to query database tables.

What Are The Rules Of Thumb When Writing SQL In Access?

The rules of thumb to consider when creating SQL statements in Access 2000 include the following:

- Terminate SQL statements with a semicolon.

- Write SQL keywords in uppercase and parameters in lowercase or mixed case.

- Use multiline statements to distinguish keywords from table names.

- Use an asterisk (*) as a wildcard to retrieve all table fields for a SQL dataset.

What Is The SQL Foundational Four?

The SQL Foundational Four is the set of four SQL keywords that drive most SQL programming activity: **SELECT, INSERT INTO, UPDATE,** and **DELETE.**

What Does The SELECT Statement Do?

The **SELECT** statement initiates data retrieval queries. The standard syntax for a SQL **SELECT** statement is:

```
SELECT (name of one or more table columns)
FROM (name of table containing the specified column(s));
```

What Does The INSERT INTO Statement Do?

The **INSERT INTO** statement lets you add single records to a table and copy records from tables or queries to other tables. The **INSERT INTO** statement is built using the following syntax:

```
INSERT INTO table name [column name]
VALUES (value1, value2};
```

What Does The UPDATE Statement Do?

The **UPDATE** statement lets you update data in one or more columns programmatically. The **UPDATE** statement is built using the following syntax:

```
UPDATE tablename or queryname
SET column = Some expression
WHERE row-specific criteria
```

What Does The DELETE Statement Do?

The **DELETE** statement removes table rows. The **DELETE** statement is built using the following syntax:

```
DELETE
FROM tablename
WHERE restriction criteria
```

Chapter 6—Let's Build A Market Research Tool

What Are The Valid SQL Aggregate Functions In Access 2000?

The aggregate functions that are valid in Access 2000 are shown in Table A.1.

Table A.1   Valid SQL aggregate functions.

Function Name	Operation
Avg()	Returns the average of all non-null column values
Count()	Returns the number of records in a table
First()	Returns the value of the first record in a recordset
Last()	Returns the value of the last record in a recordset
Max()	Returns the largest value in a recordset
Min()	Returns the smallest value in a recordset

(continued)

Table A.1 Valid SQL aggregate functions *(continued).*

Function Name	Operation
STDev()	Returns the sample standard deviation for a column
STDevP()	Returns the population standard deviation for a column
Sum()	Returns the total of all records in a table
Var()	Returns the sample variance for a column
VarP()	Returns the variance deviation for a column

What Are The Valid Domain Aggregate Functions In Access 2000?

The valid Access 2000 domain aggregate functions are shown in Table A.2.

What Is The Code Used To Build The Market Research Tool?

The code used to create the Market Research Tool is shown in Listing A.2.

Table A.2 Valid domain aggregate functions.

Function Name	Operation
DAvg()	Returns the average of all non-null column values
DCount()	Returns the number of records in a table
DFirst()	Returns the value of the first record in a recordset
DLast()	Returns the value of the last record in a recordset
DMax()	Returns the largest value in a recordset
DMin()	Returns the smallest value in a recordset
DSTDev()	Returns the sample standard deviation for a column
DSTDevP()	Returns the population standard deviation for a column
DSum()	Returns the total of all records in a table
DVar()	Returns the sample variance for a column
DVarP()	Returns the variance deviation for a column

Listing A.2   The Market Research Tool.

```
Option compare Database
Private Sub AVGQ1_Click()
'Variable Declaration Section
    Dim Stats1
'Variable Definition Section
    Stats1 = DAvg("q1", "Responses")
'Processing Logic Section
    MsgBox "The average response & _
    for Question 1 is " & Stats1
End Sub
Private Sub AVGQ2_Click()
'Variable Declaration Section
    Dim Stats2
'Variable Definition Section
    Stats2 = DAvg("q2", "Responses")
'Processing Logic Section
    MsgBox "The average response for & _
    Question 2 is " & Stats2
End Sub
Private Sub AVGQ3_Click()
'Variable Declaration Section
    Dim Stats3
'Variable Definition Section
    Stats3 = DAvg("q3", "Responses")
'Processing Logic Section
    MsgBox "The average response for & _
    Question 3 is " & Stats3
End Sub
Private Sub AVGQ4_Click()
'Variable Declaration Section
    Dim Stats4
'Variable Definition Section
    Stats4 = DAvg("q4", "Responses")
'Processing Logic Section
    MsgBox "The average response for & _
    Question 4 is " & Stats4
End Sub
Private Sub AVGQ5_Click()
'Variable Declaration Section
    Dim Stats5
'Variable Definition Section
    Stats5 = DAvg("q5", "Responses")
'Processing Logic Section
    MsgBox "The average response for & _
    Question 5 is " & Stats5
End Sub
```

Chapter 7—VBA Programming Fundamentals

What Are The Conventions To Which VBA Variables Must Adhere?

In VBA, variable names must adhere to the following conventions:

- They must begin with a letter.
- They can contain only letters, numbers, and underscore characters.
- They must be 40 characters or less.
- They cannot be a VB reserved word.

How Do You Break Long Lines Of Code In VBA?

Long lines of code are broken by placing a space followed by an underscore at the breakpoint.

What Is The DoCmd Object?

The **DoCmd** object provides VBA with command equivalents to Access 2000 macros.

What Is Syntax In The Context Of VBA?

In VBA, syntax refers to the set of rules that governs the way programming statements are written.

What Is A Constant?

A constant is a name representing a value that never changes.

What Is The RunCommand Method?

The **RunCommand** method allows VBA to execute commands that equate to the Access 2000 menu and toolbar options.

What Do Operators Operate On?

Operators can work on variables, literal numbers, constants, and expressions.

What Makes Operators Important?

Operators are used to make decisions, to assign data to variables, and to control program flow.

What Are Some Reasons To Use VBA Instead Of Macros?

Some of the reasons for using VBA instead of macros include, but are not limited to, the following:

- VBA lets you perform complex functions programmatically.

- VBA executes faster than macros.

- VBA lets you interact with other applications.

Chapter 8—Let's Work With Recordsets

What Is A Recordset?

A recordset is a Data Access Object (DAO) that contains a set of table records.

What Types Of Recordsets Are There?

There are three primary recordset types:

- *Table*—The table-type recordset is the default type for any **Recordset** object that supports Access tables.

- *Dynaset*—The dynaset-type recordset is a Data Access Object that contains a dynamic set of records not stored in the database. It can contain a table or query results.

- *Snapshot*—The snapshot-type recordset is a Data Access Object that contains a fixed view of a set of records.

How Do I Create A Recordset?

Recordsets can be created using an expression similar to the following:

```
Dim variable As Recordset
Set variable = db.OpenRecordset(contents of Recordset)
```

What Methods Are Used To Navigate Through Recordsets?

The methods used to navigate through the rows of a recordset are **MoveFirst**, **MoveLast**, **MovePrevious**, and **MoveNext**.

What Is The Code Used To Build The Recordset Navigation Panel?

The code used to create the Recordset Navigation Panel is shown in Listing A.3. Remember that breaks in the code, such as in the middle of a **MsgBox** statement, are for editorial purposes only. Do *not* break up a **MsgBox** statement.

Listing A.3   The Recordset Navigation Panel.

```
Option Compare Database

Private Sub PercentPosition_Click()
'Variable Declaration Section
Dim db As Database
Dim RecordSource
Dim percent
'Variable Definition Section
Set db = CurrentDb
Set RecordSource = db.OpenRecordset("FirstEmployees")
percent = InputBox("Please enter a percentage.")
'Processing Logic Section
    RecordSource.PercentPosition = percent
    MsgBox "The record found at this
    position contains the last name "
    & RecordSource("LastName")
End Sub

Private Sub RecordCount_Click()
'Variable Declaration Section
Dim db As Database
Dim RecordSource
'Variable Definition Section
```

```
Set db = CurrentDb
Set RecordSource = db.OpenRecordset("FirstEmployees")
    numrecs = RecordSource.RecordCount
'Processing Logic Section
    MsgBox "The number of records
    in this table is " & numrecs
End Sub


Private Sub Seek_Click()
'Variable Declaration Section
Dim db As Database
Dim recordlist
Dim SeekIt As String
Dim MatchMsg
'Variable Definition Section
Set db = CurrentDb
Set recordlist = db.OpenRecordset("FirstEmployees")
SeekIt = InputBox("Enter the last name for
the employee whose status you wish to check.")
MatchMsg = "The last name you
entered is an authorized employee."
'Processing Logic Section
        recordlist.Index = "LastName"
        recordlist.Seek "=", SeekIt
    If recordlist.NoMatch = True Then
        MsgBox "We have no employee on file
        with the last name " & SeekIt
    Else
    MsgBox MatchMsg
    End If
End Sub


Private Sub MovenRecords_Click()
'Variable Declaration Section
Dim db As Database
Dim RecordSource
Dim Advance As Integer


'Variable Definition Section
Set db = CurrentDb
Set RecordSource = db.OpenRecordset("FirstEmployees")
Advance = InputBox("Enter the number of
rows you wish to move ahead")
'Processing Logic Section
    If IsEmpty(Advance) Then
    MsgBox "Please enter a value!"
    Else
    RecordSource.Move Advance
    MsgBox "This record contains the
```

```
              last name " & RecordSource("LastName")
          End If
End Sub
Private Sub MovePrevious_Click()
'Variable Declaration Section
    Dim db As Database
    Dim RecordSource
'Variable Definition Section
    Set db = CurrentDb
    Set RecordSource =
    db.OpenRecordset("FirstEmployees")
'Processing Logic Section
  RecordSource.MoveLast
  Do While RecordSource.BOF = False
    RecordSource.MovePrevious
        If RecordSource.BOF = True Then
        MsgBox "Beginning of File, Please
        Click the MoveNext Button"
        Else
        MsgBox "This record contains the
        Last Name: " & RecordSource("LastName")
        End If
    Loop
End Sub

Private Sub MoveFirst_Click()
'Variable Declaration Section
    Dim db As Database
    Dim RecordSource
'Variable Definition Section
    Set db = CurrentDb
    Set RecordSource =
    db.OpenRecordset("FirstEmployees")
'Processing Logic Section
    RecordSource.MoveFirst
    MsgBox "The first record in this
    table contains the Last Name: " .
    & RecordSource("LastName")
End Sub

Private Sub MoveLast_Click()
'Variable Declaration Section
    Dim db As Database
    Dim RecordSource
    Dim myBookmark As String
'Variable Definition Section
    Set db = CurrentDb
    Set RecordSource =
```

```
    db.OpenRecordset("FirstEmployees")
    myBookmark = RecordSource.Bookmark
'Processing Logic Section
    RecordSource.MoveLast
    MsgBox "The last record in this table
    contains the Last Name: " & RecordSource("LastName")
    RecordSource.MoveFirst
    RecordSource.MoveNext
    RecordSource.Bookmark = myBookmark
    MsgBox "This is a Bookmark test."
    & RecordSource("LastName")
    RecordSource.Bookmark = myBookmark
    MsgBox "A successful Bookmark is
    confirmed by the Last Name: "
    & RecordSource("LastName")
End Sub

Private Sub MoveNext_Click()
'Variable Declaration Section
    Dim db As Database
    Dim RecordSource
'Variable Definition Section
    Set db = CurrentDb
    Set RecordSource =
    db.OpenRecordset("FirstEmployees")
'Processing Logic Section
    Do While RecordSource.EOF = False
    RecordSource.MoveNext
        If RecordSource.EOF = True Then
        MsgBox "End of File,
        Please Click the MovePrevious Button"
        Else
        MsgBox "This record contains the
        Last Name: " & RecordSource("LastName")
        End If
    Loop
End Sub
```

Chapter 9—Understanding SQL And VBA Operators

What Is A Bookmark?

A bookmark is a four-byte long integer that references the current row in a recordset.

What Are SQL Operators?

SQL operators are standard logical operators (=, <>,>) and comparison operators (**LIKE, IN**, and **BETWEEN...AND**).

What Is The Code Used To Create The Shoe Order Form?

The code used to create the Shoe Order Form is shown in Listing A.4.

Listing A.4   The Shoe Order Form.

```
Private Sub YourOrder_Click()
'variable declaration section
Dim Shoes_Ordered
Dim Shoes_OutofStock
Dim Dress
Dim Casual
Dim Running
Dim OrderCost
Dim CostPerPair
'variable definition section
Dress = CInt(DressShoes.Value)
Casual = CInt(CasualShoes.Value)
Running = CInt(RunningShoes.Value)
Shoes_Ordered = Dress + Casual + Running
Shoes_OutofStock=Shoes_Ordered - 5
OrderCost = Shoes_Ordered * 19.95
CostPerPair = OrderCost / Shoes_Ordered
'processing logic section
MsgBox "Your total shoe order
is " & Shoes_Ordered & " pairs!"
MsgBox "Oops! We're out of Casual Shoes,
your order is reduced to"
& Shoes_OutofStock & " pairs!"
MsgBox "Your order cost is $" & OrderCost & "."
MsgBox "Your cost per pair is $" & CostPerPair & "."
End Sub
```

Chapter 10—Let's Work With Class Modules

What Are Property Statements?

Property statements are VBA procedures executed when a property is set or retrieved:

- **Property Get**—Used to retrieve the values of class instance properties.

- **Property Let**—Used to allow users of your objects to change the value of an object property.

- **Property Set**—Used to create object properties.

What Is The Code Behind The Class Module Panel Form?

The code behind the Class Module Panel form is shown in Listing A.5.

Listing A.5   The Class Module Panel.
```
Option Compare Database
Private Sub DateStamp_Click()
Dim DS As New DateStamp
MsgBox DS.DateStamp
End Sub
Private Sub DateTimeStamp_Click()
Dim DTS As New DateTimeStamp
MsgBox DTS.DateTimeStamp
End Sub
Private Sub TimeStamp_Click()
Dim TS As New TimeStamp
MsgBox TS.TimeStamp
End Sub
```

What Is The Object Browser?

The Object Browser is a tool used to look up property and method information about all the objects within a specific database.

Chapter 11—Understanding Object-Oriented Programming With Access 2000

What Is Object-Oriented Programming?

Object-oriented programming (OOP) is a structured approach to developing software that focuses on decomposing a problem into distinct objects.

How Does Access 2000 Support OOP?

Access 2000 supports OOP using class modules.

What Is Encapsulation?

Encapsulation, also called *data hiding*, is the object-oriented principle that an object can be used without the user having any knowledge about its inner workings.

What Is Inheritance?

Inheritance is the object-oriented principle that allows object reuse without the need to reproduce the object's attributes and behaviors with each new use.

What Is Polymorphism?

Polymorphism is the object-oriented principle that allows the use of a variable of a parent class to refer to any classes derived from the parent class.

What Are AccessObjects?

AccessObjects are an Access 2000 object type. They include information about a single object instance and describe forms, reports, macros, modules, data access pages, tables, queries, views, stored procedures, and database diagrams.

Chapter 12—Creating Reports In Access 2000

What Options Are Available For Creating Reports In Access 2000?

Access 2000 provides the option to create reports using the AutoReport feature or the Report Wizard, or you can create reports manually.

What Are The Sections Of An Access 2000 Report?

Access 2000 reports are divided into the following sections: Report Header, Page Header, Detail, Page Footer, and Report Footer.

What Are The Steps For Manually Creating An Access 2000 Report?

Creating a manual report in Access 2000 involves the following five steps:

1. Select the Create Report In Design View option from the database window and choose a recordsource.

2. Sort your report data as required.

3. Add report headers and footers.

4. Display report data, text, and/or totals.

5. Arrange the report controls per your report design layout.

Chapter 13—Understanding Access Report Design

What Types Of Reports Can Be Created Using Access 2000?

Access 2000 can be used to create the following major report types:

- *Detail reports*—Documents that provide an entry for each record.

- *Summary reports*—Provide aggregate data for all the records presented in a detail report.

- *Cross-tabulation reports*—Display summarized data grouped by one set of information on the left side of the report and by another set across the top of the report

The following reports can also be created in Access:

- Reports containing graphics and charts
- Reports containing forms
- Reports containing labels
- Reports including any combination of the above

Chapter 14—Introducing Data Access Pages

What Are Data Access Pages?

Data access pages are HTML documents that can be directly bound to table data in a database.

Do Data Access Pages Have Any Special Requirements?

Yes. Designing data access pages requires that Internet Explorer 5 be installed on your development machine.

Are Data Access Pages Part Of The Access 2000 Database?

No. Data access pages are saved in the file system rather than within the Access 2000 database.

Are Data Access Pages Available In Previous Versions Of Access?

No. Data access pages are new in Access 2000.

What Is A Grouped Data Access Page?

A *grouped* data access page is a hierarchical, interactive Web page that's similar to a grouped report.

Can Data Access Pages Work With Microsoft Office Components?

Yes. You can include Office 2000 Web components such as spreadsheets, charts, and PivotTables in your data access pages.

Can I Convert Existing Web Pages To Data Access Pages?

Yes. Access 2000 provides the capability to convert existing Web pages to data access pages.

What Type Of Controls Are Used With Data Access Pages?

Data access pages use controls that are HTML intrinsic, as well as COM components.

What Type Of Data Can Be Used On Data Access Pages?

Data access pages support data from Access databases and SQL Server 6.5 or higher.

Are Data Access Pages Processed On A Web Server?

No. Data access pages are processed on the client side.

Chapter 15—Understanding Data Access Pages And The Web

What Is Scripting?

Scripting is the process of adding programming logic to HTML code using a scripting language.

Are There Different Scripting Languages?

Yes. Three of the more common scripting languages are VBScript, JScript, and JavaScript.

What Languages Are Used To Create Data Access Pages?

Generally, you'll use one or a combination of three languages to develop data access pages

- *Dynamic HTML*—Dynamic HTML is an enhancement to Cascading Style Sheets (CSS), which let you define and apply paragraph and character styles to an entire document or Web page.
- *VBScript*—VBScript, also known as *Visual Basic Scripting Edition*, is a scaled-down version of Visual Basic designed specifically for Web application development.
- *JavaScript*—JavaScript is a scripting language for the Web developed by Netscape Communications Corporation.

What Is JScript?

JScript is a Microsoft adaptation of JavaScript.

What Is Required To Publish Data Access Pages On The Web?

You'll need five elements to publish data access pages on the Web—a database, data access page files, a hosting Web server, a file transfer utility, and Internet Explorer 5.

What Is The Microsoft Script Editor?

The Microsoft Script Editor is a utility designed to assist in the development of data access pages by providing editing and debugging capabilities in a single, integrated environment.

Chapter 16—Let's Work With Form Controls

How Are Form Controls Created In Access 2000?

Form controls are created using the Access 2000 toolbox.

What Is The Code Behind The FEInterface Form?

The code used to develop the FEInterface form is shown in Listing A.6.

Listing A.6   The FEInterface form.

```
Option Compare Database
Private Sub AddRecord_Click()
DoCmd.RunCommand acCmdRecordsGoToNew
End Sub
Private Sub AddRecord2_Click()
DoCmd.RunCommand acCmdRecordsGoToNew
End Sub
Private Sub Command8_Click()
Me!FirstEmployeesID.BackColor = 16776960
End Sub
Private Sub AllOff_Click()
Me!FirstEmployeesID.Enabled = False
Me!LastName.Enabled = False
Me!FirstName.Enabled = False
Me!Title.Enabled = False
Me!EID3.Enabled = False
Me!City.Enabled = False
Me!State.Enabled = False
Me!Comments.Enabled = False
If Me!FirstEmployeesID.Enabled = False Then
Me!AllOn.Value = Enabled
End If
End Sub

Private Sub AllOn_Click()
Me!FirstEmployeesID.Enabled = True
Me!LastName.Enabled = True
```

```
Me!FirstName.Enabled = True
Me!Title.Enabled = True
Me!EID3.Enabled = True
Me!City.Enabled = True
Me!State.Enabled = True
Me!Comments.Enabled = True
If Me!FirstEmployeesID.Enabled = True Then
Me!AllOff.Value = Enabled
End If
End Sub

Private Sub ColorOff_Click()
Me!ColorOn.Enabled = True
DoCmd.GoToControl "ColorOn"
Me!ColorOn.Value = False
Me!ColorOff.Value = True
Me!ColorOff.Enabled = False
Me!FirstEmployeesID.BackColor = 16777215
Me!LastName.BackColor = 16777215
Me!FirstName.BackColor = 16777215
Me!Title.BackColor = 16777215
Me!EID3.BackColor = 16777215
Me!City.BackColor = 16777215
Me!State.BackColor = 16777215
Me!Comments.BackColor = 16777215
MsgBox "The data field colors are now normal!"
End Sub
Private Sub ColorOn_Click()
Me!ColorOff.Enabled = True
DoCmd.GoToControl "ColorOff"
Me!ColorOff.Value = False
Me!ColorOn.Value = True
Me!ColorOn.Enabled = False
Me!FirstEmployeesID.BackColor = 16776960
Me!LastName.BackColor = 16776960
Me!FirstName.BackColor = 16776960
Me!Title.BackColor = 16776960
Me!EID3.BackColor = 16776960
Me!City.BackColor = 16776960
Me!State.BackColor = 16776960
Me!Comments.BackColor = 16776960
MsgBox "The data field colors are now light blue!"
End Sub

Private Sub Command102_Click()
Debug.Print Me!ListBoxA.Selected(0)
End Sub
Private Sub Command114_Click()
```

```
Dim GetName
Dim Lname
GetName = InputBox("Enter a name")
SQLTxt = "SELECT * FROM FirstEmployees
WHERE LastName = Me!GetName;"
Do Until Lname = GetName
DoCmd.GoToRecord Record:=acNext
Loop
End Sub

Private Sub Form_Load()
  Dim lst As ListBox
 Dim intI As Integer, intJ As Integer

  Set lst = Me!ListBoxA
     'Display FirstEmployeesID, LastName,
       FirstName fields in list box.
    With lst
      .RowSourceType = "Table/Query"
      .RowSource = "FirstEmployees"
      .ColumnCount = 3
    End With

    ' Print value of each column for each row.
  For intI = 0 To lst.ListCount - 1
    For intJ = 0 To lst.ColumnCount - 1
        Debug.Print lst.Column(intJ, intI)
        Debug.Print
      Next intJ
    Next intI
End Sub

Private Sub GoBack_Click()
On Error GoTo ErrorHandling_Err2
DoCmd.GoToRecord Record:=acPrevious
ErrorHandling_Exit:
Exit Sub
ErrorHandling_Err2:
If Err.Number = 2105 Then
MsgBox "There are no previous records."
Resume ErrorHandling_Exit
Else
End If
End Sub
Private Sub GoBack2_Click()
On Error GoTo ErrorHandling_Err2
DoCmd.GoToRecord Record:=acPrevious
```

```
ErrorHandling_Exit:
Exit Sub
ErrorHandling_Err2:
If Err.Number = 2105 Then
MsgBox "There are no previous records."
Resume ErrorHandling_Exit
Else
End If
End Sub

Private Sub GoFirst_Click()
DoCmd.GoToRecord Record:=acFirst
Me!GoLast.Enabled = True
DoCmd.GoToControl "GoLast"
Me!GoFirst.Enabled = False
End Sub
Private Sub GoFirst2_Click()
DoCmd.GoToRecord Record:=acFirst
Me!GoLast.Enabled = True
DoCmd.GoToControl "GoLast"
Me!GoFirst.Enabled = False
End Sub
Private Sub GoLast_Click()
DoCmd.GoToRecord Record:=acLast
Me!GoFirst.Enabled = True
DoCmd.GoToControl "GoFirst"
Me!GoLast.Enabled = False
End Sub

Private Sub GoLast2_Click()
DoCmd.GoToRecord Record:=acLast
Me!GoFirst.Enabled = True
DoCmd.GoToControl "GoFirst"
Me!GoLast.Enabled = False
End Sub

Private Sub GoNext_Click()
DoCmd.GoToRecord Record:=acNext
Me!GoLast.Enabled = True
Me!GoFirst.Enabled = True
End Sub

Private Sub GoNext2_Click()
DoCmd.GoToRecord Record:=acNext
Me!GoLast.Enabled = True
Me!GoFirst.Enabled = True
End Sub
```

```
Private Sub HideIt_Click()
Me!Comments.Visible = False
If Me!Comments.Visible = False Then
Me!ShowIt.Value = Disabled
End If
End Sub

Private Sub ShowIt_Click()
Me!Comments.Visible = True
If Me!Comments.Visible = True Then
Me!HideIt.Value = Disabled
End If
End Sub
```

Chapter 17—Understanding Form Controls

What Does A Label Control Do?

The Label control lets you add static text to a form that's editable in Design View only.

What Does A Tab Control Do?

The Tab control is a self-contained group of pages that lets you display several screens of related data on a single form.

What Does A Text Box Control Do?

The Text Box control lets you enter or display data on a form, report, or data access page.

What Does A Toggle Button Control Do?

The Toggle Button control is used to represent a True or Yes condition while "up" and a False or No condition while "down."

What Does An Option Group Control Do?

An Option Group control lets you place a set of like controls together for the purpose of selecting one member of the control set.

What Does A Check Box Control Do?

When not selected, the Check Box control is empty and represents a False or No condition. When the Check Box control is selected, a small checkmark appears in it, indicating a True or Yes condition.

What Does An Option Button Control Do?

An Option Button control displays a filled circle when a True or Yes condition exists and an empty circle when a False or No condition exists.

What Do Combo And List Box Controls Do?

Combo and List Box controls display multiple data selections for the purpose of allowing the user to pick a single item from a range of available choices.

What Properties Are Used To Display Combo And List Box Data?

The following properties are used to display Combo and List Box data—the **BoundColumn** property, the **ColumnCount** property, and the **ColumnWidths** property.

Chapter 18—Working With Macros In Access 2000

What Is A Macro?

A macro is a set of one or more actions that each perform a particular operation, such as opening a form or printing a report.

What Is A Macro Action Argument?

A macro action argument is like a parameter to a command or function, and gives Access specific instructions on how to execute a selected macro action.

Can I Convert Macros To VBA Code?

Yes. This is accomplished by selecting Tools|Macro|Convert Macros To Visual Basic on the Access 2000 menu bar.

How Do I Run A Macro?

A macro can be run from the Macro Design window, from the Macros tab, by being triggered from a Form or Report event, or by selecting a menu or toolbar option.

Is There A Restriction On Using Comments With Macros?

Yes. Comments for macros are limited to one line of no more than 256 characters.

Chapter 19—Further Examining Macros

What Object Methods Are Used To Perform Macro Actions In VBA?

The **Application** object and the **DoCmd** object are used to perform macro actions in VBA.

What Macro Actions Don't Have A Corresponding VBA Method?

The following macro actions have no corresponding VBA method: **AddItem**, **MsgBox**, **RunApp**, **RunCode**, **SendKeys**, **SetValue**, **StopAllMacros**, and **StopMacro**.

When Should I Use Macros Rather Than VBA?

You'll typically want to use macros instead of VBA if your design requirements meet most or all of the following criteria:

- You need to prototype your application quickly.

- You're not concerned about error handling in your application.

- You need to trap keystrokes or provide a macro that runs automatically without any command-line interference.

Can I Use Macro Commands Within VBA?

Yes. Most macro commands can be performed in VBA code using the **DoCmd** object. In this scenario, the macro action becomes a method of the **DoCmd** object.

Chapter 20—Working With Command Constants And Common Dialogs

What Are Command Constants?

Command constants are intrinsic constants supplied by Access 2000, VBA, Microsoft ActiveX Data Objects (ADO), and Microsoft Data Access Objects (DAO).

How Is The TransferDatabase Method Of The DoCmd Object Used?

The **TransferDatabase** method of the **DoCmd** object is used to import data from a database such as Visual FoxPro, dBASE, Paradox, or another Access database.

How Is The TransferText Method Of The DoCmd Object Used?

The **TransferText** method of the **DoCmd** object is used to import text from a text file.

How Is The RunCommand Action Constant Used?

You use the **RunCommand** action constant to run a built-in Microsoft Access command, such as those appearing on a Microsoft Access menu bar, toolbar, or shortcut menu.

Chapter 21—Talking About Command Constants and Common Dialogs

What Is The Format For Command Constants In Access 2000?

In Access 2000, command/intrinsic constants contain a mixture of lowercase and uppercase letters and are no longer separated by an underscore. For example, **A_NORMAL** is now **acNormal**.

How Is The TransferSpreadsheet Method Of The DoCmd Object Used?

The **TransferSpreadsheet** method of the **DoCmd** object is used to import data from a spreadsheet file.

What Is The Common Dialog Control?

The Common Dialog control provides an interface between VBA/Access and the routines in the Microsoft Windows dynamic link library Commdlg.dll.

What Is The Default Database Library Supported By The VBA Integrated Development Environment (IDE)?

The default database library supported by the VBA IDE is the ActiveX Data Objects Library.

Chapter 22—Working With Functions In Access 2000

What Is A Function?

A function is a type of VBA procedure that works like a subroutine, except it returns a value to the code block that invokes it.

What Are The Six Primary Function Categories?

The six primary function categories are date and time, data conversion, math, string, variant, and user interface.

What Is The Code Behind The Master Function Palette Form?

The code behind the Master Function Palette form is shown in Listing A.7. Remember that breaks in the code, such as in the middle of a **MsgBox** statement, are for editorial purposes only. Do *not* break up a **MsgBox** statement.

Listing A.7   The Master Function Palette.

```
Option Compare Database

Private Sub Command0_Click()
    DoCmd.Close acForm, "Master Palette"
    DoCmd.OpenForm "Data Conversion Panel", acNormal
End Sub

Private Sub Command2_Click()
    DoCmd.Close acForm, "Master Palette"
    DoCmd.OpenForm "Math Functions Panel", acNormal
End Sub

Private Sub Command3_Click()
    DoCmd.Close acForm, "Master Palette"
    DoCmd.OpenForm "String Functions Panel", acNormal
End Sub
```

```
Private Sub Command4_Click()
    DoCmd.Close acForm, "Master Palette"
    DoCmd.OpenForm "Variant Functions Panel", acNormal
End Sub

Private Sub Command5_Click()
    DoCmd.Close acForm, "Master Palette"
    DoCmd.OpenForm "User Interface
    Functions Panel", acNormal
End Sub

Private Sub Form_Load()
MsgBox Example()
End Sub
Function Example()
    Example = "Thank you for using the
    Function Palette Master Control!"
End Function
Function DoingFine()
    DoingFine = "Looks like you're
    getting the hang of this!"
End Function
'-----------------------------
' Command1_Click
'
'-----------------------------
Private Sub Command1_Click()
On Error GoTo Command1_Click_Err

    DoCmd.Close acForm, "Master Palette"
    DoCmd.OpenForm "Class Module Panel",
    acNormal, "", "", , acNormal

Command1_Click_Exit:
    Exit Sub

Command1_Click_Err:
    MsgBox Error$
    Resume Command1_Click_Exit

End Sub
```

Chapter 23—Let's Talk About Functions

How Many Types Of Functions Are There?

There are two types of functions:

- *User-defined functions*—Small programs written by you, the developer, to return a value, to modify a value, or to test for some condition.

- *Built-in functions*—As the name implies, built-in functions are those that are native to Visual Basic for Applications.

Chapter 24—Client/Server Design With Access Technologies

What Does The Database Splitter Wizard Do?

The Database Splitter Wizard is an Access utility that lets you split the objects within a database into two separate MDB files.

What Is ADP?

ADP stands for Access Data Project. Access Data Projects are new in Access 2000, and allow you to design front ends for your SQL Server databases using the Access 2000 development environment.

Is It Possible To Upsize An Access Database To A More Robust Platform?

Yes. Access 2000 lets you upsize your databases to SQL Server 7 using the Database Upsizing Wizard utility under Tools | Database Utilities on the Access 2000 menu bar.

What Is Pessimistic Record Locking?

Pessimistic record locking is when the database engine locks a record as soon as a user accesses the record, and does not release the lock on the record until after the user is no longer accessing the record.

What Is Optimistic Record Locking?

Optimistic locking is when the record is only locked after it is updated, and the lock is released as soon as the entire transaction is committed.

Chapter 25—Working Further With Client/Server Database Design

What Design Model Is Typically Most Appropriate For Corporate Databases?

The most appropriate design model for databases in the corporate environment is the client/server model because all data is maintained in a single central location or a series of central locations. Also, individual users access the data by using applications specifically designed to access it, that security is improved, and databases designed under the client/server model can handle many more transactions more efficiently than other models.

What Should Be Considered When Developing An Access Client/Server Application?

Some things to keep in mind if you're thinking of building an Access client/server application include the following:

- Not all field types supported in Access are supported in every back-end database.

- Any security that you implement in Access isn't converted to your back-end database.

- Validation rules that you set up in Access need to be reestablished on the back end.

- Referential integrity isn't supported on all back ends. If it's supported on your back end, it's not automatically carried over from Access.

- Queries involving joins that were updateable within Access aren't updateable on the back-end server.

What Are Database Views?

Database views are objects that allow you to horizontally and vertically partition information from one or more tables in the database, thereby allowing a user to see only selected fields and selected rows.

What Are Stored Procedures?

Stored procedures are precompiled SQL statements located on the server machine. Stored procedures typically run faster than standard SQL statements because they are precompiled.

What Are Database Diagrams?

Database diagrams are objects that graphically represent tables, the columns they contain, and the relationships between them.

Chapter 26—Let's Write One More Access Program

How Do I Import Objects From Another Database?

You can accomplish this task by performing the following steps:

1. Select Insert | *<object type>* from the Access 2000 menu bar, select Import *<object type of your choice>* from the dialog

box that appears, and then click on OK to open the Import dialog box.

2. From the Import dialog box, locate and select the database name and then click the Import button to open the Import Objects dialog box.

3. On the Import Objects dialog box, select the options of your choice and then click on OK.

What Is A One-To-Many Relationship?

When a single table has multiple child records, the relationship between the parent table and the child tables is called a *one-to-many* relationship.

What Is The Code Behind The HRAppInterface Form?

The code behind the HRAppInterface form is shown in Listing A.8.

Listing A.8   The HRAppInterface form.

```
Option Compare Database

Private Sub AddRecord_Click()
DoCmd.RunCommand acCmdRecordsGoToNew
End Sub

Private Sub AddRecord2_Click()
DoCmd.RunCommand acCmdRecordsGoToNew
End Sub

Private Sub AddRecord3_Click()
DoCmd.RunCommand acCmdRecordsGoToNew
End Sub

Private Sub AddRecord4_Click()
DoCmd.RunCommand acCmdRecordsGoToNew
End Sub

Private Sub AddRecord5_Click()
DoCmd.RunCommand acCmdRecordsGoToNew
End Sub
```

```
Private Sub AddRecord6_Click()
DoCmd.RunCommand acCmdRecordsGoToNew
End Sub

Private Sub GetIt_Click()
Dim GetIt As Recordset
Set GetIt = Me.RecordsetClone
GetIt.FindFirst "[LastName] = '" & Me![FindIt] & "'"
Me.Bookmark = GetIt.Bookmark
Me![FindIt] = Null
MsgBox "Search complete. Click the
Employee Tab for Results!"
End Sub

Private Sub GoBack3_Click()
On Error GoTo ErrorHandling_Err2
DoCmd.GoToRecord Record:=acPrevious
ErrorHandling_Exit:
Exit Sub
ErrorHandling_Err2:
If Err.Number = 2105 Then
MsgBox "There are no previous records."
Resume ErrorHandling_Exit
Else
End If
End Sub

Private Sub GoBack4_Click()
On Error GoTo ErrorHandling_Err2
DoCmd.GoToRecord Record:=acPrevious
ErrorHandling_Exit:
Exit Sub
ErrorHandling_Err2:
If Err.Number = 2105 Then
MsgBox "There are no previous records."
Resume ErrorHandling_Exit
Else
End If
End Sub

Private Sub GoBack5_Click()
On Error GoTo ErrorHandling_Err2
DoCmd.GoToRecord Record:=acPrevious
ErrorHandling_Exit:
Exit Sub
ErrorHandling_Err2:
If Err.Number = 2105 Then
MsgBox "There are no previous records."
```

```
Resume ErrorHandling_Exit
Else
End If
End Sub

Private Sub GoBack6_Click()
On Error GoTo ErrorHandling_Err2
DoCmd.GoToRecord Record:=acPrevious
ErrorHandling_Exit:
Exit Sub
ErrorHandling_Err2:
If Err.Number = 2105 Then
MsgBox "There are no previous records."
Resume ErrorHandling_Exit
Else
End If
End Sub

Private Sub GoFirst3_Click()
DoCmd.GoToRecord Record:=acFirst
Me!GoLast.Enabled = True
DoCmd.GoToControl "GoLast"
Me!GoFirst.Enabled = False
End Sub

Private Sub GoFirst4_Click()
DoCmd.GoToRecord Record:=acFirst
Me!GoLast.Enabled = True
DoCmd.GoToControl "GoLast"
Me!GoFirst.Enabled = False
End Sub

Private Sub GoFirst5_Click()
DoCmd.GoToRecord Record:=acFirst
Me!GoLast.Enabled = True
DoCmd.GoToControl "GoLast"
Me!GoFirst.Enabled = False
End Sub

Private Sub GoFirst6_Click()
DoCmd.GoToRecord Record:=acFirst
Me!GoLast.Enabled = True
DoCmd.GoToControl "GoLast"
Me!GoFirst.Enabled = False
End Sub

Private Sub GoLast_Click()
DoCmd.GoToRecord Record:=acLast
Me!GoFirst.Enabled = True
```

```
DoCmd.GoToControl "GoFirst"
Me!GoLast.Enabled = False
End Sub
Private Sub GoBack_Click()
On Error GoTo ErrorHandling_Err2
DoCmd.GoToRecord Record:=acPrevious
ErrorHandling_Exit:
Exit Sub
ErrorHandling_Err2:
If Err.Number = 2105 Then
MsgBox "There are no previous records."
Resume ErrorHandling_Exit
Else
End If
End Sub

Private Sub GoBack2_Click()
On Error GoTo ErrorHandling_Err2
DoCmd.GoToRecord Record:=acPrevious
ErrorHandling_Exit:
Exit Sub
ErrorHandling_Err2:
If Err.Number = 2105 Then
MsgBox "There are no previous records."
Resume ErrorHandling_Exit
Else
End If
End Sub

Private Sub GoFirst_Click()
DoCmd.GoToRecord Record:=acFirst
Me!GoLast.Enabled = True
DoCmd.GoToControl "GoLast"
Me!GoFirst.Enabled = False
End Sub

Private Sub GoFirst2_Click()
DoCmd.GoToRecord Record:=acFirst
Me!GoLast.Enabled = True
DoCmd.GoToControl "GoLast"
Me!GoFirst.Enabled = False
End Sub

Private Sub GoLast3_Click()
DoCmd.GoToRecord Record:=acLast
Me!GoFirst.Enabled = True
DoCmd.GoToControl "GoFirst"
Me!GoLast.Enabled = False
End Sub
```

```
Private Sub GoLast2_Click()
DoCmd.GoToRecord Record:=acLast
Me!GoFirst.Enabled = True
DoCmd.GoToControl "GoFirst"
Me!GoLast.Enabled = False
End Sub

Private Sub GoLast4_Click()
DoCmd.GoToRecord Record:=acLast
Me!GoFirst.Enabled = True
DoCmd.GoToControl "GoFirst"
Me!GoLast.Enabled = False
End Sub

Private Sub GoLast5_Click()
DoCmd.GoToRecord Record:=acLast
Me!GoFirst.Enabled = True
DoCmd.GoToControl "GoFirst"
Me!GoLast.Enabled = False
End Sub

Private Sub GoLast6_Click()
DoCmd.GoToRecord Record:=acLast
Me!GoFirst.Enabled = True
DoCmd.GoToControl "GoFirst"
Me!GoLast.Enabled = False
End Sub

Private Sub GoNext_Click()
DoCmd.GoToRecord Record:=acNext
Me!GoLast.Enabled = True
Me!GoFirst.Enabled = True
End Sub

Private Sub GoNext2_Click()
DoCmd.GoToRecord Record:=acNext
Me!GoLast.Enabled = True
Me!GoFirst.Enabled = True
End Sub
Private Sub AllOff_Click()
Me!FirstEmployeesID.Enabled = False
Me!FirstEmployeesID2.Enabled = False
Me!FirstEmployeesID3.Enabled = False
Me!FirstEmployeesID4.Enabled = False
Me!FirstEmployeesID5.Enabled = False
Me!FirstEmployeesID6.Enabled = False
Me!LastName.Enabled = False
Me!FirstName.Enabled = False
Me!Title.Enabled = False
```

```
Me!Department.Enabled = False
Me!ClassName.Enabled = False
Me!ProjectName.Enabled = False
Me!HealthInsPrvdrName.Enabled = False
Me!HomePhone.Enabled = False
Me!HomeState.Enabled = False
Me!StreetAddressHome.Enabled = False
If Me!FirstEmployeesID.Enabled = False Then
Me!AllOn.Value = Enabled
End If
End Sub

Private Sub AllOn_Click()
Me!FirstEmployeesID.Enabled = True
Me!FirstEmployeesID2.Enabled = True
Me!FirstEmployeesID3.Enabled = True
Me!FirstEmployeesID4.Enabled = True
Me!FirstEmployeesID5.Enabled = True
Me!FirstEmployeesID6.Enabled = True
Me!LastName.Enabled = True
Me!FirstName.Enabled = True
Me!Title.Enabled = True
Me!Department.Enabled = True
Me!ClassName.Enabled = True
Me!ProjectName.Enabled = True
Me!HealthInsPrvdrName.Enabled = True
Me!HomePhone.Enabled = True
Me!HomeState.Enabled = True
Me!HomeState.Enabled = True
Me!StreetAddressHome.Enabled = True
If Me!FirstEmployeesID.Enabled = True Then
Me!AllOff.Value = Enabled
End If
End Sub

Private Sub ColorOff_Click()
Me!ColorOn.Enabled = True
DoCmd.GoToControl "ColorOn"
Me!ColorOn.Value = False
Me!ColorOff.Value = True
Me!ColorOff.Enabled = False
Me!FirstEmployeesID.BackColor = 16777215
Me!FirstEmployeesID2.BackColor = 16777215
Me!FirstEmployeesID3.BackColor = 16777215
Me!FirstEmployeesID4.BackColor = 16777215
Me!FirstEmployeesID5.BackColor = 16777215
Me!FirstEmployeesID6.BackColor = 16777215
Me!LastName.BackColor = 16777215
Me!FirstName.BackColor = 16777215
```

```
Me!Title.BackColor = 16777215
Me!Department.BackColor = 16777215
Me!ClassName.BackColor = 16777215
Me!ProjectName.BackColor = 16777215
Me!HealthInsPrvdrName.BackColor = 16777215
Me!HomePhone.BackColor = 16777215
Me!HomeState.BackColor = 16777215
Me!StreetAddressHome.BackColor = 16777215
MsgBox "Field Highlights Are Disabled!"
End Sub
Private Sub ColorOn_Click()
Me!ColorOff.Enabled = True
DoCmd.GoToControl "ColorOff"
Me!ColorOff.Value = False
Me!ColorOn.Value = True
Me!ColorOn.Enabled = False
Me!FirstEmployeesID.BackColor = 16776960
Me!FirstEmployeesID.BackColor = 16776960
Me!FirstEmployeesID2.BackColor = 16776960
Me!FirstEmployeesID3.BackColor = 16776960
Me!FirstEmployeesID4.BackColor = 16776960
Me!FirstEmployeesID5.BackColor = 16776960
Me!FirstEmployeesID6.BackColor = 16776960
Me!LastName.BackColor = 16776960
Me!FirstName.BackColor = 16776960
Me!Title.BackColor = 16776960
Me!Department.BackColor = 16776960
Me!ClassName.BackColor = 16776960
Me!ProjectName.BackColor = 16776960
Me!HealthInsPrvdrName.BackColor = 16776960
Me!HomePhone.BackColor = 16776960
Me!HomeState.BackColor = 16776960
Me!HomeState.BackColor = 16776960
Me!StreetAddressHome.BackColor = 16776960
MsgBox "Field Highlights Are Enabled!"
End Sub

Private Sub GoNext3_Click()
DoCmd.GoToRecord Record:=acNext
Me!GoLast.Enabled = True
Me!GoFirst.Enabled = True
End Sub

Private Sub GoNext4_Click()
DoCmd.GoToRecord Record:=acNext
Me!GoLast.Enabled = True
Me!GoFirst.Enabled = True
End Sub
```

```
Private Sub GoNext5_Click()
DoCmd.GoToRecord Record:=acNext
Me!GoLast.Enabled = True
Me!GoFirst.Enabled = True
End Sub

Private Sub GoNext6_Click()
DoCmd.GoToRecord Record:=acNext
Me!GoLast.Enabled = True
Me!GoFirst.Enabled = True
End Sub

Private Sub HideIt_Click()
Me!LastName.Visible = False
If Me!LastName.Visible = False Then
Me!ShowIt.Value = Disabled
End If
End Sub

Private Sub ShowIt_Click()
Me!LastName.Visible = True
If Me!LastName.Visible = True Then
Me!HideIt.Value = Disabled
End If
End Sub
```

Chapter 27—Optimizing Your Access 2000 Applications

What Areas Are Key In Optimizing Access 2000 Applications?

Optimizing Access 2000 applications typically occurs in three areas: stability, performance, and maintainability.

What Does Application Stability Involve?

Application stability has to do with how "error free" your code is and how your application reacts when errors are found.

What Does Application Performance Involve?

Application performance has to do with how efficiently your code is able to execute.

What Does Application Maintainability Involve?

Application maintainability has to do with the ease with which a third party can look at your code and repair it or enhance it.

What Are The Three Categories Of Program Errors?

The three categories of program errors are errors in syntax, errors in execution, and errors in logic.

Appendix B

Knowledge Base Key To Troubleshooting Access

As you continue your Access programming life, you'll find from time to time that there may be a problem or bug that you just can't quite figure out. This is when you'll need a ready reference to lend a hand.

This appendix is your quick reference to Access technical support articles in the Microsoft Knowledge Base. The entries that you'll find in Table B.1 are listed by Article ID, Title, and Synopsis. This layout should make it easier for you to get the answers you need. The Microsoft Knowledge Base is a feature of Microsoft's online technical support and is accessible via the Web at **http://support.microsoft.com**.

Table B.1   Key to the Microsoft Knowledge Base.

Article ID	Title	Synopsis
Q161252	Run-Time Error '3027' Using ODBCDirect to Open RecordSet	This article discusses the condition that occurs when you use an ODBCDirect connection to open a recordset and the fact that you may receive the error message "Run-time Error '3027'" if you use the **AddNew** method.
Q142999	Tips for Debugging Visual Basic for Applications Code in Microsoft Access	Microsoft Access provides debugging tools that enable you to step through your code one line at a time to examine or monitor the values of expressions and variables and to trace procedure calls.

(continued)

Table B.1 **Key to the Microsoft Knowledge Base** *(continued)*.

Article ID	Title	Synopsis
Q162068	Microsoft Access 97 Articles Available by Fax or Email: Modules, Macros, & Expressions	This article discusses how you can obtain technical support information from the Microsoft Knowledge Base by email or fax.
Q147816	Using Microsoft Access as an Automation Server	This article includes discussions of topics such as Creating A Reference To Microsoft Access, Using **GetObject()** And **CreateObject()** Functions, Understanding The **UserControl** And **Visible** Properties, Viewing An Instance Of Microsoft Access, Bypassing Startup Settings When Opening A Database, and Using A Run-Time Application.
Q95608	How to Parse Comma-Separated Text into Multiple Fields	This article demonstrates two methods you can use to parse comma-separated text in a text field and to display the text in multiple text fields.
Q89610	Tips on How to Troubleshoot Microsoft Access Macros	This article discusses Single Stepping, the Action Failed Dialog Box, the **MsgBox** action, and the **StopMacro** action as tools that can be used to isolate and locate a problem when a macro doesn't perform correctly.
Q166766	Microsoft Technical Support Guidelines for MS Access	This article presents the guidelines that Microsoft Technical Support (MTS) engineers follow when supporting Microsoft Access customers.
Q164455	Unable to Quit Access	This article addresses the condition that occurs when you select File|Exit on the Access menu bar and the program fails to quit.
Q99401	How First Line of Data Is Used to Import Delimited Text	The first line of data is extremely important when you are importing delimited text files. Microsoft Access 2.0 and earlier use the first line of data to determine the number of fields and the data type for each field.
Q97995	Multiple Users Adding Fields Causes Cross-Linking	This article discusses the fact that incorrect data appears in tables when multiple users load and modify the same database within minutes of each other. It also presents a typical scenario in which this problem occurs.
Q96904	Low Number of Share Locks Can Cause Error Message	This article discusses the issues surrounding the error message "Can't save; record is locked by another user in Microsoft Access," even when only one user (in one session on one computer) is using a database opened for shared access.

(continued)

Table B.1 **Key to the Microsoft Knowledge Base** *(continued)*.

Article ID	Title	Synopsis
Q95926	Screen Redraw Problems When Reordering Groups	This article discusses the fact that when you change the order of two group levels, the headers or footers have different heights in a report, Microsoft Access does not redraw the screen completely.
Q95927	Currency Format Causes Report Alignment Problems	This article provides resolution to the issue that in a report, if you set the **Format** property of a number control to Currency, you may have difficulty aligning the formatted numbers with numbers that are not formatted to Currency.
Q90863	Older Versions of Shared DLLs Cause MS Access Problems	This article addresses the fact that shared Dynamic Link Libraries (DLLs) in your system that are older than those supplied with Microsoft Access version 1.0 or Microsoft Windows version 3.1 can cause unexpected errors with Microsoft Access.
Q180458	Problems Outputting Report with Data-sheet Form as Subreport	This article addresses the fact that if a report contains a form as a subreport, and the form is in Datasheet view, if you try to output the report to another file format, such as text, Microsoft Excel, or Rich Text Format, you may encounter unexpected behavior based on the version of Access you are running.
Q175380	"Unrecognized database format" Using Database Documentor	When you try to run the Database Documentor on an object in a Microsoft Access 7.0 database, you may receive an error message.
Q165830	Problems Adding Records to Replicated Database Using ASP	This article discusses the fact that if you export a form based on a table in a replicated database to ASP format, you cannot add new records using the ASP form.
Q164003	Save Password Check-box Dimmed When Linking ODBC Tables	This article talks about what to do if you are unable to save the Login ID and Password locally when you link a table from an ODBC data source checkbox is dimmed in the Link Tables dialog box.
Q187690	Actions You Can't Perform Once MDB Saved as an MDE File	This article discusses the fact that Microsoft Access 97 includes a feature called Make MDE File, which you can use to keep database applications compiled and secure. The Make MDE File feature removes the text representation of your Visual Basic for Applications code and stores only the binary compiled p-code.

(continued)

Table B.1   Key to the Microsoft Knowledge Base *(continued).*

Article ID	Title	Synopsis
Q185823	MS Access ODBC Driver Does Not Expose **adFldIsNullable** to AD	This article talks about what to do when using Microsoft Active Data Objects (ADO) with the Microsoft Access ODBC driver and attempts to programmatically check the nullability of a field when the ADO Field **Attributes** property returns true even if the field is a required (non-nullable) field.
Q185425	ADO Hierarchical Recordsets via SHAPE APPEND via C++/VBA/Java	This article describes how to use **SHAPE APPEND** to produce hierarchical recordsets and how to traverse them.
Q181489	"Syntax Error in FROM clause" Opening a Jet Table	In this article you'll learn what to do when opening a Microsoft Jet table using ActiveX Data Objects (ADO) displays the following error: "Run-time error '-2147217900 (80040e14)': [Microsoft] [ODBC Microsoft Access 97 Driver] Syntax error in **FROM** clause."
Q176024	IsObject Function Help Topic Cites Incorrect Function	This article discusses the fact that the Microsoft Access 97 **IsObject** Function Help Topic contains the following sentence: "You can use the **IsNothing** function to determine if an object reference has been set to **Nothing**."
Q163628	Blank DB Icon Missing in Access 95 After Installing 97	After you install Microsoft Office 97 Professional Edition or Microsoft Access 97, if you still have Microsoft Access 7.0 on your computer the Blank Database icon in Microsoft Access 7.0 is missing.
Q162819	How to Remove the Most Recently Used (MRU) Files List	This article talks about how the most recently used (MRU) file list is the list of the last four database files that were opened in Microsoft Access, how it appears in the Startup screen for Microsoft Access and at the bottom of the File menu, and how you can remove the names of the last four opened database files by editing the Registry.
Q162374	Adding Your Own Links to the Microsoft On The Web Menu	This article demonstrates how to add your own commands or modify existing commands on the Microsoft On The Web Help menu. You can do this by adding or changing Registry keys and values for each Web site that you want to link to, using the Registry Editor.

(continued)

Table B.1   Key to the Microsoft Knowledge Base *(continued).*

Article ID	Title	Synopsis
Q153756	How to Set the Query Timeout Value for ODBC Connections	This article demonstrates how to set the **QueryTimeout** property for queries run against ODBC data sources.
Q151186	Updated Jet DLLs Available on MSL	In this article, you learn that the Msjtwng.exe file contains an update of three DLL files that are included with Microsoft Access 7.0, Microsoft Visual Basic 4.0, and Microsoft Windows NT 4.0.
Q150500	Unable to Create 32-Bit ODBC Data Source	In this article, you learn that after you install Microsoft Access 7.0 and include the Microsoft Desktop ODBC drivers, you are unable to set up a data source using the 32-bit ODBC Administrator in Control Panel.
Q149535	List of Problems Fixed in Microsoft Access 7.0a	This article lists the problems in Microsoft Access for Windows 95 version 7.0 that are fixed in Microsoft Access for Windows 95 version 7.0a.
Q148424	Troubleshooting Invalid Page Faults in MS Access 95 and 97	This article discusses the causes of invalid page faults in Microsoft Access 97 and Microsoft Access 7.0 and provides troubleshooting steps for solving invalid page fault errors.
Q109730	Network Problems May Cause "Segment Load Failure" Error	This article discusses the "Segment Load Failure" error message or another memory-conflict error message, and how in Microsoft Access 97 you may also receive a "System Process—Lost Delayed Write Error" or an "Invalid Bookmark Error" message when viewing data from linked tables.
Q104756	CanGrow or CanShrink Problems in Report Header or Footer	In this article, you learn what to do if you paste an existing text box control that has its **CanGrow** or **CanShrink** property set to Yes into a report header or footer, and the header or footer will not change.
Q103991	Memory or Disk Space Problems Using MS-DOS 6.0	Discusses what happens when you are working in Microsoft Access and receive an out of memory error message, which could also be accompanied by other messages saying you have insufficient disk space or insufficient space in your Temp directory.

(continued)

Table B.1 **Key to the Microsoft Knowledge Base** *(continued).*

Article ID	Title	Synopsis
Q103629	Word for Windows Print Merge Using Microsoft Access Data	This article discusses that there is no Microsoft Word for Windows file converter capable of reading Microsoft Access database files. In order to use data from a Microsoft Access database in a Microsoft Word for Windows print merge, the data must first be exported from Microsoft Access in a format that Microsoft Word for Windows recognizes.
Q103180	White Lines or Missing Data When Printing Reports	This article discusses the problems that may occur when you print from Microsoft Access using the Canon BJC800 or BJ10E printer drivers. Problems can include horizontal white lines appearing on the report, portions of the text not being printed, the report only printing using a lower resolution than normal, color reports printing only in monochrome, and only one page of the report printing at a time, rather than the whole document printing at once.
Q102522	"Record Lock Threshold Exceeded" with Large Action Query	If you exceed the maximum number of locks set per connection for the Novell server, you may receive an error message on the server.
Q100972	Force MS Access to Use "Snapshot" Mode for Linked Data	Because Microsoft Access addresses linked (attached) data differently than it does its own native data, this article discusses how Microsoft Access retrieves linked ODBC data.
Q99940	How to Wait for a Shelled Process to Finish	This article discusses that when you are using the Shell() function or the RunApp macro to run another program or process, Microsoft Access does not wait for the shelled process to finish.
Q98810	GPF Printing Subreport with Datasheet Default View	In this article, you learn that Reports do not have a Datasheet view as forms do; however, forms created with a default Datasheet view can be saved as reports. This can cause problems in Microsoft Access.
Q94418	Printing Microsoft Access Reports on HP Laserjet II	This article discusses why it's necessary to set the option Print TrueType As Graphics in Print Setup when you print to a Hewlett-Packard Laserjet II.

(continued)

Table B.1   Key to the Microsoft Knowledge Base *(continued)*.

Article ID	Title	Synopsis
Q93694	"Outdated COMMDLG.DLL" Error Message During Setup	This article discusses when you try to open a database and receive the following error message: "Outdated COMMDLG.DLL. Please reinstall Microsoft Access."
Q92815	Hints for Using Generic Print Driver with Forms/Reports	This article discusses a way to get Microsoft Access output from forms or reports into a text file that involves using the Windows Generic print driver and printing to a file.
Q90864	MS Access Saves Printer Information with Each Form/Report	In this article, you discover that Microsoft Access saves printer driver information with each form or report that it generates, and what this actually means.
Q90149	Exporting to SQL Server Does Not Create Indexes	This article discusses the fact that Microsoft Access allows you to export data to SQL Server back ends and the impact this has on database indexes.
Q193052	Find Bookmark Wizard Available for Download on MSL	In this article, you learn about the Find Bookmark Wizard, a Microsoft Access add-in that will search the forms, reports, and modules in an Access database for text that references either the **Bookmark** or **AbsolutePosition** property.
Q187317	Error When Installing Add-In or Wizard	Here you'll find out about issues that result when you install an add-in or wizard, such as the Microsoft Access 97 Exchange and Outlook Wizard or the Microsoft Print Relationships Wizard.
Q183628	Using the RDS Data-Factory via Standard ADO Open Method	Information about RDS (Remote Data Service), which is tightly integrated with ActiveX Data Objects (ADO). It is included in the Microsoft Data Access Components (MDAC).
Q179077	Creating a Hyperlink to a Microsoft Access Table or Query	This article describes how to insert a hyperlink that opens a Microsoft Access 97 database table or query.
Q178112	"Type Mismatch in Join Expression" Error with Filter by Form	When you use a combo box or list box control to do a Filter By Form, you may receive an error message.

(continued)

Table B.1 **Key to the Microsoft Knowledge Base** *(continued)*.

Article ID	Title	Synopsis
Q172733	Updated Version of Microsoft Jet 3.5 Available on MSL	The Jet35upd.exe file contains an update of two DLL files that are included with Microsoft Access 97, Microsoft Office 97 Professional Edition, and Microsoft Visual Basic 5.0.
Q170702	Invalid Page Fault Repairing DB after Compact Attempt	When you try to compact a database while in break mode of a module, you receive a message telling you that the database is in use by another person or program.
Q167067	PivotTable Wizard Error Using MS Excel 7.0 in MS Access 97	If you try to invoke the PivotTable Wizard when you have Microsoft Excel version 7.0 or 7.0a installed, the PivotTable Wizard will return an error message.
Q166766	Microsoft Technical Support Guidelines for MS Access	This article presents the guidelines that Microsoft Technical Support (MTS) engineers follow when supporting Microsoft Access customers.
Q166355	PivotTable Wizard Fails with Parameter Query in MS Access	When the data source that is used in the PivotTable Wizard is a query that contains a parameter, you may receive an error message when attempting to use the Wizard.
Q165472	Space in HTML File Name May Cause Web Browser Error	When you browse to an Internet page created with Microsoft Access 97, if the file name contains a space, your Web browser may return an error message.
Q165271	Synch with Replicas before Changing Design Master	Discusses the importance of synchronizing all the databases in a replica set Schema before making schema changes in the Design Master database.
Q164254	Can't Print Black Lines on Report When Spool Set to Raw	When you try to print a black line on a report that you are creating in Microsoft Access 97, the line is not printed. However, if you view the report in Print Preview, the line is present.
Q164172	Understanding Relational Database Design Available on MSL	Ureldes.doc shows you how to plan and design a database from the ground up. For practical examples, it uses the Northwind Traders sample database.
Q164008	ACC97: Subforms Appear Blank When Browsing ASP Files on NT 4.0	When you use Internet Explorer 3.0, 3.01, or 3.02 on Microsoft Windows NT 4.0 to browse an Active Server Pages (ASP) file that contains a subform, it appears blank.

(continued)

Table B.1   Key to the Microsoft Knowledge Base *(continued).*

Article ID	Title	Synopsis
Q163997	How to Completely Uninstall Microsoft Access 97	When you run the Microsoft Access Setup program in Maintenance mode, and you click the Remove All button, some Microsoft Access files are not removed from your computer.
Q162069	Access 97 Articles Available by Fax or Email: Internet Features	This article shows you how to obtain support information from the Microsoft Knowledge Base by email or fax.
Q158923	TransferDatabase/ CopyObject in Runtime May Corrupt Object	Using the /Runtime command-line option to open a database that uses **TransferDatabase** or **CopyObject** to import or export a Microsoft Access object may corrupt the object.
Q158933	Error "<Database Name> Isn't an Index in This Table"	When you run the **Repair Database** command, you may receive the following error message: "Isn't an index in this table."
Q155195	Opening Replica DB Causes "File Already Exists" Error	When you open a replica copy of a database you receive the following error message: "File already exists." When you click the OK button, the database does not open.
Q153151	Numeric Value Out of Range Error Inserting into SQL Server	When you try to insert a new record into a linked (attached) SQL Server table, you may receive the following error message: "Numeric Value Out of Range."
Q152760	DB Password with Space Becomes Invalid after Compact	When you set a database password that contains one or more spaces, the password becomes invalid after you compact the database.
Q151726	"Microsoft Access Couldn't Print Your Object" Error Msg	You may receive an error message when trying to print from Access, even though the printer driver appears to work correctly with most Microsoft Office for Windows 95 programs.
Q151164	Problems Using Instr() to Find Special Characters	When you use the **Instr()** function, you may see incorrect results when you search through a character string looking for certain ASCII characters, usually non-U.S. characters.
Q148396	How to Remove Excess Characters from Contents of a String	This article demonstrates how to use a custom function to remove excess characters from a string.

(continued)

Table B.1 Key to the Microsoft Knowledge Base *(continued)*.

Article ID	Title	Synopsis
Q147785	Imported MS Excel Spreadsheet May Have Blank Columns	When you import a Microsoft Excel spreadsheet whose cell table goes beyond the last cell that actually contains data, you may get blank columns in the Microsoft Access table
Q141796	How to Identify the Jet Database Engine Components	Jet is the default database engine for Visual Basic as well as other Microsoft applications such as Microsoft Access, Excel, Project, and Microsoft Foundation Classes (MFC). Which version of Jet you are using can be unclear—this article helps you figure it out.
Q138443	How Replication Affects AutoNumber Fields	When you convert a nonreplicable database to a replicated database, the AutoNumber fields in your tables change from incremental to random.
Q137076	Can't Use Microsoft Access Files (MDB or DDE) with Word	When you use the Mail Merge or the Insert Database command to obtain data from a Microsoft Access data file, the option for MS Access Databases (MDB) does not appear in the Files Of Type list.
Q135374	"External Table Isn't in Expected Format" Error Message	When you try to import a delimited text file, you may receive the following error message: "External table isn't in expected format."
Q132184	"Invalid Bracketing of Name <Expression Object>" Error	When you run an **ApplyFilter**, **OpenForm**, or **OpenReport** action using a macro or custom function with a **Where Condition** argument, you may receive an error message.
Q132028	Errors Using Large OLE Objects with MS SQL Server Tables	When you use large OLE objects (greater than about 400K) with Microsoft SQL Server tables, you may encounter problems.
Q132057	"Unable to Get System Fixed Font" Error Message	When you start Microsoft Access, you may receive the following two error messages: "Unable to get system fixed font" and "Can't start Microsoft Access. Please try again."
Q130857	Tips to Design Reports for Output to RTF File	This article describes tips you can use to design a report whose output you plan to save to a Rich Text Format (RTF) file using the **Output To** command.

(continued)

Table B.1   Key to the Microsoft Knowledge Base *(continued).*

Article ID	Title	Synopsis
Q124302	Setup of Data Source in Use Causes Sharing Violation Error	Setting up a Microsoft Access data source to point to an MDB file on the network that is already being accessed by another application causes a sharing violation.
Q119710	Local Microsoft Access Installation Required by ADT	This article discusses what's needed to have the full functionality of the Microsoft Access Developer's Toolkit (ADT).
Q113352	How to Refer to a Control on a Subform or Subreport	This article describes how to refer to controls on subforms or subreports, and describes some common problems you may encounter when you do so.
Q109391	GP Fault Attaching Tables with Old CTL3D.DLL File	A general protection (GP) fault may occur when you attach tables using ODBC. Or, you may notice that the borders of the ODBC dialog boxes appear unusual.
Q106181	Canceling a **DoCmd Print** Returns Error Messages	Discusses what happens when you click Cancel to cancel printing started by a macro that contains a function with a **DoCmd.PrintOut acPrintAll** statement (or **DoCmd Print A_Printall** statement).
Q101675	Sample Table Design to Support Questionnaire Applications	This article describes a table design that you can use for an application that tallies results from questionnaires and surveys.
Q101324	Access Basic Error-Handling Supplemental Information	This article supplements the information available in the Microsoft Access Language Reference manual about how to handle errors in an Access Basic application.
Q96109	Troubleshooting Setup & Installation Problems (1.x/2.0)	This article explains the troubleshooting techniques that you can use to resolve Microsoft Access setup and installation problems.
Q90152	Paradox Tables, Indexes, and Multiple Connections	If a Paradox table does not have a primary key, then it cannot be opened twice, even exclusively. This means it cannot be used in more than one place in a query or in code.
Q143163	Problems Running Microsoft Jet 3.0 on Windows NT 4.0	When you use Microsoft Jet 3.0 on Microsoft Windows NT 4.0, you may experience performance problems.

(continued)

Table B.1 **Key to the Microsoft Knowledge Base** *(continued)*.

Article ID	Title	Synopsis
Q100139	Database Normalization Basics	This article explains database normalization terminology for beginners. A basic understanding of this terminology is helpful when discussing the design of a relational database.
Q97517	How to Print Total Number of Pages on Each Page of Report	You can print the page number on each page of a report by using the Page property in a text box control in the page footer.
Q95920	Every Other Page Blank in Printed Reports (1.x/2.0)	When you print a report generated in Microsoft Access, a blank page appears between every printed page of the report or a blank mailing label appears between every printed label.
Q95806	How to Skip Used Mailing Labels and Print Duplicates	This article describes how to print multiple copies of the same mailing label and how to use a partially used page where only some of the labels are available.
Q184949	Report May Lose Formatting When Output to HTML	When you save a Microsoft Access 97 report to HTML format, column headers and fields may not be properly aligned.
Q182867	Jet Database Engine 3.x Error Messages Due to Corruption	This article discusses the three most common error messages returned by Microsoft Jet 3.x that denote some form of corruption in the database.
Q142009	How Windows Regional Settings Affect Microsoft Access	This article demonstrates how Microsoft Access handles Currency, Date/Time, and Number formats when you change the Regional Settings in the Windows 95 and Windows NT 4.0 Control Panel.
Q141373	"There is no license" Error Starting Microsoft Access	When you start Microsoft Access 7.0 or 97, you may receive an error message.
Q128809	"#Deleted" Errors with Attached ODBC Tables	When you retrieve, insert, or update records in an attached ODBC table, each field in a record contains the "#Deleted" error message. When you retrieve, insert, or update records using code, you receive the error message "Record is deleted."

Appendix C

Web Sites And Support Resources For Access, VBA, And Office 2000

Because this book can't possibly cover all there is to know about Access 2000 and VBA, the next best thing is to leave you with some idea of where to go for additional insights and assistance.

This appendix provides you with a variety of resources to supplement the knowledge you've acquired from this book. Refer to it when you need additional information and/or guidance, or when you simply have something you believe is worth sharing with the Access programming community.

Access Developer Web Sites

http://www.microsoft.com/Accessdev/

http://www.access-developer.com

http://members.xoom.com/AccessFreak/

VBA Developer Web Sites

http://msdn.microsoft.com/vbasic/

http://www.pinpub.com/vbd/

http://www.summsoft.com/vba/

Office 2000 Developer Web Site

http://www.microsoft.com/officedev/ode/ode2k.htm

Access Developer Magazines

http://www.informant.com/icgmags.asp

http://www.informant.com/mod/

http://www.advisor.com/wHome.nsf/wPages/AVmain/

http://www.zdjournals.com/ima/index.htm

Access User Group

http://www.yahoo.com/computers_and_Internet/Software/
Databases/Access/User_Groups/

Access And VBA Third-Party Products

http://www.fmsinc.com/products/index3.html

http://www.wdn.com/ems/access.htm

Access Training Programs

http://www.takethelead.fullerton.edu/CertProg/MicroAcc.htm

http://it-training.ucdavis.edu/references/access.html

Access Newsgroups

microsoft.public.access.gettingstarted

microsoft.public.access.tablesdbdesign

microsoft.public.access.queries

microsoft.public.access.forms

microsoft.public.access.formscoding

microsoft.public.access.reports

microsoft.public.access.macros

microsoft.public.access.modulesdaovba

microsoft.public.access.commandbarsui

microsoft.public.access.odbcclientsvr

microsoft.public.access.externaldata

microsoft.public.access.interopoledde

microsoft.public.access.multiuser

microsoft.public.access.replication

microsoft.public.access.security

microsoft.public.access.setupconfig

microsoft.public.access.conversion

microsoft.public.access.activexcontrol

microsoft.public.access.devtoolkits

microsoft.public.access.3rdpartyusrgrp

VBA Newsgroups

microsoft.public.access.devtoolkits

microsoft.public.access.formscoding

microsoft.public.access.macros

microsoft.public.access.queries

microsoft.public.officedev

microsoft.public.vb.ole.automation

microsoft.public.vb.database.dao

microsoft.public.vb.database.odbc

microsoft.public.vb.database.rdo

microsoft.public.word.word97vba

Appendix D

Known Jet And Data Access Object Errors

Finding out what's wrong when an error occurs can be frustrating, especially when you don't know Error 2428 from the mating ritual of the South American fire ant.

Table D.1 provides the trappable error codes and explanations associated with the Jet database engine and data access objects. Trappable errors can occur while an application is running and can be responded to using the **Error** object. See Chapters 3 and 5 for the context of the errors found in this appendix.

Table D.1   Trappable error codes.

Error Code	Error Message	What's Going On
2420	Syntax error in number.	You have a non-numeric value where a numeric value is required.
2421	Syntax error in date.	The date used in your program is not valid.
2422	Syntax error in string.	The expression used in your program contains an invalid string.
2423	Invalid use of '.', '!', or '()'.	Your program contains an expression that doesn't allow the use of delimiters.
2424	Unknown name.	You've referenced a field or property that Access doesn't recognize.
2425	Unknown function name.	You've referenced a function that Access doesn't recognize.

(continued)

605

Table D.1   **Trappable error codes** *(continued).*

Error Code	Error Message	What's Going On
2426	Function isn't available in expressions.	You've used a function that's incompatible with the expression you're trying to use.
2427	Object has no value.	You entered an expression containing an identifier for an object that has no value.
2428	Invalid arguments used with domain function.	You have entered an invalid argument in a function used to calculate totals.
2429	**In** operator without ().	When coding an SQL statement that includes the **In** operator, you must surround the list of items to test with parentheses.
2430	**Between** operator without **And**.	When using the **Between** operator to test whether a value of an expression lies within a specified range of values, specify the upper and lower limits of the range separated with the reserved word **And**.
2432	Syntax error (comma).	The expression or statement uses a comma where it doesn't belong or is missing a comma to separate arguments.
2433	Syntax error.	The wording or punctuation of the command isn't correct. It may be missing an operator, or you may have specified an operator that does not exist.
2434	Syntax error (missing operator).	The expression or statement is missing an operator.
2435	Extra).	You entered an expression that has too many closing parentheses. Delete any parenthesis that doesn't have a matching opening parenthesis.
2436	Missing),], or Item.	You entered an expression that is missing a closing parenthesis, bracket, or vertical bar. Check the expression to make sure you entered it correctly.
2437	Invalid use of vertical bars.	You entered an expression that has invalid vertical bars (|). Check the expression to make sure you entered it correctly.
2438	Syntax error.	You entered an expression that has invalid syntax. For example, an operand or operator may be missing, you may have entered an invalid character or comma, or you may have entered text without surrounding it by quotation marks. Check the expression to make sure you entered it correctly.

(continued)

Table D.1 **Trappable error codes** *(continued).*

Error Code	Error Message	What's Going On
2439	Wrong number of arguments used with function.	You entered an expression that has a function with the wrong number of arguments. Check the function to verify how many arguments it takes, or check the expression to make sure you entered it correctly.
2440	**IIf** function without ().	The **IIf** function requires parentheses around its arguments, as shown in the following syntax: **IIf(expr, truepart, falsepart)**
2442	Invalid use of parentheses.	You entered an expression that has invalid parentheses. For example, you may be trying to use the parentheses syntax for an identifier in a query. In a query, you can use only the standard identifier syntax.
2443	Invalid use of **Is** operator.	The **Is** operator is used to determine if an expression is null. You can use the **Is** operator in an expression only with **NULL** or **NOT NULL**.
2445	Expression too complex.	This expression is too complex for the Microsoft Jet database engine. Try to simplify the expression.
2446	Out of memory during calculation.	The application doesn't have enough memory to complete the calculation. Make sure you have enough RAM and an established swap file. You may need to terminate other programs, remove desktop wallpaper bitmaps, or remove unneeded device drivers to recover enough memory.
2447	Invalid use of '.', '!', or '()'.	The expression doesn't use delimiters correctly. To reference the properties of DAO objects, it is recommended that you use the property name syntax.
2448	Can't set value.	You are trying to assign a value to an object that is read-only or doesn't have a value.
3000	Reserved error <Item>; there is no message for this error.	An unexpected error occurred. The specified code identifies the conditions under which this error can occur. Contact Microsoft Product Support Services for more information.

(continued)

Table D.1   Trappable error codes *(continued)*.

Error Code	Error Message	What's Going On
3001	Invalid argument.	You tried to perform an operation that involves a routine in a DLL, and one of the arguments to the routine is invalid. Check your entry to make sure you have specified the correct arguments, and then try the operation again.
		This error also occurs when you attempt to use mutually exclusive constants in an argument to a method, such as specifying both **dbConsistent** and **dbInconsistent** in the options argument to the **OpenRecordset** method.
3005	Database \<name\> isn't a valid database name.	The specified database name doesn't follow the standard naming conventions for file names. The name may be too long for the buffer that contains the path and file name. Enter a new name, and then try the operation again.
3006	Database \<name\> is exclusively locked.	You tried to use a database that is currently open for exclusive access by another user. Wait for the other user to finish working with the database, and then try the operation again.
3007	Can't open library database \<name\>.	The specified database is an internal Microsoft Jet database engine library database, which you can't open.
3008	The table \<name\> is already opened exclusively by another user, or it is already open through the user interface and cannot be manipulated program- matically.	You tried to use a table that is currently open for exclusive access by another user, or you tried to programmatically manipulate a table that is open through the user interface. Address the appropriate condition, and then try the operation again.
3010	Table \<name\> already exists.	You tried to create or rename a table with a name that already exists in this database. Choose another name, and then try the operation again.
		In a multiuser database, this error can also occur if you delete a table, another user creates a table with the same name, and then you try to roll back the deletion of your table. To restore your table, the other user must first delete or rename the new table before you try the rollback operation again.

(continued)

Table D.1 **Trappable error codes** *(continued)*.

Error Code	Error Message	What's Going On
3012	Object <name> already exists.	You tried to create an object with a name that already exists in this database. Choose a different name, and then try the operation again.
3014	Can't open any more tables.	You've reached the limit on the number of tables that can be opened at one time. Close one or more tables, and then try the operation again.
3016	Field won't fit in record.	You tried to import or paste a field that is too large. Consider breaking the field into smaller pieces and then importing or pasting the data to multiple fields or changing the data type of the field. Records are limited to just under 2K in size, excluding Memo and OLE Object fields.
3017	The size of a field is too long.	You either tried to define or create a Text field longer than 254 characters or you tried to define a query parameter longer than 255 characters. Use a number between 1 and 254, and then try the operation again, or create a Memo field for the data.
3018	Couldn't find field <name>.	This error occurred for one of the following reasons: a) The specified field doesn't exist. b) You misspelled the field name. c) You entered an invalid field identifier. For example, **[My Table]_[My Field]** instead of **MyTable![My Field]**. d) You didn't use brackets to surround a field name that contains spaces.
3021	No current record.	This error occurs after the unsuccessful application of one of the **Find** methods or the **Seek** method, when the underlying recordset contains no records or the record has been deleted. Move to or select another record, and try the operation again.
3036	Database has reached maximum size.	To add data to this database, you must first reduce its size by deleting data.
3037	Can't open any more tables or queries.	You've reached the limit on the number of tables and queries that can be opened at one time. Close one or more tables or queries, and then try the operation again.
3039	Couldn't create index; too many indexes already defined.	You should consider deleting an existing index to make room for the new index.

(continued)

Table D.1 Trappable error codes *(continued).*

Error Code	Error Message	What's Going On
3040	Disk I/O error during read.	The disk could not be read due to an internal disk or drive failure.
3041	Can't open a database created with a previous version of your application.	You tried to access a database that is in an outdated format. Compact the database, and then try the operation again.
3047	Record is too large.	You defined or imported a table with records larger than 2K. This error occurs when you enter data into the record, not when you define the table structure. Redefine the table by making some fields shorter, removing unneeded fields, or moving some fields to other tables.
3048	Can't open any more databases.	You've reached the limit on the number of databases that can be opened at one time. Close one or more databases and try the operation again.
3049	Can't open database <name>.	It may not be a database that your application recognizes, or the file may be corrupt. You tried to open a non-Microsoft Jet database, such as a Btrieve, dBASE, or Paradox database or table, or if the specified database is a Microsoft Jet database, it is corrupted. You should attempt to repair the database. If the database can't be repaired, restore the database from a backup copy, or create a new database.
3055	Not a valid file name.	You tried to use a file name that doesn't follow the naming conventions for your operating system. Specify the file name again, and then retry the operation.
3056	Couldn't repair this database.	This database is corrupted, or it isn't a Microsoft Jet database. Restore the corrupted Microsoft Jet database from a backup copy, or create a new database.
3058	Index or primary key can't contain a null value.	This error was generated because: a) You tried to add a null value to a primary key field. b) You tried to add a new record, but didn't enter a value in the field that contains the primary key. c) You executed a query that tried to put a null value in a primary key field.

(continued)

Table D.1 Trappable error codes *(continued)*.

Error Code	Error Message	What's Going On
3059	Operation canceled by user.	You halted the operation before its normal completion.
3064	Can't open action query <name>.	You tried to open an action query using the **OpenQueryDef** method, which is an obsolete method originally valid only with select queries. The preferred method for executing an action query is to use the **Execute** method of the **QueryDef** object.
3065	Can't execute a select query.	You tried to use the **Execute** method with a select query. The **Execute** method is valid only with action queries. Select queries contain a **SELECT** statement and can return records; action queries do not.
3066	Query must have at least one destination field.	This error occurs if you don't specify any destination field names when you create a query. Select at least one destination field.
3067	Query input must contain at least one table or query.	In Microsoft Jet databases, this error occurs if you don't select a table name when you create a query. Select at least one table or query.
3070	The Microsoft Jet database engine does not recognize <name> as a valid field name or expression.	The specified name isn't a recognized field name or a valid expression. In a query, this error can occur if you enter a name that improperly refers to a database, table, or field.
3071	This expression is typed incorrectly, or it is too complex to be evaluated.	A numeric expression may contain too many complicated elements. Try simplifying the expression by assigning parts of the expression to variables.
3074	Can't repeat table <name> in **FROM** clause.	You can't list the table name more than once. Remove the extra occurrences of the table name or use an alias. If you are trying to join a table to itself, use an alias to change the second reference to the table.
3078	The Microsoft Jet database engine cannot find the input table or query <name>. Make sure it exists and that its name is spelled correctly.	This error is present when: a) The specified table or query doesn't exist. b) You misspell the table or query name. Check for missing underscores or other punctuation, and make sure you didn't enter leading spaces.
3088	Too many expressions in **ORDER BY** clause.	You created an SQL statement that has an **ORDER BY** clause with more than 10 expressions. Remove some of the fields listed in the **ORDER BY** clause.

(continued)

Table D.1 **Trappable error codes** *(continued).*

Error Code	Error Message	What's Going On
3089	Too many expressions in **DISTINCT** output.	You created an SQL statement that has an **ALL**, **DISTINCT**, or **DISTINCTROW** predicate with more than 10 expressions. Remove the **DISTINCT** reserved word, or remove some of the fields listed in the **DISTINCT** predicate.
3090	Resultant table not allowed to have more than one AutoNumber field.	You tried to execute a query that would result in a table with more than one field that has an AutoNumber data type. Change the query to include only one AutoNumber field.
3093	**ORDER BY** <clause> conflicts with **DISTINCT**.	You created an SQL statement with an **ALL**, **DISTINCT**, or **DISTINCTROW** predicate and an **ORDER BY** clause that contains a field not listed in the **SELECT** statement. Remove the **DISTINCT** reserved word, or remove the specified field from the **ORDER BY** clause.
3096	Can't have aggregate function in **WHERE** <clause>.	You can't use an aggregate function in the **WHERE** clause of an SQL statement.
3097	Can't have aggregate function in **ORDER BY** <clause>.	You can't use an aggregate function in the **ORDER BY** clause of an SQL statement.
3101	The Microsoft Jet database engine can't find a record in the table <name> with key matching field(s) <name>.	In a one-to-many relationship, you entered data on the "many" side for which there is no matching record on the "one" side
3105	Missing destination field name in **SELECT INTO** <statement>.	Enter a destination field name in the specified statement, and then try the operation again.
3106	Missing destination field name in **UPDATE** <statement>.	Enter a destination field name in the specified statement, and then try the operation again.
3113	Can't update <field name>; field not updatable.	The specified field is part of a **TableDef** or dynaset-type **Recordset** object that can't be updated, or you executed a query that combines updatable and nonupdatable **TableDef** objects, and you tried to update one of the fields in the query's results (the resulting dynaset-type **Recordset**).

(continued)

Table D.1 **Trappable error codes** *(continued)*.

Error Code	Error Message	What's Going On
3125	The database engine can't find <name>.	Make sure it is a valid parameter or alias name, that it doesn't include invalid characters or punctuation, and that the name isn't too long.
3126	Invalid bracketing of <name>.	The specified name either can't have brackets around it, or the brackets are mismatched. Check your entry to make sure the brackets are properly matched, and then try the operation again.
3127	The **INSERT INTO** statement contains the following unknown field name: <field name>.	Make sure you've typed the name correctly, and try the operation again.
3128	Specify the table containing the records you want to delete.	You tried to execute a delete query but the query doesn't specify the name of the table containing the records you want to delete.
3129	Invalid SQL statement; expected **'DELETE'**, **'INSERT'**, **'PROCEDURE'**, **'SELECT'**, or **'UPDATE'**.	Your SQL statement couldn't be recognized because it doesn't begin with one of the specified reserved words.
3130	Syntax error in **DELETE** statement.	You entered an SQL statement that has an invalid **DELETE** statement because a reserved word or argument name is misspelled or missing or the punctuation is incorrect.
3131	Syntax error in **FROM** clause.	You entered an SQL statement that has an invalid **FROM** clause because a reserved word or argument name is misspelled or missing or the punctuation is incorrect.
3134	Syntax error in **INSERT INTO** statement.	You entered an SQL statement that has an invalid **INSERT INTO** statement because a reserved word or argument name is misspelled or missing or the punctuation is incorrect.
3138	Syntax error in **ORDER BY** clause.	You entered an SQL statement that has an invalid **ORDER BY** statement because a reserved word or argument name is misspelled or missing or the punctuation is incorrect.
3141	The **SELECT** statement includes a reserved word or an argument name that is misspelled or missing, or the punctuation is incorrect.	You entered an SQL statement that has an invalid **SELECT** statement because a reserved word or argument name is misspelled or missing or the punctuation is incorrect.

(continued)

Table D.1   Trappable error codes *(continued)*.

Error Code	Error Message	What's Going On
3144	Syntax error in **UPDATE** statement.	You entered an SQL statement that has an invalid **UPDATE** statement because a reserved word or argument name is misspelled or missing or the punctuation is incorrect.
3145	Syntax error in **WHERE** clause.	You entered an SQL statement that has an invalid **WHERE** clause because a reserved word or argument name is misspelled or missing or the punctuation is incorrect.
3159	Not a valid bookmark.	This error can occur if you set the **Bookmark** property to a string that is invalid or wasn't saved from previously reading a **Bookmark** property.
3160	Table isn't open.	You tried to perform an operation on a table that hasn't been opened. Open the table, and then try the operation again.
3162	You tried to assign the Null value to a variable that isn't a Variant data type.	Use the **Dim** statement to declare the variable as a Variant, and then try the operation again.
3163	The field is too small to accept the amount of data you attempted to add.	Insert or paste less data.
3164	The field can't be updated because another user or process has locked the corresponding record or table.	You tried to change the value of a control whose **Locked** property is set to **Yes**.
3167	Record is deleted.	You referred to a record that you deleted or that another user in a multiuser environment deleted. Move to another record, and then try the operation again.
3175	Date is out of range or is in an invalid format.	Only dates from December 30, 1899, through December 30, 9999, are recognized.
3177	Not a valid table name.	The name you entered doesn't follow standard naming conventions. Enter a new name, and then try the operation again.
3179	Encountered unexpected end of file.	You tried to import a file that contains an end-of-file marker in an unexpected position.

(continued)

Table D.1 Trappable error codes *(continued)*.

Error Code	Error Message	What's Going On
3184	Couldn't execute query; couldn't find linked table.	The linked table no longer exists or has been renamed or moved. Link the table, and then try to execute the query again.
3190	Too many fields defined.	You tried to perform an operation that involves more than 255 fields. Reduce the number of fields, and then try the operation again.
3191	Can't define field more than once.	You tried to create a table in which more than one field was defined with the same name. Each field name in a table must be unique.
3192	Couldn't find output table <name>.	You tried to use an **INSERT INTO** statement with the specified table, which doesn't exist. Make sure you entered the name correctly, and then try the operation again.
3199	Couldn't find reference.	You entered a file, table, or field reference that couldn't be found. Check the spelling and punctuation to make sure you entered the reference correctly, and then try the operation again.
3200	The record cannot be deleted or changed because table <name> includes related records.	You tried to perform an operation that would have violated referential integrity rules for related tables.
3204	Database already exists.	You tried to create or rename a database using a name that already exists. Enter a different name, and then try the operation again.
3242	Invalid reference in **SELECT** statement.	You entered an invalid field or table reference in the **SELECT** statement.
3250	Couldn't build key.	When building a primary index, the Microsoft Jet database engine couldn't build a primary key. Make sure the key fields are named properly and that there are no duplicate records based on this key. This error can occur when you use the **Seek** method and pass it a value for a field that is not part of the index.
3251	Operation is not supported for this type of object.	You were attempting to execute a method or assign a value to a property that is usually valid for the object, but isn't supported in this specific instance. For example, the **Edit** method is generally valid for **Recordset** objects, but not for a snapshot-type **Recordset**.

(continued)

Table D.1 **Trappable error codes** *(continued).*

Error Code	Error Message	What's Going On
3259	Invalid field data type.	The data type specified in the **Field** object's **Type** property isn't valid.
3263	Invalid **Database** object.	The **Database** object specified isn't the result of the **OpenDatabase** method, or it has been modified and is no longer valid.
3265	Item not found in this collection.	An attempt to reference a name in a collection failed because the object doesn't exist in this collection or there is more than one object with this name in the collection, such that using its name is an ambiguous reference.
3266	Can't append a **Field** that is already a part of a **Fields** collection.	A **Field** object was specified as an argument to an **Append** operation when it already is a member of an existing **Fields** collection. Use the **Dim** statement and **CreateField** method to declare a new **Field** object and specify its values, and retry the operation with the new **Field** object.
3270	Property not found.	The specified property couldn't be found because it doesn't exist, or if the property is user-defined, it may have been deleted from the collection.
3272	Object isn't a collection.	You've referred to an object as though it were a collection.
3273	Method not applicable for this object.	You tried to use a method on an object that doesn't support that method.
3370	Can't modify the design of table <name>. It's in a read-only database.	You can't modify tables in a read-only database.
3371	Can't find table or constraint.	The table or relationship you specified doesn't exist. Specify a valid table or constraint name.
3375	Table <name> already has an index named <name>.	You're trying to create an index that already exists.
3376	Table <name> doesn't exist.	Check to see if the name you specified exists in the **TableDefs** collection.
3380	Field <name> already exists in table <name>.	You have entered the same field name twice. Rewrite your code, giving each field a unique name. You should also check to see if the field name exists in the **Fields** collection.

(continued)

Table D.1   Trappable error codes *(continued)*.

Error Code	Error Message	What's Going On
3381	There is no field named <name> in table <name>.	The specified table doesn't contain the specified field. Check the spelling of the field name. You should also check to see if the field name exists in the **Fields** collection.
3382	Size of field <name> is too long.	Text fields in Microsoft FoxPro tables can be no more than 254 characters, and in Microsoft Jet tables, no more than 255 characters. Redefine the size of the field.
3384	Can't delete a built-in property.	You are trying to delete a **Property** object defined by the Microsoft Jet database engine. You can only delete user-defined properties for which you have permission to modify the design, or ones for which this permission isn't required.
3385	User-defined properties don't support a null value.	User-defined **Property** objects can't be set to Null. Instead, use the **Delete** method on the property to remove it from its collection.
3388	Unknown function <name> in validation expression or default value on <name>.	The function you are referencing is either unknown (because the name is invalid or misspelled) or is a type of function not allowed by the **ValidationRule** or **DefaultValue** property. Among the types of functions not allowed are user-defined, SQL aggregate functions.
3421	Data type conversion error.	The Microsoft Jet database engine was unable to convert data into the type required by a method or property. This problem typically occurs if you use an argument of one type when a method or property expects another type.
3428	A problem occurred in your database. Correct the problem by repairing and compacting the database.	The database you are attempting to use has an unspecified problem and, as a result, it is marked as corrupt. To correct the problem: 1. Close the database. 2. Repair the database with the **RepairDatabase** method. In Microsoft Access, you can also do this by going to Tools|Database Utilities|Repair Database. 3. Compact the database with the **CompactDatabase** method. In Microsoft Access, you can also do this by going to Tools|Database Utilities|Compact Database.

(continued)

Table D.1   Trappable error codes *(continued).*

Error Code	Error Message	What's Going On
3575	The disk drive you are attempting to write to is full.	The disk drive does not have enough space to complete the operation. Delete unneeded files from the disk to create sufficient space for the operation. Make space available on the disk larger than the file you are attempting to save.
3576	The database you are attempting to open is already in use by another application.	If you are attempting to open the database in exclusive mode, it is possible that another application already has the database open. If you are attempting to open the database in shared mode, it is possible that another application has the database open in exclusive mode. Close the other applications using the database, and try your request again.
3584	Insufficient memory to complete operation.	Your computer ran out of memory while trying to replicate the database. Close other applications on the computer, and try the operation again.
3641	There are fewer records remaining in the record-set than you requested.	You've reached the end of the recordset.
3642	A cancel was performed on the operation.	A query has been interrupted by the data source. Some of the matching rows have not been returned. Try submitting the query again.
3643	One of the records in the recordset was deleted by another process.	One or more of the records in the recordset was deleted after the query was performed. You should refresh the recordset, and try the query again.
3647	A column requested is not being returned to the recordset.	One of the requested columns is not available.
3649	The language-specific code page was not specified or could not be found.	You have attempted to open a database that was created with a language that is not installed on your computer. You should determine what language was specified for this database when it was created, and then make sure that language is installed on your system.
3656	Error in evaluating a partial expression.	You have entered an invalid expression in a Boolean filter used to determine which records to use in a partial replica.

Index

P